AF718114

01
95
64
48a

THE LAW

OF

DEBTOR AND CREDITOR,

IN THE

UNITED STATES AND CANADA.

BY

JAMES P. HOLCOMBE,

AUTHOR OF A "DIGEST OF THE DECISIONS OF THE SUPREME COURT OF THE UNITED STATES,"
EDITOR OF "SMITH'S MERCANTILE LAW," "LEADING CASES
UPON COMMERCIAL LAW," ETC.

LAW LIBRARY
JUL 1 4 1994
GOLDEN GATE UNIVERSITY

Fred B. Rothman & Co.
Littleton, Colorado
1994

Library of Congress Cataloging-in-Publication Data

Holcombe, James Philemon, 1820-1873.
The law of debtor and creditor in the United States and Canada / by James P. Holcombe.
p. cm.
Originally published: New York : D. Appleton, 1848.
Includes index.
ISBN 0-8377-2246-2
1. Debtor and creditor--United States--States. 2. Debtor and creditor--Canada. I. Title.
KF150.Z95H64 1994
346.73'077--dc20
[347.30677]
93-43368
CIP

Printed in United States of America

The paper used in this publication meets the minimum requirements of American National Standard for Information Sciences—Permanence of Paper for Printed Library Materials, ANSI Z39.48-1984.

THE LAW

OF

DEBTOR AND CREDITOR,

IN THE

UNITED STATES AND CANADA.

BY

JAMES P. HOLCOMBE,

AUTHOR OF A "DIGEST OF THE DECISIONS OF THE SUPREME COURT OF THE UNITED STATES," EDITOR OF "SMITH'S MERCANTILE LAW," "LEADING CASES UPON COMMERCIAL LAW," ETC.

NEW-YORK:
D. APPLETON & COMPANY, 200 BROADWAY
PHILADELPHIA:
GEO. S. APPLETON, 148 CHESNUT-STREET
MDCCCXLVIII.

Entered, according to Act of Congress, in the year 1848,

By D. Appleton & Company,

In the Clerk's Office of the District Court for the Southern District of New-York.

PREFACE.

This volume has been prepared with the hope of supplying a general and acknowledged want, not only of the professional, but of the business men of our country. Its object is to present in a popular but faithful form, the most important principles of law, regulating the mercantile relation of debtor and creditor, in the States of the American Union, and in the British Provinces of Canada. The intimate commercial relations subsisting between the people of these various regions, and the great diversity of their local jurisprudence, render the information which it embodies matter of daily interest and value to our merchants and lawyers. Next in importance to a uniform system of mercantile law, is the diffusion of a knowledge of its points of conflict.

In the arrangement of the work, the leading distinction between rights and remedies, more or less prominently marked, has been every where preserved. A separate chapter is devoted to the law of each State, those provisions being discussed which seemed to possess the greatest practical value. The dignity of the several species of instruments, the rights of their respective holders, having received the same bona fide and for a valuable consideration, the order in which they are to be paid out of the assets of a decedent's estate, the period within which suits may be instituted upon each, the cases within which a writing is essential to the creation of a debt, or the efficacy of an acknowledgment, the rights secured to married women in the property of their husbands, and the exemption of her estate from liability for his debts, the statutes regulating the rights and liabilities of partners, agents, and corporators, the rates of interest and the damages upon protested bills of exchange, are considered in the first part of each chapter. The remedies to recover debts, embracing the modes of obtaining and enforcing judgments, the cases in which a debtor may be arrested, upon either mesne or final process, or in which his estate may be attached, and the proceedings thereon, the lien of judgments, the various species of execution, and the property liable to be taken upon each, the remedies against sheriffs and attorneys for failing to pay over money when collected, the organization of courts, the laws concerning the administration of the estates of insolvent and deceased persons, occupy the remaining portion. The compiler has drawn his materials from the statutes and reports of the several States, and from information furnished to him by gentlemen residing in different sections of the country. He would take this opportunity of expressing his acknowledgments to Mr. Newton Edwards of Boston, for most of the matter relating to the New England States, to Mr. George Benagh of Lynchburg, Virginia, Mr. Richard W. Walker of Florence, Alabama, and Mr. Thomas B. Holcombe of Madison, Indiana, for contributions on the laws of their respective States.

The extent of the field embraced, and the absence of any complete collection of the statute law of the States, render some inaccuracies unavoidable. The compiler hopes and believes, that they will be found to be few and unimportant.

JAMES P. HOLCOMBE.

CINCINNATI, Aug. 1st, 1848.

CONTENTS.

LAW OF DEBTOR AND CREDITOR.

MAINE.

1. *Choses in Action.*

THE common law has not been altered in Maine as to the assignability of choses in action; and except in cases governed by the mercantile law, the assignee cannot bring an action upon them in his own name.

A scrawl does not have the force of a seal; but where there is only one seal and several signatures, the recital in the instrument, "sealed with our seals," is equivalent to an adoption of the particular seal by each. (*a*)

(*a*) Bank of Cumberland *v.* Bugbee, 1 App. 27.

No recovery can be had upon any promissory note executed since August 10th, 1846, which is payable on demand at a place certain, or on demand at a place certain after the expiration of a specified time, unless the plaintiff shall prove that such demand was made at the place of payment prior to the commencement of the suit. (*a*)

2. *Damages upon Bills of Exchange.*

Where a bill of exchange, drawn or indorsed within the state, and payable in some other of the United States, is protested for non-acceptance or non-payment, the holder may recover against the acceptor, drawer, or indorser, not only the contents of the bill and interest, but in addition thereto, damages at the rate of three per cent. on the amount of the bill, if it be payable in either of the states of New Hampshire, Massachusetts, Vermont, Connecticut, Rhode Island, or New-York; at the rate of six per cent. if it be payable in New-Jersey, Pennsylvania, Delaware, Maryland, Virginia, South Carolina, Georgia, or the District of Columbia; and at the rate of nine per cent. if it be payable in any other state. (*b*)

Upon a bill of exchange drawn, accepted, or indorsed within the state for one hundred dollars or more, and payable within the state at a place seventy-five miles distant from the place where drawn, the rate of damages over and above the contents of the bill and interest is one per cent. on the principal amount.

There is no statute regulating the damages upon protested foreign bills of exchange, but in Griffith's Law Register, vol. iv. 1007, it is intimated that the decisions of Massachusetts would be recognized by the courts of Maine. These decisions were founded upon what Chief Justice Parsons, in the case of *Grimshaw* v. *Bender et als*, 6 Mass. 157, declared to be the immemorial usage of the state. "That usage is to allow the holder of the bill the money for which it was drawn, reduced to our currency at par, and also the charges of protest, with American interest on those sums from the time when the bill should have been paid; and the further sum of one-tenth of the money for which the bill

(*a*) Acts of 1846, 203. (*b*) R. S. 510,

was drawn, with interest upon it from the time that payment of the dishonored bill was demanded of the drawer. But nothing has been allowed for re-exchange, whether it is below or at par. The usage governs also in actions against indorsers and acceptors of foreign bills."

Protest.—The protest of any foreign or inland bill of exchange, or promissory note, or order, duly certified by a notary public, under his hand and official seal, shall be legal evidence of the facts stated in such protest, and also as to the notice given to the drawer or indorsers, in any court of law. (*a*)

3. *Interest.*

Six per cent. is the legal rate of interest. The excess above that rate cannot be recovered in an action upon any contract; and if it has been paid, may be recovered back by the borrower or his personal representatives, on instituting an action therefor within twelve months next after the payment. The statute does not embrace maritime contracts, such as bottomry, insurance, or the course of exchange. The latter provision does not apply to bills of exchange or promissory notes, payable to order or bearer, which have passed into the hands of an innocent indorsee for a valuable consideration. (*b*)

On all executions issued on judgments in civil actions or acknowledgments of debt, lawful interest shall be collected by the officer serving the execution, from the time judgment was rendered or the debt became payable. (*c*)

It is said in Griffith's Law Register, 1006, that interest is not recoverable on book debts, except where a demand is proved, or upon the expiration of a credit which was given for a specified time.

4. *Frauds.*

The English Statute of Frauds is substantially re-enacted, but it is provided that the consideration of any such promise, contract, or agreement, need not be set forth or expressed in the writing

(*a*) R. S. 264. (*b*) Ib. 317. (*c*) Ib. 509.

signed by the party to be charged therewith, but may be proved by any other legal evidence. (*a*)

No action can be maintained to charge a party by reason of any representation or assurance concerning the character, credit, ability or dealings of any other person, unless such representation is in writing. (*b*)

No contract for the sale of any goods for the price of thirty dollars or more, shall be allowed to be good, unless the purchaser shall accept part of the goods so sold and actually receive the same, or give something in earnest to bind the bargain, or in part payment, or some note of memorandum of the bargain in writing. (*c*)

5. *Effect of Marriage upon Rights of Property.*

Any married woman may become seized or possessed of any property, real or personal, by bequest, gift, demise, purchase, or distribution, in her own name, and as of her own property, exempt from liability for the debts or contracts of her husband: provided that such property, if acquired after marriage by conveyance from the husband without adequate consideration, or by purchase with his moneys or property, shall be liable for the payment of his prior contracted debts. (*d*)

6. *Principals, Factors, and Agents.*

Every person in whose name any merchandise shall be shipped, shall be deemed the true owner thereof, so far as to entitle the consignee of such merchandise to a lien thereon, for any moneys advanced or negotiable security given by such consignee to and for the use of the person in whose name such shipment shall have been made, and for any money or negotiable security received by the person in whose name the shipment shall have been made, to and for the use of any such consignee.

Every factor or agent intrusted with the possession of any bill of lading, custom-house permit, or warehouse keeper's receipt for the delivery of any such merchandise; and every factor or agent not having the documentary evidence of title, who shall be

(*a*) R. S. 591. (*b*) Ib. (*c*) Ib. (*d*) Acts of 1847, 23. Acts of 1844.

intrusted with the possession of any merchandise for the purpose of sale, or as a security for any advances to be made or obtained thereon, shall be deemed to be the true owner thereof, so far as to give validity to any contract made by such agent with any other person, for the sale or disposition of the whole or any part of such merchandise, for any money advanced, or negotiable instrument or other obligation in writing, given by such person upon the faith thereof. Where, however, any person accepts such merchandise in deposit, from such agent, as security for an antecedent debt, he shall not thereby acquire any other rights in or to such merchandise or document, than were possessed by the agent at the time of the deposit. The true owner may recover the merchandise deposited in repayment of any money advanced upon the same, or any balance arising from the proceeds of sale, which may remain in the hands of the person with whom it was deposited, after satisfying the amount justly due to him by reason of such deposit.

No common carrier or warehouse keeper, however, is authorized to sell or hypothecate the merchandise or property committed to him for transportation or storage. (*a*)

7. *Corporations.*

By an act of 1831, which continues to be law, all acts of incorporation thereafter granted, are made liable to be amended, altered, or repealed, at the pleasure of the legislature, in the same manner as if an express provision to that effect were therein contained, unless there shall have been inserted in such act of incorporation an express provision to the contrary.

Where the creditors of a corporation cannot find sufficient attachable property to realize their debt, the individual property of each stockholder may be taken in execution, to the amount of his stock, to satisfy the same, if contracted during the term in which he was owner of the stock. This liability of the stockholder shall continue notwithstanding a subsequent transfer of the stock, for the term of one year from the record of such transfer, and for six months from the recovery of judgment against such corporation, on a suit commenced within the year aforesaid. (*b*)

(*a*) R. S. 262. (*b*) Ib. 328.

The corporators of a manufacturing corporation are relieved from their individual liability, if the corporation contract no debts which at any time exceed the amount of capital invested in real estate, or exceed one half of the amount of capital paid in, and remaining undivided; provided the treasurer publishes a semi-annual statement under oath, of the amount of all the assessments voted by the company, and actually paid in, of the nett amount of the existing capital stock, of the amount of all debts due from the company, of the amount of capital stock invested in real estate, buildings, machinery, and other fixtures, and the last estimated value affixed to the real estate of such corporation by the assessors of the town where the same is located, and the aggregate value fixed to all the taxable property of such corporation by such assessors. (*a*)

8. *Limited Partnerships.*

Limited partnerships were authorized in Maine, by an act passed in 1836. They may be formed for the transaction of mercantile, mechanical or manufacturing business; and shall be composed of one or more persons who shall be called general partners, and to whom the general principles of the law of part nership shall apply, and one or more persons called special partners, who shall contribute a specific sum in cash to the common stock, and who shall not be liable for the debts of the concern beyond the amount so advanced. The names of the general partners only are to be used in the style of the firm under which the business is conducted, and any special partner permitting his name to be used, or making any contract respecting the concerns of the partnership, will be treated as a general partner. Suits respecting the business of the partnership to be prosecuted by or against the general partners. The parties forming this contract must sign a certificate setting forth the name under which the business is to be conducted, the name and places of residence of each of the general and also special partners, the amount of capital which each of the special partners has contributed to the common stock, the general nature of the business, the time when the

(*a*) Acts of 1844.

partnership is to commence and when it is to terminate. This certificate is to be acknowledged by all the parties before a justice of the peace, and recorded in the registry of deeds of the county or district in which the principal place of the partnership business is situated, or if there be several such places in different counties or districts, then a duly certified transcript of such certificate is to be recorded in the office of the register of deeds for every such county or district. It is also within twenty days after registry to be published in a newspaper of the county where lies the principal place of business, or if there be no such paper, then in one printed in an adjoining county, or in the newspaper published by the printer to the state, and continued for six weeks successively. If such certificate be not recorded and published, both upon the formation and the renewal of such partnership, or if it contain any statements intentionally false, or which might mislead third persons, the partnership is to be deemed a general one. The capital stock is not to be reduced during the continuance of the partnership, below the sum mentioned in the certificate, by any withdrawal of a portion of the same, or any division of interest or profits. If during the existence, or at the termination of a partnership, the common property is not sufficient to pay the debts, the special partners will be severally answerable for the same, to the amount withdrawn or received by them, from the partnership, with interest thereon from the time of such withdrawal. No general assignment in view of insolvency will be valid, unless it provides for an equal distribution of the partnership property among all the creditors in proportion to their claims, and unless notice of the assignment be given within fourteen days from its execution, in some newspaper printed in the county where the principal place of business is situated, or the adjoining county, or in the newspaper published by the printer to the state. The assent of the creditors will be presumed, unless expressly, or by some act inconsistent with assent, they dissent therefrom, within sixty days after notice of the assignment. The partnership can only be dissolved during the term specified for its existence, by giving notice of the dissolution in the same manner as of the formation. In all cases not enumerated, the members of limited partnerships are subject to the liabilities, and entitled to the immunities incident to general partnerships. (*a*)

9. *Statutes of Limitation.*

All actions of debt founded upon any contract or liability not under seal, except such as are brought on some judgment or decree of a court of record within the United States, or of a justice of the peace within the state; all actions upon a judgment rendered in any court not being a court of record, except justices of the peace within the state; all actions of assumpsit, or upon the case, founded on any contract or liability express or implied, must be brought within six years next after the cause of action has occurred. Actions brought upon promissory notes signed in the presence of an attesting witness, or upon any bill, note, or other evidences of debt issued by any bank, are excepted from the operation of the preceding limitation, but are embraced by the general limitation of twenty years, which is fixed as the term within which all personal actions or any contract not otherwise specially limited, must be brought. In actions of debt or assumpsit brought to recover the balance due upon mutual and open account current, the cause of action shall be deemed to have accrued at the time of the last item proved in such account. Where a fraud has been committed, which is the ground of action, or where the cause of action has been fraudulently concealed by a person liable thereto, the person entitled may bring suit within six years from the time of the discovery of his rights. A new promise by one of two or more joint contractors does not deprive the co-contractor of the benefit of the statute. To revive an action in any case founded upon contract, the promise or acknowledgment must be in writing. No indorsement or memorandum of a partial payment upon any promissory note, bill of exchange, or other writing, by or on behalf of the party to whom such payment was made, shall have the effect of repelling the operation of the statute. Presumption of payment is made to attach to all judgments or decrees of any court of record within the United States, or of a justice of the peace within the state, after the expiration of twenty years.

(*a*) R. S. 264

The usual saving is made of the rights of infants, feme coverts, persons non compos mentis, imprisoned, or without the limits of the United States. Where the defendant, at the period of the accruing of the cause of action, is without the state, or is absent for any length of time afterwards, such term is not to be estimated as a part of the period of limitation. (*a*)

10. *Assignments by Insolvent Debtors.*

All assignments by insolvent debtors, for the benefit of one or more creditors, shall enure equally to the benefit of all creditors who upon notice may become parties to such assignment; and shall be construed by law to pass all property, real and personal, whether specified in the assignment or not, which is not by law exempt from attachment. The assignor may require a release from creditors who become parties to the instrument which shall forever discharge him from their claims; he must, however, make an affidavit that he has assigned all his estate, real and personal, for their benefit. The assignee is required to give notice, by advertisement for three months, to enable all the creditors of the assignor to become parties. During this period, the assignee shall not be liable by reason of the possession of such property, to trustee process or attachment. (*b*)

11. *Imprisonment for Debt.*

No debtor can be arrested on mesne process, in any suit brought on a contract, express or implied, or upon any suit brought on a judgment founded upon such contract, unless the creditor or his agent makes oath before a justice of the peace that he has reason to believe and verily does believe that such debtor is about to depart or reside beyond the limits of the state, and to take with him property or means exceeding the amount required for his immediate support, and that his demand exclusive of interest is ten dollars. If the debtor is arrested after notice to his creditor, and makes a full and honest disclosure of his property, the same is held as attached for the benefit of the creditor, and the debtor may be

(*a*) R. S. 616 to 620. (*b*) Laws of Maine, 1844, 101.

discharged from imprisonment, and no execution can subsequently issue at any stage of such suit against the body of the debtor. (*a*) *See title Judgment and Execution.*

12. *Courts.*

Besides various municipal and police courts, the judicial power of the state is distributed between the Supreme Judicial Court and various District Courts. The former is held once a year in most of the counties of the state, in some of them twice. The latter are held three times a year in most of the counties, twice a year in the rest. The former consists of a chief justice and two associate justices, and has a general civil jurisdiction at law and in equity, original and concurrent with the District Courts, where the debt or damage exceeds the sum of two hundred dollars. The District Courts, besides their concurrent jurisdiction with the Supreme Court, have exclusive jurisdiction where the debt or damage demanded does not exceed two hundred dollars. (*b*)

Remedy against Sheriffs.—Any sheriff or his deputy unreasonably refusing to pay over to the person entitled, money received by him upon execution, shall forfeit to such person five times the lawful interest of the money, so long as he shall unreasonably detain it. (*c*)

13. *Judgment and Execution.*

The judgment creates no lien of itself upon the lands of the debtor. They are not bound until execution has been issued; but may be attached in the first instance on mesne process.

All the real estate of a debtor, whether in possession or reversion, or whether fraudulently conveyed, all rights of entry into land, all statutory rights to land derived from possession or improvement, and all equities of redemption, may be taken in execution for his debts. (*d*) Mere rights of action may be sold by the officer under the execution. Where possession may be taken and delivered of the estate, the officer after having it appraised and set forth by metes and bounds, may deliver possession to the creditor

(*a*) R. S. 624. (*b*) Ib. 394 and sub. (*c*) Ib. 765. (*d*) Ib. 382 to 391.

or his attorney, and upon a return of the execution to the office whence it was issued, setting forth his proceedings, and a recordation of the same in the registry of deeds for the county, the creditor will be invested with the title of the debtor: saving to the wife her right of dower. The debtor may redeem the land within one year after the levy, by paying or tendering to the creditor the sum at which they were appraised and interest from the time of the levy, and all reasonable expenses and repairs, after deducting the rents and profits received by the creditor, or which he might have received. (*a*)

If the debtor does not redeem, and the judgment is reversed on writ of error, the title to the land taken in satisfaction is lost; but if reversed on review or new trial, it is not affected. (*b*)

The real estate of a decedent may be taken in execution, and appraised and set off, or sold, and redeemed upon any judgment against the executor or administrator for the proper debt of the deceased. (*c*)

All the chattels real and personal of a debtor, except such as are specially exempted, current gold and silver coin, bank notes, and other evidences of debt issued by any moneyed corporation, and circulated as money; any share of the stock of an incorporated company, and the equity of a mortgagor of personal property to redeem, may be sold on execution. (*d*)

Where the debt remaining due amounts to ten dollars or upwards, exclusive of costs, and no express provision has been made to the contrary, execution may run against the body of the judgment debtor; and he may be arrested and imprisoned for the purpose of obtaining a discovery of his property wherewith to satisfy the same. The debtor may be released upon taking an insolvent oath, if two justices, before whom he may be examined, after notice to his creditor, and an opportunity allowed to him of interrogating the debtor, and offering any pertinent evidence, shall be satisfied that he has made a true disclosure of his condition. Any property disclosed, notes, accounts, bonds, or other contracts, may be appraised and set off to the creditor. The effect of the discharge will be to relieve the body of the debtor

(*a*) R. S. 382 to 391. (*b*) Griffith's Law Register 990, vol. 4.
(*c*) R. S. 382 to 391. (*d*) R. S. 515.

from any execution on the judgment, but in no other way to impair the creditor's rights. (*a*)

14. *Attachments, Foreign and Judicial.*

Where the goods of a non-resident, having no agent within the state, have been attached before a justice of the peace, judgment may be rendered against the debtor, as in ordinary cases, upon compliance with such order respecting notice, as the justice may make. (*b*)

On all writs returnable before a justice of peace, or municipal court, and on executions issued by such justices or courts, personal property may be attached in any county of the state. (*c*)

All civil actions may be commenced by attaching the goods and estate of the defendant. Every species of property liable to be taken in execution for debt, may be attached, and will be affected by a lien in favor of the attaching creditor, for a period of thirty days after final judgment in the case. (*d*)

Any action founded in contract, may be commenced by a trustee process or foreign attachment, which, from the time of serving the writ on the trustee, shall bind all the goods, effects, or credits of the principal defendant under his control, to answer the final judgment in the action. As many persons may be summoned as trustees, including corporations, as the plaintiff may think necessary, at any time before process has been served on the principal. A non-resident, the defendant in any suit, may be charged as trustee, to an executor or administrator in reference to a debtor legacy.

Judgment may be rendered against the trustee, his own rights and those of third persons being protected, for any goods, effects, and credits of the principal in his hands, which judgment shall discharge him from all demands of the principal defendant.

Where the principal defendant is a non-resident, the court may make such order as to notice, as the justice of the case may require.

Creditors who have taken the body of their debtor in execution, and afterwards discover goods or credits of the defendant,

(*a*) R. S. 623. (*b*) Act of 1844, 81. (*c*) Act of 1842, 7. (*d*) R. S. 484.

not attachable by ordinary process of law, may have the benefit of the trustee process. (*a*)

Attachment of Boats.—Boats and vessels employed in transporting goods upon any river, bay, or stream in the state, are rendered liable for any loss or damage to such goods, wares, or merchandise, whether in the employment of the owner or not. The attachment against the boats, however, must be issued within sixty days after the injury occurred, and not afterwards; and it will overreach any transfer, sale, mortgage, or other lien upon the property executed after the loss occurred, and be prior to the attachment. (*b*)

15. *Effect of Death upon the Rights of Creditors.*

When an estate appears, from the representation of the administrator, to be insolvent, it is the duty of the judge of probate to appoint two or more persons as commissioners to receive and examine all claims of creditors against the estate, who shall appoint convenient times and places for that purpose, and give notice of the same by advertisement. The period of six months is allowed for the presentation and proof of such claims, to be extended at the discretion of the judge for an additional term, not to exceed eighteen months from the date of the commission. Any creditor whose claim is disallowed in whole or part by the commissioners, may, by appeal from their decision, have the same determined at common law, or submit the matter to referees, to be agreed upon between them, and appointed by a rule of the probate court, whose award shall be final. Thirty days after the return of the commissioners, the judge shall make a decree for the distribution of the effects among the creditors according to the rules of law.

Every creditor of an insolvent estate who has failed to present his claim for allowance, is forever barred from recovering the same, unless further assets come to the hands of the administrator after a decree of distribution.

Debts are to be paid in the following order:—1. Expenses of

(*a*) R. S. 528 to 538. (*b*) Acts of 1846, 178.

funeral and administration. 2. Allowance from the personal estate for benefit of widow and children, made by probate judge and proportioned to the condition of the deceased and the state of his family. 3. Expenses of last sickness. 4. Debts entitled to preference under the laws of the United States. 5. Public taxes and moneys due the state. 6. All other debts.

Both real and personal property constitute assets.

NEW HAMPSHIRE.

1. ASSURANCES OR EVIDENCES OF DEBT.
2. DAMAGES ON PROTESTED BILLS OF EXCHANGE.
3. THE LAW OF USURY.
4. FRAUDS.
5. LIMITED PARTNERSHIPS AND LIABILITY OF CORPORATE INSTITUTIONS.
6. LAWS OF INSOLVENCY.
7. EFFECT OF MARRIAGE ON THE TITLE TO THE WIFE'S PROPERTY.
8. LIMITATION OF PERSONAL ACTIONS AND SAVING CLAUSES.
9. EFFECT OF DEATH ON THE RIGHTS OF CREDITORS.
10. MODE OF COLLECTING DEBTS.
11. COURTS.

1. *Assurances or Evidences of Debt.*

Grace on Promissory Notes, &c.—Days of grace are allowed on all bills of exchange, negotiable promissory notes, orders, or drafts, excepting those payable on demand, unless the instrument shows the intention of the parties to have been otherwise. (*a*)

Actions on Promissory Notes secured by Mortgage.—See title "Limitation of Personal Actions."

2. *Damages on Protested Bills of Exchange.*

There is no provision on the subject of this title.

3. *The Law of Usury.*

What rate of interest will be usurious.—In the rendition of judgments, and in all business transactions, where interest is secured or paid, it will be computed at the rate of six dollars on a

(*a*) R. S. 180.

hundred, for one year, unless a lower rate is expressly stipulated; and every person directly or indirectly receiving interest on any contract at a higher rate, will forfeit, for each offence, three times the sum so received. (*a*)

Evidence and penalty.—When any person, for the recovery of debt or damages, is sued upon any instrument, and more than legal interest has been paid or secured upon the money sued for, or is secured by such instrument, if the debtor (the creditor being living) come into court and offer to make oath, and if required by the court, actually swear, that there has been taken or secured upon the money sued for, or that there has been or is secured by the instrument sued, illegal interest, the court, in rendering judgment, will deduct from the sum lawfully due three times the amount so taken or secured, unless the creditor will swear that he has not, directly or indirectly, willingly taken or secured on the money sued for, or secured by the instrument sued, any interest above the rate aforesaid.

What is not usury.—Nothing herein contained extends to the letting of cattle or other usages of like nature among farmers, or to maritime contracts, as bottomry, insurance, or course of exchange, as heretofore used.

4. *Frauds.*

Statute of frauds.—No action can be maintained on any contract for the sale of lands, unless the agreement on which such action is brought, or some memorandum thereof, is in writing, and signed by the parties to be charged, or some person authorized by them. (*b*)

No action may be brought to charge any executor or administrator on any special promise to answer damages out of his own estate; to charge any person upon any special promise to answer for the debt, default, or miscarriage of another person; or to charge any person on any agreement that is not to be performed within one year from the time of making it; unless such promise or agreement, or some memorandum or note thereof, is in writing,

(*a*) *R.* S. 191. (*b*) Ib. 180.

and signed by the party to be charged therewith, or by some person authorized by him.

No contract for the sale of goods, wares, or merchandise, for the price of thirty-three dollars or upwards, will be valid unless the buyer accept and receive part of the property so sold, or give something in earnest to bind the bargain, or in part payment, or unless some note or memorandum thereof be made and signed by the parties, or some person duly authorized by them.

Provisions as to personal mortgages.—Possession of the mortgaged property must be delivered to and retained by the mortgagee, or the mortgage must be recorded by the clerk of the town in which the mortgagor resides, when the mortgage is made. (*a*)

The mortgagor and mortgagee must make and subscribe an affidavit, (to be appended to and recorded with the mortgage) in substance as follows: "We severally swear that the foregoing mortgage is made for the purpose of securing the debt specified in the condition thereof, and for no other purpose whatever, and that the said debt was not created for the purpose of enabling the mortgagor to execute said mortgage, but is a just debt honestly due and owing from the mortgagor to the mortgagee."

No mortgagor may execute a second or subsequent mortgage of property subject to a previous mortgage, without setting forth in the subsequent mortgage the existence of the previous one.

None of these provisions affect any transfer of property under bottomry or respondentia bonds, or of any ships or goods at sea or abroad, if the mortgagee take possession thereof as soon as may be after their arrival in this state.

Penalty for fraudulent conveyances, &c.—Any person fraudulently mortgaging, pledging, selling, alienating or conveying any of his real or personal estate amounting in value to one hundred dollars, or fraudulently concealing his personal estate of that value to prevent its attachment on mesne process or execution, may be punished by imprisonment not less than thirty days or more than a year, or by fine not exceeding double the value of such estate, or in both these ways. (*b*)

(*a*) R. S. 132. (*b*) Ib. 215.

5. *Limited Partnerships, and Liability of Corporate Institutions.*

For what purposes limited partnerships may be formed, and what constitutes general and special partners.—Limited partnerships for the transaction of mercantile, mechanical, or manufacturing business within this state (nothing herein contained authorizing such partnerships for the purpose of banking or insurance), may consist of one or more persons, to be called general partners, and to be jointly and severally responsible, as general partners now are by law, and of one or more persons, who will contribute to the common stock a specific sum in cash as capital, who will be called special partners, and will not be personally liable for any partnership debts, except as hereafter provided. (*a*)

Certificate to be signed, recorded, published, &c.—The parties forming such partnerships must make and severally sign a certificate, containing the name or firm under which the partnership is to be conducted, the names and respective places of residence of all the general and special partners, distinguishing who are general and who are special partners, the amount of capital contributed by each special partner, the general nature of the business to be transacted, and the time when the partnership is to begin and end.

The partnership will not be deemed to have been formed till such a certificate shall be acknowledged by all the partners before a justice, and recorded in the town clerk's office in the town in which the principal place of business of the partnership is situated, in a book to be kept for that purpose, open to public inspection, and if the partnership have places of business in different towns, said certificate must be recorded in each of such towns; and if any false statement shall be made in any such certificate, all the persons interested in the partnership will be liable as general partners.

The partners must for six successive weeks immediately after such certificate is recorded, publish a copy thereof in a newspaper printed in the county where their principal place of business is

(*a*) R. S. 75.

situated, and if no such paper be there printed, then in a newspaper printed in an adjoining county in this state. If such publication be not so made, the partnership will be deemed general.

On every renewal or continuation of a limited partnership beyond the time originally agreed upon, a certificate thereof must be made, acknowledged, recorded, and published, as before provided in case of the formation of such partnerships, and every partnership not renewed in conformity with these provisions will be deemed a general partnership.

Business to be done by and in the name of the general partners.—The business of the partnership must be conducted under a firm in which the names of the general partners only shall be inserted, without the addition of the word company or any other general term; and the general partners only must transact the business: and if the name of any special partner be used in such firm, with his consent or privity, or if he personally make any contract respecting the partnership concerns with any persons except the general partners, he will be deemed and treated as a general partner.

Liability of stockholders and officers of corporations.—All corporations having for their object a dividend of profits among their stockholders, hereafter incorporated, or whose charters are subject by law to alteration, amendment, or repeal, will be governed by the following provisions, and the stockholders and officers will be personally liable for the debts and civil liabilities of such corporations in the following cases only: (*a*)

1st. They will be jointly and severally liable for all debts and contracts of such corporations, till all the capital fixed and limited by such corporation has been paid in, and a certificate thereof has been made and recorded by the clerk of the town where such corporation has its place of business or is situated. And no note or obligation given by any stockholder, whether secured by pledge or otherwise, will be considered as payment of any part of the capital stock.

2d. If, on the reduction of the capital stock of any corporation, any part thereof is withdrawn and refunded to the stockholders before the payment of all debts of the corporation contracted pre-

(*a*) Laws of 1846, 321.

viously to recording the copy of a vote for that purpose in the office of the clerk of the town in which said corporation is located, or has its place of business, such of the stockholders as vote for or receive their share of the capital stock so withdrawn or refunded, will be jointly and severally liable for the payment of said last mentioned debts.

3d. Every such company will give notice annually, in May, to the governor, of the amount of all the assessments voted by the company and actually paid in, the amount of all debts due to and from such corporation, and the value of all the property and assets of said corporation, so far as the same can be ascertained, as existing on the first day of said May, which notice must be signed by the president and a majority of the directors. If any corporation fail to do so, all the stockholders thereof will be jointly and severally liable for all the debts of the corporation then existing, and for all that shall be contracted before such notice is given.

4th. If the directors of any such corporation declare and pay any dividend when the corporation is insolvent, or any dividend the payment of which would render it insolvent, they will be jointly and severally liable for all the debts of the corporation then existing, and for all that shall be thereafter contracted, so long as they respectively continue in office ; provided that the amount for which they are so liable will not exceed the amount of said dividend, and that if any director be absent when such dividend is made, or object thereto, and file his objection in writing, with the clerk of the corporation, who will record the same, he will be exempted from said liability.

5th. No loan of money may be made by any such corporation, other than banks, to stockholders therein : and if any such loan shall be made to a stockholder, the officers who make it or assent thereto will be jointly and severally liable, to the extent of such loan and interest, for all the debts of the corporation contracted before the payment of the sum so loaned.

6th. The whole amount of the debts of any corporation aforesaid other than banks must not exceed the amount of one-half the stock actually paid in, and of its other property and assets : and the whole amount of bills in circulation of any banking corporation must not at any one time exceed the capital stock actually paid in: and in case of any excess, the directors under whose administration it happens will be jointly and severally liable to the extent of such excess, for all the debts of the corporation then existing and for all those contracted while they respectively continue in office, and until the debts and circulation of said corporations respectively are reduced to the amount herein prescribed. Provided that any director who is absent at the time of contracting a debt contrary to these provisions, or who objects thereto, may exempt himself from said liability by forthwith giving notice of the fact to the stockholders, at a meeting called for that purpose.

7th. If any certificate, return or notice, made or given in pursuance of this act, be false in any material representation, all the officers who have signed the same, knowing it to be false, will be jointly and severally liable for all the debts of the corporation contracted while they were in office or stockholders therein.

The stockholders of every banking corporation hereafter incorporated, or whose charter is by law subject to amendment, alteration or repeal, will be severally liable in their individual capacity for the debts of the corporation in a sum equal to the amount of their stock in said corporation, and not otherwise: and no bank may have any other or greater rights, immunities or privileges in relation to the amount of bills or notes they may issue or have in circulation, or to any matter or thing, than are enjoyed by other corporations of like nature.

Modes of proceeding against corporations, officers, &c.—Proper actions of debt and assumpsit for the collection of such debts or liabilities may be prosecuted against one or more of said stockholders, which actions will not be abated because the other stockholders are not joined as defendants in such suits.

No such suit may be commenced till legal demand for payment has been made upon the company; and if, on such demand, the officers or stockholders discharge the debt, or expose unincumbered personal property of the company, liable to attachment, sufficient to satisfy the debt and costs, so that the same may be attached in a suit against the company, no suit will be sustained against the stockholders: but if the debt is not thus satisfied, or property exposed as aforesaid, it will be the duty of the officers to call a meeting of the stockholders of the company, and of the company, when convened, to provide means, within sixty days from the time when the demand is made, for the payment of the debt: and if it is not discharged within said sixty days, a suit may be brought against the stockholders as above provided.

6. *Laws of Insolvency.*

New Hampshire has no Insolvent Laws.

For provisions as to insolvent estates of persons deceased, see title 9th.

No assignment for the benefit of creditors is held valid in this state, unless it provides for an equal distribution of all the estate, rights, and credits of the debtor among all his creditors, in equal proportions to their respective claims; nor unless the person making the same shall have made oath that he has placed and assigned, and that the true intention of his assignment is to place in the hands of his assignee all his property of every description, except such as is exempted from attachment and execution, to be divided among all his creditors in proportion to their respective claims. (*a*)

7. *Effect of Marriage on the Title to the Wife's Property.*

Contracts before marriage.—Parties before marriage may contract that after such marriage the wife may continue to hold any real or personal estate, or rights of action, of which she is seized or possessed at the time of the marriage, to her sole and separate use, free from any interference of her husband; and she may hold and enjoy the same accordingly. (*b*)

Conveyances and bequests to married women.—Any devise, conveyance, or bequest of property, may be made to a married woman, to be held without the intervention of a trustee, to her sole and separate use, free from any interference of her husband, and she may hold such estate accordingly; and may in like manner hold any property which she may receive under any deed of trust made before or after the marriage. Such contract or conveyance, if it relate to real estate, must be recorded in the

(*a*) R. S. 134.

(*b*) Laws of 1846, 327.

registry of deeds for the county where such real estate lies. Nothing herein contained empowers any husband to convey property to his wife in any other manner, or with any other effect, than if this act had not been passed.

Married women dying intestate.—If any married woman, holding property to her separate use under this act, die intestate, all her interest in the personal property so held will vest in her husband, unless otherwise provided in the contract or conveyance, and he will have his curtesy in all lands and tenements held by his wife, as if this act had not been passed.

When marriage may not be contested after the death of one of the parties.—Any persons cohabiting and acknowledging each other as husband and wife, and generally reputed to be such for three years, and until the decease of one of them, will be deemed, after such decease, to have been legally married.

8. *Limitation of Personal Actions and Saving Clauses.*

Actions for words and personal injuries.—Actions for words, and for assault, battery, wounding, or imprisonment, must be brought within two years after the cause of action accrues. (*a*)

Other personal actions.—All other personal actions must be brought within six years after the cause of action accrues.

Debts on judgment and contracts under seal.—Actions of debt founded on any recognizance, or upon any contract under seal, must be brought within twenty years after the cause of action accrues.

Notes secured by mortgage.—Actions upon notes secured by mortgage may be brought so long as the plaintiff is entitled to commence any action upon the mortgage.

Writs of error.—Writs of error must be commenced within three years after judgment rendered.

Minors, &c., have two years after disability ceases.—Any infant, married woman, or insane person, may commence either of the personal actions aforesaid, within two years after such disability is removed.

Time of absence from state not computed.—If the defendant,

(*a*) R. S. 360.

when the cause of action accrued, or afterwards, was absent from, and residing out of, the state, the time of such absence will be excluded in the computation of the several times before limited for the commencement of personal actions.

New action in one year after judgment, if said judgment is not a bar.—If judgment be rendered against the plaintiff in any action commenced within the times before limited, or upon any writ of error brought thereon, he may commence a new action thereon within one year thereafter, in case his right of action is not barred by such judgment.

9. *Effect of death on the rights of Creditors.*

Administration to whom granted.—Administrations will be granted—

1st. To the executor named in the will.

2d. To the widow, or any of the next of kin, or such suitable person as they may nominate.

3d. To one of the devisees or creditors.

4th. To such other person as the judge may think proper.

Administrator's bond and conditions.—No person may intermeddle with the estate of any person deceased before giving bond to the judge in such sum as he shall approve, with sufficient sureties, to return to said judge a true and perfect inventory of the estate of the deceased, on oath, within three months of the date of the bond ; to administer said estate according to law ; to render to said judge an account of administration, upon oath, within one year ; to pay and deliver all the rest of the estate which shall be found remaining upon the account of the executor or administrator to such person or persons as said judge, by his decree according to law, shall limit and appoint ; and to deliver the letters of administration into the court of probate in case any will of the deceased should be approved and allowed. (*a*)

Provisions in reference to insolvent estates, the appointment of a commissioner, the proof of claims before him, &c.—Substantially the same as in Massachusetts.

The widow's allowance.—The widow of a person deceased

(*a*) R. S. 158.

testate, leaving no lineal descendant, will be entitled in addition to her dower, to one third part of all the estate remaining after the payment of debts and expenses of administration, no provision being made for her by will, or she waiving such provision.

If the deceased is intestate and leaves no such lineal descendant, the widow will be entitled to one half of all the estate remaining after the payment of debts and expenses of administration, in addition to her dower.

If the widow in either of the cases aforesaid so elect, she will be entitled, including her dower, to an amount of the estate remaining after payment of debts and expenses of administration, not exceeding that which her husband received from her or in her right during coverture.

The provisions of the three preceding sections will not be in force if a settlement is made on the wife before marriage.

The widow of a person dying intestate, leaving lineal descendants, will be entitled in addition to her dower, to one third part of the personal estate, after the payment of the debts and expenses of administration.

Distribution of personal estate.—The personal estate not bequeathed, remaining in the hands of the administrator on settlement of his account, will be distributed—

1st. To the widow, the share by law prescribed.

2d. The residue in equal shares to the same persons to whom the real estate, if there were any, would by law descend.

3d. To the state, if there be no heir or devisee.

Remedies for and against executors, &c.—Any person complained of by any administrator, heir, legatee, or creditor of a person deceased, on suspicion of having concealed, embezzled or conveyed away any of the personal estate of the deceased, may be cited before the judge and examined under oath for the discovery of the same. And in case any person so cited to appear, or appearing refuse to answer, he may be committed. (*a*)

No action will be sustained against any administrator, if commenced within one year after the original grant of administration, nor unless the demand has been exhibited to the administrator within two years after the original grant of administration and payment demanded. (*b*)

(*a*) R. S. 160. (*b*) Ib. 161.

No action can be prosecuted against an administrator where the estate is decreed to be administered as an insolvent estate.

Any person interested in the estate of a person deceased may commence an action as administrator, which will not be abated nor the attachment lost by reason of his not being administrator nor by his decease, if the administrator then or afterwards appointed shall, at the first or second term of the court, endorse the writ and prosecute the same as plaintiff.

Writs of attachment and execution against administrators, on a cause of action against the person deceased, will run only against the estate of the deceased; the administrator cannot be arrested, nor his estate attached or levied on in such an action.

If any person unlawfully intermeddle with, embezzle, alienate, waste or destroy any of the personal estate of a deceased person, he will be liable to the actions of creditors and others aggrieved, as executor in his own wrong, in double the value of the estate so intermeddled with, embezzled, alienated, wasted or destroyed. (*a*)

Any person interested in any bond given to a judge of probate may apply to the judge for an order for the suit thereof, setting forth his claim intended to be recovered in such suit, and the judge after due notice and hearing may make such order, upon the applicant giving bond, with sufficient sureties, to pay the costs which may be adjudged against him. (*b*)

10. *Mode of Collecting Debts.*

1. BY FOREIGN ATTACHMENT.

In what actions this process lies.—The same as in Massachusetts.

What attachment authorized by the writ.—The same as in Massachusetts.

Trustee, when defaulted.—If the trustee do not appear, when trustee process, duly served on him, is returnable, or if continued, at the term to which it is continued, he will be defaulted, and execution will issue against him, his proper goods and estate, for

(*a*) R. S. 158. (*b*) R. S. 169.

such amount as the plaintiff shall recover against the principal defendant in such process, not exceeding the amount alleged in such process. (*a*)

Liability of trustee, how tried.—Interrogatories as to his liability may be put to any person summoned as a trustee, which interrogatories, and the answers thereto, must be in writing, subscribed and sworn to in open court or before a justice of the peace, if the parties agree: or the question of his liability may be tried by a jury, as the plaintiff may elect.

Trustee, when liable.—Any person summoned as a trustee, having money, goods, chattels, rights, or credits of the principal defendant at the time when the writ is served on him, or at any time after service and before disclosure (such property being subject to no lien), will be adjudged a trustee therefor, and execution will issue against him for the same, or as much thereof as will satisfy said execution.

Not liable for earnings of wife of debtor, &c.—No person will be held liable as a trustee on account of the personal services or earnings of the wife of the debtor at any time, or on account of labor performed by the debtor or any of his family after service of the process, or within fifteen days prior to such service.

Liability for debt not yet due.—When the trustee is indebted to the principal defendant, and the time of payment has not expired, the court will suspend issuing execution against such trustee, as justice may require.

Liability on contracts for the delivery of specific articles.—If the trustee is under contract for the delivery of any specific article or articles to the principal defendant, or payment in any such articles, execution will issue against the trustee for such articles, or enough thereof to satisfy such execution, which must be paid and delivered to the creditor according to such contract. The creditor will be the agent of the principal defendant for the purpose of receiving such articles, and will levy his execution thereon. If not capable of division, the whole may be sold. The unsold property, and the overplus of the proceeds of the property sold are to be retained by the officer and delivered to the debtor when he may demand them.

(*a*) R. S. 208.

Liability for neglect to deliver.—If any person refuse to expose property on account of which he has been adjudged a trustee, so that execution may be levied thereon, execution will, after due notice, issue against him, his own goods and estate, for such sum as the court may think proper.

Liability for note, order, &c.; for property under lien, and for refusal to deliver such property.—If any trustee disclose the fact that he had, when the process was served on him, or afterwards, any promissory note, order, receipt, bill of exchange, bond, or other promise for the payment of money or the delivery of property belonging to the principal defendant, the court will appoint a receiver to collect and apply the proceeds to the payment of the debt and costs recovered by the plaintiff against the principal defendant, the surplus, if any, to go to the debtor.

And if it appear as aforesaid that the trustee had at the time of the service of such process, or afterwards, any personal property of said defendant, subject to a lien, pledge, or mortgage, which property, at the time of the disclosure, has not been sold by the trustee, the court will appoint a receiver to sell the same, if a greater amount than the sum due can be obtained therefor, and after paying the amount of such pledge, lien, or mortgage, to apply the balance as aforesaid.

And if any person so summoned as trustee in either of the two last mentioned cases, refuse to deliver up any such note or other property, on order of the court, execution will issue against him as trustee for the amount thereof.

Liability on negotiable note.—If any person summoned as trustee is indebted at the time of service of such process, or afterwards, to the principal defendant, by a negotiable promissory note made or payable in this state, or the parties to which at the time of making resided in this state, the court may require such debtor to appear and answer on oath all interrogatories respecting the possession, transfer, or other disposition of such note, and will give due notice to any person claiming an interest in such note, so that he may appear and show how and when the transfer was made, and the question of the validity of such transfer will be decided by the jury, if he or the plaintiff request it. If it do not appear that the note was transferred in good faith and for an adequate consideration, before the service of the trustee process, the promissor will be charged as the trustee of such debtor.

Proceedings if property is claimed by another.—If any person claim property in the hands of a supposed trustee, by assignment from the debtor or otherwise, the court will permit him to appear and maintain his right. And the testimony of the debtor, as of any other competent witness, may be taken thereon as the court shall direct.

Trial by jury.—On disclosure made by any person summoned as a trustee, the creditor may move the court that the jury try the point whether such person is trustee or not, and on payment of trustee's costs up to the time of filing such motion, unless the court restrict the same, an order will be made and an issue framed for the trial of such question. On such trial, said disclosure, the evidence of the debtor, and any other competent evidence may be offered, and judgment will be rendered on the verdict, as in other cases, against the trustees.

Judgment against trustee.—When any person is adjudged a trustee of any debtor as aforesaid, except where it is otherwise provided, judgment will be rendered and execution issue against such trustee, his own goods and estate, therefor, or for so much thereof as will satisfy the judgment against the principal defendant, in the same manner as if such suit were brought against him personally.

II. BY SUIT AT COMMON LAW.

Cases where bail may be required.—No female may be arrested or imprisoned on any writ in any action founded on contract. (*a*)

No person entitled to vote at any town meeting, on the day of such meeting, will be liable to arrest on any civil process: nor any officer or soldier, while going to, returning from, or attending at any military exercise, parade, court martial, or court of inquiry, which it may be his duty to attend: nor any executor or administrator for a cause of action against any person deceased: nor any sheriff while he remains in office: nor any person on mesne process in any real action or action of ejectment.

(*a*) R. S. 185.

No person may be arrested or imprisoned on any writ in any action founded on a contract, unless the debt or damage for which such action is brought, exclusive of costs, exceed the sum of thirteen dollars and thirty-three cents.

No person may be arrested on any writ or execution founded on a contract made after March 1, 1841, unless the plaintiff or some person in his behalf make an affidavit before a justice, on the back of the writ, that in his belief the defendant is justly indebted to said plaintiff in a sum exceeding thirteen dollars and thirty-three cents, and that he conceals his property so that no attachment or levy can be made, or that there is good reason to believe he is about to leave the state to avoid the payment of his debts. Any person so arrested may require the officer to carry him before two justices, one of them to be of the quorum, and if the facts above stated appear true to them, said defendant will be committed to jail, unless he procure sufficient bail: if they do not appear true, he will be discharged from arrest.

Time within which judgment may be obtained where there is no controversy.—In an action where there is no appearance for the defendant, judgment may be obtained at the close of the term when said action is entered.

Every species of property may be sold on execution; the debtor being to redeem real estate within a year.

Executions, when to issue, and when returnable.—No execution may issue till twenty-four hours after judgment rendered.

Executions from the Superior Court are returnable at the next regular term of the court, if within six months, otherwise within six months from the date thereof: executions from the Court of Common Pleas, at the next term thereof; and executions issued by justices within sixty days from their date.

Executions against property of persons imprisoned.—When a debtor is committed to prison on execution, the creditor on return of the same may have a further execution against the property of the debtor, although his person be not discharged, and upon the satisfaction of such execution the debtor will be discharged. (*a*)

Provisions in reference to liability of sheriffs and attorneys

(*a*) R. S. 193.

for refusing to pay over moneys collected, and as to Executions against Sheriffs.—Substantially the same as in Massachusetts.

11. *Courts.*

The judicial power is distributed between the Superior Court of Judicature, the Circuit Court, and the Court of Common Pleas, The former holds an annual, the latter a semi-annual term in each county of the state. The latter court is that in which all actions are brought for the recovery of debts and the enforcement of contracts, and all jury trials are held. There are also in each county, courts of probate.

VERMONT.

1. *Assurances and Evidences of Debt.*

Proceedings in actions of account.—If the defendant, in any action of account, plead any thing, which being true, he ought not to account, it will be tried by a jury, and if the verdict be against him, or if said defendant do not appear, or appearing, confess that he ought to account with the plaintiff, the court will render judgment that he do account, and will appoint auditors to examine and adjust the accounts between the parties. Said auditors may call for the books of the parties, and may examine under oath the parties to the suit and other witnesses, and on their report thereon to the court, judgment will be rendered on such report, if no just cause appear to the contrary, for such sum as is found to be in arrear from either party, with costs, including those of the auditors, to be paid by the successful party; such judgment to be final. (*a*)

Grace on bills and notes, and actions thereon.—Bills of exchange, drafts, and promissory notes, executed in any other state

(*a*) R. S. 36.

and payable in this state, and all such bills, drafts, and notes executed in this state and payable in any other state, will be entitled to three days grace : this provision not extending to contracts payable on demand or in any way but in money.

The indorsee of any bill or promissory note for the payment of money to any person, or order, or bearer, may maintain an action in his own name for the recovery of the money.

The holder of any bill or note, payable in money to the bearer, or to any person or bearer, may maintain an action thereon in his own name without indorsement. (*a*)

Seal of court, or public office or officer.—In cases where the seal of any court or public office or officer is required to be affixed to any paper issuing from such court or office, the word *seal* includes an impression of such official seal made on paper alone, as well as one made by means of a wafer or of wax affixed thereto. (*b*)

2. *Damages upon Protested Bills of Exchange.*

There is no provision upon the subject of this title.

The Law of Usury.

What is lawful interest.—The lawful rate of interest is six dollars on a hundred dollars for a year, and the same rate for a greater or less sum, and for a longer or shorter time.

Persons paying usurious interest may recover what.—Any person paying more than lawful interest may recover back the amount so paid above the legal interest, with interest thereon from the time of payment, in an action of assumpsit, declaring for money had and received, or goods sold and delivered, as the case may be.

Certain contracts excepted.—The foregoing provisions do not extend to the letting of cattle and other usages of like nature among farmers, or maritime contracts, bottomry, or course of exchange, as has been customary.

(*a*) R. S. 73. (*b*) Ib. 4.

4. *Frauds.*

Statute of frauds.—No action, in law or equity, may be brought,—

1st. To charge an executor or administrator on any special promise to answer damages out of his own estate:

2d. To charge any person on any special promise to answer for the debt, default, or misdoings of another:

3d. To charge any person on any agreement made on consideration of marriage:

4th. Upon any contract for the sale of lands, tenements, or hereditaments, or of any interest in or concerning them:

5th. Upon any agreement that is not to be performed within one year from the making thereof:

Unless the promise, contract, or agreement upon which such action may be brought, or some memorandum or note thereof, shall be in writing and signed by the party to be charged therewith, or by some person lawfully authorized by him; and if the contract or agreement relate to the sale of real estate, or any interest therein, such authority must be conferred in writing. (*a*)

No contract for the sale of goods, wares, or merchandise, for the price of forty dollars or more, will be valid, unless the purchaser accept and receive part of the goods so sold, or give something in earnest, to bind the bargain or in part payment, or unless some note or memorandum of the bargain be made in writing and signed by the party to be charged thereby, or by some person lawfully authorized.

No action may be brought to charge any person upon any representation or assurance made concerning the character, conduct, credit, ability, trade, or dealings of any other person, unless such representation or assurance be made in writing, and signed by the party to be charged thereby, or by some person lawfully authorized.

Provision as to mortgages of machinery.—No mortgage of any machinery used in any factory, shop, or mill, hereafter made, will be valid against any other person than the parties thereto,

(*a*) R. S. 61.

unless possession of such machinery be delivered to and retained by the mortgagee.

Fraudulent conveyances and contracts.—All fraudulent and deceitful conveyances of houses, lands, tenements, or hereditaments, or of goods and chattels, all bonds, titles, notes, contracts, and agreements, all suits, judgments, and executions, made or had, to avoid any right, debt, or duty of any other person, shall, as against the party or parties only, whose right, debt, or duty is attempted to be avoided, their heirs, executors, administrators, or assigns, be void: and any party to such proceedings, who shall justify the same to have been made, had, or executed *bona fide* and upon good consideration, or who shall alien or assign any such houses, lands, &c., so conveyed to him or them as aforesaid, shall forfeit their value, and the value of such goods and chattels, also so much money as is mentioned in such covinous bond, bill, note, contract, agreement, judgment, and execution; such forfeitures to be equally divided between the party aggrieved and the county in which such offence is committed, to be recovered by an action on the case, founded on this statute. (*a*)

5. *Limited Partnerships, and Liability of Corporate Institutions.*

The laws in reference to limited partnerships in Vermont correspond with those in Massachusetts, with the following exceptions.

If there is no newspaper printed in the county where the principal place of business of the partnership is situated, the certificate of partnership must be published in a newspaper printed in an adjoining county in this state.

The same rule holds in reference to the place of publication of the dissent of creditors from an assignment made by a partnership.

No dissolution of a limited partnership can take place, except by operation of law, before the time specified in the certificate above mentioned, unless a notice of such dissolution be recorded and published in like manner as the original certificate. The other provisions found in the Massachusetts statute in reference to notice of dissolution, are not in force in this state: nor is equity jurisdiction of questions arising under this chapter given to the Supreme Court. (*b*)

(*a*) R. S. 95. (*b*) R. S. 75.

Capital stock subject to attachment, &c.—The capital stock of any private corporation, whether owned by such corporation or individuals, will be liable to and held by attachments, and may be taken and sold on executions against such corporation. (*a*)

Provision in case of two attachments of corporate property, the first by a director and the second by another creditor.—When the property of any private corporation is attached on a writ in favor of a person who is a director of such corporation, and the same property is afterwards attached by another creditor of the corporation, who is not a director, and before the time when, by law, the first attachment should be returned, the attachment so made by such director will be postponed, and such subsequent attachment will hold the property against the attachment of such director.

After sundry provisions in reference to a general bank fund, to insolvent banks, the duties of bank commissioners, the amount of capital to be paid in, &c., the following provisions are made:

Bank charter forfeited, by what.—If any moneyed corporation, having banking powers, created or rechartered after October 1st, 1831, issue, or have outstanding or in circulation at any time an amount of notes or bills loaned or put in circulation as money, exceeding three times its capital stock then paid in and actually possessed, or neglect to make the required annual payments to the state treasurer for three months after they ought to be made, or lose one half of the capital stock paid in, or suspend the payment of its bills in specie for sixty days, or refuse to allow the officers of such corporation to be examined on oath by the bank commissioner in relation to the condition and affairs of such corporation, said corporation may be proceeded against by said commissioner and enjoined by the Court of Chancery as an insolvent corporation. (*b*)

Bank not subject to certain provisions if private property is holden.—If any banking company, hereafter incorporated, chartered or rechartered, by its act of incorporation make the private property of the stockholders holden to redeem the bills issued by such corporation, it will not be required to comply with the conditions of this chapter.

Punishment for fraudulently issuing bills, &c.—Any director or other officer of a bank, or any person interested in or having

(*a*) R. S. 79. (*b*) R. S. 80.

charge or control of the same, who shall corruptly put or cause to be put in circulation any amount of the bills of such bank beyond the amount prescribed by its charter, will be confined to hard labor in the state prison for a term not exceeding ten years.

Loans not to be made on pledge of stock.—No person may take or borrow from any bank, hereafter chartered or rechartered, any money by reason of the pledge of any stock in such bank.

How far stockholders may be indebted to a bank.—The stockholders and officers of any bank may not at any one time be directly or indirectly indebted to such bank to a greater amount than fifteen per cent. of the capital stock of such bank, actually paid in; and no individual stockholder or officer of such bank may at any one time be indebted to the same, directly or indirectly, to a greater amount than two thousand dollars: nor may any stockholder or officer, directly or indirectly, receive any loan or discount at such bank unless he procure two good and sufficient sureties for the same, neither of whom are stockholders or officers of such bank.

Penalty for disobeying provisions of the last two sections.—If any bank, directly or indirectly, make any loan or discount, contrary to the provisions of the last two sections, such corporation may be proceeded against and enjoined by the Court of Chancery as an insolvent corporation.

Bank not to loan till all its capital stock is paid in.---No bank, hereafter chartered or rechartered, may make any loans or discounts till all the capital stock is actually paid in, in gold and silver coin.

Capital stock not to be divided till charter expires.---If any bank, hereafter chartered or rechartered, shall directly or indirectly distribute or divide any portion of its capital stock among the stockholders of such corporation, before the expiration of its charter, such bank may be proceeded against and enjoined as an insolvent corporation.

6. *Insolvent Laws.*

There is no peculiar provision on the subject of this title.

7. *Effect of Marriage upon Rights of Property.*

The same observation is to be made as to this title.

8. *Limitation of Personal Actions.*

Certain specified laws, the same as in Massachusetts.—For laws of Vermont, as to actions to be brought within six years; certain actions against sheriffs; suits by aliens; limitation of actions for slander and libel; remedies in case of reversal, arrest of judgment, &c.; limitation of demands filed in set-off; limitation of suits by or in behalf of the state; new promise to be in writing; promise by one of several debtors, and proceedings in an action against such debtors; the effect of part payment (omitting the provision as to memorandum of payment purporting to be made by the party receiving such payment); see laws of Massachusetts on the same subject. (*a*)

Actions for assault and battery.—Actions for assault and battery, and false imprisonment, must be commenced within three years after the cause of action accrues.

Actions on attested notes.—Actions on attested notes must be brought within fourteen years next after the cause of action accrues thereon.

Actions of debt, or scire facias on judgment.—Actions of debt, or scire facias on judgment, must be brought within eight years next after the rendition of such judgment; and all actions of debt on specialties within eight years after the cause of action accrues.

Actions of covenant.—Actions of covenant, other than the covenants of warranty and seisin, contained in deeds of conveyance of land, must be brought within eight years next after the cause of action accrues. All actions of covenant brought on any covenant of warranty, contained in any deed of conveyance of land, must be brought within eight years next after the final decision against the title of the covenantor in such deed; and all actions of covenant brought on any covenant of seisin, contained in such deed, must be brought within fifteen years next after the cause of action accrues.

Case of defendants out of the state.—If at the time when any cause of action of a personal nature, mentioned in this chapter,

(*a*) R. S. 58.

accrues against any person, he is out of the state, the action may be commenced within the time herein limited therefor, after such person comes into the state; and if, after such cause of action has accrued, and before the statute has run, the person against whom it has accrued, is absent from, and resides out of the state, having no known property within the state which could be attached, the time of his absence will not be taken as any part of the time limited for the commencement of the action.

Case of action stayed by injunction.—Whenever the commencement of any suit is stayed by an injunction of any court of equity, the time during which such injunction is in force, will not be deemed any portion of the time limited for the commencement of such suit.

Exception for certain disabilities.—If any person, entitled to bring any action in this chapter specified, at the time when the cause of action accrues, be a minor, or married woman, insane, or imprisoned, such person may bring said action within the times herein respectively limited, after the disability is removed.

Exceptions as to certain suits against moneyed corporations.—None of the provisions of this chapter apply to suits brought to enforce payment on bills, notes, or other evidences of debt, issued by moneyed corporations.

Provisions as to written promise, &c., when to take effect.—None of the provisions of this chapter respecting the acknowledgment of a debt, or a new promise to pay it, will apply to any such acknowledgment or promise made before January 1st, 1842; but every such last mentioned acknowledgment or promise, although not made in writing, will have the same effect as if no provisions relating thereto had been herein contained.

9. *Effect of Death on the Rights of Creditors.*

Appointment and removal of executors and administrators, with the will annexed.—See laws of Massachusetts.

Personal estate, how distributed.—The personal estate of intestates will be applied as follows: (*a*)

1st. The widow, if any, will be allowed her apparel and orna-

(*a*) R. S. 47.

ments, the wearing apparel of the deceased, and such other of the personal estate as the probate court may assign her: which will not be less than one-third after the payment of the debts and charges.

2d. The widow and children constituting the family of the deceased will have such allowance as the probate court deem necessary for their maintenance during the settlement of the estate; which in case of an insolvent estate will not be longer than eight months after granting administration, nor at any time after the dower and personal estate are assigned to the widow.

3d. When any person dies, leaving children under seven years of age, having no mother, or when the mother dies before the children reach the age of seven years, an allowance will be made for the necessary maintenance of such children till they are seven years old, out of such part of the personal estate and the income of such part of the real estate as would have been assigned to their mother had she been living.

4th. If on the return of the inventory of any intestate estate, it appear that the value of such estate does not exceed one hundred and fifty dollars, the probate court may assign for the use and support of the widow and children of the intestate, or for the support of the children under seven years of age, if there be no widow, the whole of said estate, after the payment of funeral charges and expenses of administration.

5th. If the personal estate amount to more than one hundred and fifty dollars, and more than the allowance before mentioned, it will be applied to the payment of the debts of the deceased, his funeral charges, and expenses of settling the estate.

6th. The residue, if any, of the personal estate, will go to the same persons and for the same purposes, as prescribed for the disposition of real estate.

What court will grant administration.—See laws of Massachusetts, substituting the word "district" for "county."

To whom administration will be granted.—Administration will be granted:

1st. To the widow or next of kin, or both, or such persons as they request to have appointed.

2d. To one or more of the principal creditors.

3d. To such persons as the probate court may judge proper.

Examination of persons suspected of concealing, embezzling, &c., effects of the deceased.—See laws of Massachusetts.

Proceedings when personal estate is insufficient to pay debts.—See laws of Massachusetts.

Appointment of commissioners, their duties, &c.—Where letters testamentary or of administration are granted by any probate court, such court will appoint two or more commissioners to receive, examine, and adjust all claims and demands against the deceased, except where it appear that there are no debts against such deceased person, or that the value of such estate does not exceed one hundred and fifty dollars, and is assigned, as before provided, for the support of the widow and children. From the decision and report of the commissioners, allowing or disallowing any claim to the amount of twenty dollars, any executor, administrator, or creditor may appeal to the next stated session of the county court in the same county. (*a*)

Distribution of assets in case of solvent and insolvent estates.—If, on the report of commissioners and ascertaining the amount of claims against the estate, it appear that the executor or administrator has enough to pay the debts, he must pay the same within the time appointed by law: if he has not enough for that purpose, after paying the expenses of administration, he will pay the debts in the following order: 1st. The necessary funeral expenses. 2d. The expenses of the last sickness. 3d. Taxes. 4th. Debts due the state. 5th. Debts due the United States. 6th. Debts due to other creditors. If there be not assets enough to pay all the debts of any one class, each creditor will have a dividend in proportion to his claim: and no creditor of any one class will receive any payment till those of the preceding class are fully paid.

Executor and administrator, how liable for neglect to render account.—When an executor or administrator, after being duly cited by the probate court, shall neglect to render his account, he will be liable on his bond for all damages which may accrue; and his bond may be put in suit on the application of any person interested in the estate.

(*a*) R. S. 49.

10. *Mode of Collecting Debts.*

I. BY FOREIGN ATTACHMENT.

In what actions this process lies.—All actions founded on any contract, express or implied, entered into since January 1st, 1839, and all actions founded on any contract where the principal defendant has absconded from, or is resident out of this state, or is concealed within this state, brought in the county court, or before a justice when the matter in demand exceeds the sum of forty dollars, may be commenced by the trustee process. (*a*)

Form of the writ, and what attachment it authorizes, and who are liable as trustees.—See laws of Massachusetts.

Trustee when and how to be discharged; his examination on oath, his default on non-appearance, and the mode of trial when he appears.—See laws of Massachusetts. For exception in reference to trustee's disclosure, see "*Trustee's disclosure not conclusive.*"

Case in which adverse claimant may become a party to the suit; the proceedings in such case, and when principal defendant may be a witness.—See laws of Massachusetts.

Case of trustee having specific goods. What demands not attachable by this process.—No person may be adjudged a trustee,—

1st. By reason of any money or other thing due from him to the principal defendant, unless it is, at the time of the service of the writ on him, due absolutely and without depending on any contingency.

2d. By reason of any debt due from him on a judgment, so long as he is liable to an execution on the judgment.

Attachment of debt before it is payable, and case of fraudulent conveyance to trustee.—See laws of Massachusetts.

Trustee's disclosure not conclusive.—The answers and statements sworn to by any person summoned as a trustee will not be considered as conclusive in deciding how far he is chargeable, but either party may allege and prove any facts that may be material in deciding that question.

(*a*) R. S. 29.

Liability of trustee if he do not pay the sum on account of which he is adjudged a trustee.—If any person adjudged a trustee refuse or neglect to pay such sum as the court determines to be due from him to the principal defendant by the time specified in the order of court, he will be liable for the same, with interest, to the plaintiff in the action, to be recovered in an action on the case.

If debt recovered by plaintiff or the amount in the trustee's hands do not exceed ten dollars, trustee to be discharged.—If the amount of debt or damages recovered by the plaintiff in any trustee process, do not exceed ten dollars, or if the goods, effects, and credits in the hands of the trustee do not exceed in value ten dollars, the trustee will be discharged, and recover his costs against the plaintiff.

II. BY SUIT AT COMMON LAW.

Ordinary process in civil causes; and attachments, how issued; writs not to issue unless costs are secured.—The ordinary mode of process in civil causes in the several courts of this state is by writ of summons or attachment. Said writs of attachment may issue against the goods, chattels, or estate of the defendant, and for want thereof against his body. (*a*)

No writ of summons or attachment, requiring any person to appear and answer before any court in this state, will be issued unless there be sufficient security given to the defendant by way of recognizance, by some person other than the plaintiff, to the satisfaction of the authority signing such writ, that the plaintiff shall prosecute his writ to effect, and shall answer all damages, if judgment be rendered against him.

Real and personal property attached, how long held.—Personal property attached on mesne process will be held to respond to the judgment rendered on such process thirty days from the time of rendering such judgment; and unless the plaintiff, within said thirty days, take such property in execution, it will be discharged from such process; and real estate, attached on such process, will be held five calendar months after the rendition of final judgment,

(*a*) R. S. 28.

and no longer, unless such personal property or real estate be incumbered by a prior attachment, in which case such personal property will be held thirty days, and such real estate five calendar months, after such incumbrance is removed.

Arrest on mesne process.—When the body of any person is arrested on mesne process, the officer will commit him to jail unless he expose personal property sufficient to secure such officer, or procure some person to become surety to the satisfaction of such officer, by indorsing his name as bail on the back of the writ.

When courts will issue executions, and when executions are returnable.—The Supreme and County Courts, respectively, may issue execution in due form of law, in twenty-four hours after the rising of the court, on every final judgment rendered by such court, which will be made returnable within sixty days from the date thereof, or at the next term of such court (if not less than sixty days), at the election of the party.

Imprisonment of debtors.—No female may be arrested or imprisoned on any mesne process issuing in any action founded on contract, nor on any execution issuing on a judgment recovered in any such action.

No person, who is a resident citizen of this state, may be arrested or imprisoned by virtue of any mesne process issuing in an action founded on a contract, express or implied, entered into after January 1, 1839, nor by virtue of any execution, issued on a judgment recovered in an action founded on any such contract; provided, that if the plaintiff in an action on any contract made after said date, file with the authority issuing the writ an affidavit that he has good reason to believe and does believe that the defendant is about to abscond from the state, and has secreted about his person or elsewhere money or other property, such writ may issue as an attachment against, and be served upon the body of the defendant.

When the goods or chattels of the debtor cannot be found, sufficient to satisfy the execution and legal fees thereon, the officer may commit the debtor to jail.

Liability of sheriff neglecting or refusing to pay over money on execution.—If any sheriff neglect or refuse, on demand made, to pay to the creditor in any execution, his agent or attorney, all such sums of money as said sheriff shall have received on such execution, he will forfeit and must pay to the person to whose use he received such money, fifteen per cent. interest thereon while he detains the same after said demand. (*a*)

Time within which judgment may be obtained where there is no controversy.—On an action where there is no appearance for the defendant, judgment may be obtained at the close of the term when said action is entered.

11. *Courts.*

The judicial power is vested in a Supreme Court, and County Courts, or Courts of Common Pleas. The former is held once, the latter twice a year in each county of the state. The Chancery Courts have two stated sessions annually in each county.

(*a*) R. S. 11.

MASSACHUSETTS.

1. *Assurances and Evidences of Debt.*

Mutual and open accounts, how affected by limitation of actions.—See title, "*Limitation of Actions.*"

Method of proving book accounts.—The original memoranda of charges made by a party, at or near the time of the transaction to be proved, though not kept regularly in the manner of a day-book, are competent evidence, with the suppletory oath of the party, to prove the items charged, and the jury are to judge of their credit. But every memorandum of a shop-keeper or laborer is not to be admitted as his book. The charges must afford a fair presumption that they were the daily minutes of his business transactions. (*a*)

If the clerk who made the entries is dead or insane, the book is admissible on proving his handwriting. (*b*)

Where a tradesman's day-book has marks which show that the items have been transferred to a ledger, the ledger must be

(*a*) 2 Mass. R. 217. 13 Mass. R. 427. 4 Mass. R. 455. (*b*) 3 Pick. R. 396.

produced, that the other party may have advantage of any items entered therein to his credit. (*a*)

Where entries were first made on a slate, and afterwards transcribed upon a book, kept in the ledger form, such book was admitted as evidence to prove the items charged. (*b*)

Set off of mutual demands.—Mutual debts and demands between plaintiff and defendant in any action, may be set off, subject to the following restrictions:

No demand may be set off, unless founded on a judgment, or a contract, express or implied; nor unless it is for the price of real or personal estate sold, or for money paid, money had and received, or for services, or unless it is a sum that is liquidated, or one that may be ascertained by calculation; nor unless it existed at the time of the commencement of the suit, and then belonged to the defendant, nor unless it is due to him in his own right.

Any demand assigned to the defendant, with notice to the plaintiff of the assignment before the commencement of the action, may be set off as if originally payable to the defendant.

If the demand set off is founded on a bond or other contract having a penalty, only the sum equitably due will be set off.

The set off will be allowed only in actions founded on demands which could themselves be the subject of set off.

After a demand in set off is filed, the plaintiff will not be allowed to discontinue his action, unless by consent of the defendant. (*c*)

Bills of exchange and promissory notes,—Grace on: Void, if given for gaming consideration: Provisions as to notes payable on demand.—On all bills of exchange payable at sight or at a future day certain, and on all promissory negotiable notes payable at a future day certain, within this state, in which there is no express stipulation to the contrary, grace will be allowed, as it is by the custom of merchants, on foreign bills of exchange, payable at the expiration of a certain period after date or sight: but these provisions do not extend to any bill of exchange, note, or draft, payable on demand. (*d*)

All notes, or other securities or conveyances in which the

(*a*) 2 Mass. R. 569. (*b*) 13 Ib. 427. (*c*) R. S. 96. (*d*) R. S. 303.

whole or any part of the consideration is for money or goods won by gaming, or bets thereon, or for repaying money knowingly lent or advanced for any gaming or betting, or at the time and place of such gaming or betting, to any person so gaming or betting, will be void as between the parties, and as to all persons, except those who claim under them in good faith and without notice of the illegality of the consideration. (*a*)

In any action on a promissory note payable on demand, brought by an indorser against the promissor, any matter will be deemed a legal defence, and may be given in evidence, which would be a legal defence to a suit on the same note, if brought by the promissee. (*b*)

On a promissory note payable on demand, made after this act goes into operation, (act passed April 6, 1839,) a demand made within or at the expiration of sixty days from the date thereof, without grace, will be deemed to be made within a reasonable time; and any thing which is deemed equivalent to a presentment and demand on a note payable at a fixed time, or which would dispense with such presentment and demand, if it occur at or within the said sixty days, will be deemed a dishonor thereof, and will authorize the holder to give notice of such dishonor to the indorser, as upon a presentment to the promissor, and his neglect or refusal to pay the same. And no presentment of such note to the promissor and demand of payment will be deemed to be made within a reasonable time, so as to charge the indorser, unless made on or before the last of said sixty days.

Instruments importing consideration.—The words "value received" are only *prima facie* evidence of consideration. (*c*)

Contracts under seal are valid without consideration. (*d*)

The American courts have been disposed to treat the recital of the *amount* of consideration in a deed of conveyance, like the mention of the date of the deed, the quantity of land, and other recitals of quantity and value to which the attention of the parties is supposed to have been but slightly directed, and to which, therefore, the doctrine of estoppels does not apply. Hence, though the party is estopped from denying the conveyance, and

(*a*) R. S. 50. (*b*) Ib. 121. (*c*) 14 Pick. 198. 5 Ib. 391. 6 Ib. 427, 433.
(*d*) 8 Mass. Rep. 162, 200. 2 Ib. 159.

that it was for a valuable consideration, yet the weight of American authority is in favor of treating the recital as only *prima facie* evidence of the amount paid, in an action of covenant by the grantee, to recover back the consideration, or in an action of assumpsit by the grantor, to recover the price yet unpaid. (*a*)

2. *Rates of Damages on Protested Bills.*

Bills payable without the United States.—When a bill drawn or indorsed in Massachusetts, and payable without the United States, except in Africa, beyond the Cape of Good Hope, and Asia, and the islands thereof, is duly protested, the party liable for the contents must, on due notice and demand, pay the same at the current rate of exchange at the time of the demand, and damages at the rate of five per cent. on said contents, with interest thereon, computed from the date of the protest, in full of all damages, charges, and expenses. (*b*)

Bills payable beyond the Cape of Good Hope, &c.—In the excepted cases above mentioned, the contents of the bill must, on due notice and demand, pay the same at its par value, with twenty per cent. thereon, in full of all damages, interest, and charges. (*c*)

Bills payable out of the state, but within the United States.—Damages on inland bills are as follows: on bills payable in Maine, New Hampshire, Vermont, Rhode Island, Connecticut, and New-York, two per cent.; in New Jersey, Pennsylvania, Maryland, and Delaware, three per cent.; in Virginia, the District of Columbia, North Carolina, South Carolina, and Georgia, four per cent.; and within any other of the United States, or the territories thereof, five per cent. (*d*)

Bills payable within this state.—The rate of damages on bills of exchange, and orders for the payment of money, drawn or indorsed in Massachusetts, for any sum not less than one hundred dollars, payable in the state, at any place not less than seventy-five miles from the place where the same is drawn or indorsed, when such bills or orders are not duly accepted or paid,

(*a*) Greenleaf on Evidence, vol. i. sec. 26. 17 Mass. Rep. 249. 20 Pick. Rep. 247.
(*b*) R. S. 33. (*c*) Ib. 33. (*d*) Ib. 239.

are one per cent. in addition to the contents thereof, and interest on said contents. (*a*)

3. *Usury.*

The rate of interest.—The rate of interest is six per cent. per annum. (*b*)

Effect of usury on a contract.—No contract for the payment of money with interest at a greater rate than six per cent. is thereby rendered void; but whenever, in an action brought on such contract, it appears upon a special plea to that effect, that a greater rate of interest than the law allows, has been directly or indirectly reserved, taken, or received, the defendant recovers his full costs, and the plaintiff forfeits threefold the whole interest reserved or taken, and has judgment only for the balance due after deducting said threefold amount. (*c*)

Party paying usurious interest to recover back threefold the whole interest.—A party paying more than legal interest may recover back threefold the whole interest paid, by an action of debt, or by a bill in chancery, provided such action or bill be prosecuted within two years after said interest has been paid.

Debtor and creditor may be witnesses in certain actions.—In the trial of any action where it appears by the pleadings that the fact of unlawful interest having been taken or reserved is put in issue, the debtor (the creditor being living) may become a witness, and the creditor, if he offer his testimony, shall also be a witness.

4. *Frauds.*

Statute of frauds.—No action (*d*) may be brought in any of the following cases, unless the promise, contract, or agreement on which such action is brought, or some memorandum or note thereof, is in writing, signed by the party to be charged, or some person authorized by him:

1st. To charge an executor or administrator on any special promise to answer damages out of his own estate.

(*a*) R. S. 33. (*b*) 12 Pick. R. 586. R. S. 35. (*c*) 7 Pick. R. 40. (*d*) R. S. 472.

2d. To charge any person upon any special promise to answer for the debt, default, or misdoings of another.

3d. To charge any person upon an agreement made in consideration of marriage.

4th. Upon any contract for the sale of lands, tenements, or hereditaments, or of any interest in or concerning them.

5th. Upon any agreement not to be performed within one year from the making thereof.

The consideration of such promise, contract, or agreement need not be expressed in the writing, signed by the party to be charged therewith, but may be proved by any other legal evidence.

No action shall be brought on any representation or assurance concerning the character, conduct, credit, ability, trade or dealings of any other person, unless such representation or assurance be made in writing, and signed by the party to be charged thereby, or by some person authorized by him.

No contract for the sale of goods for the price of fifty dollars or more shall be valid, unless the purchaser accept and receive part of the goods sold, or give something in earnest to bind the bargain or in part payment, or unless some note or memorandum in writing of the bargain be made and signed by the party to be charged thereby, or some person authorized by him.

Provisions as to delivery of mortgaged property, &c.—No mortgage of personal property is valid against any other person than the parties thereto, unless possession of the mortgaged property be delivered to and retained by the mortgagee, or unless the mortgage be recorded by the clerk of the town where the mortgagor resides, and by the clerk of the town where he principally transacts his business. But nothing herein contained will avoid or defeat any contract of bottomry or respondentia, or the transfer, assignment or hypothecation of any ship or goods, at sea or abroad, if the mortgagee shall take possession of such ship or goods as soon as may be after the arrival thereof within this state.

A mortgage of goods which the mortgagor does not own when the mortgage is made, though he afterwards acquires them, is void as against his attaching creditors. (*a*)

(*a*) 10 Met. Rep. 481.

Frauds in general.—An act done with intent to defraud is no ground for a civil action for fraud, unless some actual damage be occasioned to the plaintiff. (*a*)

Oral representations made by the vendor previously to a written contract of sale, may be introduced to show fraud. (*b*)

All the members of a firm are liable for the fraud of one of them, or of their agent, in the course of his employment, in the sale of partnership property. (*c*)

Fraudulent conveyances.—A conveyance made to defraud creditors, though voidable by them, is valid against the grantor and his heirs. (*d*)

A conveyance with intent to defraud creditors cannot be avoided by them, unless the grantee participated in such fraudulent intent. (*e*)

In order to impeach a conveyance as fraudulent against creditors, being without consideration, or on a secret trust, it is not necessary to show that the grantor was insolvent at the time of conveying, but only that he was deeply indebted. (*f*)

A conveyance of land originally fraudulent as against creditors, is not thereby void, but only voidable, and may be purged of fraud if the fraudulent intent be abandoned, and the grant confirmed for adequate consideration. (*g*)

A fraudulent grantee cannot be held as trustee of the grantor after having paid bona fide debts of the grantor to the full amount of the property received. (*h*)

Real estate purchased by a debtor, and held by the vendor or some other person for the purpose of defrauding creditors, may be attached and taken in execution as the property of the debtor. (*i*)

A deed executed and registered without the knowledge of the grantee is valid if subsequently accepted by him. (*k*)

An assignment of chattels in trust for the payment of debts, not signed by or assented to by any creditors, renders the assignee liable as trustee of the debtor. (*l*)

(*a*) 2 Mass. R. 111. (*b*) 22 Pick. R. 546. (*c*) 1 Met. R. 560.
(*d*) 4 Mass. R. 354. 3 Ib. 573, 580. 20 Pick. R. 247.
(*e*) 12 Mass. R. 456. 12 Pick. R. 89. 14 Mass. R. 245, 250. 3 Met. R. 63.
(*f*) 19 Pick. R. 231. (*g*) 3 Met. R. 332. (*h*) 12 Mass. R. 140.
(*i*) R. S. 107. (*k*) 12 Mass. R. 456. (*l*) 9 Pick. R. 13.

Fraudulent sales of personal property.—A sale of goods procured by fraud in the vendee is not void, but voidable by the vendor; and until it is so avoided, the vendee may give a perfect title to a bona fide purchaser, without notice of the fraud. (*a*)

If on a sale the vendor makes untrue statements of matters of fact, as of his own knowledge, and the vendee is thereby deceived, he may avoid the sale, though the vendor did not know whether they were true or false. (*b*)

Where the members of a corporation are personally liable for the debts, a transfer of shares to avoid the levy of an execution for such debts upon the person or individual property is fraudulent and void as against creditors. (*c*)

The sale of goods without delivery of possession is invalid as against an attaching creditor of the vendor. (*d*)

But after an actual sale and delivery of goods, possession by the vendor is not a conclusive badge of fraud so as to render the sale void as against creditors. (*e*)

The continuance of a mortgagor in possession and use of the property after a mortgage becomes absolute, does not per se constitute fraud. (*f*)

If any person summoned as a trustee have in his possession goods, effects, or credits of the principal defendant, which he holds by a conveyance or title void as to the creditors of such defendant, he may be adjudged trustee on account of such goods, effects and credits, though the principal defendant could not have maintained an action therefor against him. (*g*)

5. *Principals, Factors, and Agents.*

Every factor or other agent intrusted with the possession of any merchandise for the purpose of sale, or any bill of lading consigning the same to such factor for that purpose, shall be deemed the true owner thereof, so as to give effect to any bona fide contracts made by such factor with any third person for the

(*a*) 12 Pick. R. 307. (*b*) 18 Ib. 95. (*c*) 17 Mass. R. 330.
(*d*) 17 Mass. R. 110. 7 Pick. R. 56. 11 Ib. 352.
(*e*) 15 Mass. R. 244. 2 Pick. R. 14 Ib. 464, 497. (*f*) 19 Pick. R. 202.
(*g*) R. S. 109, § 35. 4 Mass. R. 508. 12 Ib. 140. 5 Ib. 390.

sale of such merchandise in whole or in part. The consignee of merchandise shall have a lien thereon, to secure the payment of any money advanced, or securities given to the shipper on account of such consignment, where such consignee has no notice at the time of making the advance by the bill of lading or otherwise, that the shipper is not the bona fide owner thereof, and where also at the time of the shipment, the merchandise was in the lawful possession of the shipper. (*a*)

6. *Limited Partnerships, and Liability of Corporate Institutions.*

Limited partnerships may be formed except for banking and insurance.—Limited partnerships may be formed for the transaction of mercantile, mechanical, or manufacturing business, upon the conditions hereafter stated; but none of the provisions herein contained authorize such partnerships for the purpose of banking and insurance. (*b*)

Liabilities of general and special partners.—Said partnerships may consist of one or more persons, called general partners, to be jointly and severally responsible like other general partners, and of one or more persons contributing a specific sum in cash as capital, to be called special partners, and not to be personally liable for debts of the partnership, except as hereinafter provided.

Certificates to be made by partners, and to be acknowledged, recorded, and published.—The persons forming such partnerships must severally sign a certificate containing the name of the partnership, the names and places of residence of each of the general and special partners, specifying who are general and who are special partners, the amount of capital contributed by each special partner, the general nature of the business to be transacted, and the time when the partnership is to commence and terminate.

The partnership will not be deemed to have been formed till such a certificate shall be acknowledged by all the partners before a justice of the peace, and recorded in the registry of deeds of the county in which the principal place of the business of the partnership is situated, in a book kept for the purpose, open to

(*a*) Acts of 1845, 515. (*b*) R. S. 34.

public inspection; and if the partnership shall have places of business in different counties, a copy of the certificate certified by the register of deeds in whose office it shall be recorded must be filed and recorded in like manner in the office of the register of deeds in every such county; and if any false statement is made in such certificate, all interested in the partnership will be liable as general partners.

The partnership will be deemed general unless a copy of the certificate above-mentioned is published for six weeks next after said registry, in a newspaper printed in the county where their principal place of business is situated, or if no paper is printed there, in a newspaper printed in Boston.

Renewal of partnerships.—On every renewal of a limited partnership, a certificate thereof must be made, acknowledged, recorded, and published, as in the original formation of such partnership; otherwise it will be deemed a general partnership.

Partnership style; liability of special partners in case of deficit of assets.—The names of the general partners only are to be inserted in the firm, without the addition of the word company, or any other general term; and the business is to be transacted by the general partners only; and any special partner permitting his name to be used in the firm, or personally making any contract respecting partnership concerns with any person except the general partners, will be deemed a general partner.

While the partnership continues, no portion of the capital stock is to be withdrawn, nor any division of interest or profits to be made, so as to reduce such capital stock below the sum stated in the certificates above mentioned; and if during the existence, or at the termination of the partnership, the assets of such partnership do not suffice to pay its debts, the special partners will severally be held responsible for all sums received, withdrawn, or divided by them, with interest thereon from the time when they were withdrawn.

Assignments—when valid.—In case of insolvency, no general assignment will be valid, unless it provide for a pro ratâ distribution of the partnership property among all the creditors, excepting claims of the United States government, arising from bonds for duties, which are to be paid or secured first.

Assent of creditors to assignment, when to be presumed.—The assent of creditors to such assignment will be presumed, unless they dissent, expressly or impliedly, within sixty days after notice thereof; and notice of such assignment must be given within fourteen days after it is made, in some newspaper printed in the county where the place of business of the party making it is situated, or if there be no such newspaper, then in some newspaper printed in Boston. Partners doing business in Duke's county or Nantucket, must give such notice in some newspaper printed in Boston, within sixty days after the date of the assignment, if there is no newspaper printed in the counties, respectively, where their places of business are situated.

Suits to be by and against general partners, except in certain cases.—Suits respecting the partnership business must be brought by and against the general partners only, except where special partners are to be deemed general partners, in which case all who are deemed general partners may join or be joined in the suit, and excepting also the case above mentioned, where special partners are held severally responsible on account of sums withdrawn from the common stock.

Dissolution, how effected.—No dissolution of such partnership can take place, except by operation of law, before the time specified in the certificate, unless notice thereof is recorded in each registry where the original certificate or certificate of renewal before mentioned was recorded, and unless such notice is published six successive weeks in some newspaper printed in the county where the original certificates were published, if there be any such newspaper otherwise in one printed in Boston.

Liability of partners in cases not specially provided for.—In all cases not herein provided for, limited partners are subject to all the liabilities and entitled to all the rights of general partners.

Equity jurisdiction of Supreme Judicial Court.—The Supreme Judicial Court may hear and determine in equity all questions arising under these provisions.

Corporations to continue three years after charter expires, to close their concerns.—Corporations whose charters expire by their own limitation, or are annulled in any way, continue bodies corporate three years after such dissolution, for the purpose of prosecuting and defending suits, and closing their concerns. (*a*)

When corporations expire, receivers to be appointed.—On the expiration or annulling of the charter of any corporation, the Supreme Court may, on petition of any creditor, stockholder, or member, appoint receivers to take possession of the property and settle the affairs of the corporation: their powers to continue so long as the court shall think necessary. And said court has equity jurisdiction of all questions arising in the proceeding of such receivers.

Franchise may be attached and sold on execution: liability of the corporation in such case: right of redemption.—The franchise of any corporation authorized to receive toll, and all the rights and privileges thereof, are liable to attachment on mesne process, and may be sold on execution: the powers, duties, and liabilities of such corporation continuing the same after such sale as before. And such franchise may be redeemed by paying or tendering the purchaser the sum paid, with twelve per cent. interest thereon, without any allowance for the toll which he may have received.

Warrants of distress against corporations for damages.—A warrant of distress may issue against such corporation for damages, duly assessed, with interest thereon and reasonable costs, for any injury to property by the doings of such corporation, provided said damages remain unpaid thirty days after such assessment.

Remedy in equity against officers and members.—Money due from officers or members of a corporation for any debts thereof, or for any acts of the officers or members thereof, respecting the business thereof, may be recovered by a bill in equity to the Supreme Judicial Court.

7. *Insolvent Laws.*

Commissioner in insolvency, and his courts.—There is one commissioner in insolvency in each county, holding courts at the shire town thereof on the first Tuesday of each month, and at such other times and places as he may appoint. (*b*)

(*a*) R. S. 44.

(*b*) Insolvent Law of 1848, §§ 1 and 4.

Debtor's petition, and warrant thereon.—On the petition of any debtor owing not less than two hundred dollars, which he is unable to pay, to the commissioner for the county where he resides or has his usual place of business, such commissioner will issue a warrant to a messenger (who must be a sheriff or deputy sheriff of said county) (*a*), ordering him to take possession of all the estate of said debtor, both real and personal, and keep the same till the appointment of an assignee or assignees. (*b*)

Duties of messenger: first meeting.—Said messenger thereon takes possession of all of said estate, gives public and personal notice of the insolvency, and calls a meeting of creditors, to prove their debts and choose one or more assignees. In case no choice is made by creditors, the commissioner appoints. At this meeting the debtor must produce a full schedule of his creditors and assets. (*c*)

Duties of the assignee.—The assignee must accept in writing his appointment within four days after it is made (*d*); give bonds with sufficient sureties, if required by a majority of the creditors who have proved their claims, or by the commissioner (*e*); call such meetings of creditors as he shall be ordered by the commissioner: collect all the debtor's estate by suit or otherwise: convert the same into money, of which, with his expenses and charges, he must keep an accurate account, to be produced at the third meeting of the creditors (*f*): and pay out such dividends as may be ordered by the commissioner. The assignee may be removed by the vote of a majority of creditors, and a new one appointed. He may also be removed by the commissioner when it shall appear, on the complaint of some person interested in the estate, that he has been guilty of some fraudulent act in reference to said estate. (*g*) And he may be committed to the common jail, if he disobey any lawful order of the commissioner. (*h*)

(*a*) Laws of 1844, c. 178, § 10.

(*b*) Laws of 1838, c. 163, § 1. Laws of 1841, c. 124, § 1.

(*c*) Laws of 1838, c. 163, §§ 2, 6. By the Laws of 1848, c. 304, § 8, this schedule must be presented by the debtor to the messenger within three days after the date of the warrant, and the messenger must return the same at the first meeting.

(*d*) Laws of 1838, c, 163, § 2.

(*e*) Laws of 1844, c. 178, § 11. Insolvent Law of 1848, § 12.

(*f*) Laws of 1838, c. 163, §§ 11, 12.

(*g*) Laws of 1838, c. 163, § 11. Insolvent Law of 1848, § 12.

(*h*) Laws of 1838, c. 163, § 23.

Second meeting.—The assignee will call a second meeting of creditors by order of the commissioner, within three months from the date of the warrant to the messenger, at which meeting debts may be proved, the debtor may amend his schedules, and must make and subscribe an oath, to be filed in the case, that said schedules are correct, that his property has been fully and fairly delivered up for the benefit of his creditors, and that if any thing thereafter comes into his hands which ought to go to said creditors, it shall be delivered to the assignee for that purpose. (*a*)

Third and subsequent meetings.—The assignee will call a third meeting of creditors, by order of the commissioner, within six months after his appointment, at which meeting debts may be proved, the assignee will render a full account of all receipts and payments touching the estate of the debtor, and the commissioner will thereupon order a dividend of the estate, or of such part thereof as he shall think fit. Should any funds remain in the hands of the assignee, a second dividend will be made within eighteen months after his appointment, which will be final, unless some suit is pending, or some part of the estate outstanding. Debts proved after any dividend will not be permitted to disturb it. And if after the payment of all the debts proved against the estate, any surplus remains, it will be paid to the debtor. (*b*)

Privileged debts.—Debts due to the United States and the commonwealth: debts due to operatives in the service of the insolvent, for labor performed within sixty-five days before the insolvency, to an amount not exceeding twenty-five dollars; and costs incurred as provided in the following section, are preferred debts. (*c*)

Effect of the assignment on attachments.—The assignment dissolves all attachments of property belonging to the insolvent, made after the Insolvent Laws went into operation and before the time of the first publication of issuing the warrant, on mesne process issuing from any court of this state (*d*), even though judgment is recovered before the assignment takes effect, if the execution is not levied till after the first publication of notice (*e*);

(*a*) Laws of 1838, c. 163, §7. (*b*) Ib. c. 163, §§12, 13.

(*c*) Laws of 1838, c. 163, §12. Ib. c. 163, §24. Laws of 1841, c. 124, §6.

(*d*) Laws of 1838, c. 163, §5. 21 Pick. R. 169. (*e*) 7 Met. R. 318.

but not if the levy is commenced before the first publication. (*a*) And whenever such attachment is dissolved by proceedings under this act, the legal costs in the suit are a privileged debt, provided the debt on which the suit is founded is proved. (*b*)

Proof of debts, what debts may be proved, when they may be proved, oath before proving debts.—All debts due and payable from the debtor at the time of the first publication of the notice of issuing the warrant, may be proved and allowed against the estate at any regular meeting of the creditors; and all debts then absolutely due, though not payable till afterwards, may be proved as if payable presently, with a discount of interest, where no interest is payable by the contract till the time when the debt would become payable: and all moneys due from the debtor on any bottomry or respondentia bond, or on any policy of insurance, may be proved, in case the contingency or loss happen before making the first dividend, as if it had happened before the said first publication: and in case the debtor shall be liable for any debt in consequence of having made or indorsed any bill of exchange or promissory note before the said first publication, or in consequence of the payment by a party to any bill or note of the whole or any part thereof, or of a payment by any surety of the debtor in any contract, although such payments be made after the said first publication, provided they be made before the making of the first dividend, such debt may be proved as if it had been due and payable by the said debtor before said first publication: and all demands against the debtor on account of goods or chattels wrongfully obtained, taken, or withheld by him, may be proved to the amount of the worth of the property thus taken: and no other debt than those above mentioned may be proved. (*c*)

In cases of mutual credit or debt between the insolvent and any other person, the balance only of account will be allowed or paid on either side.

A creditor holding property of the debtor by mortgage, pledge, or lien, to secure the payment of a debt, must sell such property under the order of the commissioner, apply the proceeds to the payment of his debt, and come in as a creditor for the balance, or give up to the assignee the property so held as security, and

(*a*) 9 Met. R. 23. (*b*) Laws of 1841, c. 124, § 6. (*c*) Laws of 1838, c. 163, § 3.

come in as a creditor for his whole debt, or not prove any part of said debt.

No debt can be proved against an insolvent estate, unless the creditor make oath in substance as follows :—" I, , do swear that , of , by (or against) whom proceedings in insolvency have been instituted, at and before the date of such proceedings, was, and still is, justly and truly indebted to me in the sum of , for which sum, or any part thereof, I have not, nor has any other person to my use, to my knowledge or belief, received any security or satisfaction whatever, beyond what has been disposed of agreeably to law. And I do further swear that the said claim was not procured by me for the purpose of influencing the proceedings in this case." Said oath may be administered by any justice of the peace, where the creditor resides more than five miles from the place of meeting of the creditors.

Examination of debtor, and of any person suspected of concealing, &c., debtors' effects.—The debtor must, at any time before the granting of his certificate of discharge, on due notice, attend and submit to an examination on oath, before the commissioner and the assignees, on all matters relating to his estate and the due settlement thereof according to law ; said examination to be in writing, when so required by the commissioner, and to be signed by the debtor and filed with the other proceedings. (*a*)

The commissioner before whom any matter is pending in insolvency, may, on complaint, under oath, of any person interested in the estate, cite before him any person suspected of having fraudulently received, concealed, embezzled, or conveyed away any of the estate of the insolvent, to be examined on oath, and if the person so cited refuse to appear and answer all lawfully propounded interrogatories, he may be committed to the common jail until he submit to the order of the commissioner. (*b*)

Causes of proceeding against an insolvent on petition of creditors.—If any person arrested on mesne process in any civil action for one hundred dollars or upward, founded on a demand in its nature provable against the estate of an insolvent debtor, do not give bail thereon on or before the return day of such process: or if any person be actually imprisoned more than thirty days on

(*a*) Laws of 1838, c. 163, § 6. (*b*) Laws of 1846, c. 168, § 1.

mesne process or execution, in any civil action founded on such contract, for one hundred dollars or upwards: or if any person whose goods or estate are attached on mesne process in any civil action founded on such contract, for one hundred dollars or upwards, do not within fourteen days from the return day of the writ, if the term of the court to which the process is returnable shall so lòng continue, or on or before the last day of said term, if said court shall sooner rise, dissolve the attachment, any creditor having a demand against such person to the amount of one hundred dollars (although the debt may not have become payable), in its nature provable against his estate, may within ninety days, and not after, petition the commissioner for the county where the debtor resides, that a warrant may issue against the estate of said debtor, and the usual proceedings in insolvency be had. And if the facts set forth in such petition appear to be true, the commissioner will issue a warrant, and the usual proceedings in insolvency will be had, as if on a voluntary petition of said debtor. (*a*) And if any person remove himself, or his property, or any part thereof, from the commonwealth, with intent to defraud his creditors, or conceal himself to avoid arrest, or his property or any part thereof to prevent its being attached or taken on any legal process, or procure himself or his property to be arrested, attached, or taken on any legal process, or make any fraudulent conveyance or transfer of his property, or any part thereof, then any of his creditors whose claims provable against his estate amount to one hundred dollars, may apply by petition, stating the facts and the nature of said claim or claims, verified by oath, to the commissioner of the county where the debtor resides or last resided, praying that his estate may be seized and distributed according to law; and after due notice to the debtor, and a hearing of the petitioners and debtor, or his default to appear, if the facts stated in said petition appear to be true, the master will issue his warrant to take possession of the estate of said debtor, and the usual proceedings in insolvency will be had. (*b*)

Insolvency of Copartners.—A warrant may be issued against partners on their petition, or that of one of them, or on the petition

(*a*) Laws of 1838, c. 163, § 19. Laws of 1844, c. 178, § 12.
(*b*) Laws of 1844, c. 178, § 9.

of a creditor, in the manner herein provided for. On such warrant the joint stock and property of the company and the separate estate of each of the partners will be taken, excepting the parts exempted from attachment, and the joint and separate creditors may prove their respective debts. The assignees will be chosen by the company creditors, and they will keep separate accounts of the joint property of the company and the separate estate of each member, and after deducting from the whole amount received by the assignees all their expenses and disbursements, the net proceeds of the joint stock will go to pay the company creditors, and the net proceeds of the separate estate of each partner will be appropriated to pay his separate creditors. If any balance remain from the separate estate of any partner, after paying his separate debts, it will be added to the joint stock; and any balance of the joint stock, after payment of the joint debts, will be appropriated among the several estates of the separate partners. When the general partners in any limited partnership formed according to the thirty-fourth chapter of the Revised Statutes, become insolvent, the same proceedings may be had, except that the separate estates and separate debts of the special partner in such limited partnerships will not be subject to any of the proceedings against such partnerships. (*a*)

Discharge, when granted—what prevents it from being granted, or makes it void after it is granted, &c.—No insolvent whose assets do not pay fifty per cent. of the claims proved against his estate can receive a discharge under this act (act went into effect June 9th, 1848), or the acts to which it is in addition, unless a majority in number and value of his creditors who have proved their claims assent thereto, in writing, within six months after the date of the assignment; and in no case will a certificate of discharge be granted till the third meeting of creditors; and such discharge will be null and void, if the debtor, or any person in his behalf shall have procured the assent of any creditor thereto by any pecuniary consideration. (*b*)

No claim for necessaries furnished the debtor or his family will be barred by the discharge, unless such claim be proved against the estate.

(*a*) Laws of 1838, c. 163, § 21. (*b*) Laws of 1848, c. 304, § 10.

No discharge of a debtor will be granted or valid, if said debtor be a second time insolvent under these acts, and the assets of his estate fail to pay fifty per cent. of the claims proved against him, unless three-fourths in value of the creditors whose claims are proved shall assent thereto in writing.

No discharge will be granted or valid if said debtor shall be a third time insolvent under these acts. (*a*)

A certificate of discharge granted to a debtor will be void if he have willfully sworn falsely as to any material fact in the course of the proceedings, or have fraudulently concealed any of his estate or effects, or books or writings relating thereto, or if in contemplation of becoming insolvent, or obtaining a discharge under this act, he make any payment, assignment, sale, or transfer, either absolute or conditional, of any part of his estate, with a view to give a preference to any creditor or any person who is or may be liable as an indorser or surety for such debtor, or to any other person who may have claim or demand against him: provided that this clause shall not apply to security given for the performance of any contract, when the agreement for such security is part of the original contract, and the security is given at the time of making the contract. (*b*)

No discharge will be granted or valid, if a debtor within six months before the filing the petition by or against him, procure his estate, real or personal, to be attached, sequestered, or seized on execution, or being insolvent or in contemplation of insolvency, directly or indirectly make any assignment, sale, transfer, or conveyance, absolute or conditional, of any part of his estate, real or personal, intending to give a preference to a pre-existing creditor, or any person who is or may be liable as indorser or surety for such debtor, unless such debtor make it appear that, at the time of making such preference, he had reasonable cause to believe himself solvent. (*c*)

No discharge will be granted or valid if the debtor, when insolvent, within one year next before the filing of the petition by or against him, pay or secure, in whole or in part, any borrowed money or pre-existing debt, or any liability of his or for him, if the

(*a*) Laws of 1844, c. 178, §§ 5, 6. (*b*) Laws of 1838, c. 163, § 10.

(*c*) Laws of 1841, c. 124, § 3.

creditor proves that, at the time of making said payment or giving said security, the debtor had reasonable and sufficient cause to believe himself insolvent. (*a*)

8. *Effect of Marriage upon the title to the Wife's Property.*

Contract before marriage that the wife may hold her property independent of her husband.—The parties to an intended marriage may previously enter into a contract that the wife shall hold the whole or any part of her estate independently of her husband: such contract to contain a clear schedule of said estate, and to be recorded, before the marriage, or within ninety days thereafter, in the registry of deeds for the county where the husband resides at the time of the record, or if he be not a resident of Massachusetts, in the registry of deeds of the county where the wife resides at the time of such record, if made before the marriage, or where she last resided, if made after the marriage: said contract to be void, if not so recorded.

Conveyance, devise, or bequest of property to a married woman, for her sole use, without a trustee: effect of not recording the same, &c.—A married woman may receive a conveyance, devise, or bequest of any estate, to be held independently of her husband, without the intervention of a trustee; such estate to be liable to attachment by a creditor of the husband, unless such grant or conveyance be recorded within ninety days from its delivery in the registry of deeds for the county where the grantor then resides, or if he do not reside in Massachusetts, in the county where the grantee resides.

Rights and remedies of and against a married woman, as to her separate estate.—Any married woman owning estate secured, conveyed, devised, or bequeathed to her under this act, has the same rights and powers, is entitled to the same remedies, in her own name, and is under the same liabilities in respect to such property, as if she were unmarried; and such property may be attached and taken on execution, as if she held the same, being unmarried.

In whom and how separate estate, held under this act, vests,

(*a*) Laws of 1844, c. 178, § 8.

the owner dying intestate.—If a married woman, holding property under this act, die intestate, her right and interest in the personal property vests in her husband, unless otherwise provided in the contracts and conveyances before mentioned, and he has his courtesy in her lands and tenements: provided, however, that he take administration on the estate of the deceased, and hold such personal property, and all the wife's interest in real estate, saving his estate by the courtesy, subject to the payment of all her debts, incurred before or after marriage.

Separate estate of a married woman, how to be used and invested.—None of the separate estate held under this act is to be employed in trade or commerce; but must be invested in real estate, stocks of the United States, state stocks, corporation stocks, personal securities, or furniture in the actual possession of the woman. (*a*)

9. *Limitation of Personal Actions and Saving Clauses.*

Certain actions to be brought within six years.—(*b*) Actions of debt founded on any contract not under seal, except such as are brought on the judgment or decree of some court of record of the United States, or of some one of the states; (*c*) actions on judgments rendered in any court not of record; actions for arrears of rent; actions of assumpsit or case founded on any contract or liability; (*d*) actions for waste and trespass upon land; (*e*) actions of replevin and all other actions for taking, detaining, or injuring goods and chattels, and all other actions on the case, except for slander and libel, must be commenced within six years after the cause of action accrues.

Others to be brought within two years.—Actions for assault and battery, false imprisonment, slander, and libel must be commenced within two years after tne cause of action accrues.

Certain actions against sheriffs, within four years.—Actions against sheriffs for the misconduct or neglect of deputies must

(*a*) R. S. 208. (*b*) Ib. 120.

(*c*) 2 Mason's R. 311. 1 Ib. 243. 22 Pickering's R. 430.

(*d*) 2 Galliston's R. 477. (*e*) 7 Pickering's R. 153.

be commenced within four years after the cause of action accrues. (*a*)

Exceptions as to certain notes.—None of the above provisions apply to any action on a promissory note signed in the presence of an attesting witness, provided the action be brought by the original payee or his executor or administrator, nor to any action brought on bills, notes, or other evidences of debt issued by any bank. (*b*)

And as to suits on accounts current.—In actions of debt and assumpsit for the balance on an open or mutual account current, the cause of action is deemed to have accrued at the time of the last item proved. (*c*)

Exceptions for certain disabilities.—In the case of a person under twenty-one years of age, or a married woman, insane, imprisoned, or absent from the United States at the time when the cause of action accrues, the statute of limitations begins to run immediately on the removal of such disability. (*d*)

General limitation of twenty years.—Personal actions on any contract not limited by any other law of the commonwealth, must be brought within twenty years after the cause of action accrues.

Case of defendants out of the state.—In the case of a person absent from the state when the cause of action accrues, the statute of limitation begins to run on his return to the state; and in case of residence out of the state after the cause of action accrues, the time of such absence is not reckoned as part of the time limited for the commencement of the action. (*e*)

Case of the death of either party.—In case of the death of either party within the time herein limited for the commencement of actions, or within thirty days thereafter, if the cause of action survives, the action must be commenced by or against the executor or administrator of the deceased within two years after the grant of letters testamentary or of administration.

Suits by aliens.—In case of suits by aliens, the time of the

(*a*) 9 Greenleaf's R. 74.

(*b*) 16 Mass. R. 290, 314. 4 Pick. R. 382. 8 Ib. 246. 19 Ib. 43. 23 Ib. 282.

(*c*) 2 Mass. R. 217. 3 Pick. R. 96. 8 Ib. 187. 6 Ib. 362. 4 Greenleaf's R. 337. 6 Ib. 308. 3 Metcalf's R. 216.

(*d*) 14 Mass. R. 203. 17 Ib. 180. 10 Ib. 29.

(*e*) 3 Mass. R. 271. 7 Ib. 515. 1 Pick. R. 263. 17 Mass. R. 55.

continuance of a war between the United States and the country of which such aliens are subjects or citizens, is not deemed a part of the periods herein limited for the commencement of actions.

Remedy in case of reversal, arrest of judgment, &c.—If in any action duly commenced within the time herein limited, the writ fails of sufficient service or return, by unavoidable accident, or by any default or neglect of the officer, or if the writ is abated, or the action otherwise avoided or defeated by the death of one of the parties, or for any matter of form, or if, after verdict for the plaintiff, the judgment is arrested, or if a judgment for the plaintiff is reversed on writ of error, the plaintiff may commence a new action for the same cause within one year after the abatement or other determination of the original suit, or after reversal of the judgment, and if the cause of action survives, his executor or administrator may, in case of his death, commence such new action within the said one year. (*a*)

Case of fraudulent concealment by defendant.—In case of fraudulent concealment by a defendant of the cause of any action herein mentioned from the person entitled thereto, the statute of limitations begins to run from the time when the person so entitled discovers that he has such cause of action. (*b*)

Acknowledgment or new promise.—In actions of debt or upon the case founded on any contract, any acknowledgment or promise intended to take the case out of the statute of limitations must be made in writing, signed by the party chargeable thereby.

An acknowledgment within six years by the executor or administrator of the debtor, that the debt is undischarged, will take it out of the statute of limitations. (*c*)

An acknowledgment that a note is due, or a promise to pay it, made within six years by the principal, takes it out of the statute of limitations as respects the surety. (*d*)

So an acknowledgment by one of several joint debtors takes the case out of the statute as against all. (*e*)

An acknowledgment made to a stranger in the absence of the plaintiff will take a demand out of the statute. (*f*)

(*a*) 2 Pick. R. 605. (*b*) 3 Mass. R. 201. 1 Pick. R. 435. 3 Ib. 74. 9 Ib. 212. (*c*) 8 Mass. R. 133. 16 Ib. 428. (*d*) 4 Pick. R. 382. (*e*) 3 Ib. 291. (*f*) 4 Ib. 110.

Promise by one of several debtors.—In the case of joint contractors, or joint executors or administrators of any contractor, no one of them will lose the benefit of the provisions herein contained, so as to be chargeable on any acknowledgment or promise made or signed by any other or others of them, nor by reason only of any payment made by any other or others of them. (*a*)

Effect of part payment.—No memorandum of any payment of principal or interest made on any promissory note or other writing by or on behalf of the party to whom such payment purports to be made is deemed sufficient proof of payment to take the case out of the statute of limitations.

Limitation of demands filed in set off.—All the provisions herein mentioned apply to debts on contract, alleged by way of set off; and the time of limitation of such debt is to be computed as if an action had been commenced therefor when the plaintiff's action was commenced.

Limitation of actions on penal statutes.—Suits for penalties, on penal statutes, brought by private persons, must be commenced within one year after the offence is committed; such suits brought by or in behalf of the commonwealth must be brought within two years.

Presumption of payment of a judgment.—Every judgment and decree in any court of record of the United States, or of this or any other state, is presumed to be paid and satisfied at the expiration of twenty years after the rendition of the judgment or decree.

Provisions as to written promise, &c., when to take effect.—The provisions herein contained respecting the acknowledgment of a debt or a new promise to pay it, apply only to such acknowledgment or promise made before the first day of October, one thousand eight hundred and thirty-four.

Limitation of actions against executors and administrators.—Actions by creditors of a deceased person against the executor or administrator must be commenced within four years of the time when his bond is given, except when assets are received after

(*a*) 2 Pick. R. 581. 4 Ib. 382. 3 Ib. 291. 7 Greenl. R. 26.

the expiration of the four years, or the right of action accrues after that time. (*a*)

Computation of periods mentioned in statute of limitations.—In the computation of the periods mentioned in the statute of limitations, the day on which the cause of action accrued is to be included. (*b*)

Statute of limitations, not affecting trusts.—The general statute of limitations of six years does not affect trusts. (*c*)

10. *Effect of Death on the Rights of Creditors.*

Appointment and removal of executors and administrators, with the will annexed, and bond to be given by them.—Every executor and administrator with the will annexed, before entering on his duties, must give bond to the judge of probate, with sufficient sureties, in such sum as such judge directs, to return to the probate court within three months a true inventory of all the real and personal estate to be administered; to duly administer all such estate as may at any time come to the possession of such executor or administrator; and to render on oath a true account of his administration within one year, and at other times when required by said judge.

If any person appointed an executor refuse the trust, or do not give bonds, as above provided, within twenty days after probate of the will, the judge of probate will commit administration to such person as would have been entitled thereto, had the deceased died intestate.

The judge of probate may remove an executor or administrator who neglects to settle the estate according to law, or becomes insane, or otherwise incapable of discharging the trust, or unsuitable for it. (*d*)

Distribution of personal estate of intestates.—The personal estate of intestates is to be distributed as follows :

1. The widow, if any, is allowed her articles of apparel and ornaments, and such necessaries for the use of herself and family as the judge shall order.

(*a*) R. S. 66. 11 Pick. R. 173. 20 Ib. 321. (*b*) 15 Mass. R. 193.
(*c*) 5 Pick. R. 321. (*d*) R. S. 63.

2. The personal estate remaining after such allowance, is to be applied to the payment of the debts of the deceased, the charges of his funeral, and of settling his estate.

3. The residue of personal estate, if any, is to be distributed among the heirs, as real estate would be, excepting that alienage will be no impediment to receiving a share; that, if the intestate were a married woman, her husband will receive all the residue of the personal estate; that, if the intestate leave a widow and issue, the widow will receive one-third of said residue; that, if there be no issue, the widow will receive one-half thereof; that, if the intestate leave no kindred, the widow will receive the whole of said residue; and that, if there be no widow, the whole will escheat to the commonwealth. (*a*)

What court will grant administration.—The judge of probate of any county wherein deceased was an inhabitant or resident, will grant administration on his estate; and if deceased were resident in any other state or country, leaving estate to be administered in this state, administration will be granted by the judge of probate of any county where the property is situated.

To whom administration will be granted.—The order of persons entitled to administration on the estate of an intestate are,

1. The widow, or next of kin, or both.

2. One or more of the principal creditors, if there be any competent and willing to undertake the trust, and if there be none such, the judge will appoint whom he thinks fit, provided,

3. That if the deceased were a married woman, administration will be granted to her husband, unless she has made some testamentary disposition of her separate estate which makes it proper to appoint some other person.

4. That if deceased were an alien and left no widow or next of kin in this state, administration will be granted to the consul or vice-consul of the nation to which he belonged.

Examination of persons suspected of concealing effects of the deceased.—Upon complaint to the judge of probate, any person suspected of concealing, embezzling, or conveying away effects of the deceased, may be examined on oath; and if he refuse to appear and answer all lawful interrogatories, he may be committed to the common jail.

(*a*) R. S. 64.

Proceedings when personal estate is insufficient to pay debts.—When the personal estate of the deceased is insufficient to pay the debts and charges of administration, real estate may be sold for this purpose, upon due license from the judge.

Proceedings when the estate is insolvent.—An insolvent estate, after discharging expenses of the last sickness, funeral, and administration, will be applied to the payment of debts in the following order:

1. Debts entitled to a preference under the laws of the United States.

2. Public rates and taxes, and sums due the commonwealth for duties on auction sales, and other excise duties.

3. Debts due all other persons. (*a*)

When it shall appear to the judge that the estate is probably insolvent, he will appoint commissioners to examine all claims, and return to the probate court a list thereof with the sum they have allowed on each claim, within six months (or eighteen months, if so much is required) from the date of the commission. Appeals may be made from the decision of the commissioners to the courts of common law.

After thirty days from the return of the commissioners, the judge will order a distribution of the effects among the creditors, and if the whole assets are not then distributed, further distribution will be made as the judge shall order.

Time within which original administration will be granted.—No original administration will be granted after the expiration of twenty years from the death of the testator or intestate. (*b*)

Remedies for enforcing a settlement.—The administration bond may be put in suit by any creditor, for his own benefit, whenever he has recovered judgment against the executors or administrators, and they have neglected to pay his debt on demand, or show property to be taken in execution for that purpose; or when the amount due him has been ascertained by the decree of distribution, and the executors or administrators neglect to pay on demand. (*c*)

Such suit may be brought by the next of kin to recover his share of the personal estate, after a decree of the court ascertain-

(*a*) R. S. 68. (*b*) Ib. 64. (*c*) Ib. 70.

ing the amount due him, if the administrator or executor neglect to pay on demand; and generally it may be brought by any person interested in the estate who may be authorized by the judge.

Suits on administration bonds must be brought in the Supreme Judicial Court for the county in which the administration bond is taken. (*a*)

If the effects of the deceased are sold or embezzled by any person who has not taken out letters testamentary or of administration thereon, and given bond as executor or administrator, he will be liable to the actions of all persons aggrieved, as an executor in his own wrong.

No executor or administrator, after due notice of his appointment, will be held to answer to the suit of a creditor of the deceased, unless commenced within four years from the time of giving the administration bond, except when assets are received after the expiration of said four years. (*b*)

No executor or administrator will be held to answer to the suit of any creditor of the deceased, within one year after the giving of the administration bond, except for the recovery of a demand that would not be affected by the insolvency of the estate, or unless such suit be brought after the estate has been represented insolvent for the purpose of ascertaining a contested claim.

If, in consequence of unreasonable delay on the part of any executor or administrator to convert the estate of the deceased into money, said estate shall be taken in execution by any creditor of the deceased, such executor or administrator will be liable in an action on his bond for all damages occasioned thereby.

The bond of any executor or administrator neglecting to render an account when duly cited by the judge, may be put in suit, and if he persist in such neglect, judgment will be rendered against him, and he will be held liable as if he had been an executor in his own wrong. (*c*)

(*a*) R. S. 64. (*b*) Ib. 66. (*c*) Ib. 68.

11. *Mode of Collecting Debts.*

I. BY FOREIGN ATTACHMENT.

In what actions this process lies.—All personal actions may be commenced by trustee process, except actions of replevin, actions on the case for malicious prosecution, or for slander, either by writing or speaking, and actions of trespass for assault and battery. (*a*)

Attachment of what—authorized by the writ.—The writ authorizes an attachment of the goods and estate of the principal defendant in his own hands, and also of any goods, effects, or credits of said defendant in the hands of any person or corporation summoned as a trustee, which goods, &c., will be held to respond to the final judgment, as in the ordinary process. (*b*)

Payments made and liabilities incurred after service of the writ, but before such service is known to the trustee.—If after the service on the trustee, but before he has knowledge thereof, he in good faith makes any payment, or becomes in any way liable to any third person for or on account of the goods, effects, or credits in his hands, or has delivered the same to the original defendant, or to any other person entitled thereto, he will be allowed therefor as if such payment or delivery had been made, or liability incurred, before the service of the writ on him. (*c*)

Trustee when and how discharged.—If the supposed trustee appear in person or by attorney, and declare in writing, that he had not, when the writ was served on him, any goods, effects, or credits of the principal, and submit himself thereupon to examination on oath, and if the plaintiff decline to examine him, or on examination his declaration appear to the court true, he will be discharged.

Examination of trustee.—If the plaintiff proceed to examine the supposed trustee on his declaration, he must propose interrogatories in writing, to be answered in writing, signed, and sworn to; and if the person so summoned admit that he has goods, ef-

(*a*) R. S. 109.

(*b*) 3 Pick. R. 302. 7 Mass. R. 259. 6 Pick. R. 120. 2 Mass. R. 37.

(*c*) 3 Pick. R. 65.

fects, or credits of the principal, or wish to refer that question to the court upon the facts, he may make a declaration, setting forth such facts as he may deem material, and submit himself thereupon to a further examination on oath.

Trustee not appearing, to be defaulted.—Any person duly summoned as a trustee, neglecting to answer, will be defaulted and adjudged a trustee.

Mode of trial when trustee appears.—The answers and statements sworn to by any person summoned as a trustee, will be considered as true in deciding how far he is chargeable, but either party may allege and prove any other facts not stated or denied by the supposed trustee, that may be material in deciding that question.

Adverse claimant may become a party, when.—An adverse claimant of the property in the hands of the supposed trustee may be admitted as a party to the suit, so far as it respects his title to said property.

Principal defendant may be a witness.—Upon any trial between the attaching creditor and any other person claiming the same effects, the principal defendant may be examined as a witness for either party, if there be no other objection to his competency except his being a party to the original suit.

Trustee having specific goods.—Any person chargeable as a trustee by reason of goods or chattels other than money, which he holds or is bound to deliver to the principal defendant, must deliver the same, or so much thereof as may be necessary, to the officer holding the execution, and he will sell the same, and apply and account for the proceeds as in the case of a common execution.

Liability of trustee for non-delivery of such goods.—If any trustee refuse or neglect to deliver any goods in his hands, when lawfully required by the officer serving the execution, he will be liable to the plaintiff in the action for the value thereof, after deducting the amount of his lien thereon, if there be any, to be recovered as money is recovered when not paid on the first execution, pursuant to the judgment against a trustee.

What demands not attachable by this process.—No person will be adjudged a trustee,—

1. By reason of having drawn, accepted, made, or indorsed any negotiable bill, draft, note, or other security:

2. By reason of money or any other thing received or collected by him as a sheriff or other officer by force of an execution or other legal process in favor of the principal defendant in the foreign attachment, although the same have been previously demanded of him by the principal defendant: (*a*)

3. By reason of any money in his hands as a public officer, and for which he is accountable, merely as such officer, to the principal defendant: (*b*)

4. By reason of money or other thing due from him to the principal defendant, unless it be, at the time of the service of the writ on him, due absolutely and without depending on any contingency: (*c*)

5. By reason of any debt due from him on a judgment, so long as he is liable to an execution on the judgment. (*d*)

Debt may be attached before it is payable.—Any money or other thing due to the principal defendant, may be attached before it has become payable, provided it be due absolutely and without contingency; but the trustee will not be bound to pay or deliver it before the time appointed by the contract.

Fraudulent conveyance to the trustee.—Any person, summoned as a trustee, having in his possession goods, effects, or credits of the principal defendant, held by a conveyance or title that is void as to creditors of the defendant, may be adjudged a trustee, on account of such goods, &c., though the principal defendant could not have maintained an action therefor against him. (*e*)

Proceedings on scire facias.—Any person adjudged a trustee who does not satisfy the execution in the original suit (if it be not otherwise satisfied), will be liable to a writ of scire facias, and if, after due notice, he neglect to appear and answer thereto, he will be defaulted; and if he was not examined in the original

(*a*) 3 Mass. R. 289. 5 Ib. 319. (*b*) 7 Ib. 259.

(*c*) 3 Mass. R. 33, 68. 6 Pick. R. 120. 3 Ib. 1, 65.

(*d*) 2 Mass. R. 94. 3 Ib. 121.

(*e*) 4 Mass. R. 508. 12 Ib. 140. 5 Ib. 390.

suit, judgment will be rendered and execution will issue against him, his own goods and estate, for the sum remaining unsatisfied on the judgment against the original defendant. If the trustee have been examined in the original suit, judgment on the scire facias will be rendered on the facts stated on that examination, for the amount with which the trustee was originally chargeable, or so much thereof as will satisfy the judgment against the principal defendant. If the trustee appear and answer to the scire facias, not having been before examined, the whole matter will be open for examination, as in the original suit.

Costs of trustee.—Any person summoned as a trustee, appearing at the first term, and submitting himself to examination as before provided, will be allowed to retain his costs for travel and attendance, and such sum as the court may allow for necessary expenses, out of the effects in his hands. If any person who is summoned as a trustee and dwells in the county where the writ is returnable, is defaulted in the original suit, and a writ of scire facias is issued, he will be personally liable for the costs of the suit in the scire facias, unless he has paid over all such effects on the original execution, or was prevented from appearing in the original suit by absence from the state or some other cause deemed sufficient by the court.

II. BY SUIT AT COMMON LAW.

How writs may be framed.—Original writs may be framed either to attach the goods or estate of the defendant, and for want thereof to take his body; or it may be an original summons, either with or without an order to attach the goods or estate. In actions against corporations, and in other cases in which goods and estate may be attached, but the defendant is not liable to arrest, the writ of attachment and original summons may be combined in one, requiring the officer to attach the goods and estate, and to summon the defendant.

Attachment on mesne process.—The attachment of property upon a writ is one of the most common and effectual means of securing a debt. The effect of such attachment is fully discussed in the cases cited below. (*a*) It is held in this commonwealth that an attachment of property on mesne process is a security or lien on property, and that it could not be impaired or destroyed by any thing contained in the United States bankrupt law. (*b*) Both an attachment and arrest cannot be made on the same writ, and the one last made will be void. (*c*)

Where bail may be required.—No person may be arrested or held to bail on a demand arising on any contract made after July 4, 1834, unless the plaintiff or some person in his behalf make oath before a justice of the peace that said plaintiff has a demand against the defendant, on the cause of action stated in the writ, which the deponent believes to be justly due, and on which he expects that the plaintiff will recover ten dollars or upwards, and that the deponent has reasonable cause to believe that the defendant is about to depart beyond the jurisdiction of the court to which the writ is returnable, and not to return till after judgment may probably be recovered in said suit, so that he cannot be arrested on the first execution, if any, which may issue in such suit. (*d*)

Females cannot be imprisoned on mense process or execution on any contract made after July 1, 1831, except in a judgment against them as trustees for ten dollars and upwards. (*e*)

No member of the house of representatives may be arrested or held to bail on mesne process, during his going to or returning from, or attending, the general assembly. (*f*)

Time within which judgment may be obtained when there is no controversy.—In cases that have been defaulted, and where verdict has been rendered and no further action taken by the losing party, judgment is rendered as of the last day of the term, unless otherwise expressly ordered by the court; but where the terms are very long, as in Suffolk county, it is usual, after waiting the time prescribed by the rules for filing exceptions or making a motion for a new trial, to order judgment to be entered as of a particular day, in which case the day must be noted by the

(*a*) 10 Met. R. 320. 2 Story's R. 131. 3 Ib. 428. 7 Law Reporter, 77.
(*b*) Colby's Practice, 114. (*c*) 3 Mass. R. 561. 13 Ib. 73.
(*d*) R. S. 90. (*e*) Ib. 97. (*f*) Constitution of Mass. §10.

clerk on his docket. It is never allowed till the last day, at the first term. (*a*)

How long after judgment, goods attached on mesne process may be held.—If final judgment be rendered for the plaintiff, goods and estate attached on mesne process will be held for thirty days after judgment, in order to their being taken on execution; and if the attachment is made in the county of Nantucket, and the judgment is rendered in any other county, or if the judgment is rendered in Nantucket, and the attachment is made in any other county, the goods and estate will be held for sixty days after final judgment. (*b*)

Execution.—The party obtaining a final judgment in any civil transaction, may take out his execution at any time after twenty-four hours after judgment rendered, and these hours are exclusive of the Lord's Day. If an execution be sooner issued and levied, the levy is void. (*c*) He may also take it out within one year, but not afterward. If he take it out within such time, and it be returned at any time within a year after the return day of that which preceded it, he may have an alias execution, except that if the debtor have been surrendered by his bail, the creditor may sue out an execution after the surrender, though more than a year has elapsed after the return day of the next preceding execution. (*d*) A *pluries* execution may be obtained in the same way, and any number of *pluries* from year to year. If the creditor neglect to keep his execution alive in this manner, he can resort to a scire facias, or an action of debt, to revive his judgment.

Both real and personal property may be sold upon execution; the debtor being allowed one year to redeem real estate, on payment of debt, costs and interest.

No female may be imprisoned on mesne process or execution for any debt founded on a contract made after July 1, 1831, except on a judgment against her as a trustee, for ten dollars or more, in a process of foreign attachment.

When the plaintiff has the body of the defendant in execution, his right to proceed against his property is suspended. (*e*) But

(*a*) R. S. 97. Colby's Practice, 992. (*b*) R. S. 90.
(*c*) 8 Met. R. 496. R. S. 87. (*d*) R. S. 97.
(*e*) 11 New Hampshire R. 311. Colby's Practice, 295.

a creditor may sue out a writ upon his judgment, though an execution be out at the same time, unless the debtor have been actually seized upon such execution. (*a*)

Liabilities of attorneys and sheriffs refusing to pay over moneys collected.—An attorney may be removed by the Supreme Judicial Court or the Court of Common Pleas for any deceit, malpractice, or other gross misconduct, and shall moreover be liable in damages to the party injured thereby, and to such other punishment as may be provided by the law. (*b*)

If any officer unreasonably neglect to pay any money collected by him on execution when demanded by the creditor therein, he will forfeit and must pay to the creditor five times the lawful interest of the money from the time of the demand until it is paid. (*c*)

The sheriff is responsible for the official misconduct of his deputies. (*d*)

When the condition of the official bond of any sheriff is broken, to the injury of any person, such person may at his own expense institute a suit thereon in the name of the treasurer of the commonwealth; the writ to be indorsed with the name of the person for whose benefit the suit is brought, or of his attorney, and the same proceedings to be had thereon, to final judgment and execution, as in a suit by a creditor on an administration bond. (*e*)

No sheriff can be arrested on mesne process or execution in a civil action, but any such execution will be issued against his goods, chattels, and lands; and if it be returned unsatisfied, the creditor may file before the governor and council an attested copy of such execution and return, giving notice also of such proceedings to said sheriff; and if such sheriff do not within thirty days after said notice pay the whole debt with reasonable costs of the copies and notifications above mentioned, the governor will remove him from office. After such removal, and the appointment of another sheriff, the creditor, his first execution being returned unsatisfied, may take out an *alias* execution, which will run against the body, as well as the estate. (*e*)

(*a*) 9 Met. R. 23. (*b*) R. S. 88. (*c*) Ib. 97. (*d*) Ib. 14.
(*e*) R. S. 14.

12. *Courts.*

The judicial power is distributed between the Supreme Judicial Court, and the Court of Common Pleas. The former has original as well as appellate jurisdiction in actions arising upon contract. The latter have a general concurrent jurisdiction in the same class of cases. The former is held once a year in each county of the state, the latter three times a year in some and four times in others. There are also courts of probate, and the municipal courts of the city of Boston.

RHODE ISLAND.

1. *Assurances and Evidences of Debt.*

Action against drawer and endorser of foreign bills.—See title 2d—"*Rates of damages on protested bills.*"

2. *Rates of Damages on Protested Bills.*

Damages and interest on foreign bills.—When any foreign bill of exchange is drawn or indorsed within this state, for the payment of any sum of money, and such bill is returned from any place or country without the limits of the United States, protested for non-acceptance or non-payment, the drawer or indorser will be subject to the payment of ten per cent. damages thereon, and charges of protest, and the bill will carry an interest of six per cent. per annum from the date of the protest. (*a*)

(*a*) R. S. 287. Reference is made throughout this chapter to "The Public Laws of the State of Rhode Island and Providence Plantations," revised and finally enacted January, 1844. Published by Knowles and Vose, Providence, 1844.

Action against drawer and indorser may be joint or several.—Any person having a right to demand any sum of money upon a foreign protested bill of exchange as aforesaid, may commence and prosecute an action for principal, damages, interest, and charges of protest, against the drawers or indorsers, jointly or severally, or against either of them separately,.and judgment will be given for such principal, damages, and charges, and interest upon such principal at the rate aforesaid, to the time of such judgment, together with costs of suit.

Damages and interest on inland bills.—When any inland bill of exchange is drawn or indorsed within this state, for the payment of any sum of money without the same, and such bill is protested for non-acceptance or non-payment, the drawer or indorser will be subject to the payment of five per cent. damages thereon, and charges of protest, and the bill will carry an interest of six per cent. per annum from the date of the protest.

3. *Law of Usury.*

Rate of interest established.—The lawful rate of interest in this state is six per cent. (*a*)

Usury being pleaded, the court may admit the parties as witnesses: judgment, how entered: certain usages excepted from these provisions.—If suit be commenced on any specialty, contract, promise, or assurance, made in this state after the passing of this act, and the defendant specially plead that higher interest than the rate aforesaid was taken, or thereby secured or agreed for, the court will admit the defendant as a witness, on issue joined in such suit, and also the plaintiff on his own motion: and if such agreement be found usurious, the plaintiff will have judgment for the principal sum of money, or real value of the goods, wares, or other commodity as aforesaid, with legal interest thereon, with costs: nothing herein contained extending to the letting of cattle, or other like usages among farmers, or to maritime contracts among merchants, as bottomry, insurance, or course of exchange, as has been heretofore accustomed.

(*a*) R. S. 286.

4. *Frauds*

Actions not to be brought in certain cases, unless on promises in writing.—No action may be brought whereby to charge any executor or administrator on his special promise to answer any debt or damage out of his own estate, or whereby to charge the defendant upon his special promise to answer for the debt, default or miscarriage of another person: or to charge any person upon any agreement made on consideration of marriage: or on any contract for the sale of lands, tenements, or hereditaments, or the making of any lease thereof for a longer time than one year: or upon any agreement which is not to be performed within one year from the making thereof, unless the promise or agreement on which such action is brought, or some note or memorandum thereof is in writing, and signed by the party to be charged therewith, or some other person lawfully authorized. (*a*)

Fraudulent conveyances, &c., to be void.—Every gift, grant, or conveyance of lands, tenements, hereditaments, goods or chattels, or of any rent, interest, or profit out of the same, by writing or otherwise, and every note, bill, bond, contract, suit, judgment or execution, had or made or contrived, of fraud, covin, collusion, or guile, to the intent or purpose to delay, hinder, or defraud creditors, or to deceive or defraud those who may purchase bona fide the same estate, real or personal, will be deemed, as against the person or persons, his, her, or their legal representatives or assigns, whose rights or interests, by such devices and practices as aforesaid, are or might be, injured, delayed or defrauded, utterly void.

5. *Limited Partnerships.*

The laws of Rhode Island on this subject are the same with those of Massachusetts, with the following exceptions: (*b*)

The sections in reference to the equity power of the Supreme Court, and the presumption of assent of creditors to a partnership assignment, are not found in the laws of Rhode Island.

(*a*) R. S. 222. (*b*) Ib. 282.

The certificate required to be made by all the parties to a limited partnership must be acknowledged by said parties before some justice of the peace or public notary, and filed in the office of the clerk of the town in which the principal place of business of the partnership is situated, and recorded by such clerk in a book kept for that purpose. If the partnership have places of business in different towns, the certificate must be filed and recorded in like manner in the office of the clerk of every such town.

The partners must publish a copy of the certificate for six successive weeks immediately after the registry thereof, in at least two newspapers printed in this state: the partnership to be deemed general in case such publication be not made.

In case of the insolvency of any limited partnership, no special partner will, under any circumstances, be allowed to claim as a creditor till the legal claims of all the other creditors of the partnership shall be satisfied.

No dissolution of a limited partnership will take place, except by operation of law, before the time specified in the certificate before mentioned, unless notice of such dissolution be recorded in the clerk's office, where the original certificate, or the certificate of renewal or continuation of the partnership was recorded, and in every other clerk's office where a copy of such certificate was recorded, and unless such notice be published for six successive weeks in at least two newspapers printed in this state.

6. *Principals and Agents.*

Person in whose name merchandise is shipped, deemed the owner, &c.: consignee to have lien thereon for advances, unless notified who is the true owner.—Every person in whose name merchandise is shipped will be deemed the true owner thereof, so as to entitle the consignee thereof to a lien thereon for moneys advanced or negotiable security given by such consignee, to or for the use of such owner: provided such consignee shall not have notice by bill of lading or otherwise, at or before the advancing of any money or security by him, or at or before the receiving such money or security by the person in whose name the shipment has been made, that such person is not the bona fide owner thereof.

Person intrusted with goods for sale, &c., deemed the owner: may sell or pledge them in case, &c.—Any person intrusted with and in possession of goods delivered to him for the purposes of sale, and any person intrusted with and in possession of any bill of lading, receipt, or certificate of a warehouse keeper or inspector, or any warrant or order for the delivery of goods, will be deemed to be the true owner of such goods, or of the goods mentioned and described in such documents respectively, so far as to give the same validity, force, and effect, to any contracts thereafter entered into by him with any person for the sale or disposition of the same, or for the deposit or pledge thereof, as a security for any money or other property advanced, or any negotiable instrument or other obligation in writing given upon the faith of such goods, or of such several documents, or either of them, as if the same contract had been so made by the bona fide owner of such goods: provided that the person so contracted with shall not have notice, by such document or otherwise, that the person so intrusted as aforesaid is not the bona fide owner.

Person accepting such merchandise in deposit, &c., will acquire no other right than the agent had therein.—Any person accepting or taking any such merchandise, goods, or document, in deposit or pledge from any such agent as a security for any antecedent debt or demand, will not acquire thereby or enforce any right or interest in or to such goods, merchandise, or document, other than was possessed or might have been enforced by such agent at the time of such deposit or pledge.

Any person may purchase of an agent: sale and purchase valid, unless notified that the agent is not authorized to sell.—Any person may contract with an agent intrusted with goods, or to whom the same may be consigned, for the purchase of such goods, and receive the same and pay for them to such agent; and such contract and payment will be binding and good against the owner of such goods, notwithstanding the purchaser shall have notice that the person making such contract, or in whose behalf the same is made, is an agent: provided that such contract and payment be made in the usual and ordinary course of business, and that such purchaser shall not, when such contract is entered into or such payment made, have notice that such agent is not authorized to sell said goods or to receive said money.

Owner of goods may recover them from his agent before sold, &c.: may demand of purchaser sum agreed to be paid for them, recover them if pledged, &c.—Nothing herein contained will be deemed to prevent the true owner of any such goods shipped, intrusted, or deposited as aforesaid, from demanding and recovering the same from his factor or agent, before the same shall have been so sold, deposited, or pledged, nor to prevent such owner from demanding and receiving from any such purchaser the sum agreed to be paid for the purchase of such goods, subject to any right of set-off on the part of such purchaser against such agent or factor: not to prevent any such owner from demanding and recovering such goods from any person with whom the same may have been so deposited or pledged as a security for any money or other property advanced, or any negotiable security or obligation in writing given as aforesaid, upon repayment of such money or restoration of such other property, and satisfaction of such security or obligation in writing so advanced, together with such further sum as shall, with the amount so advanced by such depositary or pawnee, be equal to the money or other property and security or obligation in writing, if any, advanced by such agent or factor to such owner, or to the amount for which such agent or factor has a lien on the same goods: nor to prevent such owner from recovering from such depositary or pawnee any balance or sum of money remaining in his hands as the produce of the sale of such goods, after deducting thereout the amount of the money or other property or security in writing so advanced: and the amount so set off and retained by such purchaser or paid by such owner on redeeming such goods, or in any manner allowed by him on recovering the same or the produce of the sale thereof, will be deemed and taken as so much paid by him to and for the use of such agent or factor.

Common carrier, &c., prohibited from selling or pledging.—Nothing in this act authorizes a common carrier, warehouse-keeper, or other person to whom merchandise or other property may be committed for transportation or storage only, to sell or pledge the same.

Penalty on agent for fraud.—If any such agent or factor deposit or pledge any goods, wares, or merchandise, or any such document as is herein before mentioned, which shall have been intrusted or consigned as aforesaid to his care or management, with any person as a security for money or other property borrowed or received by such agent or factor, and shall apply or dispose of any of the proceeds thereof to his own use, in violation of good faith, or with intent to defraud any such owner of such goods, the person so offending will be deemed guilty of a misdemeanor; and on conviction thereof on indictment, will be fined not more than one thousand dollars, or be imprisoned not exceeding five years.

7. *Laws of Insolvency.*

Petitions in insolvency, by whom and to whom to be made: exhibits to be filed therewith: and what court has jurisdiction of the matter.—Any inhabitant of this state, who shall have resided and been domiciled here three years next preceding the preferring his petition, (this term of residence the court may dispense with when they think it just and consistent with the true intent of this section,) and whose debts exceed one hundred dollars, and who is or shall be insolvent, may petition the Supreme Court for the benefit of this act: and must exhibit and file with said petition under oath, a statement of all his debts, and to whom due, and of the losses and misfortunes by which his insolvency has been caused, and a true inventory of all his estate, both real and personal, in possession or action, remainder, or reversion, excepting wearing apparel not exceeding in value one hundred dollars. The clerk of said court will give due notice to creditors. And said Supreme Court have full jurisdiction over said petition, and power to carry into effect all the provisions of this act. (*a*)

Examination of petitioners, &c.—Said petitioners will be strictly examined by the court and any creditors who desire it, in reference to all matters pertaining to their estate, conduct, and circumstances, so far as the interests of the creditors may have been or may be liable to be affected thereby, and said court may require

(*a*) R. S. 210.

them to produce satisfactory evidence of all such facts as they may deem material to a full understanding of the merits of each case. And no discharge will be granted, unless, upon full investigation and hearing of such testimony (if any), the court consider said petitioner entitled thereto.

Effect of such petition on proceedings for collection of debts.—On the reception of such petition, said court will have power, in their discretion, to stay all proceedings against the body and estate, or either, of the petitioner, for the collection of debts: and to cause said petitioner to be liberated from jail, on giving sufficient bonds, conditioned to return to jail in ten days after the rising of the court at which such petition shall be finally disposed of, unless such petitioner receive a certificate of discharge from said court.

Assignment.—Whenever the benefit of this act is extended to any such petitioner, he must at the same term, before receiving his certificate of discharge, make, acknowledge, and deliver to such assignee or assignees as the court appoint, an assignment in trust of all his estate, real and personal, of any kind whatsoever.

Fraudulent conveyances by petitioner.—If any petitioner, before making his assignment, convey lands, goods, debts, demands, or property of any kind whatever, with intent to defraud his creditors, all the property so assigned will nevertheless vest in the assignee; and every person receiving any such conveyance, and willfully concealing such property, will forfeit double the value thereof, for the benefit of the creditors: and any person suspected of such concealment, may, on application of the assignee, be brought before said Supreme Court, and examined on oath respecting the same.

Assignees, by whom called to account, &c.—Such assignee or assignees may be called to account, and discharged by said court, and others be appointed in their places.

Duties of assignees.—Said assignee must, before proceeding to act, be sworn before said court, and if required give bonds for the faithful performance of the trust: give due notice, as by law required, that creditors may prove their claims against the estate, for which purpose not less than six nor more than eighteen months from the first publication of notice will be allowed at the discretion of the court. It will be the duty of the assignee to examine the insolvent touching the claims against his estate, and to require him to produce any paper which may be of use in deciding any of said claims. At the expiration of the time allowed for proving claims, the assignee will forthwith make division of the net produce of said estate among the creditors, in proportion to their respective debts, allowing to the insolvent those articles which are exempted from attachment, and deducting the necessary expenses of settling the estate and the reasonable compensation of the assignee.

Appeal to the general assembly from decree of the Supreme Court.—Any petitioner, or any creditor of a petitioner, may appeal from the final decision of the Supreme Court, on the petition, to the general assembly, upon filing notice of such appeal in the clerk's office of the Supreme Court in the county in which such petition shall have been so tried and decided. When the prayer of the petition shall have been granted by the Supreme Court, and the creditor appeals from such decision, all proceedings for debt against the person of the petitioner will be stayed till the trial of the petitioner in the general assembly, or until said assembly shall otherwise direct.

Effect of discharge: effect of fraud and perjury on such discharge.—Insolvent debtors, obtaining a discharge under this act, without fraud or perjury are not liable to arrest or bodily restraint on account of any debt, covenant, contract (except a promise of marriage), agreement, or pecuniary obligation of any kind, not originating in tort or criminal conduct, contracted, entered into, or incurred prior to the filing of the petition; but any creditor may sue out an original summons against him, and on final judgment in favor of such creditor, execution will issue, not running against the body of said insolvent, nor can his real estate be attached thereon, unless at the time of the attachment he be absent from the state or concealed therein. If the plaintiff on trial prove any fraudulent proceedings or practices on the part of said defendant, by him concealed from said court, for the purpose of fraudulently obtaining his discharge, said plaintiff will have judgment for his debt and damages (being first proved and ascertained) as if no such discharge had ever been granted to the defendant; and in all cases thereafter said discharge will be considered null and void.

Provisions in reference to the sett-off of mutual debts, and the form of oath to be taken by the insolvent.—Substantially the same as under the Insolvent Laws of Massachusetts.

Preferred debts.—All debts due to this state or any town therein for taxes, or to the United States, will be considered preferred debts, to be paid before any dividend is made.

Man marrying a woman discharged under this act, liable for what debts of hers.—A man intermarrying with a woman who has been discharged under this act, will be liable for debts incurred on any contract entered into by his wife before the benefit of this act was extended to her, only to the amount of such property as came into his possession or under his control by her marriage, excluding her wearing apparel.

8. *Effect of Marriage upon the Title to the Wife's Property.*

Certain property possessed by a woman before marriage, &c., secured to her sole use.—The real estate, chattels real, household furniture, plate, jewels, stock, or shares in the capital stock of any incorporated company of this state, or debts secured by mortgage on property within this state, which are the property of any woman before marriage, or which may become the property of any woman after marriage, are so far secured to her sole and separate use, that the same, and the rents, profits, and income, will not be liable to be attached or in any way taken for the debts of the husband, either before or after his death; and on the death of the husband, in the life-time of the wife, will be and remain her sole and separate property. In case of the sale of any such property, the proceeds may be invested in the wife's name in any of the kinds of property aforesaid, and be secured to and holden by the wife in the same manner as the property sold. (*a*)

Furniture, stocks, mortgages, &c, possessed by wife, not to be sold, &c., unless by joint deed, except, &c.—The chattels real, household furniture, plate, jewels, stock or shares, or debts, as aforesaid, so held as aforesaid, cannot be sold, leased, or conveyed by the husband, unless by deed in which the wife joins as grantor; said deed to be acknowledged as by law provided in the case of

(*a*) R. S. 270.

real estate of marriage; but whenever said household furniture, plate, or jewels are sold by her husband as his own property, to one purchasing the same bona fide, and without actual or constructive notice of the right of the wife thereto, such sale will vest in such purchaser a good and valid title thereto.

Disposal by married woman of her personal property by will.—Any married woman, more than eighteen years old, may dispose of her personal estate secured to her by this act, by will executed in the common form.

Property liable for debts of wife contracted before marriage.—The property secured to any married woman by this act will be liable to attachment or levy for her debts, contracted before marriage, as if she had continued sole; and nothing herein contained will be construed to impair any right of lien thereon, or any legal remedy for the enforcement thereof.

To what the provisions of this act apply.—Nothing herein contained will impair the rights of the husband as tenant by courtesy, or his right to administer on the estate of his wife, in case she dies intestate, or will authorize any husband to give to or settle upon his wife any of his property in any other manner or with any other effect than if this act had not been passed.

9. *Limitation of Personal Actions.*

Certain actions to be brought within six years; others within four; others within two; covenant, &c., within twenty.—All actions of trespass, trespass and ejectment, detinue or replevin; all actions of account and upon the case, except on such accounts as concern trade or merchandise between merchant and merchant, their factors or servants; all actions of debt founded on any contract without specialty; all actions of debt for arrearages of rent; actions of debt for other causes, and all actions of covenant, brought at any time after this act goes into operation, must be commenced and sued within the time hereinafter directed, viz.: Said actions upon the case, except for slander, and said actions of account, and the said actions for debt, founded on any contracts without specialty, or brought for arrearages of rent, and all actions of detinue and replevin must be commenced within six years after the cause of action accrues; said actions of trespass, and trespass and ejectment, within four years after the cause of action accrues; actions upon the case for words, within two years after the cause of action accrues; and all actions of debt, other than those before specified, and all actions of covenant, within twenty years next after the cause of such actions accrues. (*a*)

If defendant be without the state, &c., when suit may be commenced.—If any person go out of the state after cause of action has accrued, but before said action is barred under this act, the time of his absence will not be reckoned in computing the time of limitation.

If plaintiff be under age, &c.—If any person be under twenty-one years of age, feme covert, non compos mentis, imprisoned or beyond the limits of the United States, when the cause of action accrue, such person may bring such action within the time herein before limited, after such impediment is removed.

Case of the death of either party.—If any person for or against whom any of said actions accrue, die before the time limited for bringing the same, or within thirty days after the expiration of said time, and the cause of action survive, such action may be commenced by or against the executor or administrator of the deceased person, at any time within one year after the granting of letters testamentary or of administration.

Case of abatement or arrest of judgment.—If any action duly commenced within the time herein limited therefor, be abated or otherwise avoided or defeated by the death of any party thereto, or for any matter, or if, after verdict for the plaintiff, the judgment be arrested, the plaintiff may commence a new action for the same cause at any time within one year after the abatement or other determination of said original suit; and if the cause of action legally survives, his executor or administrator may, in case of his death, commence said new action within the said one year.

(*a*) R. S. 220.

10. *Effect of Death on the Rights of Creditors.*

When executor must prove will, or decline the trust, &c.—Every executor of the will of any person deceased, knowing of his appointment, who does not prove said will, or present it, and declare his refusal in writing, within thirty days from said decease will forfeit ten dollars per month from the expiration of said thirty days till he prove or present the same as aforesaid.

If executor decline his office, to whom administration will be granted.—Upon such neglect or refusal of an executor, administration will be committed to one or more of the devisees or legatees, or of the principal creditors, or such other person as the court think fit.

Who will be executors in their own wrong.—Any person alienating or embezzling any of the personal estate of any deceased person, before he has taken out letters of administration, and exhibited a true inventory of all the known estate of said person deceased, will be liable to all persons aggrieved, as an executor in his own wrong.

Executor's bond, and proceedings in case such bond is not given.—Every executor must give bond with sufficient sureties, before entering on his trust, to return a true inventory of all the testator's personal estate to the court of probate within three months, and to render an account of his proceedings, as administrators are bound to do; unless said executor be a residuary legatee, in which case bond may be given by him to pay the debts and legacies of the testator. In case such executor neglect or refuse for twenty days to give bond as aforesaid, administration with the will annexed may be committed to some other person.

Personal property of intestate, how to be disposed of.—If any person die possessed of any personal estate, the same will stand chargeable with the payment of all the just debts and funeral charges of the deceased, and the expenses of settling his estate; the surplus remaining thereafter, unbequeathed, will be distributed as follows:—one-third thereof to the widow of the deceased, unless the intestate died without issue, in which case she will have one-half; the residue to be distributed among the heirs in the same manner as real estate.

To whom administration will be committed.—Administration of an intestate's estate will be granted to the widow or next of kin, being upwards of twenty-one years of age, or both, as the court may think proper, within thirty days; and if at the expiration of that time they neglect to take out or apply for letters of administration, the court will commit administration to some suitable person.

Bond to be given by administrator.—Substantially the same as in Massachusetts.

Proceedings in case the estate is insolvent.—On due representation by the executors or administrators of any insolvent estate, three commissioners will be appointed by the court of probate, whose duties will be substantially the same as those of commissioners in like cases in Massachusetts. The distribution of such estate will also be the same as in that state.

Any creditor whose claim is rejected by the commissioners, may sue for the same in the common law courts, after giving due notice in the office of the clerk of probate. If the executor or administrator be dissatisfied with any creditor's claim allowed, it will be stricken from the commissioners' report. And executors and administrators may submit any claim mentioned in this section to reference, the decision of the referees thereon to be final.

If any creditor do not make out his claim with the commissioners during the existence of their commission, or at common law, or before referees, as herein provided for, he will be for ever barred of his action therefor against the executor or administrator; unless there be estate remaining in the hands of such executor or administrator upon the settlement of his account with the court of probate, after deducting the amount of claims allowed by the commissioners from the amount of the estate of the testator or intestate, remaining in the hands of such executor or administrator, to be applied to the payment of the debts of said testator or intestate.

The pendency of any commission as aforesaid will be no bar to any action against the executor or administrator, after the expiration of two years from the granting of letters testamentary or of administration.

11. *Mode of Collecting Debts.*

I. BY FOREIGN ATTACHMENT.

What is liable to attachment by this process.—When any person resides or is absent out of the state, or conceals himself therein so that his body cannot be arrested, and when any incorporated company established out of this state is indebted to any person, then the personal estate of such absent or concealed person or foreign corporation, lying in the hands of their attorney, agent, factor, trustee, or debtor, will be liable to be attached, the plaintiff giving special order therefor on the back of his writ, to answer any just debt or demand. (*a*)

How plaintiff in such suit may recover amount in the hands of garnishee.—If it appear that, at the time of the service of said writ on said garnishee, there was personal estate of defendant in his hands, then the plaintiff, after having recovered judgment against such defendant, may bring his action against such garnishee, to recover so much as will satisfy such judgment with interest and costs, if there shall appear by said garnishee's account to be a sufficiency for the same, otherwise for so much as shall appear by said account to be in his hands; and if it appear that several garnishees had property of the defendant as aforesaid, said plaintiff may sue each separately, and recover the amount in his hands, until such plaintiff receive full payment of his judgment against the defendant, with interest and costs; provided, always, that any garnishee, after final judgment against the defendant, may satisfy such judgment or any part thereof, to the amount of the estate attached in his hands, before any suit shall be brought against him therefor.

Liability of garnishee who, after due service, refuses to render an account.—If any person, body corporate, or copartnership after due service upon them as garnishee, neglect or refuse to render an account on oath, as required, of what personal estate of the defendant they had at the time of such service, such garnishee will be liable to satisfy the judgment that the plaintiff may obtain against the defendant in such case, to be recovered by special

(*a*) R. S. 109.

action on the case. If several garnishees so neglect or refuse in the same case, the plaintiff must bring his action against them all jointly.

Persons served with copy may defend the suit in the name of the defendant.—Any person duly summoned as garnishee may file an answer and defend the suit in behalf and in the name of the defendant.

Mariners' wages, &c., not liable to attachment.—Mariners' wages are not liable to attachment under this act, till after the termination of the voyage in which such wages have been earned; nor is any debt which is secured by bill of exchange or negotiable promissory note.

Shares in a bank, &c., liable to attachment.—The stock or shares of any body corporate established out of this state, and the stock or shares of any person who shall reside or be absent from this state, or shall conceal himself therein, in any bank, insurance company, or other incorporated company within this state, will be liable to be attached to answer to any just claim; and whenever any writ is sued out as aforesaid, the plaintiff or his attorney must, on the back of said writ, direct the officer charged with the service thereof to attach the defendant's stock or shares in such company.

II. BY SUIT AT COMMON LAW.

Attachment of real and personal estate.—Whenever a writ authorizing an arrest is delivered to an officer for service, if, after using his best endeavors, he cannot find the body of the defendant within his precinct, he will attach his goods and chattels to the amount commanded in the writ, if so much can be found, and may attach property of any less value, if so ordered by the plaintiff or his attorney on the back of the writ.

When a writ is taken out from any Court of Common Pleas, against any person whose body or personal estate cannot be found within this state, the words "real estate" may be added in the writ next to the words "goods and chattels," and the officer will attach the real estate of the defendant in the same manner as personal estate; and in all cases where real estate is attached, and

8

the plaintiff recovers judgment, execution will be granted against the real estate attached as aforesaid. And in all cases where execution is issued on any judgment where real estate was not attached on the original writ, if no personal estate can be found, nor the debtor's body, the party obtaining judgment may cause execution to be levied on real estate.

When judgment will be entered: time within which judgment may be obtained in cases where there is no controversy.—Every judgment will be entered as of the last day of the term in which it is rendered, unless otherwise ordered by the court.

In a defaulted action, where service is made on the person, judgment may be obtained at the term when such action is entered.

Arrest—when permitted.—The body of any male debtor may be arrested on mesne process or execution, in any civil action for debt.

Writs against females—how issued and served.—Every original writ issued against a female, founded on a contract not under seal, must be a writ of summons, and not a writ of arrest. No execution will issue against the body of any female, on any judgment founded on a contract not under seal, where the debt or damages recovered do not exceed the sum of fifty dollars. In such cases, executions will issue against the goods, chattels, and real estate of the defendants. (*a*)

Execution issued in a suit commenced by attachment—when to be levied on property attached.—When a writ has been served by attachment of real or personal estate, and judgment is for the plaintiff, the execution issued thereon must be levied on the property so attached, as soon as may be; and if the same be not so levied before the return day thereof, the property attached will be discharged. (*b*)

Executions, when to be issued, and when returned.—Executions will not be issued from the Supreme Court or Court of Common Pleas till the expiration of five days next after the rising of the court at which such judgment is rendered; and every execution issued from either of said courts will be made returnable to the next succeeding term thereof, and must be returned within

(*a*) R. S. 124   (*b*) R. S. 114.

five days from the day appointed for the sitting of the court from which it issued.

Executions, original or alias, may be issued at any time within six years from the rendition of the judgment originally, or from the return day of the last execution. (*a*)

12. *Courts.*

The judicial power is vested in a Supreme Court, and a Court of Common Pleas for each of the five counties in the state. These courts have a general and almost concurrent civil jurisdiction. The former is held once, the latter are held twice a year in each county.

(*a*) R. S. 138, 140.

CONNECTICUT.

1. ASSURANCES AND EVIDENCES OF DEBT.
2. RATE OF DAMAGES ON PROTESTED BILLS.
3. THE LAW OF USURY
4. FRAUDS.
5. LIMITED PARTNERSHIPS, AND LIABILITY OF CORPORATE INSTITUTIONS.
6. LAWS OF INSOLVENCY.
7. LIMITATION OF PERSONAL ACTIONS.
8. EFFECT OF MARRIAGE UPON RIGHTS OF PROPERTY
9. EFFECT OF DEATH ON THE RIGHTS OF CREDITORS
10. MODE OF COLLECTING DEBTS.
11. COURTS.

1. *Assurances and Evidences of Debt.*

Book accounts.—In all actions of debt on book, tried on the general issue, the evidence of the parties, and of any other persons interested, taken in or out of court, in the manner and form required in other cases, may be admitted by the court. (*a*)

When the defendant in any action of debt on book has made any plea under which it is lawful to give in evidence any book account in favor of the defendant against the plaintiff, the court may on motion of the plaintiff, order that oyer be given to the plaintiff of the book of the defendant, forthwith, or at such time as the court may prescribe. (*b*)

In actions of debt on book, where the account is alleged to be over seventeen dollars, the court may appoint not more than three persons to audit and adjust the accounts between the parties, on whose award judgment will be rendered. (*c*)

(*a*) R. S. title 10. 10 Conn. R. 179. 2 Root's R. 59, 130, 188.
(*b*) 1 Root's R. 273. 6 Conn. R. 14. (*c*) 8 Conn. R. 500. 3 Day's R. 300.

What notes negotiable.—All promissory notes, duly executed, to the amount of thirty-five dollars, or more, for the payment of money only, made payable to any person or persons, on his, her, or their order, or to the bearer, are assignable, according to the custom of merchants and the law relating to inland bills of exchange; nothing herein contained to vary the jurisdiction of the court in relation to the maker of such note, nor to authorize any person or persons to issue bills of credit to be used as a general currency or medium of trade, in lieu of money. (*a*)

2. *Rate of Damages on Protested Bills.*

When any bill of exchange, hereafter to be drawn or negotiated within this state, on any person or persons of or in any state, territory, or district of the United States, is returned unpaid, having been duly protested for non-payment in the manner usual in cases of foreign bills of exchange, the person or persons to whom the same is or may be payable will be entitled to recover of the drawer or drawers, or the indorser or indorsers of such bill of exchange the damages hereafter specified, besides the principal sum for which said bill was drawn, with lawful interest on the aggregate amount of such principal sum and damages, from the time at which notice of protest was given and the payment of said principal sum and damages was demanded, to wit: if such bill was drawn on any person or persons of or in the city of New-York, two per cent. on the principal sum specified in such bill; if upon any person or persons of or in the states of New Hampshire, Vermont, Maine, Massachusetts, Rhode Island, New-York (excepting the city of New-York), New Jersey, Pennsylvania, Delaware, Maryland, or Virginia, or of or in the District of Columbia, three per cent. upon such principal sum; if upon any person or persons of or in the states of North Carolina, South Carolina, Ohio, or Georgia, five per cent. upon such principal sum; or if upon any person or persons of or in any other state, territory, or district of the United States, eight per cent. upon such principal sum; such damages, so to be recovered and received, to be in lieu of interest and all other charges, to the

(*a*) R. S. title 72.

time at which the notice of such protest and demand of payment was made and given as aforesaid; and the amount of such bill and the damages payable thereon, as above specified, will be ascertained and determined without any reference to the rate of exchange existing at the time of such notice and demand of payment. (*a*)

3. *The Law of Usury.*

What is lawful interest.—Lawful interest in this state is six per cent.

Usurious contracts void.—All bonds, contracts, mortgages, and assurance whatever, made for the payment of any principal or money lent, or covenanted to be lent upon or for usury, whereby more than lawful interest is reserved or taken, will be utterly void. (*b*)

Penalty for taking usury.—Any person taking usury in any form will forfeit the money or other property lent, bargained, sold, or agreed for in the usurious bargain or agreement, one-half to the prosecutor and the other half to the treasury of the state. (*c*)

In an action on any contract, if the defendant inform the court that such contract was made on a usurious consideration, the court, as a court of equity, may examine the parties, and receive any other proper testimony thereon. If plaintiff refuses to be thus examined, he will become nonsuit, and defendant will recover costs.

And if the court find that the contract was given on usurious consideration, they will adjust the same in equity, and give judgment for the plaintiff to recover no more than the value of the goods or the principal sum of money which the defendant received, without interest or any advance on the same. (*d*)

(*a*) R. S. title 72.

(*b*) R. S. title 115. 5 Conn. R. 156. 3 Day's R. 68, 268, 356. 1 Root's R. 294.

(*c*) 4 Day's R. 37, 114. 2 Conn. R. 345.

(*d*) 5 Conn. R. 183. 8 Ib. 35. 1 Root's R. 115, 129, 137, 255, 267, 367.

4. *Frauds.*

Statute of frauds.—No suit in law or equity may be brought or maintained on any contract or agreement whereby to charge any executor or administrator on any special promise to answer damages out of his own estate ; or whereby to charge the defendant on any special promise to answer for the debt, default, or miscarriage of another person; or to charge any person on any agreement made upon consideration of marriage; or upon any contract for the sale of lands, tenements, or hereditaments, or any interest in or concerning them ; or on any agreement that is not to be performed within the space of one year from the making thereof; unless the contract or agreement upon which such action is brought, or some memorandum or note thereof, is made in writing, and signed by the party to be charged therewith, or some other person thereunto by him authorized. (*a*)

No contract for the sale of any goods, wares, and merchandise, for the price of thirty-five dollars or upwards, will be considered valid, unless the buyer accept part of the goods so sold, and recover the same, or give something in earnest, to bind the bargain, or in part payment, or some note or memorandum in writing of the said bargain be made and signed by the parties to be charged, or their agents lawfully authorized.

Fraudulent conveyances and the penalty for making them.—All fraudulent and deceitful conveyances of real or personal estate, and all bonds, suits, judgments, executions, or contracts, made with intent to avoid any debt or duty of others, will be void, as against those persons only, their heirs, executors, administrators, or assigns, whose debt or duty is endeavored to be avoided. (*b*)

And all the parties to such fraudulent contract, knowing the fraud, who shall wittingly justify the same, as being done bona fide and on good consideration, will forfeit one year's value of the land, and the whole value of the goods and chattels, and

(*a*) R. S. title 39. 10 Conn. R. 198. 2 Day's R. 225, 457, 535. 1 Root's R. 57, 59, 73, 77, 89, 142, 172, 549.

(*b*) 10 Conn. R. 54. 4 Day's R. 284. 5 Ib. 227, 534, 384, 345. 1 Root's R. 478.

whatever money is contained in such fraudulent bond or contract. (*a*)

Assignment for the benefit of creditors to be void unless it comply with certain provisions.—All conveyances and assignment of lands, tenements, goods, chattels, or choses in action hereafter made, directly or indirectly, by any person in failing circumstances, with a view to his insolvency, to any person or persons in trust for his creditors, or any of them, will, as against the creditors of the person making such conveyance or assignment, be fraudulent and void, unless the same be made in writing for the benefit of all said creditors, in proportion to their claims, and be lodged for record at the office of the court of probate for the district where the assigner or assigners, or some of them reside. (*b*)

5. *Limited Partnerships, and Liability of Corporate Institutions.*

Purposes for which limited partnerships may be formed: of whom said partnership may consist: liability of each class of partners, and name of the firm.—The same as in Massachusetts.

Certificate to be furnished by partners.—Provisions as to certificate to be signed by partners, the same as in Massachusetts, except that the partners must make and sign such certificate before one of the judges of the Superior Court, or a judge of the county court, and it must be registered in the office of the town clerk of the town in which the principal business of the partnership is carried on, and in like manner in every town where the partnership has places of business. And at the time of making such registry it will be the duty of such of the general partners as are authorized by the partnership to transact and manage the concerns to make oath of the actual and bona fide advance or payment of the sum or sums by the special partners, according to the registry of the amount of the same: and no such capital may be advanced to the common stock of the partnership, by the special partners, but in cash payments: and if any person be guilty of willful false swearing in the premises, he will be deemed guilty of perjury. In case the provisions herein contained in

(*a*) 4 Conn. R. 342. 8 Ib. 532. (*b*) 10 Conn. R. 291. 9 Ib. 492.

reference to said registry are neglected, or a false registry made, all the partners will be held liable as general partners. (*a*)

Capital not to be withdrawn.—No part of the capital furnished by special partners may be withdrawn at any time within the period during which the partnership is continued: nor will any special partner be allowed to claim as a creditor in case of the insolvency or bankruptcy of the partnership.

Publication of terms of partnership.—It will be the duty of the partners in any partnership formed under this act to publish the terms of the partnership, so registered as aforesaid, for at least six weeks after such registry, in at least one newspaper, published in the county in which their business is or is to be carried on, and in case no newspaper is published in said county then in a newspaper published in an adjoining county.

Suits to be brought by and against general partners only.—The same as in Massachusetts.

Capital of corporate institutions limited.—The amount of capital stock in every joint stock corporation will be fixed and limited by the stockholders, in their articles of association, in no case to be less than four thousand dollars, nor more than two hundred thousand dollars, and to be divided into shares of twenty-five dollars each. (*b*)

Withdrawal of capital stock before payment of the debts of the company.—If the capital stock of any such corporation be withdrawn and refunded to the stockholders, before the payment of all the debts of the company for which such stock would have been liable, the stockholders will be liable to any such creditor of said company, in an action founded on this statute, to the amount refunded respectively as aforesaid.

Officers intentionally neglecting to perform certain requirements of the act.—If the president, directors, or secretary of any such corporation neglect or refuse to comply with the fifteenth, sixteenth, and seventeenth sections of the act whereof these sections are a part, respecting the publication of articles of association, making and recording the certificate required by law, increase of capital stock, annual returns, and transfer of stock, such of them so neglecting or refusing will jointly and severally

(*a*) R. S. title 77.

(*b*) Ib. title 14.

be liable in an action founded on this statute, for all debts of said company contracted after such neglect and refusal.

Liability of directors if a dividend is paid when the company is insolvent.—If the directors of any such corporation declare and pay a dividend when the company is insolvent, or any dividend, the payment of which would render it insolvent, knowing said company to be insolvent, or that such dividend would render it so, the directors assenting thereto will be jointly and severally liable, in an action founded on this statute, for all debts due from said company, at the time of such dividend.

Penalty on corporations for violating any of the provisions of this act.—If any corporation established under the authority of this act, violate any of the provisions of said act, and said company thereby become insolvent, the directors ordering or assenting to such violation will jointly and severally be liable in an action founded on this statute, for all debts contracted after such violation.

Liability of private property of stockholders on certain contracts.—Neither the person nor the private property of the stockholders of manufacturing companies now (1818) incorporated in this state, will be liable for or on account of any contract made by such company after the fourth day of July next, made for the sole benefit of said company: provided that no company may take the benefit of this act unless by said fourth of July it lodge a certificate with the town clerk of that town where the factory of such company is situated, containing the amount of the capital stock of such companies. (*a*)

6. *Laws of Insolvency.*

Petition by insolvent debtor.—On petition of any inhabitant of this state to the superior court, held in the county where he or she is an inhabitant, representing that he or she is insolvent, and praying for relief, such court, as a court of chancery, will have cognizance of the case, and if it appear on hearing that the petitioner has a fair character for probity and industry, is not justly chargeable with idleness or mismanagement in his or her affairs:

(*a*) R. S. title 64.

that he or she has become insolvent, and has not conveyed away estate with intent to defraud his or her creditors, he or she will be deemed an insolvent debtor under this act. (*a*)

Notice to creditors out of the state.—On application of the debtor to either of the judges of said court, he will grant an order directing notice of such petition to be given to the creditors of such debtor living without this state; and on proof that such order has been complied with, the court may proceed to hear and determine such petition at the term when it is made returnable.

Commissioners, their powers and duties.—When any person is adjudged an insolvent debtor, such court may appoint two or three commissioners, sworn to execute faithfully the trusts reposed in them, to whom within thirty days from the rising of the court aforesaid, such insolvent debtor will make an assignment under oath of all his or her estate, except that which is exempted from attachment. The commissioner or any creditor may examine said debtor, on oath, as to any matters touching his estate. And it will be the duty of said commissioners to convert all the effects and estate so assigned to them into money, as speedily as may be, for the use of the creditors of said debtor.

Said commissioners will receive, adjust, and ascertain the debts due and owing by said insolvent to such creditors as shall seasonably present and prove their claims. Said commissioners, within thirty days after the making of said assignment, will give such public notice of their meetings as said court shall direct; and they will meet three different times within six months from the time of said public notice, unless by order of the court the time of the last meeting be further extended. No claim will be admitted after such last meeting, but as soon as may be thereafter the commissioners will examine and decide on all claims which then remain undecided. And said commissioners will average all claims allowed, upon the avails of the estate which shall come to their possession, first deducting therefrom all claims that may be allowed in favor of this state, and a reasonable amount for their services and expenses, and will pay over to each creditor, whose debt has been proved and allowed, his or her ratable share or dividend.

(*a*) R. S. title 53. 4 Conn. R. 1. 2 Conn. R. 503. 8 Conn. R. 480

Certificate of discharge.—If, on the examination above mentioned, it be the opinion of said commissioners that said insolvent has made a full and fair disclosure and assignment of his or her estate, they will deliver to him a certificate under their hands, the he or she has made such assignment in conformity with this act, which certificate will protect the person of said insolvent from arrest or imprisonment on any debt or demand due or owing to any creditor named in his or her petition, at the date thereof, or to any other creditor claiming or receiving any share or dividend from his or her estate, under this act.

Powers of superior court over commissioners.—The superior court which shall have appointed, will have power, for cause shown, to remove any commissioner, and fill any vacancy; and may on motion of one-fourth of the creditors in value, and reasonable notice to said commissioners, hear and decree concerning any proceedings by them had, or any neglect charged against them, after granting the said certificate; and may by any proper process in chancery, as occasion may require, compel said commissioners to execute their trust in such manner as the court shall adjudge that the provisions of this act require.

7. *Limitation of Personal Actions.*

Actions on specialties.—Actions on bonds or writings obligatory, contracts under seal, or promissory notes not negotiable, must be brought within seventeen years after the cause of action accrues; provided, however, that persons legally incapable to bring such actions when the cause of action accrues, may bring the same at any time within four years after such incapacity ceases. (*a*)

Actions of account, book debt, and assumpsit.—Actions of account, debt on book or on simple contract, or of assumpsit, founded on implied contract or on any contract in writing not under seal, except promissory notes not negotiable, are limited to six years after the cause of action accrues; provided, however, that persons legally incapable of bringing such actions when the

(*a*) R. S. title 60.

cause of action accrues may bring them at any time within three years after such incapacity ceases.

Actions of trespass on the case.—Actions of trespass on the case are limited to six years after the right of action accrues.

Actions on express contracts not reduced to writing, trespass, and case for words.—Actions upon express contract, other actions of book debt, on proper subjects thereof, not reduced to writing, or some note or memorandum thereof made in writing and signed by the party to be charged therewith, or some other person lawfully authorized ; actions of trespass and actions upon the case for words, are limited to three years after the right of action accrues.

Actions on penal statutes.—Actions for forfeitures on penal statutes are limited to one year after the offence committed.

Actions against officers for neglect of duty.—Actions against sheriffs, deputy sheriffs, and constables, for neglect of duty, are limited to two years after the right of action accrues.

Time of commencing new suit after reversal or arrest of judgment.—If in any of said suits or actions, judgment be given for the plaintiff, and the same be reversed by error, or a verdict pass for the plaintiff, and upon matter alleged in arrest of judgment, the judgment be given against the plaintiff, that he take nothing by his writ, declaration, or bill, the party plaintiff, his heirs, executors, or adminstrators, may commence a new suit within a year after such judgment reversed or given against the plaintiff. In the several cases aforesaid, the time of the defendant's absence from the state is to be excluded from the computation.

Writs of error and petitions for new trial.—Writs of error brought for the reversal of any judgment, and petitions for new trial in cases where final judgment has been rendered in chancery or at law, are limited to three years after the rendering of such judgment.

8. *Effect of Marriage upon Rights of Property.*

The interest of any married man in the real estate of his wife, whether possessed by her at the time of marriage, or acquired during coverture, cannot be taken on an execution against him during the life of the wife, or the life or lives of children the issue of such marriage. This act does not affect the remedy upon any contracts made prior to the 1st of July, 1845. (*a*)

9. *Effect of Death on Rights of Creditors.*

When executor should prove a will, and proceedings in case he refuse the trust.—The executor of the will of any person deceased must prove it within thirty days after the testator's decease, or present the will and declare his refusal of the executorship. In the latter case, the court of probate will commit the administration of the estate, with the will annexed, to the widow or next of kin, or one or more of the principal creditors. (*b*)

What court will grant administration, and the nature of the bond given by administrators and executors.—Substantially the same as in Massachusetts.

Liability of persons embezzling or concealing the effects of a deceased person.—Persons selling or embezzling any effects of the deceased, before taking out administration and exhibiting a true inventory of all the known estate, will be liable to the actions of any persons aggrieved as executors in their own wrong.

Persons refusing to deliver or give a satisfactory account to the executor or administrator of any effects in their hands belonging to the estate of the deceased, may be bound over by any justice of the peace to appear before the next probate court. If he refuse to be examined on oath before said court, or to answer the interrogatories put to him by said court, he may be committed to prison, there to remain till he conforms to the law.

Removal of executor or administrator.—If any executor or administrator, by reason of absence, sickness, or insanity, become incapable of executing his trust, or neglect or refuse to do the duties thereof, or waste the estate, and be unable personally to respond in damages, he may be removed from office by the court of probate, on due complaint by any heir, devisee, legatee, creditor, or surety in an administration bond, who has been injured or may be exposed to injury, and proof of the facts stated in such complaint.

(*a*) Acts of 1845, p. 36. (*b*) R. S. title 31.

On such removal, a new executor or administrator will be appointed by the court of probate, who will receive all the property of the deceased, and perform all the duties of the first executor or administrator.

Distribution of real and personal estate of a person dying intestate.—The court of probate will distribute the estate, both real and personal, of any person dying intestate, (unless the persons interested in the estate agree upon a division,) in manner following:

One-third part of the personal estate to the wife of the intestate, if there be any, and one-third of the lands and houses during life, where she has not been otherwise endowed before marriage, and all the residue of the real and personal estate, by equal proportions, according to its value at the time of distribution, to and among the children, and their legal representatives, if any of them are dead, excepting children who receive estate, by settlement of the intestate, in his life time, equal to the share of the others; and children advanced by settlement or portion, not equal to the shares of the rest, will have enough to make all the shares equal.

Certain specified changes may be made in this method of distribution, for the better accommodation of the heirs of any estate.

If any child die before he or she become of age, and before marriage, or before any legal disposition thereof, and before marriage, the portion of such child will be equally divided among the surviving children and their legal representatives.

If there be no children or legal representatives of them, one moiety of the personal estate will go to the wife, for ever, and one-third of the real estate for the term of life; and the residue of the estate, both real and personal, except as hereinafter provided, will be distributed and set off equally to the brothers and sisters of the intestate, of the whole blood, and those who legally represent them: if there be no such kindred, then to the parent or parents: if there be no parent, then equally to every of the brothers and sisters of the half blood, and those who legally represent them: if there be no parent, or brother, or sister, or legal representatives of them, then equally to the next of kin in equal degree: kindred of the whole blood to take the preference to kindred of the half blood in equal degree: no representatives to be admitted among collaterals, after the representatives of brothers and sisters. Provided, that all the real estate of the intestate received from his or her parent, ancestor, or other kindred, will belong equally to the brothers and sisters of the intestate and their legal representatives of the blood of the person or ancestor from whom such estate came or descended: if there be no such brothers and sisters or legal representatives, then equally to the brothers of such person or ancestor and their legal representatives: if there be none such, it will be set off and divided like other real estate. If there be no wife, all the estate will be divided among the children and heirs in manner aforesaid.

Time for granting administration and proving will, limited.—Administration will not be granted on the estate of any deceased person after the expiration of seven years from his death.

No will will be allowed to be proved by any court of probate after the expiration of ten years from the death of the testator: provided, that when any minor is interested in the estate, three years will be allowed, after he obtains his majority, to take out administration thereon, or to prove and allow the will.

Insolvent estates.—In case of insolvent estates, commissioners will be appointed, claims received, and a report made by them, substantially as provided by the laws of Massachusetts. If, upon such report, the estate appears to be insolvent, sale of all the property, real and personal, will be made, except certain necessary household goods for the widow, and the proceeds applied to the funeral expenses and incident charges of settling and selling the estate: debts due for the last sickness of the deceased, taxes and debts due to the state, and the debts of the several creditors, as allowed by the commissioners, in proportion to the sum found to be due.

10. *Mode of Collecting Debts.*

1. BY FOREIGN ATTACHMENT.

What is attachable by trustee process.—The effects of absent or absconding debtors, concealed in the hands of their attorneys, agents, factors, or trustees, so that they cannot be found or come at to be attached, and debts due from any person to such debtors, are attachable by trustee process. (*a*)

(*a*) R. S. title 37.

Proceedings on trial of suits against trustees, judgment, execution, &c.—Such attorney, agent, factor, trustee, or debtor, may defend his principal in such suit. If defendant be not in the state, and do not appear by himself or attorney, and said attorney, agent, &c., do not appear to defend, the court may continue the action one or two terms.

If the plaintiff obtain execution, the officer serving the same will make demand of the amount due thereon from the trustee and principal defendant, and if the trustee do not expose the effects in his hands, and the debtor do not pay the debt, a writ of scire facias may be brought against said trustee. If, on trial, it appear that he has in his hands effects of said debtor, or is indebted to him, or if he is defaulted, or refuses to disclose on oath, execution will issue against him, to be paid out of his own goods or estate, with lawful costs; unless it appear on the trial that the effects are of less value and the debt of less amount than the judgment recovered against such absent or absconding debtor, in which judgment will be rendered to the value of the goods or the amount of the debt. (*a*)

When demand must be made of trustee; limitation of scire facias.—Effects or debts of an absent or absconding debtor will not be holden or secured in the hands of his attorney, agent, factor, trustee, or debtor, by virtue of any judgment rendered against the debtor, unless demanded of them within sixty days after the rendition of the judgment. And no writ of scire facias may be maintained against such attorney, agent, &c., unless the same be brought within one year next after the right of taking out or bringing the same shall have accrued. (*b*)

Debtors discharged from imprisonment, &c., to be deemed absconding debtors.—Whenever the person of any debtor shall be discharged from imprisonment or shall not be liable thereto, at the suit of any of his or her creditors, he or she shall, as to such creditor or creditors, be deemed an absconding debtor, within the meaning of this act, and may be proceeded against as such.

No debt less than ten dollars, for personal labor or services, to be subject to foreign attachment.—No debt under ten dollars

(*a*) 8 Conn. R. 111. Kirby's R. 157, 421, 376. 1 Root's R. 138, 507, 295, 557, 276, 548, 473, 550. (*b*) 1 Root's R. 324.

which shall have accrued by reason of the personal labor or services of the person to whom the same may be due, may be taken or holden by virtue of any foreign attachment instituted against such person under this act.

II. BY SUIT AT COMMON LAW.

Process in civil actions.—The process in civil actions is by summons, or attachment against the goods and chattels of the defendant, and for want thereof, against his lands, or in some cases against his person. (*a*)

Imprisonment.—No person can be arrested upon any process, mesne or final, in an action founded simply upon contract. A party may be arrested on the ground of fraud, fraudulent obtaining of credit, fraudulent removing, concealing, or conveying of property. Every prisoner, upon giving bond, may obtain the liberties of the jail.

No female can be imprisoned for any debt incurred since 1826.

Time within which judgment may be obtained where there is no controversy.—In an action where there is no appearance for the defendant, judgment may be obtained at the close of the term when said action is entered.

When estate attached must be levied on by execution.—No estate attached on mesne process will be held to respond the judgment obtained by the plaintiff at whose suit the same is attached, either against the debtor, or any other creditor, unless said judgment creditor take out execution on such judgment, and have the same levied on goods or personal estate, within sixty days after final judgment, or on real estate, and have the same appraised and recorded within four months after such judgment has been obtained; or if said goods or estate are encumbered by any prior attachment, the execution to be levied as aforesaid within the respective terms aforesaid, after such incumbrance is removed.

Executions will be granted against what; and when they may be levied on the body.—Executions will be granted against the goods, chattels, lands, and in some cases the body of the debtor

(*a*) R. S. title 2.

By act of 1847, homesteads not exceeding in value three hundred dollars, with the necessary repairs and additions, though above that sum, are exempt from execution. There are also exempted various minor articles.

Liability of sheriff neglecting or refusing to pay over moneys collected.—Any sheriff neglecting or refusing to pay over moneys collected on execution, after the same have been duly demanded of him, will be liable to the party entitled to the same in the sum of two per cent. per month from the time of such demand till payment is made. (*a*)

12. *Courts.*

Besides the Probate and Appellate Courts, there is a Superior Court of Judicature, and there are County Courts, invested with general original jurisdiction at law and in equity in civil cases. The former court is held annually in each of the counties of the state. Two or more sessions of the County Courts are held each year, in the different counties of the state.

(*a*) R. S. title 93.

NEW-YORK.

1. *Bills of Exchange and Promissory Notes.*

Negotiability of and action on.—Promissory notes for the payment of money to any person or order or to bearer, are negotiable in the same manner as inland bills of exchange by the custom of merchants; and this, whether executed by natural or artificial persons. The payees, endorsees, and holders of the same may maintain actions thereon, in like manner as on inland bills of exchange. A promissory note payable to the order of the maker, or of a fictitious person shall have the same validity, if negotiated, as against the maker and all persons having knowledge of the facts, as if payable to bearer.

Acceptance.—No person in this state can be charged as the acceptor of a bill of exchange, unless the acceptance is in writing. If the acceptance is written on a paper other than the bill, it will only bind the acceptor in favor of a person to whom the acceptance has been shown, and who on the faith thereof has received the bill for a valuable consideration. Where a written acceptance is refused, the holder may protest the bill for non acceptance. An unconditional promise in writing to accept a bill before it is drawn, is deemed an actual acceptance in favor of every person who upon the faith thereof has received the bill for a valuable consideration.

Rate of damages upon protested bills.—The following rate of damages is allowed upon bills of exchange drawn or negotiated within the state which have been protested for non-payment: three per cent. on bills drawn upon any person at a place in either of the states of Maine, New Hampshire, Vermont, Massachusetts, Rhode Island, Connecticut, New Jersey, Pennsylvania, Ohio, Delaware, Maryland, Virginia, or the District of Columbia: five per cent. on bills drawn upon any person at any place in North or South Carolina, Georgia, Kentucky, or Tennessee: ten per cent. on bills drawn upon any person at any place in any other state or territory of the United States, or at any other place on or adjacent to this continent and north of the equator, or in any British or other foreign possessions in the West Indies, or elsewhere in the western Atlantic ocean: ten per cent. on bills drawn upon any person in any place or port in Europe. The damages are in lieu of interest, charges of protest and all other charges incurred previous to giving notice of non-payment; but from such time the holder of the bill may recover lawful interest upon the aggregate amount of principal and damages. Where the contents of the bill are expressed in the money of account of the United States, the amount of the principal sum and damages is to be determined without any reference to the rate of exchange between the place at which and on which the bill is drawn; but where the contents of the bill are payable in foreign currency, the amount due is to be ascertained by the rate of exchange, or the value of the foreign currency at the time of the demand of payment. The same rate of damages is allowed on the protest of bills for non-acceptance: the damages in either case to be recovered only by the holder of a bill who has purchased the same or some interest therein for a valuable consideration. (*a*)

2. *Interest.*

Seven per cent. is the legal rate of interest, and all contracts or assurances for a higher rate are void, and if the usurious inter-

(*a*) R. C. ii. 53.

est has been paid it may be recovered back. Wherever a borrower files a bill in chancery for discovery or relief or both, the court shall not require any offer to pay the lawful interest or principal, but shall, if the usury be established, declare the contract void, and order the usurious security to be delivered up and cancelled. (*a*) In the computation of interest a month is to be considered as the twelfth part of the year, and as consisting of thirty days.

3. *Frauds.*

Besides the statute respecting fraudulent conveyances of real estate, various conveyances and contracts relative to goods, chattels and choses in action are declared fraudulent. All conveyances, deeds of gift, transfers, or assignments, verbal or written, of goods, chattels or things in action made in trust for the use of the person making the same are void as against the creditors, existing or subsequent of such person. All sales by a vendor, of goods and chattels in his possession or under his control, and every assignment of goods and chattels by way of mortgage or security, or upon any condition whatever, unless the same be accompanied by an immediate delivery, and followed by an actual and continued change of possession of the thing sold, mortgaged or assigned, are presumed to be fraudulent and void, as against the creditors of the vendor, or the person making the assignment, or subsequent purchasers in good faith, and the burthen of establishing the fairness of such sale or assignment is imposed upon the persons claiming under them. The creditors embraced by this provision, are all persons who may be creditors of the vendor or assignor at any time while such goods and chattels remain in his possession or under his control.

A mortgage of personal property unaccompanied by any change of possession will be valid, if filed according to the direction of the statute, in the city or town where the mortgagor resides at the time of the execution thereof, or in case of his non-residence in the city or town where the mortgaged property is then situate ; a copy of the mortgage and a statement of the interest of the mortgagee therein, to be filed anew, at the expiration of a year.

(*a*) R. S. ii. 56.

All conveyances or assignments of either real or personal estate made with the intent to hinder, delay or defraud creditors are void.

No grant or assignment of any existing trust in lands, goods, or choses in action, will be valid, unless made in writing. The following agreements are void, unless the same, or some note or memorandum thereof, expressing the consideration, be in writing, and subscribed by the party to be charged therewith. 1. Every agreement that by its terms is not to be performed within one year from the making thereof. 2. Every special promise to answer for the debt, default, or miscarriage of another person. 3. Every agreement, promise, or undertaking made upon consideration of marriage, except mutual promises to marry. All contracts for the sale of goods, chattels or choses in action for the price of fifty dollars or more, are void, unless 1. A note or memorandum of the contract be made in writing, and subscribed by the parties to be charged thereby: or 2. Unless the buyer receive or accept part of such goods, or the evidences, or some of them of such things in action: or 3. Unless the buyer at the time, pay some part of the purchase money.

A memorandum by an auctioneer in his sale book, at the time of the sale of any goods at public auction, specifying the nature and price of the property sold, the terms of the sale, the name of the purchaser, and the name of the person on whose account the sale is made, is deemed a note of the contract of sale within the meaning of the law. (*a*)

4. *Principals, Factors, and Agents.*

The nominal shipper of merchandise is deemed the true owner thereof, so far as to entitle the consignee, who has no notice by the bill of lading or otherwise, that he is not the bona fide owner, to a lien thereon for any money advanced or negotiable security given by him to such shipper, or for any money or security received by such shipper for his use. An agent intrusted with the possession of a bill of lading or other documentary evidence of title, or intrusted with the possession of merchandise for the purposes of sale or as a security for advances to be obtained thereon,

(*a*) R. S. ii. 194.

is deemed the true owner so far as to give validity to any contracts by him for its sale, or for a loan of money, or advance of negotiable security on its faith. Where, however, the person making advances is advised that the factor is not the owner, the courts have held that he is not entitled to the protection of the act. (*a*) The depositary of such merchandise as a security for an antecedent debt, acquires no other rights therein, than were possessed by the agent at the time of the deposit.

The true owner of merchandise thus deposited may reclaim it, upon repayment of the money advanced, or restoration of the security given on its faith, and upon satisfaction of such lien as may exist thereon in favor of the agent depositing the same: or he may recover from such depositary any balance of the proceeds arising from the sale of such merchandise, which may remain after satisfying his just dues. Common carriers, warehouse keepers, and persons to whom property has been committed for transportation or storage, are not agents within the meaning of the factor's act. (*b*)

5. *Effect of Marriage upon the Rights of Property.*

The real and personal property owned by any female hereafter married, at the time of her marriage, and the rents, issues, and profits thereof remain her sole and separate property, as if she were a single female, and are neither subject to the disposal of her husband, nor liable for his debts. The real and personal property, and rents and profits thereof, of a female now married, shall not be subject to the disposal of her husband; but shall be her sole and separate property, as if she were a feme sole; except that it shall be liable for the debts of her husband heretofore contracted. Married women may take and hold to their own separate use, free from the control of their husbands, or any liability for their debts, any real or personal property coming to them from any other person than the husband, by gift, grant, devise, or bequest. (*c*)

This law was enacted 7th April, 1848.

(*a*) Stevens *v.* Wilson, 6 Hill 512. (*b*) Acts of 1830. (*c*) Ib. of 1848.

6. *Limitation of Actions.*

An action upon a judgment or decree of any court of the United States, or of any state or territory within the United States, or an action upon a sealed instrument, must be brought within twenty years. An action upon a contract obligation or liability expressed or implied, excepting those already mentioned; an action upon a liability created by statute, other than a penalty or forfeiture; an action for taking, detaining, or injuring any goods or chattels, including actions for the specific recovery of personal property, or an action for relief on the ground of fraud, must be commenced within six years. The cause of action is not deemed to have accrued until a discovery by the aggrieved party of the facts constituting the fraud. An action against a sheriff or coroner upon an official liability, must be brought within three years, excepting that an action for an escape must be brought within one year. In an action brought to recover a balance due upon mutual open and current accounts, where there have been reciprocal demands between the parties, the cause of action is deemed to have accrued from the time of the last item in the account on the adverse side.

Where a person is out of the state at or after the time when any cause of action has accrued, such period of absence is not deemed a part of the limitation. If any person entitled to an action is at the time of its accruing, an infant, feme covert, lunatic, or imprisoned upon a criminal proceeding for a term less than that of his natural life, the time of such disability is not to be considered a part of the period of limitation.

Acknowledgment in writing.—Where the time for commencing an action arising on contract has expired, the cause of action can only be revived by an acknowledgment or new promise in writing, signed by the party to be charged thereby.

7. *Limited Partnerships.*

Limited partnerships for the transaction of any mercantile, mechanical, or manufacturing business, not including banking or insurance, within this state, may be formed by two or more persons.

Such partnerships may consist of one or more persons, who shall be called general partners, and who shall be jointly and severally responsible as general partners now are by law; and of one or more persons who shall contribute, in actual cash payments, a specific sum as capital to the common stock, who shall be called special partners, and who shall not be liable for the debts of the partnership, beyond the fund so contributed by him or them to the capital.

The general partners only shall be authorized to transact business and sign for the partnership, and to bind the same.

The persons desirous of joining such partnership, shall make and severally sign a certificate which shall contain,

1st. The name or firm under which such partnership is to be conducted; 2d. The general nature of the business intended to be transacted; 3d. The names of all the general and special partners interested therein, distinguishing which are general and which are special partners, and their respective places of residence; 4th. The amount of capital which each special partner shall have contributed to the common stock; 5th. The period at which the partnership is to commence, and the period at which it will terminate. This certificate must be acknowledged or proved, and certified before the same persons and in the same manner as conveyances of land; and when thus acknowledged and certified, it must be filed in the office of the clerk of the county in which the principal place of the partnership business is situated, and recorded by him in a book kept for that purpose. If the partnership have places of business in different counties, a transcript of the certificate and acknowledgment shall be filed and recorded in each. An affidavit of one or more of the general partners shall be filed with the original certificate, stating that the sums therein specified to have been contributed to the common stock, have been actually and in good faith paid in cash. The partnership will not be considered as formed until these requisitions of the law have been complied with; and if any false statement is made in the certificate or affidavit, all the parties interested will be deemed general partners. The terms of the partnership must be published for six weeks after the registry, in two newspapers to be designated by the clerk of the county in which the registry is made, and published in the senate district in which the business is carried on, or it will be deemed general.

Every renewal or continuance, of such partnership, beyond the time originally fixed for its duration, shall be certified, acknowledged, and recorded, and an affidavit of a general partner be made and filed, and notice be given in the manner herein required for its original formation; and every such partnership which shall be otherwise renewed or continued, shall be deemed a general partnership.

Every alteration which shall be made in the names of the partners, in the nature of the business, or in the capital or shares thereof, or in any other matter specified in the original certificate, shall be deemed a dissolution of the partnership; and every such partnership, which shall in any manner be carried on after any such alteration shall have been made, shall be deemed a general partnership, unless renewed as a special partnership, according to the provisions of the last section.

The business of the partnership shall be conducted under a firm, in which the names of the general partners only shall be inserted, without the addition of the word "company," or any other general term; and if the name of any special partner shall be used in such firm, with his privity, he shall be deemed a general partner.

Suits in relation to the business of the partnership may be brought and conducted, by and against the general partners, in the same manner as if there were no special partners.

Special partners may from time to time, examine into the condition of the partnership concerns, and advise as to their management, but shall not transact any business on account thereof, as agent or otherwise; and any violation of this provision will subject them to the responsibilities of general partners. The special partners are not to withdraw any part of the capital stock contributed by them, during the continuance of the partnership, in the shape of dividends, profits, or otherwise. All sales or transfers of partnership property, in contemplation of insolvency, or of the insolvency of any partner, with a view to give preference to any creditor of such partnership or insolvent partner, over the other creditors of the partnership, and all other assurance, executed for the same purpose, are void as against the creditors of the partnership. The same provision is applicable to a similar transfer by a general or special partner of his own effects. In case of the bankruptcy of the partnership, no special partner can claim as a creditor until the claims of all creditors of the partnership have been satisfied. No dissolution of a partnership may take place previous to the time specified in the certificate of its formation or renewal, until a notice thereof has been filed and recorded as in the case of the original certificate; and also published once a week for four weeks in the state newspaper, and in a newspaper printed in each of the counties where the partnership has a place of business. Any special partner concurring or participating in the violation of these provisions, liable as a general partner. (*a*)

General provision as to partnership.—One of several joint debtors, or one partner upon the dissolution of a partnership, may compromise with one or all of the joint creditors, and thus exonerate himself from all several or individual liability; which composition shall be valid and binding upon the parties to it, but in no manner release the other partners, or impair the creditors' right to proceed against them. (*b*)

8. *Effect of Death upon the Rights of Creditors.*

Jurisdiction of Surrogates.—The estates of deceased persons are administered under the control of the Courts of Surrogates. These courts are not courts of record, but of peculiar and special jurisdiction, and any person claiming under their orders must show that the court had acquired jurisdiction in the mode pointed out by law. The surrogate is a local officer, confined in the execution of his duties to the county for which he has been appointed. He is invested with authority to take the proof of wills of real and personal estate in the cases prescribed by law, and also to take the proof of any will relative to real estate situated within the county of such surrogate, when the testator in such will has died

(*a*) R. S. ii. 48 to 52. (*b*) Ib. ii. 61.

out of the state, not being an inhabitant thereof, nor leaving any assets therein; to grant letters testamentary and of administration; to direct and control the conduct and settle the accounts of executors and administrators; to enforce the payment of debts and legacies and the distribution of the estates of intestates; to order the sale and disposition of the real estates of deceased persons; to administer justice in all matters relating to the affairs of deceased persons, according to the provisions of the statutes of the state. (*a*)

Administration.—In cases of intestacy, administration is first granted to the relatives of the deceased, and if there be none such, then to his creditors; the creditor first applying, if there be no disqualification, to have the preference.

Assets.—The following property is deemed assets, and goes to the executor or administrator to be applied and distributed as a part of the personal estate, and to be included in the inventory which he is required to make thereof—1. Leases for years: lands held by the deceased from year to year: and estates held by him for the life of another person. 2. The interest which may remain in the deceased at the time of his death in a term for years, after the expiration of any estate for years therein granted by him or any other person. 3. The interest in lands devised to an executor for a term of years for the payment of debts. 4. Things annexed to a freehold, or to any building, for the purpose of trade or manufacture, and not fixed into the wall of a house, so as to be essential to its support. 5. The crops growing on the land of the deceased at the time of his death. 6. Every kind of produce raised annually by labor and cultivation, excepting grass growing and fruit not gathered. 7. Rent reserved to the deceased which had accrued at the time of his death. 8. Debts secured by mortgages, bonds, notes or bills; accounts, money, and bank bills, or other circulating medium, things in action, and stock in any company, whether incorporated or not. 9. Goods, wares, merchandise, utensils, furniture, cattle, provisions, and every other species of personal property, unless specially excepted. (*b*)

Liability of real estate for payment of debts.—The general rule that the personal estate is the primary fund for the payment

(*a*) R. S. ii. 220. Ib. 73 to 117.

(*b*) R. S. ii. 89.

of debts, and must first be applied thereto, prevails in New-York; but in case of its deficiency, the executor or administrator may mortgage, lease, or sell, under the direction of the Surrogate's Court, so much of the real estate as may be requisite for the payment of debts. Such sale may be ordered either upon the application of the executor or administrator, setting forth and establishing in his petition the facts necessary to justify such sale, or upon the application of a creditor where the executor or administrator has rendered his account, and it appears therefrom that there are not sufficient assets to pay the debts of the deceased. The proceeds of the sale will be distributed among creditors, in proportion to their respective debts, without giving any preference to bonds or other specialties, or to any demands on account of any suit being brought thereon. The executor is not authorized to sell the personal estate, unless he has ascertained that a sale will be necessary to enable him to pay the debts, and discharge the legacies; and then only so much of the property as will be requisite for those purposes.

Order in payment of debts.—The following order is to be observed in the payment of debts: 1. Debts entitled to a preference under the laws of the United States. 2. Taxes assessed upon the estate of the deceased previous to his death. 3. Judgments docketed, and decrees enrolled against the deceased, according to the priority thereof, respectively. 4. All recognizances, bonds, sealed instruments, notes, bills, and unliquidated demands and accounts. No preference is to be given to debts due and payable over debts of the same class not due and payable; nor, except in the third class of cases, to any debt of one class over other debts of the same class: nor can such preference be acquired by commencing a suit for the recovery of any debt, or the obtaining a judgment thereon against the executor or administrator.

Notice to creditors, and settlement of their claims.—An executor or administrator, within six months from the granting of letters testamentary or of administration, must insert a notice once in each week for six months in a newspaper printed in the county, and in so many other newspapers as the surrogate may deem most likely to give notice to the creditors of the deceased, requiring all persons having claims against his estate to exhibit the same with the vouchers thereof, to the executor or administrator at a time and place to be specified in the notice; the day named to be at least six months from the first publication of the notice. Where an executor doubts the justness of any claim, the same may be referred to three disinterested persons, to be approved by the surrogate: where he disputes or rejects a claim, and no reference is made, the claimant must within six months from the maturity of his demand, commence a suit for its recovery, or be for ever barred from maintaining any action thereon. Where suit is brought upon any claim not presented within the time prescribed after the publication of notice, the executor or administrator is not chargeable with any assets which he may have paid in satisfaction of any claims of an inferior degree, or of any legacies, or in making distribution to the next of kin, before such suit was commenced, but such creditor may recover from any legatee or next of kin, the portion of assets which he may have received. (*a*)

Liability of executors and administrators.—All actions upon contract may be maintained by or against executors or administrators, which might have been maintained by or against their respective testators. Executors or administrators cannot be held to bail in any action brought against them in their representative character, unless it be to charge them with waste.

Settlement of account.—At the expiration of eighteen months from the appointment of an executor or administrator, he may be required, upon the application of any person having a demand against the estate of the deceased, to render an account of his proceedings in the discharge of his trust, and the surrogate may make such order as shall be just and equitable in the premises. The executor or administrator may also, at the end of the same period, voluntarily produce an account of his proceedings before the surrogate, and after due notice to the parties interested in the estate, require the same to be judicially examined and settled, and procure a decree confirming or correcting such disposition of the property of the estate as he may have made, and directing him in the legal distribution of any which may still remain in his

(*a*) R. S. ii. 90.

hands.(*a*) If, upon such application, there is any creditor or other person interested, residing in any other state of the United States or Canada, the citation requiring their appearance must either be published once in each week for three months, in the state paper, or be personally served on such creditors at least forty days before the return thereof. The allowance of an account upon final settlement is conclusive evidence of the following facts only: 1. That the charges made in such account for moneys paid to creditors, legatees, the next of kin, and for necessary expenses, are correct. 2. That such executor or administrator has been charged all the interest for moneys received by him, and embraced in his account, for which he was legally accountable. 3. That the moneys stated in such account as collected, were all that were collectable of the debts stated in such account, at the time of the settlement thereof. 4. That the allowances in such account for the decrease in the value of any assets, and the charges therein for the increase in such value, were correctly made. (*b*)

Time for payment of debts.—The surrogate having jurisdiction may decree the payment of any debt, or a proportional part, upon the application of a creditor, at any time after six months have elapsed from the granting of letters testamentary or of administration. No execution, however, can issue upon a judgment against an executor or administrator until an account of his administration has been rendered and settled, or unless on an order of the surrogate who appointed him; and if account has been rendered to the surrogate by such executor or administrator, execution shall only issue for the sum that shall have appeared upon the settlement of such account to be a just proportion of the assets applicable to the judgment. For this purpose, it is further provided, that where a creditor shall have obtained a judgment against any executor or administrator, after a trial at law upon the merits, he may at any time thereafter apply to the surrogate having jurisdiction for an order against such executor or administrator to show cause why an execution should not be issued upon such judgment. The executor or administrator shall

(*a*) Dayton's Law of Surrogates, 188; a work in which the entire subject of this title is elaborately examined.

(*b*) R. S. ii. 158.

thereupon be cited to appear and account before the surrogate; and if upon such accounting, it shall appear that there are assets in his hands, properly applicable in whole or in part to the payment of the judgment so obtained, the surrogate shall order that execution be issued for such amount. (*a*)

Limitation of actions against.—When the defendant to any action not barred by the statutes of limitation, dies during its pendency and before judgment, a new action may be commenced against his executors or administrators within one year from the granting of letters testamentary or of administration. (*b*) The term of eighteen months from the death of any testator or intestate, shall not be deemed a part of the time limited by law for commencing actions against his representatives. (*c*)

9. *Attachment.* (*d*)

When it may be issued.—The real and personal property of a debtor may be attached for the payment of his debts in the following cases: 1. Whenever such debtor, being an inhabitant of the state, shall secretly depart therefrom, with intent to defraud his creditors or to avoid the service of civil process, or shall keep himself concealed therein, with the like intent. 2. Whenever a non-resident of the state shall be indebted on a contract made within the state, or to a creditor residing within the state, although upon a contract made elsewhere. The application for the attachment must be in writing, verified by the affidavit of the creditor, or of the person making the application, on his behalf. It must specify the sum in which the debtor is indebted to the complainant, over and above all just discounts, and the grounds of the application; and the facts and circumstances to verify these grounds must also be established by the affidavit of two disinterested witnesses. Where the officer to whom the application is made is satisfied with the evidence adduced, he may issue warrants to the sheriff of every county in which such debtor may have any property, commanding him to attach and safely keep all the real and personal estate of such debtor within his county, excepting

(*a*) R. S. ii. 88, 116. (*b*) Ib. ii. 298. (*c*) Ib. ii. 443. (*d*) Ib. ii. 62 to 74.

articles exempt by law from execution, with all books and papers relating to same.

Notice.—Upon issuing any warrant of attachment, the officer shall also direct that a notice of the character hereafter described, be published in the state paper, and in a newspaper printed in the city of New-York, and in a newspaper printed in the county to which the attachment has issued, if there be one, and if there be none in such county, then in a newspaper printed nearest to such county; this notice to be published once in each week for three months, in the case of an absconding or concealed debtor, and for nine months in the case of a non-resident debtor; the notice in the case of an absconding or concealed debtor must state that an attachment has issued against the estate of such debtor, and that the same will be sold for the payment of his debts, unless he appears and discharges the attachment according to law, within three months from the first publication of such notice; and that the payment of any debts and delivery of any property belonging to such debtor, to him or for his use, and the transfer of any property by him, for any purpose whatever, are forbidden by law and are void. The notice in the case of non-resident debtors pursues a similar form, substituting "nine months," for "three," and then proceeding thus, "and that the payment of any debts due to him by residents of this state, and the delivery to him, or for his use, of any property within the state belonging to him, and the transfer of any such property by him, are forbidden and void. And such payment or delivery will be deemed fraudulent."

Assurances executed by debtor after publication of notice.—All sales, assignments, mortgages, and conveyances of any part of the real or personal estate, including things in action of an absconding or concealed debtor, made after the first publication of such notice, in payment of or as a security for any pre-existing or prior debt, or for any other consideration, and all judgments confessed by him after that time, are absolutely void as to his creditors. The same nullity belongs to any disposition by a non-resident debtor, after the first publication of notice, of his estate real or personal, in New-York.

Interposition of other creditors.—Any other creditor whose debt is then due, may become a party to the proceeding, on filing with the officer who issued the warrant, an affidavit specifying the sum in which the debtor is indebted to him, over and above all discounts, and a petition stating his desire to be deemed an attaching creditor ; whereupon he will be entitled to the privileges, and subject to the obligation of the creditor at whose instance the attachment issued. Where any subsequent warrant of attachment, issued pursuant to the provisions of this act, is levied upon any property of such debtor, such subsequent warrant and seizure will be deemed in all respects a part of the proceedings upon the first application.

Proceedings upon the warrant.—The sheriff is to make and return an inventory of the property seized, and the books and papers relating thereto, and collect all the debts and credits of the debtor. He is authorized to sell any perishable property at auction, excepting vessels. Where there is a controversy as to the title of the debtor to any goods or effects other than vessels, seized as his property, the sheriff shall summon a jury for the trial of the right; and if their verdict is for the claimant, the property shall forthwith be delivered to him, unless the attaching creditor shall sufficiently indemnify the officer for its detention. Where goods are shipped for transportation out of the state, without notice of the issuing of the attachment, at the time of the shipment, the levy of the attachment will not prevent their departure, unless the attaching creditor or his agent executes bond with sufficient sureties to indemnify the owner or master for all expenses, damages, &c., to which he may be subjected by the unlading of such vessel, and the necessary detention therefor. Where a domestic or foreign vessel is seized upon an attachment, there is a provision by which any adverse claimant of such vessel may recover the possession. In the former case, the claimant must give bonds to establish his ownership, in a suit brought against him. In the latter case, upon the affidavit of the claimant or his agent, as to the ownership, the vessel must be delivered, unless the attaching creditors give bond to prosecute the attachment with effect, and to pay all damages which may ensue from such seizure

Proceedings upon petition to contest the warrant.—Where any debtor or any person to whom he has made payments, or delivered property for a valuable consideration, after publication of the notice of attachment, desires to contest the fact of his being a non-resident, concealed, or absconding debtor, he may present a petition for that purpose to the officer who issued the warrant, verified by affidavit, and upon his executing a bond in the sum of one hundred dollars with surety, conditioned to establish the truth of his petition, the officer may either proceed in a summary way to hear the proofs and allegations of the parties, and adjudicate upon the question, or submit the case to a jury; and if the allegations of the petition are established, the warrant will be discharged. The pendency of the petition in no manner affects proceedings upon the warrant, except that no property other than that which is perishable will be sold, nor any payment made of debts, until a determination of the controversy.

Application for discharge of warrant.—The debtor may, at any time before the appointment of trustees, apply to the officer who issued the attachment, for its discharge, which will be granted, upon his executing a bond with sufficient sureties, in double the amount sworn to by the attaching creditors, conditioned to pay to each of such creditors, the sum justly due to him at the time of issuing the attachment, with interest. Such bond may be prosecuted by the attaching creditors, jointly or separately, at any time within six months from the date.

Appointment of trustees.—If the debtor does not appear and satisfy his creditors within the time for that purpose specified in the notice, nor discharge the warrant, the officer by whom it was issued shall, within three months from the expiration of the time so limited, and upon due proof of the publication of the same, appoint three or more fit persons to be trustees for all the creditors of the debtors; and unless this appointment is made within the period thus prescribed, the warrant of attachment will be considered as discharged and annulled. Every person indebted to, or having in his possession, property of the defendant in the attachment, after the first publication of the notice, must account and answer for such debt or property to the trustees. It is the duty of the trustees, within one month from the time of their appointment, to record the same in the office of the clerk of every county in which property has been seized under the warrant.

Duties of trustees.—See title, "*Rights and duties of trustees and assignees.*"

Attachment of vessels.—Debts amounting to fifty dollars or upwards, contracted by the master, owner, agent, or consignee of any ship or vessel within the state, on account of work done, or materials or articles furnished in the state, towards the building or repairing, furnishing or equipping such vessel, or such provisions and stores, furnished within the state, as were proper at the time for the use of such vessel, or on account of wharfage and the expense of keeping the vessel in port, are liens upon the vessel, tackle, apparel, and furniture, to be preferred to all other liens except mariners' wages. Such lien ceases, however, whenever the vessel leaves the state, or when she leaves the port where the debt was contracted for another within the state, in twelve days after such departure. (*a*)

10. *Insolvent Laws.*

Voluntary assignments on the application of an insolvent and his creditors. (*b*)—The object of this proceeding is to procure for the insolvent a discharge from certain obligations, and an exoneration of his person from future arrest in any action founded upon an existing indebtedness or liability. The petition must be signed by the debtor, and creditors residing in the United States, whose claims amount to two-thirds of the debts owing by him to persons residing within the United States. The petition must be accompanied by an affidavit from each creditor, stating that the sum therein specified is justly due, or will become due at a time mentioned, also the nature of the demand and the evidence and consideration thereof, and that neither the petitioner nor any one for his use hath received from the insolvent or any other person, payment of any demand or any part thereof, in money or in any other way whatever, or any gift or reward upon an express or implied confidence that he should become a petitioner for such insolvent. The insolvent must accompany the petition with a schedule, containing a full and true account of all of his creditors, their places of residence, amount, nature, evidences, and securities of their claims, as well as a full and true inventory of his entire estate, real and personal, legal and equitable, and all incumbrances

(*a*) R. S. ii. 587.

(*b*) Ib. 76 to 82.

thereon, and books and securities relating thereto. He must also annex to his petition and schedule an affidavit of the truth of the same, and that he has not at any time or in any manner whatever, disposed of, or made over any part of his estate for the future benefit of himself or his family, or in order to defraud any of his creditors, and that he has in no instance acknowledged a debt for a greater sum than he honestly and truly owed, and that he has not paid, or secured to be paid, or in any way compounded with his creditors, for the purpose of fraudulently obtaining the prayer of his petition.

Upon the receipt of these papers, it is the duty of the officer to make an order, requiring all creditors to show cause at a day and place to be named therein, why an assignment of the insolvent's estate should not be made, and he discharged from his debts. The officer is at the same time to direct a notice of the contents of this order to be published in the state newspaper, and in the newspaper of the county where the application is made, or if there be none, then in the newspaper nearest thereto; and if one-fourth part of the debts owing by such insolvent have accrued in the city of New-York, or be owing to creditors residing there, then in a newspaper of that city to be designated by him. If all the creditors of the insolvent reside within one hundred miles of the place where they are required to show cause, the notice must be published once in each week, for four weeks successively; otherwise once in each week for ten weeks successively. Any creditor desirous of opposing the discharge, may appear at the appointed time and place, and file his objections in writing, which, with the proofs and allegations of the parties, shall be submitted for determination to a jury. At the hearing, the insolvent may be examined upon oath, touching his estate and condition; and if it appears that he has collected any debts or demands, or made any transfer of any part of his personal or real estate, since the execution of his schedule, he will be required to pay or secure to be paid within thirty days to his assignees, the full amount or value of the same, excepting such portion as has been necessarily expended in his support or that of his family. In default thereof, or if it appear that the insolvent, in contemplation of insolvency or of petitioning for a discharge under this act, has made any sale or transfer, absolute or conditional, of any part of his estate or interest therein, or has confessed a judgment or given any security with a view to give a preference for an antecedent debt to any creditor, he will be debarred. If the officer before whom the application is pending, is satisfied that the insolvent has fairly complied with the requisitions of the law, he shall direct him to make an assignment of his entire estate, excepting such articles as may be deemed necessary for his own use, to such person or persons as the petitioning creditors, or those owning the major part of the claims, shall nominate. The assignment shall vest in the assignees all the interest which the insolvent may possess at the time of executing the same, in any estate, real or personal, legal or equitable, and any contingent interest which may accrue to him within three years. The insolvent, upon the execution and proof of this assignment, is entitled to a discharge from all debts due at that time, or to become due afterwards, but contracted previously, founded upon contracts made or to be executed within the state, and from all debts owing to persons resident within the state at the time of the first publication of the notice of the application for such discharge, or owing to persons not residing within the state, but who have united in the petition for the discharge, or accepted a dividend from the estate; and also from all liabilities incurred by reason of the making or indorsing of any promissory note or bill of exchange previous to the execution of the assignment, or in consequence of the payment by any party to such instrument of the whole or any part of the money to be secured thereby, whether such payment be made prior or subsequent to the execution of the assignment. Such discharge will also exonerate the insolvent from arrest or imprisonment, upon any proceeding founded upon contracts or liabilities previously incurred. The discharge will be rendered null and void by reason of any perjury, fraud, or collusion on the part of the insolvent in the premises.

Voluntary assignments by an insolvent debtor. (*a*)—Proceedings similar to those which have just been described, may be had upon the application of an insolvent debtor, praying that his estate may be assigned for the benefit of all his creditors, and his person thereafter exempted from arrest or imprisonment by reason of

(*a*) R. S. 86 to 88.

debts arising out of contracts or liabilities previously incurred; and if in prison to be released from imprisonment, and the discharge which may be granted shall have that operation. The liability however of the property of the insolvent is in no manner affected by this discharge.

Voluntary assignments by debtors imprisoned in execution. (*a*)—A debtor whose body has been taken in execution, may at any time, if the demand against him does not exceed five hundred dollars, or after the lapse of three months, if it does, be released from imprisonment, upon filing a petition for that purpose, accompanied by a full and true account of his condition as it was at the time of his imprisonment, and as it is at the period of his application, and an affidavit that such account is true, and that he has not in any manner disposed of any part of his property, with a view to his future benefit, or to defraud his creditors. If, upon notice served on the creditors, at whose instance he is imprisoned, and an opportunity afforded them to contest the allegations of the petition, the court or officer shall be satisfied that the proceedings on the part of the petitioner have been just and fair, they may order him to make an assignment of his property to persons designated for the benefit of the creditors upon whose executions he is imprisoned, and upon the execution thereof shall direct his discharge, his property still remaining liable. The assignees shall forthwith collect, sell, and distribute the proceeds of the insolvent's estate among the creditors by whom his body had been taken in execution previous to his petition, in proportion to the amounts due to them respectively. If a debtor remains in prison for the space of three months without applying for his discharge, he may be required by his creditor in writing to make application for the benefit of this act; and for default thereof for the space of thirty days after personal service of the notice, he will be forever debarred from doing so.

Proceedings by creditors to compel assignment by insolvent debtors. (*b*)—Where any person has been imprisoned for more than sixty days in any civil action, any creditor having a claim amounting to twenty-five dollars, upon which suit might then be brought, may file a petition to compel an assignment of such

(*a*) R. S. 88 to 91. (*b*) Ib. ii. 82 to 85.

debtor's estate, and if two-thirds in amount of the creditors of such debtor residing in the United States, upon being made parties to the proceeding by a notice served on them, shall unite in the petition, and no good cause appear to the contrary, the officer making the order shall require the debtor by a certain specified day to deliver an account of his creditors, and an inventory of his estate upon oath, and to execute an assignment thereof. Unless that number unite in the petition, it will be dismissed. If upon being served with this order, the imprisoned debtor comply with it, and in all respects conform to the requisitions of the act concerning the voluntary assignments of insolvent debtors, he will be entitled to the discharge which is provided in that act. If he fails to obey the order, and shows no sufficient reason for his neglect, the officer by whom it was made may execute an assignment of all the estate of such debtor to the persons nominated by the petitioning creditors as assignees, for the benefit of all the creditors, which shall have the same operation and effect as if it had been voluntarily executed by the debtor upon the day of the first publication of notice to his creditors. Every debtor thus refractory will be afterwards precluded from obtaining any discharge from his imprisonment, except upon his petition and that of his creditors, under the act providing for the voluntary assignment of insolvent debtors; upon which petition the proceedings pointed out in that act may be had, except that the assignment must be made to the assignees appointed under the provisions of this chapter.

General provisions as to attachments and assignments. (*a*)—Applications for warrants of attachment, for the appointment of trustees, for the discharge of an insolvent debtor to compel an assignment, for the exemption of a debtor's person from imprisonment or arrest, may be made to circuit judges, supreme court commissioners, first judges of county courts, and any other judges of such courts of the degree of counselor of law in the supreme court, recorders of cities.

Corporations are deemed creditors within the meaning of the provisions of these acts, and may present or unite in a petition as other creditors. Whenever partners or joint companies are creditors of any debtor, the petition or affidavit may be signed by

(*a*) R. S. ii. 91 to 95.

either of the partners or one of the company. Creditors residing out of the state may present or unite in a petition in the same manner as resident creditors; their affidavits will be received when sworn to before a judge or clerk of a court of record of the state, district, or territory in which they reside, duly authenticated under the seal of such court.

Whenever any petitioning creditor has purchased a debt or demand against the estate of the insolvent, for a less sum than its nominal amount, he shall be deemed a creditor to the amount only of the sum actually paid. No creditor can become a petitioner in respect to a debt secured by mortgage, judgment, or other assurance, unless he relinquishes such security for the common benefit of all his creditors. Every discharge is to be recorded by the clerk of the county in which it was granted, and every assignment by the clerk of the county in which it was executed.

Rights and duties of trustees and assignes. (*a*)—Assignees appointed under the various provisions which have been enumerated, are declared to be trustees of the estate of the debtor in relation to whose property, they have been appointed, for the benefit of his creditors. They have power to sue for, and recover all the estate or rights in action of the debtor as fully as he could have done himself before their appointment: to sell such estate at public auction, from time on reasonable notice and credit, and execute conveyances therefor, to discharge all incumbrances upon the estate of the debtor, and make any settlement or composition with his creditors. Trustees upon their appointment are to give notice thereof, and to require all the debtors and creditors of the insolvent, at a time and place specified, to be present, and in the one case to discharge their indebtedness, and in the other to deliver their accounts; and shall also require all persons having in their possession any property of the insolvent, to surrender the same. This notice is to be published for three weeks; in the case of an insolvent or imprisoned debtor, in a newspaper printed in the county where application was made; in the case of a non-resident, concealed, or absconding debtor, in the newspapers in which the notice of attachment was printed. In case of any controversy arising between the trustees, and these parties, the

(*a*) R. S. ii. 95 to 106.

same may be referred to the arbitration of three indifferent persons. The trustees are to keep a regular account of the moneys received by them, and are to convert the real and personal estate of the insolvent into money as speedily as possible. Within fifteen months from the time of their appointment, the trustees shall call a general meeting of the creditors by a notice published in the same manner as the notice of their appointment, at a period not more than three nor less than two months distant. At this meeting the accounts and demands for and against the estate are to be fairly adjusted, as far as the same can be ascertained; the amount of money in the hands of trustees declared. After payment of costs and necessary expenses and debts, entitled to priority under the laws of the United States, the trustees are to distribute the residue of the proceeds among the creditors in proportion to the amount of their respective claims. An allowance may be made to the debtor in certain cases, provided it does not exceed five hundred dollars. The trustees are to render an account of their administration to the Court of Common Pleas in which they reside, or to the Supreme Court, under whose supervision their trust is to be executed, and who may remove them and appoint new trustees in their place, and finally discharge them from all responsibility.

11. *Proceedings in Civil Suits.*

Commencement of actions. (*a*)—Civil actions are commenced by the service of a summons. When the person on whom the service is to be made, cannot after due diligence be found within the state, and that fact as well as the existence of a cause of action against the defendant is established by affidavit to the satisfaction of the court from which the writ emanates, or a judge thereof, and also that the defendant is a resident of the state, or has property therein, the court or judge may grant an order that the service be made by the publication of the summons in two newspapers, which the judge may designate as most likely to give notice to the person to be served, and for such length of time not less than thirty days, as the judge shall deem reasonable A copy

(*a*) Code of Procedure 132, Suppl. 8.

of the summons is also to be deposited in the post-office, directed to the person to be served, at his place of residence, unless it appear to the judge that such residence is neither known to the party making the application, nor can be ascertained by him in the use of reasonable diligence. Personal service of the summons out of the state, is equivalent to publication and deposit in the post-office. Where the summons has been neither personally served on the defendant, nor received by him through the post-office, he or his representatives may, on application and showing of cause, be allowed to defend the action at any time before judgment; or be allowed to defend after judgment within one year after notice thereof, and within seven years after the rendition of the same, upon such terms as may be just; and if the defence be successful, and the judgment, or any part thereof, have been collected, restitution may be enforced.

Arrest.—A defendant may be arrested upon the order of a judge of the court in which the action is brought, or from a county judge in the following cases:

1. Where it is made to appear upon the affidavit of the plaintiff or some other person, that a sufficient cause of action exists, and that the defendant is not a resident of the state, or is about to remove therefrom; or

2. Where the suit is for the recovery of damages, on a cause of action not arising out of contract, or for a fine or penalty, or on a promise to marry, or for moneys collected by a public officer or by an attorney in the course of his employment as such, or by any person in a fiduciary capacity, or for any misconduct or neglect in office, or in a professional employment, or where the action is to recover the possession of personal property unjustly detained.

In either of the last mentioned cases, the sufficiency of the cause of action must also be established by affidavit. No female can be arrested in an action arising on contract, or in any other action, except for a willful injury to person, character or property. (*a*)

The Code of Procedure in which the preceding provisions are contained, expressly declares that they are in no way to affect the

(*a*) Code of Procedure 162. R. S. ii. 106 to 114.

act to abolish imprisonment for debt, and to punish fraudulent debtors. Under that act, in all cases where a defendant could not be arrested or imprisoned, the plaintiff who had either commenced a suit or obtained a judgment against him in a court of record, might obtain from the judge of the court, or officer authorized to perform his duties, a warrant to arrest the defendant, on establishing by the affidavit of the plaintiff or some other person, that there is a debt due from the defendant to the plaintiff, amounting to more than fifty dollars, and specifying the nature and amount thereof as near as may be, for which the defendant cannot be arrested or imprisoned, and establishing one or more of the following particulars:

1st. That the defendant is about to remove any of his property out of the jurisdiction of the court in which the suit is brought, with intent to defraud his creditors; or

2d. That the defendant has property or rights in action which he fraudulently conceals, or that he has rights in action or some interest in public or corporate stock, money or evidences of debt, which he unjustly refuses to apply to the payment of any judgment or decree which shall have been rendered against him, belonging to the complainant; or

3d. That he has assigned, removed or disposed of, or is about to dispose of any of his property, with intent to defraud his creditors; or

4th. That the defendant fraudulently contracted the debt or incurred the obligation respecting which suit is brought.

Upon being arrested by virtue of this warrant, the defendant may appear before the officer by whom it was issued, and controvert by his own affidavit or otherwise any of its allegations; and such officer shall have power to compel the attendance and testimony of witnesses, and to hear and determine upon the evidence submitted to him in the premises. The defendant may have the hearing adjourned or postponed upon sufficient cause shown, and his entering into bond with security in double the amount of the debt, conditioned that until the final decision of the matter pending before the officer he will not remove any property which he then has out of the jurisdiction of the court in which the suit is brought, with intent to defraud his creditors:

and that he will not assign or dispose of such property with a view or intent to give a preference to any creditor for any debt antecedent to such assignment. If the allegations of the complainant are substantiated to the satisfaction of the officer, he shall direct the defendant to be committed to the jail of the county in which the hearing is had, until discharged according to law.

This commitment is not to be granted if the defendant shall either pay the demand with costs of suit, or give security therefor within sixty days, or make and deliver an inventory of his estate, and account of his creditors, and execute an assignment of his property as hereinafter provided, or enter into bond with security that he will apply for such an assignment and discharge within thirty days, or in a case where the particular fraudulent intent established against the defendant is a contemplated removal of his property, if the defendant will give bond and security that he will not remove any property which he has out of the jurisdiction of the court with intent to defraud his creditors, nor dispose of any such property with such intent, or with a view to give a preference to any creditor for any debt antecedent to such assignment or disposition, until the demand of the plaintiff has been satisfied, or three months elapsed from the rendition of a final judgment in the suit brought by him. The construction of this act was considered in the matter of Prime, 1 Barb. S. C. R. 296, and it was there held that the proceedings under it were never for the benefit of the creditors at large, except in the case of an assignment after the debtor has been convicted of a misdemeanor; and that previous to the execution of the assignment they were for the benefit of the prosecuting creditor alone.

Judgment and execution.—Execution may be issued upon a judgment as soon as it is rendered. After the lapse of five years from the entry of the judgment an execution can be issued only by leave of the court on motion, with notice to the adverse party. Before such leave will be granted, it must be established by oath of the party or other proof, that the judgment or some part thereof remains unsatisfied and due. There are three kinds of execution, one against the property of the judgment debtor, one against his person, and the third for the delivery of the possession of real or personal property. If the action was one in which the defendant might have been arrested, an execution against the person of the judgment debtor may be issued to any county within the jurisdiction of the court, after the return of an execution against his property unsatisfied in whole or in part. If it be against the property of the judgment debtor, it requires the sheriff to satisfy the judgment out of the personal property of such debtor, or if sufficient cannot be found, then out of the real property belonging to him on the day when the judgment was docketed, or at any time thereafter. When an execution against the property of the judgment debtor, issued to the sheriff of the county where he resides, or if he resides out of the state, to the sheriff of the county where the judgment roll is filed, has been returned unsatisfied in whole or in part, the judgment creditor may obtain an order from a judge of the court, or a county judge of the county to which the execution was issued, requiring the judgment debtor to appear and make discovery on oath, concerning his property, before such judge, at a time and place specified in the order. At such time witnesses may be required to appear and testify as upon the trial of an issue: and an adverse claim to any property of the judgment debtor disclosed or discovered, may be tried. The judge may order any property of the judgment debtor not exempt from execution, in the hands either of himself or any other person, or due to the judgment debtor, to be applied towards the satisfaction of the judgment. (*a*)

Where real estate is sold upon execution, within one year from the time of the sale, the party whose right and title were sold, or in case of his death, his heirs, devisees, grantees, or other representatives, are entitled to redeem the estate so sold, by paying to the purchaser, his personal representatives or assigns, or to the officer who made the sale, the amount bid by such purchaser at the sale, with interest at the rate of ten per cent. from the time of sale; upon which payment the sale of the premises so redeemed, and the certificates thereof, are to be null and void. The right of the debtor to redeem expires at the end of the year; but within three months thereafter any judgment creditor of such debtor may redeem, upon paying the amount of the purchase-money, with seven per cent. interest. (*b*)

(*a*) Code of Procedure, 198 Suppl.

(*b*) R. S. ii. 293, 294, 295.

12. *Courts.*

The jurisdiction in civil actions is distributed between the Court of Appeals, the Supreme Court, Circuit Courts, and Courts of Oyer and Terminer, the County Courts, the Justice's Courts, and the various Municipal Courts. The Supreme Court consists of thirty-two judges, four of whom are elected by each of the eight judicial districts into which the state is divided. Its business is distributed between general and special terms, and circuits, and courts of oyer and terminer. Six general terms are held annually in each judicial district. These general terms are in the nature of courts of appeal. The number of special terms, circuit courts, and courts of oyer and terminer in each county, varies with its population and business; there being, for example, eleven in the county and city of New-York, and three in the county of Broome. The governor designates the times and places of holding these courts, and the judges by whom they are held.

NEW JERSEY.

1. CHOSES IN ACTION.
2. BILLS OF EXCHANGE AND PROMISSORY NOTES.
3. INTEREST.
4. FRAUDS.
5. CORPORATIONS.
6. LIMITED PARTNERSHIPS.
7. ASSIGNMENTS BY INSOLVENT DEBTOR.
8. LIMITATION OF ACTIONS.
9. EFFECT OF DEATH UPON THE RIGHTS OF CREDITORS.
10. IMPRISONMENT FOR DEBT UPON MESNE PROCESS.
11. ATTACHMENT.
12. JUDGMENT AND EXECUTION.
13. INSOLVENT LAW.
14. COURTS.

1. *Choses in Action.*

A scroll affixed to any instrument for the payment of money has the force and obligation of a seal. (*a*) But deeds for any other purpose must be sealed with wax or a wafer. (*b*) The words in an instrument for payment of money, " witness my hand and seal," are sufficient to show that a scroll was intended as a seal. (*c*)

All bonds, bills and other writings obligatory for the payment of money, may be assigned, and the assignee may maintain an action thereon in his own name. (*d*)

2. *Bills of Exchange and Promissory Notes.*

All notes in writing made and signed by any person or persons, body politic or corporate, or their authorized agents, for the pay-

(*a*) Elmer's Digest, 354.
(*b*) Perrine *v.* Cheeseman, 6 Hals. 174.
(*c*) Force *v.* Craig, 2 Hals. 272.
(*d*) Elmer's Digest, 354.

ment of a sum of money therein mentioned to any other person, or body politic or corporate, or their order, or unto bearer, may be assigned and endorsed over in succession to any other person natural or artificial, in the same manner as inland bills of exchange, and such assignee or endorsee may maintain an action either against the maker of the note, or any prior endorser. The plaintiff in such suit must however allow all just set offs, not only as against himself, but as against the assignor of the note, before notice of the assignment to the defendant: *unless it shall be expressed on the face of the note, that the sum therein mentioned, is to be paid without defalcation or discount.* (*a*)

All inland bills of exchange for the sum of eight dollars and upwards, must be presented for acceptance and payment, and protested for non-acceptance or non-payment, in the same manner as foreign bills; a justice of the peace being authorized to make a protest in the want or default of a notary public.

3. *Interest.*

The rate of interest in New Jersey was fixed at seven per cent. in 1797, and remained unaltered until 1823, when it was reduced to six per cent. All contracts on which a higher interest is reserved or taken are declared to be utterly void. A penalty is inflicted upon the lender of money at usury, of the full amount of the debt, to be recovered by action of debt or case in any court of record; one half for the benefit of the state, and the other half to the use of the prosecutor. A borrower may compel a discovery from the lender of the whole transaction by a bill in chancery; and upon tender of the principal sum, be relieved of all interest and costs of suit. (*b*)

4. *Frauds.*

The English statute of frauds and perjuries has been substantially enacted in New Jersey.

(*a*) Elmer's Digest. 445, 446. (*b*) Ib. 261.

5. *Corporations.*

All sales, assignments and conveyances by any incorporated company, in contemplation of insolvency, except to a bona fide purchaser for a valuable consideration without notice, are declared to be utterly null and void as against creditors.

6. *Limited Partnerships.*

Limited partnerships were authorized by an act passed the 9th of February, 1837, and which went into operation on the 1st of April of the same year. They must be confined to the transaction of mercantile, manufacturing, or mechanical business. They may consist of one or more partners, who shall be called general partners, and who shall be jointly and severally responsible as general partners now are by law, and one or more persons who shall contribute in actual cash payments a specific sum, as capital to the common stock, to be called special partners, and who shall not be liable for the debts of the partnership, beyond the sum so contributed to the capital. The general partners only are authorized to transact the business of the partnership, and sign its name; and the business of the firm is to be conducted in the name of the general partners only, without the addition of the word "company," or any other general term; and if any special partner allows his name to be used in the firm, he shall be deemed a general partner. A special partner may from time to time examine into the state and progress of the partnership concerns, and advise as to their management, but the transaction of any business for the partnership, or acting in the capacity of its agent or attorney, will involve a special partner in the liabilities of a general partner. If by the payment of interest or profits to any special partner, the original capital has been reduced, the partner receiving the same shall be bound to make good his share of capital with interest. Every transfer, sale, assignment, or security given by a general or special partner, of the effects of the partnership, or of their separate effects, in contemplation of insolvency, with intent to prefer one or more creditors, shall be considered fraudulent and void as against the creditors of the partnership, and any special partner participating in or assenting to any such arrangement, shall be held liable as a general partner. When the partnership becomes insolvent, no special partner can under any circumstances claim as a creditor, until the claims of all the other creditors of the partnership are satisfied.

To form a limited partnership, the parties must severally sign a certificate, containing the name under which the partnership is to be conducted, the general nature of the business to be transacted, the names of all the general and special partners interested therein, distinguishing which are general and which are special partners, and their respective places of residence, the amount of capital contributed by each partner to the common stock, the period at which the partnership is to commence, and at which it will terminate. This certificate shall be acknowledged by the several persons signing the same, before an officer authorized by law to take the proof and acknowledgment of deeds, (to wit, the chancellor of the state, or one of the justices of the supreme court, or a master in chancery, or one of the judges of the court of common pleas,) and such officer is to certify the acknowledgment, under his proper signature, on the instrument itself, which is then to be filed in the office of the clerk of the county where the principal place of the business of the partnership is situated, to be recorded by him at large, in a book kept for the purpose: and if the partnership has places of business situate in several counties, a transcript of this record, duly certified by the clerk, shall be filed and recorded in like manner in each. At the time of filing the original certificate, one or more of the general partners shall file an affidavit in the same office, stating that the sums specified in the certificate to have been contributed by each of the special partners to the common stock, have been actually and bona fide paid in cash. The partnership is not to be deemed to have been formed, until the preceding requisitions of the law have been complied with; and any false statement in the certificate or affidavit will render all the persons interested in the partnership liable for its engagements as general partners. The terms of the partnership shall be published immediately after their registry for at least six weeks, in some newspaper published in the county or counties where the business is to be conducted, and if there is no such newspaper, then in a newspaper published in the county nearest to the place of business; and if this publication is not made, the partnership shall be deemed general. Every alteration in the partnership, or renewal or continuance thereof, beyond the original term fixed for its duration, shall be deemed a new partnership, and all the requisites prescribed for its original formation must be observed. No dissolution of such partnership can take place by acts of the parties, previous to the time specified in the certificate of its formation or renewal, unless a notice of the same be filed and recorded in the clerk's office in which the original certificate was recorded, and published once in each week for four weeks, in a newspaper circulating in each of the counties where the partnership may have places of business. (*a*)

7. *Assignments by Insolvent Debtors.*

All assignments for the benefit of creditors are made to enure in proportion to their respective demands, to their equal benefit; and all preferences of one creditor over another, excepting mortgage and judgment creditors, (where the judgment has not been by confession, for the purpose of giving preference,) are to be deemed fraudulent and void. (*b*)

The absolute transfer of a part of his estate by a debtor upon the eve of insolvency, to a particular creditor in payment of his debt, is valid. The assignment which the law repudiates, is the unequal assignment among the creditors of his entire estate. (*c*)

An assignment of personal property situate in New Jersey, made in New-York, by a citizen of that state, and in conformity with its laws, will not pass the title, if the assignment is of a character prohibited by the laws of the latter state. (*d*)

The debtor is required to annex to his assignment an inventory, verified by his oath, of his entire estate, real and personal, and a list of all his creditors, with the amount of their respective claims. The assignees, after giving notice to the creditors for

(*a*) Elmer's Digest, 376 to 378. (*b*) Ib. 16.

(*c*) Tillou *v.* Britton, 2 Hals. 121. 2 South, 738.

(*d*) Varnum *v.* Camp, 1 Green, 326.

the term of thirty days in two newspapers published in their vicinity, and entering into bond, with security, for the faithful performance of their trust, may proceed to sell the property, and perform all other duties necessary to carry into effect the objects of the assignment. At the expiration of six months, the assignee having given additional notice for the term of six weeks next preceding, to the creditors of the insolvent, must file with the clerk of the county, wherein the debtor resided at the time of the assignment, a true list of all persons claiming to be creditors, and a statement of their respective amounts, and at the next term of the Court of Common Pleas, any controversy between the assignee and the creditors as to particular claims, may be adjusted by the court. The assignee shall then proceed, from time to time, to make an equal dividend among the creditors of the assets which have come to hand. All creditors who do not exhibit their claims within the term of six months, as aforesaid, are to be barred of a dividend, unless there should be a surplus after satisfaction of the debts exhibited, or unless such creditors should find other estate not accounted for by the assignee, before distribution. The creditors who thus become parties to the assignment, and they only, are forever barred from any future action at law or in equity against the debtor and his representatives, unless they should be able to establish fraud in the debtor, with respect to the assignment, by concealing part of his estate or otherwise. (*a*)

8. *Limitation of Actions.*

All actions of detinue, trover, and replevin, all actions of debt, founded upon any lending or contract without specialty, all actions of account and upon the case, except such as concern the trade of merchandise between merchant and merchant, their factors and servants, must be commenced within six years from the time of the accruing of the cause of action.

All actions of debt upon any sealed instrument for the payment of money, must be brought within sixteen years after the cause of action has accrued, or within sixteen years after the indorsement of a payment on the bond. Judgments of any court

(*a*) Elmer's Digest, 17, 18, 19.

of record within the state may be revived by scire facias or action of debt within twenty years next after the date of such judgment, and not after. (*a*)

Upon judgments rendered in the courts of a sister state, there is no statutory limitation, but from an unexplained forbearance of twenty years, a presumption of payment would arise, which would extinguish the judgment. (*b*)

The exception in the statute in regard to merchants' accounts, has been extended by equitable construction, so as to embrace the accounts of other persons not merchants, between whom there have been mutual dealings and credits; some of which are of more than six years, and others less. This equitable extension properly takes place in the case of mutual current accounts, or wherever any such connection appears between them as may fairly amount to an admission of unsettled accounts between the parties. (*c*)

There is no law requiring an acknowledgment to be in writing to take a case out of the statute of limitation, but it must be an express promise to pay, or a direct and unqualified admission of a previous subsisting debt, which the party is liable and willing to pay. (*d*)

There is a saving clause in favor of infants, feme coverts, and lunatics, of the period of their limitation after the removal of the disability. (*e*)

A period of non-residence or absence from the state is not to be computed as a part of the term of limitation. (*f*)

9. *Effect of Death upon the Rights of Creditors.*

Where the executor or administrator does not represent an estate as insolvent, debts are to be paid according to the order of priority fixed by the common law, except so far as it is controlled by the laws of Congress, giving preference to debts, of whatever dignity, due to the United States. To enable the personal repre-

(*a*) Elmer's Digest, 316.

(*b*) Gulick *v.* Loder, 1 Green 68.

(*c*) Belles *v.* Belles, 4 Hals. 339.

(*d*) Ib. and Conover *v.* Conover, Saxe's Ch. Rep. 404.

(*e*) Elmer's Digest, 316.

(*f*) Ib. 318.

sentative to examine into the condition of the estate, and ascertain both the amount of assets and the extent of indebtedness, no creditor can bring an action against him, within six months after the decease of the testator or intestate, unless upon a suggestion of fraud, or for the physician's bill during the last sickness, funeral charges and expenses, and any judgments entered of record against such decedent during his lifetime, all of which are to be first paid out of either the personal or real estate. (*a*)

Real estate cannot be sold, nor in any manner affected by a judgment against an executor or administrator. (*b*) But where a creditor has obtained judgment against an executor or administrator, and the personal estate is insufficient to satisfy the execution, he may require such representative to apply to the proper Orphan's Court for an order to sell the land of the decedent, and upon his neglect or refusal for the space of six months, the creditor himself may apply. (*c*)

Where an executor or administrator believes that the personal estate is insufficient to pay the debts of the deceased, it is his duty, as soon as may be convenient, to exhibit under oath a true and full account of the personal estate and debts so far as he can discover the same, to the Orphan's Court of the county where the real estate, of which his testator or intestate died seized, is situate, and ask their aid in the premises: upon which the court is to make an order, directing all persons interested in such real estate to appear at a certain day therein mentioned, not less than two months from the making thereof, to show cause why so much of said real estate should not be sold, as will be sufficient to pay the debts of the decedent. This order is to be advertised for six weeks successively, at three of the most public places in the county, and in one or more newspapers. If the court upon a hearing shall be satisfied of the insufficiency of the personal estate, it may order the executor or administrator to sell the whole, or so much as it may deem necessary to discharge the debts of the estate. No part of the realty is however to be sold until the executor has applied all the personal estate which has come to his hands to the payment of debts. (*d*)

The executor upon giving notice two months beforehand of the time and place, may proceed to sell so much of the realty as was

(*a*) Elmer's Digest, 169. (*b*) Ib. 489. (*c*) Ib. 362. (*d*) Ib. 490.

embraced by the order of the court, and the moneys arising from the same are to be applied by him as assets of the estate. (*a*)

Where the real and personal estate of a deceased person shall not be sufficient to pay his debts, the proceeds arising from the same shall be distributed among his creditors in proportion to the sums which are due to them respectively, except the debts which have been already specified. (*c*)

Where an executor or administrator shall state upon a written application to the Orphan's Court of the proper county, on oath or affirmation, that the whole estate of the testator or intestate is, according to his knowledge or belief, insufficient to pay all his debts, it is the duty of the court to direct him to give public notice by advertisement or otherwise, for the space of two months, to the creditors, to exhibit their claims within some period to be designated, not less than six nor more than eighteen months. At the next term after the expiration of this period, the executor or administrator is to report the amount of the respective demands exhibited, and the form by which evidenced, public notice being previously given of the same, and at the time of making such report to exhibit also a true and just account of the personal and real estate of the decedent, and its value. Any creditor or person interested, may appear at such term, and contest by filing exceptions any item in the report or account to be determined by the court, upon the proofs and allegations. The court may then declare the estate to be insolvent, and direct the executor or administrator to sell both the real and personal estate, and distribute the proceeds in proportion to the sums found due to them respectively. Creditors may present to the executor or administrator, not only the debts which are due, but those to become due, a reasonable rebate of interest being made. No creditor in the event of the estate proving insolvent, who does not exhibit his claim within the time limited by the court, shall prosecute the same at any future period, unless he shall discover some other estate, not inventoried or accounted for the executor or administrator before distribution, in which case he may receive his ratable proportion of the same. (*a*)

No alienation of the real estate of a testator or intestate, by

(*a*) Elmer's Digest, 490. (*b*) Ib. 169. (*c*) Ib. 170.

his heirs or devisees within one year from the time of his death, shall prejudice the rights of creditors, or relieve the same from liability for debt. (*a*)

The heirs and devisees of a decedent may be sued by his creditors, either by specialty or simple contract, or whether mentioned in the instrument of debt or not, and execution had, to the value of the land descended or devised. (*b*)

10. *Imprisonment for Debt upon Mesne Process.*

The writ of capias ad respondendum shall not be awarded, issued or served, in any action founded upon contract express or implied, except upon proof being made on oath or affirmation, before a justice of the Supreme Court of the state or before one of the commissioners, to take bail and affidavit in said court, establishing one of the following particulars:

1. That there is a debt or demand, founded upon contract, express or implied, due to the plaintiff from the defendant, specifying the nature and particulars of said debt or demand, and that the defendant is about to remove any of his property out of the jurisdiction of the court in which an action is to be commenced, with intent to defraud his creditors; or

2. That the defendant has property or rights in action which he fraudulently conceals; or

3. That he has assigned, removed, or disposed of, or is about to assign, remove, or dispose of, any of his property with the intent to defraud his creditors. Such judge or commissioner shall then make an order to hold the defendant to bail, in such sum as the plaintiff or his agent shall swear to be due from the defendant. (*c*)

By the recent constitution of New Jersey, imprisonment for debt in any action, or upon any judgment founded upon contract, unless in cases of fraud, is abolished.

No female can be imprisoned either on mesne or final process in any civil action.

(*a*) Elmer's Digest, 493. (*b*) Ib. 232. (*c*) Acts of 1842, 130.

11. *Attachment.*

A creditor whether residing in or out of the state, may obtain an attachment against a non-resident or an absconding debtor. In the former case, the applicant for the writ of attachment must make oath or affirmation before any justice of the peace or judge of a court of record within the state, that the person against whose estate such attachment is to be issued, is not, to his knowledge or belief, resident at that time in the state, and that he owes the plaintiff a certain sum of money, specifying as nearly as he can, the amount of the debt or balance. (*a*) In the latter case, the oath must be that the applicant verily believes that his debtor absconds from his creditors and is not, to his knowledge or belief, resident in the state at that time. This oath having been filed with the clerk of the Court of Common Pleas, or Supreme Court, an attachment may be issued against the rights and credits, goods and chattels, moneys and effects, lands and tenements of the debtor, wherever to be found, which writ will bind the personal estate of the defendant from the time of its levy, the real estate from the time of its emanation. (*b*)

Where two or more are jointly bound or indebted either as joint obligors, partners, or otherwise, the writ of attachment may be issued against the separate or joint estate, or both of such joint debtors, or any of them. (*c*)

An attachment, however, cannot be issued against one absent partner, if the other resides in the state ; but if all the partners abscond, then it may be issued against all, or if all the partners reside abroad ; or if dead, against their non-resident representatives. (*d*)

An attachment is a proceeding *in rem*, and wholly inconsistent with the law of administration of estates, and cannot therefore issue against an executor or administrator upon a liability of a deceased person. (*e*) It may be issued against any absent or absconding female, in a proper case, or against any corporation, whether created by the laws of the state or not. (*f*)

(*a*) Elmer's Digest, 25. (*b*) Ib. 20. (*c*) Ib. 25.

(*d*) Curtis *v*. Hollinshead, 2 Green 402. 3 Gr. 17.

(*e*) Haight *v*. Bergh, 3 Green 183. (*f*) Acts of 1839, 63.

The affidavit of the plaintiff in attachment is not conclusive evidence of the facts which it states, but the attachment may be quashed, if it appears to the court upon inquiry, that the defendant is a resident of the state, or that he did not leave home with intent to abscond, and that the plaintiff had no reasonable ground for believing the contrary, (*a*)

The defendant may release his property from the attachment, by giving bond to the plaintiff, with surety, conditioned for the safe return of the property attached, in case judgment shall be rendered against him. (*b*)

On the return of the writ of attachment, it is the duty of the clerk to give notice of its pendency by advertisement in some newspaper selected by the court, that other creditors of the defendant may become parties to the proceeding. The court at the same time is required to appoint three auditors for the purpose of hearing and adjusting all claims against the defendant, whose duty it is made to report at the first or second term thereafter, as the case may require, the sum due to each creditor. For the purpose of discovering any property of the defendant, which may be concealed, the auditors are empowered to summon and examine upon oath, touching the same, the wife of the defendant or any other person, and also to authorize the sheriff to break open any house or depository, where there is reason to believe the property of the defendant may be concealed. Where judgment is entered against the defendant upon the report of the auditors, by default, a scire facias may issue against any garnishee to appear and show cause why the plaintiff should not have execution of the money or effects of the defendant in his hands, and he may appear and tender the same to the plaintiff, and if they are accepted, be discharged with his costs; or if he does not appear, the plaintiff may have an inquisition as to the value of the property of the defendant in his hands, and recover a judgment for the amount: or if he does appear and deny the possession of the defendant's property, the question may be tried by a jury, and judgment rendered according to the facts, in behalf of the garnishee, or against him. (*c*)

(*a*) City Bank *v.* Merrit, 1 Green 131. Branson *v.* Shinn, 1 Green 250.
(*b*) Acts of 1839, 64. (*c*) Elmer's Digest, 23.

The auditors, after judgment, may proceed by virtue of an order of court for that purpose, to sell the estate, real and personal, of the defendant, and after public notice through the newspapers, requiring a meeting of the creditors, it is the duty of the auditors to distribute the proceeds ratably among all the creditors in proportion to the amount of their respective debts as ascertained by the report and judgment. (*a*)

Justices of the peace have jurisdiction in cases of attachment, when the debt does not exceed fifty dollars. (*b*)

12. *Judgment and Execution.*

Both real and personal property may be levied upon and sold on executions issued upon the judgments of any court of record. A judgment only binds land from the time of its actual entry on the minutes or records of the court. Writs of execution bind personal property from the time of their delivery to the officer. Where sundry writs of execution are issued against the goods and chattels, lands and tenements of the same person, and there is not sufficient property to satisfy all the executions, that execution which was first delivered to the officer shall first be satisfied. When there are several judgments binding the lands of the same debtor, and only one creditor takes out an execution against the same, the purchaser shall hold the land conveyed free from all the other judgments. Land cannot be sold upon any execution, if sufficient goods and chattels of the defendant can be found to satisfy the same, unless the defendant requests the sheriff in writing to proceed first to sell the land, and enters into bond with sufficient surety for the forthcoming of the goods and chattels levied on by the writ of fieri facias, to answer its exigency. (*c*)

A judgment and execution constitutes no lien upon mere equitable rights, which are not susceptible of delivery or possession. There must be a seisin, and this term has reference always to a legal title. The same principle is established as to mere equitable interests in personal property. They are not subject to levy and sale. (*d*)

(*a*) Elmer's Digest, 24. (*b*) Ib. 27. (*c*) Ib. 486 to 496. (*d*) Sax. 298.

The writ of capias ad satisfaciendum cannot be issued upon any judgment founded on a contract, express or implied, unless satisfactory proof be made before a justice of the Supreme Court, or a commissioner to take bail and affidavits in said court, to be certified by the justice or commissioner, establishing one of the particulars necessary to obtain a writ of capias, or that the defendant has rights or credits, moneys or effects, either in his own possession or in that of any other person or persons to his use, of the value of fifty dollars or over, which he unlawfully or unjustly refuses to apply in payment of such judgment. (*a*) (See "*Imprisonment for Debt.*")

Where any execution against the property of a defendant has been returned unsatisfied in whole or in part, leaving a balance due exceeding one hundred dollars, exclusive of costs, the plaintiff in such execution may file a bill in chancery to compel the discovery of any property or chose in action belonging to the defendant in such judgment, and of any property or chose in action due to him or held in trust for him, except such property as is now reserved by law, and to prevent the transfer of any such property, money, or chose in action, or the payment or delivery thereof to the defendant, except when such trust has been created by, or the fund in question has proceeded from some other person than the debtor himself. And upon the discovery of any such personal property, money, or chose in action, the court shall decree satisfaction out of the same, of the sum remaining due upon such judgments. (*b*)

The share or interest of a defendant in any joint-stock company, or other institution incorporated by the state, may be taken and sold under the writ of fieri facias as in the case of goods and chattels. (*c*)

13. *Insolvent Laws.*

Any person arrested or held in custody in any civil action, upon mesne or final process, may obtain his discharge from all debts due at the time, or contracted previously, but to become

(*a*) Acts of 1842, 132. (*b*) Acts of 1845, 141, 142. (*c*) Acts of 1842, 132.

due at a subsequent time, so far as regards the imprisonment of his person, by taking the benefit of the insolvent laws.

For this purpose, he may present a petition to the Inferior Court of Common Pleas, at any stated term, setting forth the causes of his imprisonment, with a true account of his personal and real estate, and an inventory of his deeds, notes, books of account, vouchers and securities, and a list of his creditors with the money due and owing them. The court shall then appoint a time (not less than forty days from the period of the application) and place for hearing what can be said for or against the liberation of the debtor, and the debtor must give thirty days' notice thereof in writing to each of his creditors, by personal service, or being left at their usual places of residence, where they reside in the state, and by publication in a newspaper of the state for the same period. If the court upon hearing and examination of the petition, account, and inventory, by interrogatories to the debtor or otherwise, shall be satisfied with his conduct, they may appoint one or more freeholders of the county as assignees, to whom the debtor is forthwith to execute an assignment of his estate both real and personal, and upon the making of this assignment and filing it with the clerk, they may direct the sheriff to discharge the debtor from confinement on account of any debts previously contracted. The assignees are to proceed to collect the estate of the debtor, and convert it into money, to give notice to creditors to present their claims, to examine and adjust the same, any controversy respecting such debts to be referred to two arbitrators not creditors of the insolvent, and within eighteen months to distribute among the creditors who have become parties to the proceeding, the money on hand, and then again at the expiration of each year, until a final settlement has been made.

All creditors who do not come in, and prove their debts within eighteen months after the assignment, if a division of the whole estate be made, will receive no dividend; but if the whole be not divided, and the debt be proved before the time appointed for a second division, then the creditor shall have his first dividend, but after the second division, such creditors are entirely barred. *(a)*

(*a*) Elmer's Digest, 250 to 258.

14. *Courts.*

The original civil jurisdiction is distributed between a Court of Chancery, Supreme Court, Circuit Courts, and Courts of Common Pleas.

The judges of the Supreme Court, hold Circuit Courts twice a year in each county. The Courts of Common Pleas are held four times a year in each county.

PENNSYLVANIA.

1. *Choses in Action.*

All bonds, specialties and notes in writing, payable to any person, or order, or assigns, for a sum of money, may be transferred by assignment so as to vest the assignee with a similar power, and so toties quoties, and so as also to enable the assignee to prosecute any action at law upon the same, which might have been instituted by the original payee. All assignments, however, of bonds and specialties must be under hand and seal, and before two or more credible witnesses. (*a*)

All promissory notes, bearing date in the city or county of Philadelphia, whereby any person promises to pay to any other person, or to their order, for value in account or for value received, without defalcation or set-off (the last words to be inserted in the body of the bill), are held by the indorsees, discharged of any claim of set-off or defalcation on the part of the drawer or indorsers. (*b*)

(*a*) Purdon's Digest, 144. (*b*) Ib. 962.

2. *Damages upon Protested Bills of Exchange.*

Upon all foreign bills of exchange, drawn or negotiated within this state, which shall be returned unpaid, with a legal protest therefor, the following damages may be recovered from the drawers or indorsers, in addition to the principal sum and charges of protest, together with lawful interest upon such principal sum, damages and charges of protest, from the time at which notice of the protest was given, and payment of the principal, damages, and protest charges demanded: if drawn upon any person without the state, but within some other part of the United States, excepting the state of Louisiana, five per cent. damages upon the principal sum; if drawn as before, upon any person in Louisiana, or any other place in North America, or the islands thereof, except the northwest coast of America or Mexico, or in any of the West India or Bahama islands, ten per cent. upon the principal sum; if upon any person in the island of Madeira, the Canaries, the Azores, the Cape De Verd islands, the Spanish Main or Mexico, fifteen per cent. upon such principal sum; if upon any person in any place in Europe, or the islands thereof, twenty per cent. upon such principal sum; if upon any person in any other part of the world, twenty-five per cent. upon such principal sum. The damages thus allowed are to be in lieu of interest, and all other charges except charges of protest, to the time when notice of the protest and demand of payment shall have been given. The amount of the bill and the damages payable thereon, are to be determined by the rate of exchange, or value of the money or currency mentioned in the bill, at the time of notice of protest and demand of payment. (*a*)

3. *Interest.*

The legal rate of interest is six per cent., and no more can be recovered in any action. Where usurious interest is taken, the lender is liable to a forfeiture of the principal, to be recovered in a qui tam action; but in a suit against the borrower, the lender only loses the usurious excess. (*b*)

(*a*) P. D. 140. (*b*) Ib. 649.

4. *Limitation of Actions.*

All actions of account, and upon the case, other than such accounts as concern the trade of merchandise between merchant and merchant, their factors and servants, all actions of debt grounded upon any contract or lending without specialty, all actions of debt for arrearages of rent, must be brought within six years after the cause of action has accrued. There is a saving of the period of limitation in favor of infants, feme coverts, persons non compos mentis, imprisoned at the period the cause of action accrues, after the removal of their disabilities. Where the person liable to an action is beyond seas at the time it accrues, the bar of the statute does not commence until after his return. (*a*)

5. *Factors.*

Consignees or factors who fraudulently pledge for their own use any merchandise or document, intrusted to them as a security for money borrowed, or negotiable instrument, are liable to a fine of two thousand dollars, and imprisonment for five years.

Wherever any person intrusted with merchandise, and having authority to sell or consign the same, shall ship or otherwise transmit the same to any other person, such other person shall have a lien thereon,—

1. For any money advanced or negotiable security given by him on the faith of such consignment, to or for the use of the person in whose name such merchandise was shipped or transmitted.

2. For any money or negotiable security received for the use of such consignee, by the person in whose name such merchandise was shipped or transmitted.

This lien, however, does not exist in any case where the consignee has notice, by the bill of lading or otherwise, before the time of such advance or receipt, that the person in whose name the merchandise was shipped or transmitted is not the actual owner thereof.

(*a*) P. D. 768.

Where a consignee or factor having possession of merchandise with authority to sell the same, or having possession of any bill of lading, certificate, receipt or order for the delivery of merchandise, with the like authority, deposits or pledges such merchandise with any other person as a security for money advanced, or a negotiable instrument given him on its faith, such bailee acquires thereby the same interest in and authority over the said merchandise, as if such consignee had been the actual owner: provided, however, that if such person has notice in any way that the person making the deposit or pledge is only a factor, or if the same is made without notice of this fact, but as a security for a previously existing debt, then the bailee of such merchandise or document only acquires the rights and interest therein which were possessed or might have been enforced at the time by the factor against his principal.

The actual owner of such merchandise may, however, recover the same before the deposit, from the factor or his assignees, or afterwards may recover the same, upon tendering the money or negotiable instrument advanced to the consignee upon its faith, and also the sum or instrument advanced thereon by the consignee to the owner. The owner may also recover from the bailee of the consignee any balance arising from the proceeds of the merchandise which may remain in his hands, after deducting therefrom the amount of money, or of the negotiable instrument given by him to the consignee upon its faith. (*a*)

6. *Limited Partnerships.*

Limited partnerships for agricultural, mechanical, manufacturing, or mercantile business, were authorized by an act passed in **1836**. The general provisions of this act are similar to those elsewhere detailed. It provides, however, for the sale, by a general or special partner, or their personal representatives, of the interest of either in such partnership, so as not thereby to produce a dissolution of the partnership. On the insolvency of a special partner, the partnership is not thereby dissolved, but his interest may be sold by the assignees for the benefit of his creditors. Such transfer, however, is in every instance to be acknowledged, cer-

(*a*) P. D. 486.

tified, and recorded, as in the case of the original formation of the partnership. The record is to be made in the office of the recorder of deeds of the county in which the principal place of business of the partnership is situated; and where it has places of business situate in several counties, a transcript of such certificate, duly certified, is to be filed in their respective offices. (*a*)

7. *Attachment.*

Foreign attachment.—A writ of attachment may issue against the real or personal estate of any debtor who does not reside within the commonwealth, on the application of his creditor. In every such writ a clause of summons against any person having goods or chattels of the defendant in his possession, may be inserted; or if the garnishee is not an inhabitant of the county, or about to depart therefrom, a clause of capias; such fact as well as his indebtedness to, or possession of the goods and chattels of the defendant, being first verified by affidavit. The goods and chattels, as well as the real estate attached, are bound from the execution of the writ. In the case of real estate, however, it is the duty of the sheriff to file a description of the property attached, within five days, in the office of the prothonotary of the court. (*b*)

Attachments may issue against a foreign corporation, or against a female, but will be dissolved upon their appearance by attorney, and giving security for the debt or demand, or depositing in lieu thereof, a sufficient sum of money. The plaintiff, if he has filed his declaration at the third term of the court, after the execution of the writ, may take judgment against the defendant, unless he has previously dissolved the attachment. Where the defendant does not dissolve the attachment by giving bail or security, he may enter his appearance and defend the suit, without prejudice to the lien created by the attachment, and if a judgment be rendered against him, it shall not only have the force and effect of an ordinary judgment in attachment, but of a judgment in an action commenced by summons. Where judgment has been rendered by default or otherwise against the defendant, a

(*a*) P. D. 920. (*b*) Ib. 50.

writ of scire facias may issue against the garnishee, commanding him to appear and show cause why the plaintiff should not have execution of his judgment, of the estate and effects of the defendant attached in his hands; when the plaintiff may examine the garnishee by written interrogatories touching said premises, and on his failure to appear or answer, execution may issue against him for an amount sufficient to satisfy the demand of the plaintiff with costs of suit. The plaintiff may also have a similar execution after a verdict in his favor, on such scire facias. Where judgment has been rendered against the defendant by default, the plaintiff, before taking out any execution, must enter into bond with sufficient security, that if the defendant appear in twelve months and disprove the debt recovered against him, or discharge the same with costs, he will restore to him the goods and effects, or the value thereof, attached and condemned, or so much as shall be disproved or discharged. (*a*)

Domestic attachment.—Writs of domestic attachment with summons of garnishment may be issued by the Court of Common Pleas of any county in which a debtor may reside, upon an affidavit being previously made and filed by his creditor, or some one in his behalf, of the fact of the indebtedness, and also, that the debtor has absconded from the place of his usual abode within the county, or has remained absent from the commonwealth, or has confined himself within his own house, or concealed himself elsewhere, with design in either case to defraud his creditors; or that the debtor, not having become an inhabitant, confines or conceals himself within the county, with intent to avoid the service of process and to defraud his creditors. The form of the writ, its mode of service, and the lien created by it, do not vary substantially from the case of foreign attachments. The creditor may sue out with the original writ or afterwards, other writs of attachment, directed to other counties, in which the debtor may have goods or chattels, lands or tenements. Any other creditor, upon affidavit of his debt, may suggest his name upon the record, and prosecute the attachment, if the first creditor fail to do so, or to establish his right as a creditor. Upon the return of the writ, the court shall appoint three honest and discreet men, not being

(*a*) P. D. 522.

creditors of the defendant, to be trustees of his estate, and the officer shall deliver over to them any money or personal property of the defendant which he may have in his hands by virtue of the attachment. The trustees shall immediately give notice of their appointment by publication for six successive weeks, in a newspaper published in the county where the attachment is issued, or in such other manner as the court may direct, and require all persons indebted to the defendant, or having his property in their possession, to pay or deliver over the same to them, and desire all creditors of the defendant to present their respective claims and accounts. The entire estate of the debtor is vested in such trustees, and it is their duty to prosecute all actions concerning the same. They may sell his goods and chattels at any time after the term next succeeding that to which the writ was returnable, and his real estate at any term after the third succeeding that to which the original writ was returnable, and may also dispose for the benefit of creditors of any debts due or becoming due to the defendant. At some time after the expiration of six months from the giving the notice already described, the trustees, having previously given public notice of the time and place fixed upon by them for the purpose, shall receive from the several creditors evidence of their claims, and after determining the same, state their accounts, and ascertain the proportionate sum coming to each creditor, and file a report in the office of the prothonotary of the court from which attachment issued. The prothonotary shall give notice of the filing of the report by advertisement, as in the case of the accounts of assignees under a voluntary assignment, and at the next term after the filing of the report, if no exceptions are filed, the same may be confirmed by the court, and the trustees proceed to distribution accordingly. If the whole estate has not been distributed upon such report, the trustees may, at the expiration of three months after the order of the court upon such report, proceed to make a second dividend of all such moneys as have come to their hands after the first dividend, and so on from time to time until the entire estate has been distributed. No preference is to be given in the distribution to debts due by specialty. (*a*)

(*a*) P. D. 325.

The court may at any time before a final decree of distribution, upon the application of the defendant denying and disproving the allegations upon which the attachment was granted, dissolve the same absolutely, or upon such terms as it may deem equitable.

Jurisdiction to grant writs of attachment where the debt does not exceed one hundred dollars, is conferred under somewhat similar restrictions upon justices of the peace. (*a*)

Attachment of vessels.—Ships and vessels of all kinds, built, repaired or fitted out within the state, are subject to a lien in favor of mechanics or tradesmen, for work done or materials supplied for the building, equipping or repairing such boat, on the engagement of the master or owners, in preference to other debts. This lien continues from the time the debt is contracted, until the vessel proceeds on her next voyage. (*b*)

8. *Imprisonment for Debt.*

No person can be arrested or imprisoned on any civil process, in any suit or proceeding instituted for the recovery of any money due upon any judgment or decree founded upon contract, or due upon any contract, express or implied, or for the recovery of any damages for the non-performance of any contract, except on proceeding as for contempt, to enforce civil remedies, actions for fines or penalties, or on promises to marry, for moneys collected by any public officer, or for any misconduct or neglect in office or in any professional employment. A party may obtain a warrant of arrest in other cases, where upon application to the judge of the court in which suit has been instituted or judgment obtained, he satisfies the judge, by his own affidavit or that of some other person or persons, that there is a debt or demand due to the applicant from the other party to the suit or judgment, pointing out its nature and amount, and also establishes one or more of the following particulars:

1st. That such party is about to remove some of his property from without the jurisdiction of the court in which suit is brought, for the purpose of defrauding his creditors, or

(*a*) P. D. 330. (*b*) Dunlop's Statutes, 677.

2d. That he has property which he fraudulently conceals, or

3d. That he has rights in action, or some interest in public or corporate stock, money or evidence of debt, which he unjustly refuses to apply to the payment of some judgment against him belonging to the complainant, or

4th. That he has assigned, removed or disposed of, or is about to dispose of, some of his property, with the intent to defraud his creditors, or

5th. That he fraudulently contracted the debt, or incurred the obligation respecting which suit is brought.

The defendant, upon being arrested, may appear before the judge and controvert the truth or sufficiency of the plaintiff's allegations, and if with success he will be discharged; otherwise he will be committed to prison, to be detained until discharged by law. The commitment will not be granted, where the defendant pays the demand; or in case it is a judgment, gives security for its payment at the time when it could be collected at law; or if the arrest has been founded on an allegation of a fraudulent design to remove his property out of the jurisdiction of the court, gives bond with approved security that he will not so remove any property which he then has, and that he will not assign, convey or dispose of any of his property with such intent, or with a view to give a preference to any creditor for any debt antecedent to such disposition, until the demand of the complainant has been satisfied, or until thirty days after final judgment shall be rendered in the suit brought for the recovery of such demand: or where the defendant enters into bond with sufficient security, conditioned that he will apply within thirty days, for the benefit of the insolvent laws of the commonwealth, and comply with the requisitions of such laws, and in case of his failure to obtain his discharge as an insolvent debtor, surrender himself to the jail of the county. (*a*)

Any person committed, or who has given bond as above provided, may apply for the benefit of the insolvent act, upon which proceedings similar to those described in the subsequent title will be had, and an assignment executed to trustees, invested with similar powers and duties.

(*a*) P. D., Stroud's edition, 581.

9. *Judgment and Execution.*

Judgments only bind lands, tenements or hereditaments, as against bona fide purchasers, from the time when they are actually signed; goods and chattels from the time of the delivery of the writ to the officer. A judgment is a lien upon all the interest, legal or equitable, of the debtor, in land situated in the county where the judgment is rendered, or in a county in which a transcript of the judgment is recorded. It is not a lien, however, upon after purchased lands. (*a*)

The lien of a judgment does not continue beyond five years, unless revived by scire facias, or agreement of the parties, filed and docketed. (*b*)

Execution may issue at any time within a year and day from the rendition of a judgment, or the expiration of a stay of execution, where such is indorsed thereon. Unless taken out during this period, the judgment becomes dormant, and must be revived by scire facias. In all actions instituted for the recovery of money due by contract, or damages arising from a breach of contract, except actions of debt and scire facias upon judgments, and actions of scire facias upon mortgages, if the defendant has an estate in fee simple, within the respective county, worth, in the opinion of the court, the sum for which the plaintiff may be entitled to have execution, or if the defendant shall give approved security for the payment of such sum, with interest and costs, he shall be entitled to a stay of execution for six months if the debt does not exceed two hundred dollars, for nine months if it exceeds two hundred, and does not exceed five hundred dollars, for twelve months if the sum exceeds five hundred dollars. The plaintiff may have execution for the satisfaction of his debt against the personal and real estate of his debtor, and in some cases against his body. Coin, bank notes, current bills, stocks, money deposited in bank, debts, equities of redemption in personal property, may be seized and sold under a writ of fieri facias. Where stock, deposits or debts are levied upon, the proceedings to realize the same are similar to a garnishment in foreign attachment. Where

(*a*) 6 Binney 135. (*b*) P. D. 658.

real estate is taken in execution, it is the duty of the officer to summon an inquest to ascertain whether the rents and profits of such estate, beyond all reprise, will be sufficient within seven years to satisfy the judgment upon which the execution was issued, with the interest and costs of suit. If the clear profits of the real estate will, in the opinion of the inquest, be sufficient to pay the debt or damages and costs, the sheriff shall, by the inquest, assess the clear annual value of the rents and profits; and make return thereof, with his writ, to court. Upon the return of the writ, the plaintiff may have a writ of liberari facias to deliver the said real estate, with the appurtenances, to him, at the valuation fixed by the inquest, to be holden by him, his executors or assigns, until his debt, with interest, is discharged: or the plaintiff, instead of suing out the writ of liberari facias, may demise the premises to the defendant, to retain possession of the same, at the annual valuation fixed by the inquest. If the defendant decline taking the estate on such demise, the plaintiff may sell it upon a venditioni exponas: or, if the inquest return that the clear annual profits will not be sufficient to pay the debt and damages within seven years, it may be sold at once upon such writ. (*a*)

10. *Administration of Estates.*

Fund for the payment of debts.—In Pennsylvania both real and personal property are liable for the debts of a decedent, (*b*) but the personal estate is to be resorted to in the first instance, even for debts with which the real estate is charged; (*c*) except where they have been contracted by other than the decedent, as where real estate has been purchased subject to a mortgage. (*d*) Where, however, a testator directs payment of his debts to be made out of some particular fund, the provision must be followed,

(*a*) P. D. 440 to 470.

(*b*) Act of 24th Feb., 1834; Purdon's Dig. ed. 7th, 473–484; Graff *v.* Smith, 1 Dall. 481; Benner *v.* Phillips, 9 W. and S. 20.

(*c*) Keysey's Estate, 9 S. & R. 72; Todd *v.* Todd's Ex'rs. 1 S. & R. 953; Walker's Estate, 3 R. 237.

(*d*) Keysey's Est. 9 S. & R. 72.

but the personal estate cannot be so exempted as against creditors, though it may as against heirs and devisees, where the intention is clear not merely to charge the real estate but to exempt the personal. (*a*) There is no distinction in these respects between legal and equitable assets; both are equally liable to both legal and equitable debts. (*b*) On the death of a partner, if there be no joint fund nor solvent partner remaining, both partnership and separate creditors come pari passu upon his estate.(*c*) It is to be presumed that as after acquired lands may pass by will, they may be charged with the payment of debts. (*d*)

Duration of lien of debts upon land.—Debts, except secured by mortgage or judgment, are a lien upon lands in the hands of heirs, devisees, and purchasers. This lien expires at the end of five years from the decease of the debtor, unless suit be commenced and duly prosecuted, within that period. (*e*) Where, however, a debt, demand, or covenant, is not payable within the five years, a written statement thereof is to be filed in the connty where the lands are situate, and then the debt, demand, or covenant, becomes a lien from five years after the time it falls due. (*f*)

Judgments bind the land for five years after the death, though they otherwise would have expired within that time, and they have not been revived; they take precedence according to their priority at the time of the death; and after the expiration of the five years they may be revived by scire facias, to which the widow and heirs need not be made parties. (*g*) Where there is, however, a direction to sell for the payment of debts, given to the executor, it does not come within the provisions of the act, as a trust arises, and the lien continues till presumption of payment arises. (*h*) The act, in this respect, is one of limitation and

(*a*) Bryant *v.* Hunter, 3 W. C. C. R. 242; Todd *v.* Todd's Ex'rs, 1 S. & R. 453; Martin *v.* Fry, 17 S. & R. 426; Walker's Est. 3 R. 237, 242; 9 W. 60.

(*b*) Sperry's Est. 1 Ash. 347. (*c*) Ib. Bell *v.* Newman, 5 S. & R. 78.

(*d*) Act of April 8, 1833, § 10; Walker's Est. 3 R. 242.

(*e*) Act of 1834; Purd. Dig. 476; Kerper *v.* Hock, 1 W. 14; Penn *v.* Hamilton, 2 W. 60; Fetterman *v.* Murphy, 4 W. 429.

(*f*) Act of 1834.

(*g*) Purd. Dig. 476; McMillan *v.* Red, 4 W. & S. 237; Chambers *v.* Carson, 2 Wh. 365; Christman *v.* Fritz, 13 S. & R. 1; Guier *v.* Kelley, 2 Binn. 229.

(*h*) 2 Browne 294; Alexander *v.* McMurray, 8 W. 504; Steel *v.* Henry, 9 W. 523.

repose in its nature, and after the period assigned the lien is absolutely discharged, though the existence of the debt was known to the heirs or purchasers, (*a*) and even though a voluntary conveyance is made to defraud creditors. (*b*) Though, by the act of 1834, the widow and heirs, if the real estate is to be charged, must be made parties, yet this lien is not discharged by a judgment against personal representatives alone. (*c*)

Order of payment of debts.—The order of the payment of debts of decedents is as follows:

1. Debts due the United States, which are entitled to precedence by act of congress, (*d*) and which are to be preferred to those in the order established by the act of assembly, (*e*) though such preference is not thereby given. (*f*) Notice of such debt must be, however, given to the executor or administrator, otherwise payments are to be made according to the act of assembly, and such payments will not amount to a devastavit. (*g*)

2. Funeral expenses, medicine furnished and medical advice given during the last illness of the decedent, and servants' wages not exceeding one year, payment of all of which may be compelled within a year after the letters of administration are granted. (*h*)

In the term "servants" are comprised domestic servants, persons who make part of a family, and who are employed to assist in the economy of a house or its appurtenances. (*i*)

But this preference is extinguished where security is taken, as by a servant's obtaining a single bill for his wages. (*k*)

3. Rents for not exceeding one year.

4. All other debts equally, except

(*a*) Kerper *v.* Hock, 1 W. 14; Quiglay *v.* Beatty, 4 W. 13; Hemphile *v.* Carpenter, 6 W. 22; Seitzinger *v.* Fisher, 1 W. & S. 293; Bailey *v.* Bowman, 6 W. & S. 118.

(*b*) Shorman *v.* Farmer's Bank, 5 W. & S. 373.

(*c*) Murphy's Appeal, 8 W. & S. 165; Beaner *v.* Phillips, 9 W. & S. 131; Atherton *v.* Atherton, 2 Barr. 113.

(*d*) Act of March 3, 1797, §3; Fisher *v.* Blight, 2 Cr. 353; U. S. *v.* Hooe, 3 Ib. 73.

(*e*) Purd. Dig. 475.

(*f*) Conn. *v.* Lewis, 6 Binn. 266; Fisher *v.* Blight, ib. Supr.

(*g*) Ib.; 16 Johns. 79.

(*h*) Act of 1834; Purd. Dig. 475.

(*i*) Ex parte Meason, 5 Binn. 167; Boniface *v.* Scott. 3 S. & R. 351; Miller's Est. 1 Ash. 323.

(*k*) Silver *v.* Williams, 17 S. & R. 292.

5. Debts due to the commonwealth, which are to be paid last.(*a*) Payment of none of these can be compelled until one year after letters of administration issue. (*b*)

Where however the laws of a decedent's domicil give a preference to its own citizens over the citizens of Pennsylvania, the like preference is to obtain in favor of the latter. (*c*)

This order of payment relates to personal assets only; and judgments and mortgages recorded in the lifetime of the decedent, (*d*) which were a lien on the real estate at the time of the party's death, are nevertheless entitled to priority of payment in the proceeds of such real estate, according to date of their lien, (*e*) and so where the commonwealth obtains a judgment in the lifetime of the party, notwithstandlng its postponement to other creditors by the act of assembly, (*f*) still on the sale of real estate it is the duty of a lien creditor to see that the proceeds are first applied to the discharge of his lien, and he will be considered, in regard to the debtor, as paid all that a due attention to his interests will entitle him to receive. (*g*)

After the personal estate is exhausted in the payment of debts, the executor or administrator, on application to the Orphans' Court, will be permitted to sell such part of the real estate as may be further necessary for the satisfaction of debts and legacies, without notice to heirs, &c.; (*h*) but where the assets have been once sufficient, such an order will not be granted. (*i*)

Where a creditor is executor or administrator he is not entitled to retain his debt to the prejudice of others of equal degree, but that he takes pro rata with the rest. (*k*)

Marshaling assets.—The questions arising in the marshaling of assets in equity are not of frequent occurrence in Pennsylvania, though the English doctrine may, as a general rule, be understood to be accepted. The rule with regard to the priority of application

(*a*) Act of 1834; Purd. Dig. 475. (*b*) Ib. 476. (*c*) Ib.

(*d*) Adams' Appeal, 1 P. R. 447.

(*e*) Moliere *v.* Noe, 4 Dall. 454; Girard *v.* McDermott, 5 S. R. 128.

(*f*) Ramsey's Appeal, 4 W. 71.

(*g*) Binney *v.* Comm. 1 P. R. 240; Beaner *v.* Phillips, 9 W. & S. 21.

(*h*) Act of March 29, 1832, § 31; Purd. Dig. 891.

(*i*) Pry's Appeal, 8 W. 233.

(*k*) Ex parte Meason, 5 Binn. 167.

of real estate after the exhaustion of personal is to apply 1. Real estate devised for the payment of debts: 2. Real estate descended: 3. Real estate specifically devised subject to a general charge of debts. (*a*)

Where one creditor has a lien on two funds, and another has a lien upon only one of them, the latter has the right in equity to compel the former to resort in the first instance to the other fund. (*b*) Debts, after the personalty has been fully administered, are to be paid out of land, to the exclusion of legacies with which it had been charged. (*c*)

Remedies.—The remedies for the enforcement of payment of debts are against the executor or administrator at common law, where the right of action survives; upon the administration bond, and in the Orphans' Court, where the estate is insolvent, or money has been paid into that court.

What actions survive.—All personal actions, except actions for slander, libel, and for injuries to the person, survive against executors and administrators, and if any such suits have been commenced during a party's lifetime they do not abate by his death, but his executor or administrator may be compelled by *scire facias* to become a party to such actions. (*d*) No legal proceedings are in any way destroyed by the death, resignation, or removal of executors or administrators, but their successors may be made parties in like manner. (*e*) The death of a defendant after a sequestration under order of the Orphans' Court, does not abate it; (*f*) nor is a domestic attachment in any wise affected by it; notice, however, of the pendency of the attachment must be given to the personal representatives. (*g*) Though formerly a foreign attachment would not lie against executors, as it was supposed that it might interfere with the distribution of assets; yet now, by act of assembly, legacies and distributive shares, except due to married women, may be attached in the hands of an executor or administrator, by creditors of the parties interested therein. A foreign attachment brought against the decedent him-

(*a*) Comm. *v.* Shelby, 13 S. & R. 348. (*b*) Cowden's Est. 1 Barr. 273.
(*c*) Hoover *v.* Hoover, 5 Barr. 365. (*d*) Act of 1834; Purd. Dig. 476.
(*e*) Ib. (*f*) Act of March 29, 1832; Purd. Dig. 894.
(*g*) Act of June 13, 1836; Purd. Dig. 326.

self, during his lifetime, will not abate by his death after final judgment. (*a*)

Wherever any injury to the person or to property, thougn accompanied by actual force, has been productive of benefit to a decedent or to his estate, or has added to the assets in the hands of his representatives, an action for the recovery of damages, or for chattels where they exist in specie, may be had. (*b*) Thus replevin, detinue, and in some cases, perhaps, trover, will lie, where goods have come into hands of the executor or administrator, or money had and received where they have been sold. (*c*) Where an immediate injury to personal property, or some special damage is caused by the breach of a promise of marriage, it seems that the same rule applies. (*d*) It was held, however, prior to the act of assembly of 1834, (*e*) that trespass vi et armis for seizing a vessel, could not survive against the administrator of a defendant. (*f*)

On application to the Orphans' Court, the executor or administrator may be required to execute any written or parol contract for the conveyance of land, which might have been enforced in equity, left incomplete by the death of his decedent. (*g*) By such proceeding, however, the right of dower is not divested. (*h*)

Pleading etc. therein.—Judgment is generally, in actions against an executor or administrator as such, to be satisfied out of the decedent's assets only, but he will be liable out of his own estate:

1. Where he has wasted the decedent's goods; in which case if the sheriff return that there are no goods of the decedent, and that the executor has wasted them, or if judgment be obtained in an action of debt suggesting a devastavit, execution can be taken out against his own goods. (*i*) Formerly, also, if the executor pleaded falsely, or neglected to aver that the assets were insuffi-

(*a*) Fitch *v.* Ross, 4 S. & R. 564.

(*b*) Reed *v.* Cist, 7 S. & R. 184; Heach *v.* Metzer, 6 S. & R. 272; Reist *v.* Heilbrenner, 11 S. & R. 131; Keste *v.* Boyd, 16 S. & R. 272; Penrod *v.* Morrison, 2 P. R. 126.

(*c*) Ib.

(*d*) Lallimonde *v.* Simmons, 13 S. & R. 183.

(*e*) P. D. 476.

(*f*) Nicholson *v.* Elton, 13 S. & R. 415.

(*g*) Act of 1834; Purd. Dig. 475.

(*h*) Riddleberger *v.* Mentzer, 7 W. 141; Covert *v.* Hertzog, 4 Barr. 145.

(*i*) Swearingen *v.* Pendleton, 4 S. & R. 393.

cient, and there were no sufficient assets, he would in some cases be liable for the whole debt, and in all for the costs. But the severity of the common law in this respect is now much mitigated, and since the revised act (*a*) an omission to plead plene administravit in an action brought against the executor or administrator, is no admission of assets; and no mispleading or lack of pleading will make him liable for any debt or damages recovered beyond the amount of assets that have actually come into his hands. (*b*)

(2.) Where he promises upon sufficient consideration to pay any debt of his decedent himself, in which case he alone will be liable (*c*); and so it is upon all contracts and promises made by him, though exclusively for the benefit of the estate. (*d*)

The executor or administrator is not bound to plead the statute of limitations where he believes the debt to be due (*e*); and therefore a payment of a debt so borrowed is not a devastavit. (*f*) But the parties interested in the estate have in some cases been allowed to make use of the statute against the will of the administrator. The acknowledgment, nevertheless, by an executor or administrator of a debt barred by the statute does not stop its running. (*g*)

A set off arising from the falling due of a debt or demand after the death of the party, can only be made by or against his representatives, where the estate is solvent. (*h*)

Judgment.—It is a rule that the surviving parties to an action are competent to litigate it, and therefore where one of several joint defendants dies before judgment, and judgment nevertheless is taken against all, it is irregular as to all. (*i*) If the decease occur after judgment, then execution cannot be taken out against the personalty of the decedent, but the debt nevertheless is a lien on his real estate, and may be revived by scire facias. (*k*) A judg-

(*a*) Purd. Dig. 490. (*b*) Ib. (*c*) Geyer *v.* Smith, 1 Dall. 347.

(*d*) Friez *v.* Thomas, 1 Wh. 71; Grier *v.* Houston, 8 S. & R. 402.

(*e*) Smith Est. 1 Ash. 352. (*f*) In re McFarland, 4 Barr. 129.

(*g*) Fritz *v.* Thomas, 1 Wh. 66; Forney *v.* Benedict, 5 Barr. 226.

(*h*) Bosler *v.* Exchange Bank, 4 Barr. 32.

(*i*) Comm. *v.* Miller, 8 S. & R. 456; Lewis *v.* Ash, 2 Miles 110; Ins. Co. *v.* Spang, 5 Barr. 113.

(*k*) Ib.; Stoner *v.* Stroman, 9 W. & S. 89.

ment, however, obtained against joint defendants, when one was dead at the time, is not absolutely void. (*a*)

Under the act of 1834, land cannot be reached in the hands of the widow and heirs, without making them parties in some way. The proper mode of procedure in actions, whether commenced before or after a decedent's death, is to obtain judgment first against the personal representatives, which is sufficient for satisfaction out of the personal assets. Having thus obtained judgment, if the creditor wishes to charge the land, the next is to make the owners of the land parties by scire facias. These will be admitted to contest the suit on original grounds. If the plaintiff be then successful, he can have execution on a judgment de terris. (*b*)

Administration bond.—The bond given by an administrator on his entrance upon his duties, is held to the use of such parties as may be interested in the fund in his hands, and for any neglect of duty, such as non-payment of a debt, or a devastavit. (*c*) Suit may be brought upon it by the commonwealth to the use of such parties, and after scire facias upon the judgment to determine the amount of the claims, the party first suing will be entitled out of the penalty to the whole of his claim, even to the exclusion of others. (*d*) Judgment may be so obtained against both the administrator and his sureties. (*e*)

Orphans' Court.—The Orphans' Court has the control of the conduct of executors and administrators; and may remove or discharge them. (*f*) It has also jurisdiction in the distribution of assets among creditors, when the estate is insolvent, and auditors may be appointed for the purpose. This power is exercised upon the application of any creditor, executor, or administrator, or party in interest. (*g*) If the estate be solvent this jurisdiction

(*a*) Warder *v.* Tainter, 4 W. 281.

(*b*) Act of 1834, Purd. Dig. 478; Murphy's Appeal, 8 W. & S. 165; Benner *v.* Phillips, 9 W. & S. 131; Atherton *v.* Atherton, 2 Barr. 13.

(*c*) Yard *v.* Lea's Ex'rs, 3 Yeates 345.

(*d*) Act of 1836, Purd. Dig. 145; Dallas *v.* Chaloner's Ex'rs, 3 Dall. 501; 4 Dall. 106, in notis.

(*e*) Zeigler *v.* Sprenkle, 7 W. & S. 173.

(*f*) Purd. Dig. 885, etc.

(*g*) Act of March 29, 1832, § 19; April 14, 1835; April 13, 1840; Purd. Dig. 885, etc.

cannot be exercised, (*a*) except where the proceeds of real estate have been paid into court. (*b*) It may also entertain exceptions to auditor's accounts. (*c*) But a creditor can never come into the Orphans' Court to compel payment of a litigated debt. (*d*)

Registers.—The registers of the different counties have jurisdiction within the same to receive the probate of wills, to grant letters testamentary and of administration, to pass and file the accounts of executors, administrators and guardians. (*e*)

Persons entitled to administration.—When administration is granted of the estate of any deceased person, the husband, if the decedent was a married woman, is entitled to administer; in other cases, it will be granted to the widow, or next of kin, or both, or in the event of their refusal or incompetency, to one or more of the principal creditors. (*f*)

Notice to creditors.—Every executor or administrator upon the granting of letters testamentary or of administration, shall give notice thereof, by publication once a week, for six successive weeks together, in a newspaper published at or near the place where the deceased resided; and in such notice, they must request all persons having claims or demands against the estate, to present them.

Time for payment of debts.—No executor or administrator can be compelled to pay any debt of the decedent, except such as are by law preferred in the order of payment to rents, nor to make any distribution of his estate, until the expiration of a year from the granting of administration.

Settlement of account.—The executor or administrator must render an account of his administration to the proper register, within one year from the grant of letters, accompanied by the necessary vouchers and evidence. The register upon allowing and filing the account, shall present a certified copy of the same, to the Orphans' Court of the respective county, at its stated meeting, being not less than thirty days distant from the time of such filing and allowance. And he shall give notice of the same to all persons interested by public advertisement, enumerating the

(*a*) Mett's Appeal, 1 Wh. 7; Warner's App. 2 Wh. 295; Latimer's Est. 2 Ash. 520.
(*b*) Tilghman's Est. 5 Wh. 44. (*c*) Purd. Dig. 835.
(*d*) Warner's Appeal, 2 Wh. 296. (*e*) D. L 453. (*f*) Ib. 458.

accounts to be presented at any one time to the court, and setting forth in substance, that the accountants have settled their accounts in the office of the said register, and that the same will be presented for confirmation to the Orphans' Court, at a certain time and place specified. Unless the notice has been given pursuant to law, no such account will be allowed and confirmed. Unless the parties interested agree to a different arrangement, the court will either examine the accounts or refer the same to auditors. Where any of the heirs, distributees, or creditors reside out of the United States, or out of the state, the court may if it thinks proper prescribe any additional notice to be given to such persons. (*a*)

11. *Insolvent Laws.*

The abolition of imprisonment for debt arising from contract under the acts before recited, has, except in certain enumerated cases, obviated the necessity of considering the provisions of the insolvent laws, except where the cause of arrest is in tort, or in the enumerated cases specially excepted. (*b*)

In the cases excepted from this act, and in all civil actions for damages arising from tort, the party may, on application to the Common Pleas of the county in which he was arrested or held to bail, or if neither arrested nor held to bail, of the county in which he resides, on giving bond to present himself at the next term of the court, and petition for the benefit of the insolvent laws, be released from custody. (*c*)

This petition, and that required in the act abolishing imprisonment for debt, must be accompanied by schedules containing statements,—

1. *Of all effects whatsoever and wheresoever situate.* In this are included debts due the petitioner, unless they be absolutely desperate. (*d*) But rights of action for mere personal torts need not be returned. (*e*) A bare possibility not coupled with any interest is excluded. (*f*)

(*a*) D. L. 468. (*b*) Kelley *v.* Henderson, 1 Barr. 495.
(*c*) See Act of 1836; Purd. Dig. 606. (*d*) Ingraham on Insolvency 56, 57.
(*e*) Sommer *v.* Wilt, 4 S. & R. 28; McFarlane *v.* Brun, 11 S. & R. 121.
(*f*) Lessee & Humphreys *v.* Humphreys, 2 Dall. 233.

2. *Of all debts due by him, containing the names of his creditors, the amount, and the nature or character of the debts, so far as he can ascertain the same.* It would seem that an omission of the name of a creditor by mistake, misapprehension, or accident, will not vitiate, and that the question turns almost entirely on the bona or mala fide with which the party acted. (*a*) Gross negligence, however, will raise a presumption of fraud in such case. (*b*)

3. *Of the cause of his insolvency and the extent of his losses, if any.* (*c*) The facts contained in the petition and statements must be verified on oath.

On the presentation of the petition, a time is fixed for the hearing, and notice given to creditors, for at least fifteen days. At the hearing, if, after a full exhibition of all the debtor's affairs, and an examination upon oath of the debtor in regard to them, no presumption of fraud arises, an assignment of all his estate, property, and effects whatsoever, is executed by him, an oath having been previously administered to him, to trustees nominated by two-thirds in number and value of the creditors attending in person or by attorney, or in default of such nomination, by the court; and thereupon the court will make an order discharging the debtor's person from all liability thereafter for any debt or damage accruing before the time of the order.

The trustee must give notice, at least five weeks, to all indebted to the insolvent, and to all creditors, for the presentation of accounts. They are then to collect debts, convert real estate into personal, and make distribution within twelve months, unless the time be enlarged on application to the court. A day is fixed for the presentation of proofs of debts by creditors, of which due public notice must be given, and thereupon a report is to be filed by the trustees, according to which distribution is to be made. No preference, however, is allowed to specialty creditors, but bona fide mortgages, judgments, and executions binding the personal property, are entitled to precedence of payment according to the priority of their lien. Where rent is due, goods liable to distress are not to be removed till it is paid. (*d*)

(*a*) Ex parte Scott, Ing. Ins. 81. (*b*) Ex parte Phillips, ib. 82.

(*c*) See Baker's case, 1 Binn. 452; Act of 1836; Purd. Dig. 607.

(*d*) Purd. Dig. 608.

The trustees have the power to compound or to settle debts by arbitration, and the same rights and liability in regard to set-off as their insolvent would have had. (*a*)

By the discharge of the debtor no other creditors are affected than those who have had due notice; and the liabilities of no other persons are thereby affected. (*b*)

The execution of the assignment vests in the trustees all the property of the debtor whatever, subject to all liens by mortgage or otherwise, and it is their duty to take it into possession. The trustees are capable of suing for and recovering the same in their own name.

The property by the assignment is divested, even though the trustees omit or refuse to act; (*c*) therefore the payment of a debt to the insolvent after assignment is invalid, though made without notice of the assignment. (*d*)

No bona fide conveyance for a valuable consideration before the date of the assignment, or if made in another county, before the recording of the assignment in such other county, or if of personal property, before public notice given by the trustees, to one who has had no actual notice of the petition or assignment, is in any way invalidated by the execution of the assignment. (*e*) The insolvent is also entitled to retain all such articles as are exempted from levy and sale on execution. (*f*)

The trustees may recover and dispose of all real and personal estate which the insolvent may have transferred by a voluntary conveyance, with intent to defraud his creditors, (*g*) and they have also the power to set aside all fraudulent or irregular assignments previously made. (*h*)

The choses of action of a wife which have not been reduced into possession before the assignment do not pass to the trustees, but the beneficial interest remains therein to her use. (*i*)

After all claims of creditors are satisfied, any surplus that re mains is to be paid to the insolvent or his legal representatives.

(*a*) Purd. Dig. 608. (*b*) Ib.
(*c*) Willis *v.* Row, 3 Y. 520; Ruby *v.* Glenn, 5 W. 77.
(*d*) Wickershand *v.* Nicholson, 14 S. & R. 118. (*e*) Purd. Dig. 611.
(*f*) Ib. 611. (*g*) Ib. See also Miller *v.* Samuel, 7 Pa. Law Jour. Sup. C. 377.
(*h*) Englebert *v.* Blanfit, 2 Wh. 240. (*i*) Purd. Dig. 611.

The after acquired estate of the debtor is of course subject to execution for so much of his debts as the insolvent assignment does not satisfy; but if a majority in number and in value of the creditors of any insolvent residing in the United States or having a known attorney therein, shall consent in writing thereto, an order may be made by the court, on application of the debtor, and notice given, to exempt all after acquired property from execution for any debt or cause of action existing previously to such discharge, for seven years thereafter; and if, contrary to such order, an execution issues, it will be set aside, on application to the court, with costs. (*a*)

If upon the hearing of any petitioner it appears to the court that there is just ground to believe, either,— (*b*)

1. That the insolvency of the petitioner arose from losses by gambling, or by the purchase of lottery tickets; or

2. That the petitioner has embezzled or applied to his own use any money or other property with which he has been intrusted, either as bailee, agent, or depositary; or

3. That he has concealed any part of his estate or effects, or conveyed the same in such a manner as, and with the intent, to defraud his creditors; it is the duty of the court to commit him to jail for trial at the Court of Quarter Sessions.

If upon such trial he is convicted, he is guilty of a misdemeanor, and subject to imprisonment for the terms specified by the act. (*c*)

There are other penal provisions, which it is unnecessary to enumerate.

No one, however, is entitled to the benefit of the act for the abolition of arrest and imprisonment for debt, who has not been a resident in the state for twenty days previous to the commencement of suit against him, (*d*) nor for the benefit of the insolvent laws, who has not been a resident for six months or been imprisoned for three months immediately previous to his application. (*e*)

Voluntary assignments.—A voluntary conveyance by a debtor in failing circumstances, of property not subject to any lien, in trust for the benefit of creditors, has always been considered in

(*a*) Purd. Dig. 611. (*b*) Ib. 612. (*c*) Ib. 612. (*d*) Ib. 582. (*e*) Ib. 607.

Pennsylvania as valid and founded on sufficient consideration, (*a*) and the legal estate passes thereby to the assignees, though their assent is not expressed. (*b*) Formerly, also, it was no objection to the validity of an assignment, that it gave a preference to certain creditors, or excluded those who should not execute a release within a fixed time, (*c*) even though the surplus was to be paid to the debtor. (*d*) By the act of 17th April, 1843, however, all assignments for the payment of debts in which a preference is given to one or more creditors, except for the wages of labor, not exceeding in all fifty dollars, are to be held and construed to enure for the benefit of *all* creditors in proportion to their respective demands. (*e*) It would seem that an assignment for releasing the creditors only, is within the meaning of the act. (*f*) The preference referred to is only that given by the assignment itself, and a judgment confessed at the same time with such a voluntary conveyance to certain bona fide creditors, in order to give them a priority, is not affected by the pvovisions of this act. (*g*)

It is essential that the assignment should be put entirely out of the assignor's control, for otherwise an execution will be preferred to it. (*h*) There must be an actual transfer of the property from the assignor to the assignee; (*i*) but the assignee need not take possession till the thirty days limited by act of assembly for making an inventory have expired; (*k*) and indeed the retention of possession by the assignor, after the recording of the assignment and appraisement, is never per se fraudulent. (*l*)

The assignment must be of the whole of the debtor's property, whether partnership or separate, and must contain words apt

(*a*) Beard *v*. Smith, 4 Dall. 35 note; Wilt *v*. Franklin, 1 Binn. 514; See cases in Wharton's Digest, 4th ed. tit. Debtor and Creditor, D.

(*b*) Gray *v*. Hill, 10 S. & R. 436.

(*c*) Wilt *v*. Franklin, 1 Binn. 514; Lippincott *v*. Barker, 2 Binn. 186; Hower *v*. Geesaman, 17 S. & R. 254.

(*d*) Livingston *v*. Bell, 3 W. 198.

(*e*) Purd. Dig. 90

(*f*) Seal *v*. Duffy, 4 Burr. 275, Gibson C. J.

(*g*) Blakely's Appeal, 7 Pennsylvania Law Journal 333.

(*h*) McKinney *v*. Rhoads, 5 W. 343.

(*i*) Hower *v*. Geesaman, 17 S. & R. 254.

(*k*) Mitchell *v*. Willock, 2 W. & S. 253.

(*l*) Titler *v*. Maitland, 5 W. & S. 307; Dallam *v*. Fitler, 6 W. & S. 323.

to carry it, and the reservation of any interest whatever will render it fraudulent and void, not only as to the part reserved, but as to the whole. (*a*)

A legacy to a wife will not pass by a voluntary assignment, (*b*) and it would appear that a wife's survivorship in her choses in action is never so barred. (*c*) The consideration of this point is now, however, unnecessary, as by the act of 11th April, 1848, (*d*) all property, real and personal, of a married woman, is exempted entirely from her husband's control and from liability for his debts. Where one in an assignment transfers goods belonging to another, the creditors of the latter cannot claim a dividend among those of the former. (*e*)

Before the act of 1843, just referred to, it has been held that the time fixed by the assignment within which its conditions must be complied with, must be reasonable, and not indefinite or too distant, (*f*) and that, therefore, as by an act of assembly the accounts of the trustees must be settled within a year, a provision directing payment not to be made for more than a year is void against non-assenting creditors. (*g*)

The assignment must be recorded within thirty days after its execution, (*h*) in the county in which the debtor resides, or it will be considered as null and void against creditors. It will still, however, remain valid as against a subsequent voluntary assignee, (*i*) and dissenting creditors can only avoid it pro tanto. (*k*) If the assignor should take the benefit of the insolvent laws, such an assignment could only after that time be avoided by his trustees. (*l*)

The assignees under a voluntary assignment must also, within thirty days after the execution of the assignment, file an inventory or schedule of the property so assigned, in the Common Pleas

(*a*) Thomas *v.* Jenks, 5 R. 221; Hennessey *v.* The Western Bank, 6 W. & S. 300; In re Wilson, 4 Barr. 430; Miller *v.* Samuel, 7 Pa. Law Journ. 379.

(*b*) Skinner's Appeal, 5 Barr. 262.

(*c*) Hartman *v.* Dowdel, 1 Rawle 279; ib.

(*d*) Pamph. D. 536.

(*e*) Dyott's Estate, 2 W. & S. 557.

(*f*) Pierpont *v.* Graham, 4 W. C. C. R. 232.

(*g*) Sherer *v.* Lantzenheizer, 6 W. 543.

(*h*) Act of 1818, Purd. Dig. 89.

(*i*) Seal *v.* Duffy, 4 Barr. 274.

(*k*) Ib. See also Miller *v.* Samuel, ib. Sup.

(*l*) Ib.

of the county where the assignor resides. (*a*) Appraisers are then to be appointed by the court, who are to return an appraisement of the value of the estate; when this is done and the appraisement is filed, the assignees are to give bond. After the expiration of a year the assignee or assignees may be compelled, by citation in the Common Pleas, to appear and exhibit their accounts. (*b*)

The accounts of trustees are to be published under order of court, with notice that they will be allowed at a certain time, unless cause to the contrary be previously shown.

The Court of Common Pleas of the proper county have as complete jurisdiction over assignees, as over other trustees. They may be removed and new ones appointed, or they may be compelled to give just security.

After the purposes of the trust have expired, the court may compel the conveyance by the trustees of the legal estate, on application of the party interested. (*c*)

12. *Courts.*

The judicial power is invested in a Supreme Court, three District Courts, and sixteen Courts of Common Pleas. The judges of the Supreme Court hold Circuit Courts in the various counties. The jurisdiction of the District Courts, within their respective districts, is concurrent with that of the Courts of Common Pleas in the different counties.

(*a*) Act of 1836; Purd. Dig. 85. (*b*) Ib.

(*c*) Purd. Dig. 85, 86.

OHIO.

1. BILLS OF EXCHANGE AND PROMISSORY NOTES.
2. INTEREST.
3. FACTORS.
4. LIMITED PARTNERSHIPS.
5. FRAUDS.
6. EFFECT OF MARRIAGE UPON RIGHTS OF PROPERTY.
7. LIMITATION OF ACTIONS.
8. EFFECT OF DEATH UPON THE RIGHTS OF CREDITORS.
9. ATTACHMENT.
10. INSOLVENT LAWS.
11. IMPRISONMENT FOR DEBT.
12. JUDGMENT AND EXECUTION.
13. COURTS.

1. *Bills of Exchange and Promissory Notes.*

All bonds, promissory notes, and bills of exchange drawn for a certain sum of money, and made payable to bearer, order, or assigns, are *negotiable* by indorsement thereon, so as absolutely to vest the property thereof in each and every indorsee successively; who may maintain actions against the makers, drawers, or indorsers. Such bonds, notes, and bills, are entitled to days of grace; and if indorsed after the day on which they are payable, and suit be brought by the indorsee against the maker, drawer, or obligor, the defendant may have the same defence he might have had if the action had been brought by the person to whom the instrument was originally made. If indorsed on or before the day on which it is made payable, the defendant may give in evidence any money actually paid before the instrument was indorsed to the plaintiff, on proving that the plaintiff had notice of such payment before the indorsement. (*a*)

(*a*) Swan's Statutes of Ohio, 587, 588.

On foreign bills of exchange, drawn on persons without the United States, the damages for protest are twelve per cent.: and on bills drawn on persons within the United States, and without the state of Ohio, the damages are six per cent. In both cases, the bills bear interest at six per cent. from the date of protest. (*a*)

No damages are recoverable upon any bill of exchange, foreign or inland, on account of protest, which may hereafter be drawn in the state, and which shall be protested for non-acceptance or non-payment, or which shall contain a waiver of protest, if it shall have been agreed or intended by and between the drawer or indorser, and the payee or indorsee of such bill at the time of its delivery, that the same should or might be paid at any other place than that upon which it was drawn, or by any other person or company than the person or company upon whom it was drawn. (*b*)

2. *Interest.*

The law regulating interest is as follows:—All creditors shall be entitled to receive interest on all money after the same shall become due, either on bond, bill, promissory note, or other instrument of writing, or contract for money or property; on all balances due on settlement; on money withheld by unreasonable and vexatious delay of payment; on all judgments from their date; on all decrees in chancery for the payment of money from the time specified for payment, or if no time be specified from the entering of the decree, until such debt, money or property is paid; at the rate of six per cent. per annum, and no more. (*c*)

Under this statute, it has been decided that a contract to pay more than six per cent. cannot be enforced in the courts of Ohio. The principal with lawful interest may be recovered. (*d*)

But when a bank charter declares that the bank shall not take more than six per cent. interest, and it loans money at a greater rate, the contract is totally void both for principal and interest. (*e*)

(*a*) Swan's Statutes of Ohio, 589.

(*b*) Acts of 1846, 69.

(*c*) Swan's Statutes of Ohio, 465.

(*d*) 7 Ohio Reports, part i. 80.

(*e*) Bank of Chillicothe *v.* Swayne, 8 Ohio 257.

3. *Factors.*

The Factor's Act of New-York has been substantially re-enacted in Ohio, with the addition of some penal clauses. (*a*)

4. *Limited Partnerships.*

Limited partnerships were authorized in Ohio by an act passed in 1846. (*b*) The provisions of this law do not differ materially from those of New-York.

5. *Frauds.*

The English statute of Frauds and Perjuries, and against fraudulent conveyances, have been re-enacted with no substantial variation.

By an act passed in 1835, all assignments of property thereafter executed by debtors to trustees in contemplation of insolvency, and with design to secure one class of creditors and defraud others, are made to enure equally for the benefit of all the creditors of the debtor in proportion to their demands.

6. *Effect of Marriage upon Rights of Property.*

The interest of the husband in real estate, belonging to his wife at the time of marriage, or acquired by her during coverture in any other manner than by purchase with his money or conveyance from him, cannot be taken in execution and sold for his debts during the life of the wife, and the life or lives of the heir or heirs of her body. All conveyances during such period, by the husband, of his interest in the estate so possessed or acquired, are of no effect, unless executed in the manner required to pass the estate of the wife. No interest of the husband in any chose in action of the wife not reduced by him into possession can be taken by any process of law or chancery, for the payment of his debts. Articles of furniture and household goods possessed by

(*a*) Acts of 1844, 49.

(*b*) See Acts of 1846, 29.

the wife at the time of marriage, or acquired after coverture by gift, or bequest, or with her separate money, are exempt for a like period, from liability for the husband's debts.

7. *Limitation of Actions.*

Actions must be brought within the several times mentioned below after the cause of such action shall have accrued.

1. Actions upon the case, covenant, and debt, founded upon a specialty, or any agreement, contract or promise in writing, within fifteen years.

2. Actions upon the case, and debt, founded upon any simple contract not in writing, and actions on the case for consequential damages, within six years.

3. Actions of trespass to property, real or personal; actions of detinue, trover and replevin, within four years.

4. Actions of trespass on the person, slander, libel, malicious prosecution, false imprisonment; actions against officers for malfeasance, or non-feasance in office, and actions of debt qui tam, within one year.

If the person, at the time the cause of action accrues, is an infant, feme covert, insane, or imprisoned, the statute does not begin to run until the removal of the disability.

If the defendant was out of the state or his residence unknown, the statute does not begin to run until his return or his residence is known.

An action on a contract, barred by the laws where the contract was made, is barred in the courts of this state, if the contract was made by persons resident at the time without this state. (*a*)

8. *Effect of Death on the Rights of Creditors.*

On the death of a householder sufficient provisions or other property is allowed to his widow or children to support them for twelve months; and in addition, a variety of articles: wheels, looms, stones, books not to exceed fifty dollars, one cow, twelve sheep, yarn, flax, wearing apparel, beds, cooking utensils, the

(*a*) Swan's Statutes of Ohio, 554, 555.

ornaments of the widow—table articles are not to be considered as assets in the hands of the personal representative, but remain with the family. (*a*)

The personal representative is to pay the debts of the deceased and distribute the assets in the following order:

1. The expenses of the funeral, the last sickness, and of administration.

2. The allowance made to the widow and children for twelve months.

3. Debts entitled to a preference under the laws of the United States.

4. Public rates, and taxes, and sums due the state for sales at auction.

5. All debts due to other persons.

No payments shall be made to creditors of any one class until those of a preceding class, of whose claims the personal representative has had notice, have been fully paid. Claims against the estate must be authenticated by satisfactory vouchers, and the affidavit of the claimant, that the claim is justly due, that no payments have been made thereon, and that there are no offsets against the same. (*b*)

Suit cannot be brought against an executor or administrator, until the expiration of eighteen months from the date of his bond, or of the further time allowed by the court for the collection of the assets of the estate; unless it be for the recovery of a demand that would not be affected by the insolvency of the estate, or unless it be brought after an estate has been represented insolvent, for the purpose of ascertaining a claim that is contested; or unless the claim has been exhibited, and has been disputed or rejected. (*c*)

As soon as the executor or administrator discovers that the personal estate of the decedent is not sufficient to pay the debts, with the allowance to the widow and children and expenses of administration, it is his duty to petition the Court of Common Pleas for authority to sell the realty.

The widow and heirs, or persons having the next estate of inheritance from the deceased are made defendants; and notice in

(*a*) Swan's Statutes of Ohio, 346, 347. (*b*) Ib. 353. (*c*) Ib. 356.

writing of the petition, is served on them at least fourteen days before the court can make an order of sale. If their names are unknown, or their residence is unknown, or they reside out of the state, the executor or administrator may make an affidavit of that fact, on filing his petition, and give them notice in a public newspaper of the county four weeks successively, previous to the term at which an order of sale is asked.

Any person interested in the estate may prevent a sale of the same, by giving bond to the executor or administrator, in a sum and with sureties to be approved by the court, conditioned to pay all debts, mentioned in the petition and found due, with the charges of administering and the allowance in money to the widow; so far as the personal estate shall be insufficient therefor.

The court on being satisfied of the due notification to the defendants of the petition, and of the necessity of the sale, make an order for the same. The land is sold by the executor or administrator at two-thirds of its appraised value, if improved; at one-half, if unimproved. If two unsuccessful offers to sell have been made, the court may direct the amount for which the land may be sold; or may order a new appraisement. The executor or administrator makes a return of his proceedings to the court at the next term, and if the sale has been correctly made, the court confirms it, and directs him to make a deed to the purchaser, who is thereby invested with the title of the deceased. The money is applied first, to pay the charges of the sale; next, to the payment of mortgages and judgments, according to their respective priorities of lien; and third, to the discharge of claims in the order mentioned previously for the payment of debts. (*a*)

When an executor or administrator represents an estate as insolvent, the court may appoint two or more commissioners to receive and examine all claims, and return to the court a list thereof, with the sum allowed on each. The commissioners notify creditors of their proceedings, by advertisement in some public places of the township, or in such other manner as the court may direct. Six months are allowed creditors to present and prove their claims, and such further time as the court may order, not to exceed eighteen months. At the expiration of the

(*a*) Swan's Statutes of Ohio, 360–366.

time to prove debts, the commissioners make their report, and thirty days after the report, the court orders a distribution of the effects.

Any person whose claim is disallowed, in whole or in part, by the commissioners, and any executor or administrator who is not satisfied with the allowance of any claim, may appeal from the decision of the commissioners to the Court of Common Pleas. If the court are notified of the appeal before the order for distribution is made, they may suspend the order or direct a sum to be retained sufficient to give the claimant a pro rata share. (*a*)

If the court does not think proper to appoint commissioners, the executor or administrator shall act in their place, and the proceedings are substantially the same. (*b*)

9. *Attachment.*

A writ of attachment against the lands, tenements, goods, chattels, rights, credits, moneys, and effects of a debtor may be issued from the Court of Common Pleas, on the filing of an oath or affirmation by the creditor or his agent that the debtor has absconded, to the injury of his creditors, or that he is not a resident of the state.

Where two or more are bound, as joint obligors or otherwise, the writ may issue against their separate or joint estates, or both; but the writ can issue against neither, unless the fact of non-residence or of absconding, sworn to in the affidavit, is affirmed as to every one of the obligors.

The writ is served by the sheriff in the presence of two freeholders of the county, who make, under oath, an inventory and appraisement of all the property attached, and the property is bound from the time the writ is thus served.

If the plaintiff or some other credible person shall make oath that any person (naming him) has property belonging to the defendant in his possession, and if the officer cannot come at such property, such *garnishee* shall be duly notified of the suit and required to appear in court and answer all questions touching the property of the defendant, in his possession, or within his know-

(*a*) Swan's Statutes of Ohio, 376–378. (*b*) Ib. 379.

ledge: and from the day he is notified he is liable to the attachment of creditors, for the property in his hands or the money and credits due from him to the defendant.

Notice of the suit is given by advertisement, and it must stand three terms before judgment. The defendant may appear at any time before judgment, and by putting in special bail, or surrendering himself into custody, discharge his property.

All the creditors who file their claims in time shall have the equal benefit of the act, and if the property attached is not sufficient to pay the claims of all, a distribution shall be made among the several creditors in proportion to the amount of their claims.

It is provided that no judgment shall be rendered in attachment, except for causes arising out of, founded upon, or sounding in contract; or upon the judgment or decree of some court of law or chancery. (*a*)

10. *Insolvent Law.*

The constitution of Ohio provides that "the person of a debtor, where there is not strong presumption of fraud, shall not be continued in prison, after delivering up his estate for the benefit of his creditors, in such manner as shall be prescribed by law." In pursuance of this provision, was passed the law for the relief of insolvent debtors. By this act the debtor is exempt from imprisonment on account of any debt due by him at the time he applies for the benefit of it, on the condition of honestly surrendering all his property for the general benefit of all his creditors. His future acquisitions, however, remain liable. Two classes of persons may take the benefit of this act. 1. All persons not under arrest who have resided two years in the state, and six months in the county. 2. All persons under arrest in a civil action, whether on mesne or final process, and whether residents in the state, or not. An officer, appointed by the Court of Common Pleas and called the commissioner of insolvents, is empowered to receive from applicants an assignment of their property and distribute the proceeds among their creditors. The assignment is made under oath, and vests in the commissioner the title to the property; who sells the same, at public vendue, and duly notifies the creditors, by advertisement, to present their claims for dividend.

(*a*) Swan's Statutes of Ohio, 88–93.

Real estate must be appraised by three disinterested freeholders, and cannot be sold for less than two-thirds of its appraised value. The proceedings before the commissioner are preliminary to a final examination before the court. But to secure the applicant from imprisonment in the meantime, the commissioner grants a certificate containing a schedule of all the specified debts, which secures him from imprisonment for any of those debts until he can be heard in court. The debtor files his petition in court, setting forth his application to the commissioner and praying for the relief contemplated by the act. The court directs the creditors to be called, and after hearing objections if any are made, and on being satisfied that all has been fair and honest, they grant a final certificate, containing the same schedule, the effect of which is forever to exempt the applicant from imprisonment, within the state, for any of the specified debts. (*a*)

By the act of 1844, it is declared that the certificate shall not protect the applicant from arrest for any debt accruing while acting as a public officer, executor, administrator, guardian, or in any other fiduciary character. (*b*)

11. *Imprisonment for Debt.*

Imprisonment on mesne process.—Members of congress and members and officers of the legislature are privileged from arrest, during their attendance on their respective bodies, and while going and returning. Judges and officers of courts, attorneys, suitors, witnesses, and jurors are also privileged while attending court and while going and returning. Females are exempt from imprisonment in all cases where the cause of action is founded on a contract, express or implied; insolvents, upon any debt mentioned in the schedule, except debts of a fiduciary character; voters, while exercising their franchise; militia, while on duty, and soldiers of the United States during their term of service. (*c*)

It is provided that no person shall be arrested or imprisoned on any mesne or final writ or process, in any action for the recovery of a debt due on any contract or agreement, or for the reco-

(*a*) Swan's Statutes of Ohio, 440. (*b*) General Laws, xlii. 29.

(*c*) Swan's Practice and Precedents, i. 120.

very of damages for the non-performance of any contract, promise, or agreement, or for the recovery of damages in any action of trespass, or on any judgment or decree founded on any such contract, promise, or agreement, or for damages for the non-performance thereof, or on any judgment in an action of trespass, or for consequential damages, unless the creditor, his agent or attorney, shall file an affidavit stating that there is a demand of one hundred dollars or upwards justly due such creditor, specifying, as near as may be, the nature and amount thereof, and establishing one or more of the following particulars :

1. That the defendant is about to remove his property out of the jurisdiction of the court, with intent to defraud his creditors : or,

2. That he is about to convert his property into money for the purpose of placing it beyond the reach of his creditors : or,

3. That he has property or rights in action which he fraudulently conceals : or,

4. That he has assigned, removed, or disposed of his property, or is about to do so, with intent to defraud his creditors : or,

5. That he fraudulently contracted the debt, or incurred the obligation for which suit is about to be brought : or,

6. That the defendant is about to remove his person out of the state or county with intent to defraud his creditors : or,

7. That he has converted his property into money, to place it beyond the reach of creditors : or,

8. That he is not a citizen or resident of this state. (*a*)

On the filing of the affidavit a capias ad respondendum is issued, and the defendant, when taken, is in the custody of the sheriff, who is responsible for his appearance, and may require him to give a sufficient bail-bond, and, on failure to do so, may commit him to prison. If the sheriff chooses to bear the responsibility, he may release him without security. (*b*) On the return day of the capias, or on the succeeding day, special bail may be put in by the defendant, or by the sheriff to save himself. (*c*)

It seems that the non-imprisonment laws do not apply to actions not sounding in contract, and where the action of trespass

(*a*) Swan's Statutes of Ohio, 647–649, and General Laws, xli. 28.

(*b*) Ib. 650.

(*c*) Ib. 652.

will not lie, nor to actions on promises to marry, nor to actions for moneys collected by a public officer or attorney, nor tc actions for misconduct in office. In these several classes of cases, the plaintiff may have special bail whenever the court in term or any judge in vacation shall, from the particular circumstances, order such special bail to be given. (*a*)

Imprisonment on capias ad satisfaciendum.—On any judgment or decree, the court in term, or a judge in vacation, may order a capias ad satisfaciendum against the debtor, after being satisfied by the affidavit of the creditor or his attorney, and such other testimony as he may present, of the existence of any of the following particulars:

1. That the debtor has removed or is about to remove his property out of the jurisdiction of the court, to prevent the collection of the money due on the judgment or decree: or,

2. That he has property, rights in action, evidences of debt, or some interest or stock in some corporation or company, which he fraudulently conceals, or unjustly refuses to apply to the payment of the debt: or,

3. That he has assigned or disposed of, or is about to assign or dispose of his property or rights in action, with intent to defraud his creditors or give an unfair preference to some of them: or,

4. That he has converted or is about to convert his property into money, to prevent its being taken on execution: or,

5. That he fraudulently contracted the debt or incurred the obligation on which the judgment or decree was rendered: or,

6. That he is about to remove his body out of the jurisdiction of the court: or,

7. That he is not a citizen or resident of the state. (*b*)

The person taken by a writ of capias ad satisfaciendum may be discharged by delivering to the officer real or personal property sufficient to satisfy the judgment and costs, on which the writ issued. (*c*)

He may also, on demand, be carried before the commissioner

(*a*) Swan's Practice and Precedents, i, 127.

(*b*) Swan's Statutes of Ohio, 648, 649.

(*c*) Ib. 483.

of insolvents, and be released, by availing himself of the provisions of the law for the relief of insolvent debtors. (*a*)

12. *Judgment and Execution.*

Lands, tenements, goods, and chattels, are liable to be taken in execution, and sold for the payment of debts. All lands and tenements in a county where a judgment is entered, are bound by it from the first day of the term of its rendition. Other lands, as well as goods and chattels, are bound from the time they are seized in execution. The execution is first to be levied on goods and chattels; and, for want of these, on the realty. When two or more writs of execution against the same debtor, are sued out during the term in which judgment was rendered, or within ten days thereafter, and when two or more executions against the same debtor are delivered to the officer on the same day, no preference shall be given to any of such writs. If a sufficient sum is not made to satisfy all the executions, the amount realized shall be distributed to the several creditors pro rata. In other cases, the writ of execution first delivered is first satisfied.

Notice of sales of goods and chattels on execution must be given, at least ten days before the day of sale, by advertisement in a newspaper printed in the county, or in case no newspaper be printed therein, by advertisements in five public places in the county, two of which must be put up in the township where the sale is to be had. (*b*)

Both real and personal property is appraised by three disinterested freeholders, and cannot be sold for less than two-thirds of its appraised value. (*c*)

Lands sold by the state for any debts or taxes due thereto, are not subject to the appraisement laws. And the property of clerks, sheriffs, coroners, constables, justices, and collectors of taxes, when levied on for moneys received by them, are also sold without valuation.

When two-thirds of the appraised value of lands and tenements, levied on, amounts to a sum sufficient to satisfy the execu-

(*a*) Swan's Statutes of Ohio, 441. (*b*) Ib. 467–72.

(*c*) General Laws, xli. 10, and Swan, 473.

tion and costs, the lien of the judgment on the residue of the debtor's estate is divested in favor of any other bona fide judgment creditor. Sales of lands are made at the court-house door, and notice, by advertisement, given in some newspaper printed in the county; or in case no newspaper be printed in the county, then in some newspaper in general circulation therein, and by putting up an advertisement at the court-house door and in five other public places in the county, two of which must be in the township where the lands lie. After the officer has made the sale, he reports his proceedings to the court, and if they have been correct, the court directs him to make a deed to the purchaser. The reversal of the judgment does not affect the title of the purchaser; but the former owner of the land looks to judgment creditor for compensation. A judgment on which execution is not levied in one year, ceases to operate as a lien on the estate of the debtor, to the prejudice of any other bona fide judgment creditor. The lien continues, however, for one year after the disability, occasioned by an appeal, writ of error, or injunction, is removed. (*a*)

13. *Courts.*

The judicial power of this state, in all civil cases of original cognizance, is distributed between a Supreme Court, which holds an annual term in each county of the state, and Courts of Common Pleas. There are also, in the city of Cincinnati, two courts of general jurisdiction in cases founded on contract: the Superior and the Commercial Courts of Cincinnati.

(*a*) Swan's Statutes of Ohio, 474, 479.

INDIANA.

1. *Bills of Exchange and Promissory Notes.*

Bills of exchange, both foreign and inland, are governed by the law merchant.

All notes, bonds, or other instruments in writing, for the payment of money or delivery of any article, or the conveyance of property, or to perform any condition therein mentioned, are assignable and negotiable by indorsement thereon, so as absolutely to transfer and vest the property thereof in each and every indorsee successively, who may maintain an action in his own name. But the maker of the instrument may set up any legal or equitable defence, which he had, as against the payee before notice of the assignment. He may also show any just matters of payment, or other defence which he had, as against any assignor, before notice of the assignment by such assignor, and which he might have set up and shown, had an action been brought against him, on such instrument, by such assignor. The assignee must *use due diligence* to recover against the maker, and if he fails, may resort to the party who assigned the instrument to him. (*a*)

If the maker of the note is notoriously insolvent, the assignee may sue the assignor, without having previously sued the maker. —2 *Blckf.* 243.

An assignee cannot sue a remote assignor.—1 *Blckf.* 55.

All notes in writing, negotiable and payable at any chartered bank in this state, in which such bank has any beneficial interest, and drawn for the payment of a sum of money certain and payable to order, assigns, or bearer, shall have the same effect and be negotiable in like manner as inland bills of exchange, according to the custom of merchants. (*b*)

The damages allowed for the non-acceptance or non-payment of bills of exchange, drawn within this state and duly protested, are ten per cent. when the bill is drawn on any person at a place out of the United States, and five per cent. when the bill is drawn on any person at any place in the United States or its territories, but without the state of Indiana. Such damages shall be in lieu of interest, charges of protest, and all other charges incurred previous to and at the time of giving notice of non-payment or non-acceptance; but the holder may recover interest from the time at which notice of such protest shall have been given. (*b*)

2. *Interest.*

The rate of interest is fixed at six per cent. per annum.

Interest is allowed on all moneys after they become due, on bond, bill, promissory note, or other instrument in writing; on money due on the settlement of accounts, from the day the balance shall have been ascertained; on money received to the use of another, and retained without the owner's consent, express or implied, from the reception thereof; and on money due and withheld by vexatious and unreasonable delay of payment. On judgments and decrees, interest is allowed from the date of signing the same.

A contract is not rendered void by usury; but where unlawful interest has been, directly or indirectly, reserved, contracted

(*a*) Revised Statutes of 1843, 576. (*b*) Ib. 579.

for, or received, the defendant shall recover his full costs, if sued, and the plaintiff shall only recover judgment for the principal sum due him, without interest thereon; and if he has already received any part of the interest, the same shall be deducted from the principal sum, and judgment rendered for the balance.

Illegal interest which has been paid, may be recovered back, if suit be brought within one year after the payment of the same. A party violating the law against usury, may be compelled to answer, on oath, to a bill of discovery, but is thereby exempted from any penal liability or criminal prosecution. (*a*)

3. *Effect of Marriage on the Rights of Property.*

The real estate possessed by a feme sole before marriage, or fairly acquired during coverture, or any interest therein, or rents and profits arising therefrom, cannot be taken on execution for the debts of her husband, but are deemed to be the separate property of the wife, as free from any claim of the husband or his legal representatives as if she had never been married. Such property, however, is liable for her debts contracted before marriage. (*b*)

4. *Statute of Frauds and Perjuries.*

The English statute has been re-enacted with some additions.

The consideration of a promise or agreement need not be in writing.

Any representation as to the character or credit of a person must be in writing, to charge the person making it.

The statute of 27 Elizabeth, rendering void conveyances to defraud purchasers, and the statute of 13 Elizabeth, rendering void conveyances and assignments to defraud or hinder creditors, have been re-enacted.

It is also provided that the question of fraudulent intent shall be deemed a question of fact and not of law; and that no conveyance or charge shall be adjudged fraudulent, as against creditors or purchasers, solely on the ground that it was not founded on a valuable consideration. (*c*)

(*a*) R. S. of 1843, 580, 581. (*b*) Acts of 1847, 45.
(*c*) R, S. of 1843, 588–590.

5. *Corporations.*

The statute, besides embodying some of the provisions of the common law, declares, that all corporations whose charters shall expire by their own limitation, or shall be annulled by forfeiture or otherwise, shall be continued bodies corporate for the term of three years, for the purpose of prosecuting and defending suits, and to dispose of their property and divide their stock; but not to continue the business of the corporation.

It is also provided that at any time within the said three years, any creditor or stockholder may apply to the Circuit Court of the county in which the corporation has its principal place of business, to appoint receivers or trustees to take charge of the estate and effects of the corporation, and to collect the debts thereof, with power to prosecute and defend all suits that may be necessary for the purpose, and to do all other acts proper for the final settlement of the business of the corporation. The powers of the receivers may be continued beyond the three years, and as long as the court shall think necessary for the purposes aforesaid.

The receivers shall pay the debts of the corporation, and if there be any balance remaining, shall distribute the same among those entitled thereto, as having been stockholders or members of the corporation, or their legal representatives; where no person is entitled to receive the balance of assets, it shall be paid into the state treasury. (*a*)

6. *Limited Partnerships.*

Limited partnerships for mercantile, mechanical, or manufacturing business may be formed; but not for banking or insurance.

The partnership must consist of one or more persons, to be called general partners, and to be responsible as general partners now are by law; and one or more persons to be called special partners, who shall contribute to the common stock a specific sum, in actual cash payment, and shall not be personally liable for any debts of the partnership, except in the cases hereinafter mentioned.

(*a*) R. S. of 1843, 586.

The persons forming the partnership shall make and sign a certificate, which shall contain the name or firm under which such partnership is to be conducted, the names and places of residence of all the general and special partners, distinguishing who are general and who are special partners, the amount of capital which each special partner has contributed to the common stock, the general nature of the business to be transacted, and the time when the partnership is to commence and to terminate. If any false statement is made in the certificate, all the partners shall be liable as general partners. The certificate must be acknowledged before a justice of the peace, and recorded in the county where the principal place of business of the partnership is situated; and if the partnership has several places of business in different counties, a certified copy of the certificate shall be filed in the recorder's office of each county. For six successive weeks a copy of the certificate shall be published in a newspaper printed in the county where the principal place of business is situated; and if no paper be there printed, then in a newspaper printed nearest thereto in this state. If such publication is not made, the partnership shall be deemed general.

On every renewal or continuation of the partnership, all the above provisions must be complied with or the partnership will be deemed general.

The names of the general partners only shall be used, without the addition of the word "company," or any other general term; the general partners only shall transact the business; and any special partner shall be treated as a general partner who permits his name to be used in the partnership business, or makes any contract personally concerning the partnership.

During the continuance of the partnership, no part of the capital stock shall be withdrawn, nor any division of interest or profit be made so as to reduce such capital stock below the sum stated in the certificate; and if at any time during the continuance or at the termination of the partnership, the assets shall not be sufficient to pay the partnership debts, then the special partners shall severally be held responsible for all sums by them in any way received, withdrawn, or divided, with interest thereon from the time when they were so withdrawn respectively.

Suits must be brought by and against the general partners, except where the special partners are to be treated as general partners, or are severally liable on account of sums received or withdrawn as above mentioned.

No dissolution of the partnership shall be valid unless a notice thereof shall be recorded in the recorder's office in which the certificate was recorded, and also published for six successive weeks in some newspaper printed in the county where the certicates of the formation of such partnership were published; and if no paper be printed in that county, then the dissolution must be published in a newspaper printed nearest thereto.

No assignment by the partnership in case of insolvency shall be valid, which does not provide for an equal distribution of the assets to all the creditors.

Notice of the assignment must be published within fourteen days, and the assent of the creditors shall be presumed unless within sixty days after notice thereof they dissent. (*a*)

7. *Limitations of Actions.*

All actions on bonds, bills, notes, or *any contract in writing*, and on all judgments and decrees of any court of record, may be brought within twenty years after the cause of action shall have accrued.

The following actions must be commenced within six years after the cause of action shall accrue, viz.: actions of debt; actions upon judgments rendered before a justice of the peace, or in any court not being a court of record; actions for arrears of rent; actions of assumpsit and on the case, except slander and libel; actions of waste and trespass on lands; actions of replevin, and all other actions for taking, detaining, or injuring goods or chattels. Of course, where any of the above named actions are founded on a contract in writing, the limitation of six years does not apply.

All actions for assault and battery and for false imprisonment, must be begun within three years.

All actions for slanderous words and for libel must be com-

(*a*) R. S. of 1843, 583–586.

menced within one year after the cause of the action shall have accrued.

In all actions of debt or assumpsit, where there are mutual and open accounts current between the parties, the cause of action shall be deemed to have accrued at the time of the last item proved in such account.

An action may be brought within one year after the usual disabilities are removed, viz. : infancy, coverture, insanity, imprisonment, and absence from the United States.

Where the defendant is out of the state when the cause of action accrues, the statute is suspended until his return.

Where the party dies and the right of action survives, the action may be brought within eighteen months after the expiration of the time limited by statute, and the death of the party.

In actions of debt or upon the case founded upon any contract, no acknowledgment or promise shall be evidence of a new or continuing contract, whereby to take any case out of the statute, or to deprive any party of the benefit thereof, unless such acknowledgment or promise be made in writing signed by the party chargeable thereby.

Where there are joint contractors the promise of one shall not affect the others, but suit may be instituted against the party making the new promise. (*a*)

8. *Insolvent Law.*

Every insolvent debtor, whether civil process has been issued against him or not, may obtain relief by executing an assignment of all his property, real and personal, for the benefit of his creditors, except so much as is by law exempt from execution. Such debtor files a petition in the Circuit Court, setting forth the circumstances of his indebtedness, together with a schedule containing an account of all his creditors, and an exact inventory of all his estate. The petition and schedule is verified by an affidavit as to the truth of the same, and also minutely disclaiming all acts of fraud to the injury of creditors. The court, after due publication of

(*a*) R. S. of 1843, 685, 686.

the pendency of the petition, proceeds to hear the application of the petitioner, and also the proofs and allegations of all and any of the creditors who may appear and show cause against granting the prayer of the petition. On being satisfied that the petitioner is entitled to his discharge, an order is made that he assign all his property to trustees named by the court; and on compliance therewith, he receives his discharge. The effect thereof is simply to release his person from arrest or imprisonment in any suit previously instituted, or for any debt previously contracted. It does not exempt any property, owned or acquired by the insolvent after his discharge, from the payment of all just debts and demands whenever contracted.

The assignment vests in the trustees all the interest of the insolvent in his estate, of which they become the legal owners for the benefit of creditors.

The assignment of his real estate must be by deed duly executed and recorded.

The trustees have full powers to sue, in their own names or otherwise, and recover all the estate and things in action of the insolvent; to sell, at public auction, from time to time as may be expedient, all the estate, real and personal, vested in them, and to convey, transfer, and deliver the same; to redeem mortgages, and sell property subject thereto; to settle, compound, and compromise accounts; to adjust controversies respecting the estate, by arbitration or otherwise; to submit cases to the court; and in general to exercise the rights of owners over the insolvent's property, for the benefit of creditors.

The trustees, immediately on their appointment, shall give notice thereof in a newspaper printed in the county. They also give notice, within twelve months from their appointment, to all the creditors to present their claims; which notice is to be published for four months in a newspaper in the county, and set up in three of the most public places thereof, specifying a time and place, when and where the creditors must present their accounts for adjustment. If a creditor fails to exhibit his claim, he is not entitled to any share in the distribution. After the trustees have converted the estate into money and paid necessary expenses, they distribute the proceeds among the creditors, pro rata, without giving preference to any debts or demands, except moneys owing by the insolvent as executor, administrator, guardian, or trustee; and if there be not sufficient to pay his debts, owing as executor, administrator, guardian, or trustee, then a distribution shall be made among such debts in proportion to their amounts. Debts not due shall share in the distribution after deducting a rebate of legal interest.

If the insolvent has been guilty of any fraud in his application, his discharge may be set aside, within three years, on petition of any person interested. But a judgment declaring such discharge null, will not affect the assignment; and the trustees proceed, in all respects, in the performance of their trust as if such judgment had not been rendered. (*a*)

9. *Attachment.*

The real and personal property of a debtor who is an inhabitant of the state, may be attached whenever his creditor, in person or by agent, makes an affidavit that the debtor is secretly leaving the state, or has left the state, to defraud his creditors or avoid service of process, or that he keeps himself so concealed that process cannot be served upon him, with intent to defraud his creditors. But no writ of attachment shall issue unless the debtor has been absent more than one year, if his family remain in the county, and properly explain the cause of his absence; or unless he is secretly removing his property. Before the writ issues the creditor must give an approved bond, conditioned for the prosecution of his writ, and the payment of all damages to the debtor if the proceedings should be wrongful and oppressive.

If the amount claimed does not exceed one hundred dollars, and it is not necessary to attach the land of the debtor, the proceedings may be had before a justice; otherwise, in the Circuit Court. Both the real and personal property are bound from the service of the writ.

After notice in a public newspaper of the pendency of the proceedings, the court hears the plaintiff's claim, and awards execution against the property attached. The proceedings are

(*a*) R. S. of 1843, 467–480.

in rem unless the defendant personally appears. When the property has been attached, it may be released and delivered to the debtor, on his executing a bond payable to the state of Indiana, with approved sureties, conditioned to take good care of the property, and deliver the same on demand, if judgment be recovered against him in the attachment suit.

A garnishee, or person holding property of the defendant, or indebted to him, may, upon affidavit, be summoned to answer, under oath, all questions that may be put to him, touching the rights, property, decrees, judgments, bonds, bills, notes, accounts, contracts or credits of the defendant in his hands, or within his knowledge, agency, or control. From the time that process is served on the garnishee, he is accountable to the plaintiff in attachment for the money, property, or credits in his hands, or due or owing by him to the defendant. Proceedings may be had against the garnishee alone, when the writ of attachment is returned "no property found."

Each and every creditor of the defendant, on filing his affidavit and bond, may, at any time before the final adjustment of the suit, be permitted to prove his claim, and to have any person summoned as a *garnishee;* and when final judgment is rendered, the several creditors are paid, in proportion to the amount of their claims, as adjusted by the court.

The attachment debtor may appear and plead, as of course, without giving bond; but no such appearance or pleading shall operate to discharge the property attached.

Whenever any person, other than the defendant, may claim any personal property attached, the officer, previous to any further proceedings, shall cause the right of property to be tried, as in cases of property taken in execution; and the claimant shall have reasonable time to procure testimony.

The property, both real and personal, of non-residents, may be attached for any debt or demand against them; and the proceedings in foreign attachment approximate as closely as possible to those in domestic attachment. It is provided that the property and interest of joint owners, either as partners or otherwise, shall be liable by suit against all or any of them who may be indebted, by their proper names, or their names of repute, or their partnership names and style; and the estates, property and interest which may have descended to non-resident heirs or devisees, or become vested in non-resident executors or administrators, are also liable for debts or other demands against said decedent's estates. But the property and interest of one or more joint owners, who are not indebted, shall not be affected by the proceedings against joint owners who are indebted.

After due publication of the pendency of the writ, the cause is continued from one term until the next before the court proceeds to adjudicate thereon. And after judgment is rendered, the creditor cannot receive the amount of his claim until he gives bond, with approved sureties, payable to the defendant, conditioned to answer any suit the defendant may bring against him within twelve months, and to pay such defendant all sums he may have received, and which were not justly due and owing. (*a*)

Attachment against boats.—Boats and vessels of all descriptions, which are either built, repaired or equipped within the jurisdiction of the state, or which may come within such jurisdiction, are liable for all debts contracted by the master, owner or consignee thereof, on account of work done, or supplies or materials furnished, on account of, or towards the building, repairing, furnishing or equipping such boats: and the debts so contracted shall be a lien upon such boats, their tackle, apparel and furniture, and shall have preference over all debts due from the owner, master or consignee thereof, except the wages of mariners and boatmen. (*b*)

10. *Imprisonment for Debt.*

Special bail shall not be required, in any case, unless the plaintiff, his agent, or attorney, shall make an affidavit, specifying the plaintiff's right to recover an existing debt or damages from the defendant, and also stating that he believes the defendant is about to leave the state taking with him property subject to execution, or money or effects which should be applied to the payment of plaintiff's debt or damages, with intent to defraud him. When the affidavit is filed, any judge of the court or the clerk may make an

(*a*) R. S. of 1843, 762–774. (*b*) Ib. 778.

order for bail which is endorsed on the writ of capias ad respondum, and also the amount of the debt or damages.

If bail is not given, the party is committed to prison and held there until final judgment; and for a time not to exceed ten days afterwards, in order that the plaintiff may take his body in execution. But the defendant may sue out a writ of habeas corpus, and compel the plaintiff to prove the truth of the allegations in his affidavit; and if he fails to do so, the defendant is discharged.

The bail are only liable for the amount of property, money or effects which the plaintiff may show the defendant to have possessed at the time of making his affidavit. (*a*)

No capias ad satisfaciendum shall issue against a judgment debtor, unless the creditor first files an affidavit charging the debtor with fraudulently removing, concealing or conveying away his property subject to execution, with intent to defraud and delay such creditor, or charging that the debtor has moneys, rights, credits or effects with which the judgment or decree might be paid, and which he fraudulently withholds and conceals, to delay and defraud his creditor. The affidavit may also state that the debtor has not been held to bail in the original action, and a capias ad respondum may issue.

On filing the affidavit, a scire facias issues requiring the debtor to appear and show cause why the writ of ca sa should not issue against him. The debtor may appear and plead to the scire facias, and an issue to the country be made up; and if he fails to appear after two returns of "not found" to the scire facias, the court may determine the allegations of the affidavit in his absence, and grant the writ. (*b*)

11. *Judgments and Executions.*

Whenever a judgment is rendered in any court of record for any debt, damages, sum of money, or costs, execution may be issued against the goods, chattels, lands and tenements, of the judgment debtor. (*c*)

Real estate, which may be sold on execution, includes all realty in possession, reversion, or remainder, all realty fraudulently

(*a*) R. S. of 1843, 672. (*b*) Ib. 753. (*c*) Ib. 742.

conveyed to the injury of creditors, all rights of redeeming mortgaged lands, and all lands held by a land office certificate, and all realty held in trust on an execution against the cestui que trust.

All judgments in the Supreme, Circuit, and Probate Courts, and all final decrees in Chancery for any debt, damages, sum of money, or costs, shall operate as a lien on all the realty of the debtor in the county where the judgment or decree is rendered, and bind from the rendition thereof.

Any person interested may obtain from the clerk of the court a certified copy of the judgment or decree, and file the same in the office of the clerk of any Circuit Court in the state; and from the time such copy is filed, recorded, and entered in the judgment docket of any county, it shall operate as a lien on all the realty of the debtor in that county.

A judgment or decree ceases to be a lien after ten years from its rendition; but the time during which the party, recovering such judgment or decree, is restrained from proceeding thereon, by appeal, writ of error, or injunction, constitutes no part of the term.

Any recognizance, taken by any court or by any officer, shall bind the real estate of the principal therein, from the time of taking the same; but only binds the real estate of the surety from the time that a judgment of forfeiture is rendered.

An execution to another county binds the realty from the time of the levy; and the lien continues until the sale, if due diligence is used.

The equitable interest growing out of contracts for the purchase of lands cannot be sold on execution; but when an execution has been returned unsatisfied, in whole or in part, the creditor may file his bill in Chancery to prevent the transfer of such contract, and to subject the same to the payment of his debt; and the court may order the interest of the debtor in the contract to be sold, or may transfer the same to the complainant, as they may deem most conducive to the interest of the parties.

The reversal of any judgment or decree, by virtue of which any real estate has been sold, or the title thereto decreed, shall not avoid any such sale or title, if the person to be affected thereby shall be, or shall claim under a bona fide purchaser, without notice, and not under a party to the record, or attorney of one. (*a*)

A stay of execution, for certain periods, in proportion to the amount recovered, the longest of which is one hundred and eighty days when the sum and costs exceed one hundred dollars, may be had by putting in bail. One or more sufficient freehold sureties enter into a recognizance for the payment of the judgment, interest, and costs, accrued and to accrue. The recognizance may be taken by the clerk, before the writ issues, or by the sheriff, after he has received it. The recognizance is made a record, and has the force and effect of a judgment confessed in a court of record. Execution on the judgment stayed, and on the recognizance, shall issue jointly against the parties thereto; but the levy shall first be made on the property of the defendants in the original judgment. No stay is allowed on judgments against an attorney for money collected, or against persons or corporations for money deposited with them, or against clerks, sheriffs, coroners, treasurers, trustees of funds, and other public officers acting in a fiduciary capacity.

When judgment is rendered against two or more persons, any of whom are sureties for the others, no stay of execution shall be allowed, if such sureties object at the time of rendering the judgment, unless the bail for the stay of execution will specially undertake to pay the judgment, in case the amount cannot be made from the principal debtor. (*b*)

An execution binds the goods and chattels from the time of its delivery to the officer, who indorses on it the exact date of its reception, but if there be several executions, whether issued from a court of record or not, in the hands of different officers, that execution, without regard to the time of its delivery, under which the first levy is made, shall have the preference and hold the property.

In judgments on the bonds of any officer at the suit of the state of Indiana, the real and personal estate of the debtor shall be bound from the date of the process by which such suit was instituted. (*c*) The debtor may designate the property to be le-

(*a*) R. S. of 1843, 454–466. (*b*) Ib. 736–739. (*c*) Ib. 743–44.

vied on, and if he fails to do so, the officer may select; but the personal estate shall be sold before the realty is levied on. (*a*)

All property taken in execution must be appraised, and cannot sell for less than its fair value. Each party chooses a disinterested householder as appraisers, who, in case of disagreement, choose a third; the appraisement of any two of them being taken as the value of the property. (*b*)

There shall be no valuation or appraisement of property on judgments against state, county, or township officers, against executors, administrators, or guardians, for mis-feasance, mal-feasance, or non-feasance, against attorneys, for moneys collected, against banks, insurance companies, and savings institutions, or against the principal in any delivery bond. (*c*)

By the act of February 13th, 1843, it is provided, that after the first day of June, 1843, any person, for a consideration arising wholly after that time, may agree in writing to pay any sum of money, without relief from valuation or appraisement laws; and judgment shall be rendered accordingly. (*d*)

The amount of property exempt from execution shall not exceed the value of one hundred and twenty-five dollars. (*e*)

Remedy against sheriff or attorney failing to pay over money collected.—A sheriff failing to levy upon or sell property liable to an execution, or to return a writ of execution at the proper time, or to pay over the amount received by him to the person entitled, becomes liable, not only for the amount of the execution with interest and costs, but ten per cent. damages on the principal sum. This penalty may be recovered, either by action on the official bond of the officer, or upon motion, after ten days previous notice to the court to which the execution is returnable. (*f*)

Where an attorney fails to pay over money collected by him to the person entitled, the latter, upon filing a complaint in the clerk's office of the court upon whose process the money was collected, at least ten days before the sitting of such court, may recover a judgment for the amount thus collected, with interest and costs and ten per cent. damages: the court shall also suspend the attorney from practice for any length of time in its discretion. (*g*)

(*a*) R. S. of 1843, 746. (*b*) Ib. 1044. (*c*) Ib. 1047.
(*d*) Ind. Justice, 319. (*e*) R. S. 1046. (*f*) Ib. 756. (*g*) Ib. 662.

12. *Effect of Death on the Rights of Creditors.*

When an estate is solvent, the personal representative pays the debts of the decedent in the following order.

1. The expense of administration.
2. The funeral expenses and those of the last sickness.
3. Taxes assessed previous to decedent's death.
4. Judgments, decrees, mortgages, and debts of record.
5. All judgments of courts, not of record, and all recognizances, bonds, notes, bills, demands, and unliquidated accounts whatsoever.

No executor or administrator can give preference in the payment of any debt over other debts of the same class; except that the Probate Court may authorize him to pay rents due at decedent's death, in preference to debts of the fourth class.

A debt due and payable, has no preference over one not due of the same class; nor does the commencement of a suit or the recovery of a judgment thereon entitle such debt to any preference over other debts of the same class.

No action can be brought against any executor or administrator as such, until the expiration of one year from the date of his appointment.

Every creditor of a decedent must file a statement of his demand, in the clerk's office of the Probate Court, within one year from the appointment of the personal representatives, and any creditor who fails to do so shall be barred of any preference in the payment of his debt on account of its superior dignity. The creditor must also within the year give notice of his claim to the executor or administrator, personally if he resides in the county where administration is granted; otherwise, by filing the notice in the clerk's office of the same.

No executor or administrator is personally liable, on account of any debt or claim, for having paid a debt of inferior dignity thereto, before notice that a statement of the debt was filed as required, unless such inferior debt shall have been paid before the expiration of the time within which the statement is required to be filed.

A debt not due may be paid, by an order of the Probate Court, a rebate of the legal interest being deducted.

The personal representative may require from every creditor satisfactory vouchers in support of his claims: or the affidavit of the claimant, that the debt is justly due and owing, that no payments have been made thereon, and that there are no set-offs against the same. (a)

When an executor or administrator discovers that the personal estate is insufficient to pay the debts and liabilities of the decedent, he may petition the Probate Court for an order to sell the real estate. His petition must state the amount of personalty, his application of the same, the debts outstanding, the names and ages of the heirs, devisees and legatees if known; and must describe so much of the real estate as he may think necessary to sell.

Before an order of sale is made, due notice of the petition, and of the time and place of hearing the same, must be given to the heirs, devisees and legatees, personally if they reside in the state, otherwise by publication. An inventory and appraisement of the realty, made in the manner prescribed for personal estate, shall be filed in the clerk's office of the Probate Court.

If no good cause to the contrary be shown, the court will order such a portion of the realty to be sold as may be necessary, and the sale may be made privately or at auction as the court shall deem most expedient. But it cannot be sold for a less amount, with reference to its appraised value, than real estate can be sold for at the time under execution. Instead of selling the realty, the executor or administrator may be empowered to lease or mortgage the same, if the necessary amount of money can be procured upon such lease or mortgage.

Any of the persons interested in the real estate may prevent the sale, lease, or mortgage of the same, by giving bond to the executor or administrator, in a sum and with sureties to be approved by the court, conditioned to pay all debts and liabilities which shall be eventually found to be due from the estate, so far as the personalty shall not be sufficient or liable therefor.

When a creditor has obtained a judgment against an executor or administrator, and the execution thereon is unsatisfied for want of personalty, he may petition the Probate Court for a sale of the realty to discharge his judgment. The personal representatives

(a) R. S. of 1843, 521–524.

and the heirs, devisees, and legatees of the deceased must be made defendants and duly notified. The court, on being satisfied of the truth of the plaintiff's claim, shall require the executor or administrator to file his petition to convert the realty into assets for the payment of debts. (*a*)

When an executor or administrator discovers that an estate is insolvent, it is his duty to petition the Probate Court to settle the same as such. This petition sets forth the condition of the estate, the outstanding debts, the probable deficiency, and makes the heirs, devisees and legatees defendants, and is verified by his affidavit. The court, on being satisfied of the truth of the petition, declares the estate insolvent, and directs notice to be given to the creditors, by publication, requiring them to present their claims within ten months from the date of the notice or they will not be entitled to payment. After filing the petition, suits against the estate are suspended, unless waste or fraud be alleged.

After proof of due publication, the court proceeds to hear and determine all claims filed within the time allowed by law, or within such further time as the court, for good cause, may allow; which further time shall not exceed twelve months. Issues may be made up and the claims tried by a jury.

After the estate has been converted into money, the personal representative pays the same into the Probate Court; and it shall constitute a fund to be paid out in the following order: 1. Expenses of administration. 2. Funeral expenses. 3. Expenses of last sickness. 4. All other demands which have been allowed, pro rata, without regard to their dignity. No lien is postponed or defeated; and if the estate bound is not enough to pay the lien, the balance unpaid shall share in the fund aforesaid, on being filed and allowed as other claims. (*b*)

13. *Courts.*

The general original jurisdiction in civil cases is intrusted to the Circuit Courts, which hold two terms in the year, in each county, one in the spring, the other in the fall. There are also Probate Courts, and Magistrates' Courts.

(*a*) R. S. of 1843, 527–534. (*b*) Ib. 535–540.

ILLINOIS.

1. *Choses in Action.*

All joint obligations and covenants are to be construed as joint and several. (*a*)

2. *Bills of Exchange and Promissory Notes.*

The principles of commercial law as to bills of exchange, have not been altered by statute; but promissory notes, for money or any article of personal property, whether under seal or not, stand upon a peculiar footing. They may be assigned by indorsement, so as to vest the property therein in successive assignees, and authorize such assignees to maintain any action for the recovery thereof, which might have been maintained by the obligee or payee. A note, however, to A B or bearer cannot be sued upon by the holder as bearer: the note must be assigned by indorsement, to enable any other than the payee to sue.

(*a*) R. S. 299.

No demand and notice is necessary to recover against the assignor or indorser of a promissory note; but the assignee must use due diligence for the recovery of the money or property due thereon, or damages in lieu thereof, by prosecuting a suit against the maker, unless the institution of such suit would have been unavailing, or unless the maker of the assigned instrument had absconded or left the state before its maturity.

Rate of damages upon protested bills.—Where any foreign bill of exchange, expressed to be for value received, has been duly protested for non-acceptance or non-payment, the drawers or indorsers thereof, upon being duly notified, shall pay the amount of the bill, with legal interest from the time at which it should have been paid, and ten per cent. damages, with the costs and charges of protest in addition. The drawers or indorsers of a similar bill, drawn upon any person or body politic, out of the state, but within the United States, and who have been duly notified of its protest for non-acceptance or non-payment, shall be liable for the amount of the bill, with legal interest, and in addition, five per cent. damages, with the costs and charges of protest. (*a*)

3. *Interest.*

Six per cent. is the legal and established rate of interest, except upon township loans of school funds, when twelve may be taken. (*b*) An agreement is not rendered void by the reservation of usurious interest; but wherever that fact appears in any action, the creditor can only have judgment for the amount of his debt, after deducting threefold the amount of the interest, one-third of which is set apart for the defendant, and the remaining two-thirds appropriated to the county treasury. Where the usurious excess has been paid, the penalty, threefold the amount of the interest, may be recovered by the debtor on instituting an action therefor within two years from the accruing of the right of action. Usury cannot be set up as a defence against a note in the hands of a bona fide assignee. (*c*)

(*a*) R. S. 384. (*b*) R. S. 294. (*c*) Conkling *v.* Underhill, 3 Scam. 388.

4. *Statute of Frauds.*

The English statute of frauds and perjuries has been re-enacted, with no substantial alteration except the addition of the words "promise or agreement" to the clause requiring a writing. (*a*)

5. *Assignment by Insolvent Debtors.*

There is no law depriving a failing debtor of the right to prefer one creditor to another by assignment.

6. *Limited Partnerships.*

By an act passed in 1847, limited partnerships have been authorized in Illinois on the same terms, and subject to the same restrictions, as in the state of New York.

7. *Limitation of Actions.*

All actions of trespass, detinue, trover, and replevin, for taking away goods and chattels, all actions for arrearages of rent due on a parol demise, and all actions of account and upon the case, except such as concern the trade of merchandise between merchant and merchant, their factors or agents, must be commenced within five years after the cause of action has accrued.

All actions of debt or covenant, for rent founded upon any lease under seal, and all actions of debt or covenant founded upon any single or penal bill, promissory note, or writing obligatory for the direct payment of money, or the delivery of property, or the performance of covenants, or upon any award under the hand and seal of arbitrators, for the payment of money only, must be commenced within sixteen years from the time when the cause of action accrued, or where any payment has been made upon such instrument, within sixteen years from the time of such payment.

Judgments of any court of record, may be revived by action

(*a*) R. S. 258.

of debt, or scire facias, within twenty years from the rendition of the same.

The time during which a party liable to any of the causes of action specified, may be out of the state, is not reckoned a part of the limitation. There is also the usual saving in favor of infants, feme coverts, and persons non compos, of the period of limitation after the removal of their respective disabilities. (*a*)

8. *Attachment.*

Any creditor or his agent may obtain a writ of attachment from the clerk of such court directed to the sheriff of his county, commanding him to attach the estate of any kind whatever of his debtor, wherever found, or so much as will satisfy the claim of the creditor, with interest and costs, (*b*) upon filing an affidavit in the clerk's office of any Circuit Court, setting forth that a person named therein is indebted to such creditor in a sum exceeding twenty dollars, and also the nature and amount of such indebtedness as near as may be, and stating that such debtor has departed or is about to depart from the state, with the intention of removing his effects therefrom; or is about to remove his property from the state to the injury of such creditor, or that such debtor conceals himself, or defies the sheriff, so that the process cannot be served upon him, or is a non-resident of the state.

Before the clerk issues any writ of attachment, he must take bond with security from the plaintiff or his agent, conditioned to pay all damage and costs which may ensue by reason of the same to the defendant or any other person interested. Where two or more persons are jointly indebted, either as partners or otherwise, and an affidavit is filed sufficient to bring any one of them within the provisions of this law, the writ of attachment may issue against his effects. Where two or more persons are jointly indebted, and are non-residents, writs of attachment may issue against the separate estate of any or all of them, their heirs, executors, or administrators.

The plaintiff in any action of debt, covenant, trespass, or on the

(*a*) R. S. 348. (*b*) Ib. 63.

case upon premises, commenced by summons, may at any time sue out an attachment against the estate real and personal of his debtor, before judgment, upon filing a sufficient affidavit and bond, and the proceedings shall be the same, as near as may be, as upon an original attachment. (*a*)

When the sheriff cannot find property of the defendant sufficient to satisfy the debt, he shall summon as garnishees, all persons designated by the plaintiff, as having effects or choses in action of the defendant in their possession, or as being in any wise indebted to him. It is the duty of such garnishee to appear before the court upon the return day of the writ, and to make a full disclosure on oath as to the estate of the defendant, under his control, and to answer all interrogatories propounded to him, touching the same. The plaintiff, upon alleging that such garnishee has not made a true return, may have a jury impanneled to ascertain the same, and the court shall grant the same judgment, as if the finding of the jury had been confessed by the garnishee.

A conditional judgment may be entered up against a garnishee failing to appear at the appointed time, and if upon a scire facias on such judgment issued and served, he still makes default, an absolute judgment may be rendered against him for the amount of the plaintiff's judgment against the defendant with costs. All goods and effects whatsoever of the defendant in the hands of the garnishee are also liable to satisfy such judgment.

Upon the return of the writ of attachment, it is the duty of the clerk of the court, to give notice for four weeks successively, by advertisement, in the newspaper most convenient to the place, of the pendency of the attachment, at whose suit, against whose estate, and for what sum, and that unless the defendant appear, give bail, and plead within the time limited, judgment will be rendered against him and the estate so attached sold. The plaintiff however must establish the existence of his debt, by legal testimony.

Where judgment is entered by default against the estate of the defendant, no execution can issue thereon, except against the property attached.

The usual provisions are made for the trial of the right of property, for the sale of perishable goods, for allowance of set-

(*a*) R. S. 70.

off, for dissolution of the attachment, and return of the property upon giving bond for payment of the judgment, &c. Where several attachments against the same person, are returned to the same term, or a civil judgment entered at same term in any action against the person who is defendant in the attachment, the respective creditors are to be paid pro rata out of the common effects; provided, however, that creditor retaking removed property shall have preference.

Where a writ of attachment is levied upon real estate, the sheriff must file a certificate of the fact with the recorder of the county where the same is situated, and until the filing of such certificate such levy shall not take effect as to creditors or bona fide purchasers without notice. (*a*)

The attachment law is to be construed most liberally for the detection of fraud.

No attachment is to be quashed for any insufficiency in the original affidavit, writ or bond, provided that the plaintiff or some credible person for him, causes a sufficient affidavit or bond to be filed at such time as the court may direct.

The provisions for attachments before a justice of the peace are substantially the same. The debt must not exceed one hundred dollars. (*b*)

Attachment against boats, &c.—A lien is given upon all boats built in or running upon the waters of this state, in favor of mechanics, tradesmen, and others, who have performed labor or advanced supplies for the building, equipping, or repairing the same, upon the engagement of the owner, master, or consignee. Unless this lien, however, is asserted within three months from the time of the accruing of the debt, it will not be allowed to prejudice other creditors, subsequent incumbrances, or purchasers. (*c*)

9. *Proceedings in Civil Suits.*

Arrest.—In all actions commenced in any court of record, and founded upon any specialty, bill, or note in writing, or on the judgment of any court, foreign or domestic, and in all actions of covenant and account, and actions on verbal contracts or assump-

(*a*) R. S. 315. (*b*) Ib. 58 to 62. (*c*) Ib. 71.

sits in law, in which the plaintiff or other credible person can ascertain the sum due, or damages sustained, and that the same will be in danger of being lost, or that the benefit of whatever judgment may be obtained will be in danger unless the defendant or defendants are held to bail, and such person will make affidavit of the facts before the clerk of the court from which the process issues, or a justice of the peace of the state; or when the plaintiff resides abroad, before any judge of a court of record, notary public, or other officer of the state or kingdom in which he resides, and who may be duly authorized to administer an oath; upon the delivery of such affidavit to the clerk of the court from which the process emanates, such clerk shall issue a capias, and indorse thereon an order to the sheriff to hold the defendant to bail in the sum mentioned in the affidavit.

Where the defendant is discharged as an insolvent debtor the bail will not be liable, unless judgment has been previously recovered against him. Such discharge may be obtained by going before a probate judge, and delivering up all his property. (*a*)

Judgment and execution.—When a judgment has been recovered against any person, his goods and chattels, lands and tenements, (including his interest in any contract for the sale or incumbrance of real estate,) and in some cases his body, may be taken in execution for its satisfaction.

The judgment binds the lands of the debtor from the last day of the term of the court in which it was rendered for the period of seven years, provided that execution has issued at some time within a year from the date of the judgment, unless stayed by injunction or some order of court. After the lapse of seven years, the judgment ceases to be a lien as against bona fide purchasers, or subsequent incumbrances by mortgage, judgment, or otherwise.

The goods and chattels of the defendant are only bound from the time of the delivery of the execution to the sheriff.

Where any writ of execution or attachment is sent from the court of one county to an officer of another, and levied upon real estate in such county, the officer must make and file a certificate thereof in the recorder's office of such county; and until the same

(*a*) R. S. 80.

is filed, the levy will not take effect as against creditors or bona fide purchasers without notice.

Where lands are sold upon execution, the defendant, his heirs, representatives, or grantees, may redeem the same within twelve months, by paying to the purchaser the amount of the purchase money and ten per cent. interest. After the expiration of twelve months, and before the expiration of fifteen months, any judgment creditor of the debtor may redeem upon the same terms, an opportunity being offered for any other persons to purchase the property by bidding an amount greater than the redemption money tendered by such creditor.

Where the sheriff has levied upon personal property by virtue of any writ of execution, the defendant may retain the same upon giving bond and security for its forthcoming at the day and place mentioned, in the condition. If this bond is broken the sheriff may proceed to levy upon the defendant's property, and if this be not sufficient, the property of the security, and offer the same for sale, allowing no further indulgence. (*a*)

Garnishment.—Where the officer returns upon any execution "no property found," and the plaintiff or other credible person makes oath that the defendant has no property in his possession, within the *knowledge* of the affiant, liable to execution, and that affiant has good reason to believe that another person named is indebted to defendant, or has some estate belonging to defendant in his hands, such person may be summoned as a garnishee, and proceedings had against him as in the case of attachment. (*b*)

Imprisonment upon a ca. sa., and discharge under insolvent act.—The constitution of Illinois provides that no person shall be imprisoned for debt unless upon refusal to deliver up his estate for the benefit of his creditors, in such manner as may be prescribed by law, or in cases where there is a strong presumption of fraud. The insolvent debtor's act (*c*)provides that where any debtor refuses to surrender his property in satisfaction of an execution against him, upon affidavit of such fact by the plaintiff in the execution or his agent, a writ of capias ad satisfaciendum may be issued against the body of such debtor. Where the debtor desires to release his person from such imprisonment, he may ap-

(*a*) R. S. 300 to 308. (*b*) Ib, 307. (*c*) Ib. 282.

ply for a discharge to the probate judge of the county in which the arrest is made. Such debtor shall make a full and just inventory of his entire estate, and also of all his debts, and verify the truth and fairness of the same by affidavit, and also, that he has in no manner disposed of any portion of his estate to the injury of his creditors, or to secure for himself any future advantage. Any creditor may contest the truth of such schedule, and for this purpose witnesses may be examined, and the debtor interrogated on oath. The probate judge may, if the proceedings of the debtor seem fair and just, appoint an assignee to whom such debtor shall transfer all his estate, and also grant to the debtor a discharge which will release him from imprisonment, and also exempt him from arrest on account of any debt mentioned in the schedule, until such discharge is vacated by due course of law. The creditor may appeal from the decision of the Probate Court, to the Circuit Court, who may impannel a jury to determine the controversy.

It is the duty of the assignee thus appointed, to collect the estate of the debtor, and convert the same into money as soon as may be, and distribute the proceeds among the creditors as in the case of the insolvent estates of deceased persons. The proceedings of the assignee are under the control and subject to the revision of the Probate Court.

Where a party desires to contest the allegation of fraud or refusal to surrender his property upon which he has been arrested, he may go before the probate justice of the county and have the allegations tried by a jury of seven householders.

10. *Effect of Death upon the Rights of Creditors.*

The estates of deceased persons are administered under the eye and control of the Courts of Probate, which are established in each county of the state. It is the duty of the executor or administrator, within three months from the granting of letters testamentary or of administration, to make out and return to the office of the probate judge an inventory of the estate of the deceased. He shall also fix upon a certain term of the Court of Probate, within nine months from the period of his qualification, for adjusting and settling all claims against the estate of the deceased, and give notice thereof by publication in a newspaper, and also at the door of the court-house and other public places. If no objection is made by any party interested, to any claim then presented, the same may be established by the affidavit of the claimant. If any such claim is disputed, it must be adjudicated according to law.

No execution can be issued against any executor or administrator for the period of one year from his qualification, nor can any suit be instituted against him, except in a few special cases, until the expiration of such period. No suit can be brought against an executor or administrator for any cause, unless brought within one year after such representative has settled his accounts with the Court of Probate. All demands not exhibited within two years from the grant of letters testamentary or of administration, will be forever barred unless the creditor find other estate of the deceased, not inventoried or accounted for by the executor, in which his claim may be paid pro rata, out of the subsequently discovered estate. The term of two years is saved for infants, feme coverts, and persons non compos mentis, after the removal of their disability.

Demands against deceased persons are divided into the following classes:

1st. Expenses of funeral and last sickness.

2d. Expenses of administration, and physician's bill during last sickness.

3d. Amount due by the deceased as an executor, administrator or guardian.

4th. All other demands, without regard to quality or dignity, which shall be exhibited within two years from the grant of administration.

Claims which have been allowed by the Court of Probate are to be paid in the order of the preceding classification; and when al. the demands of one class cannot be satisfied, they must be paid pro rata.

When it appears that the personal estate is insufficient to discharge all the debts of the deceased, the executor or administrator may obtain an order from the Circuit Court for a sale of so much of the realty as will supply the deficiency; and the proceeds of such sale shall be distributed in the same order as other assets. The real estate is not however to be sold, until the personalty has been exhausted. The Court of Probate, upon the application of any party in interest, may coerce the executor or administrator to make immediate application to the Circuit Court for the sale of such real estate.

All executors or administrators shall exhibit their accounts for settlement to the Court of Probate from which their letters were obtained, at the first term of such court after the expiration of one year from the date of the letters; and in like manner every twelve months thereafter, until such administration is completed. (*a*)

11. *Courts.*

A judge of the Supreme Court holds a Circuit Court in each county of the state, in the spring and fall, which is invested with general original jurisdiction in civil causes.

(*a*) R. S. 535 to 565.

MICHIGAN.

1. *Bills of Exchange and Promissory Notes.*

Notes in writing for the payment of a sum of money to any person or bearer, are negotiable as inland bills of exchange according to the custom of merchants, and the payees and indorsees of every such note, or any holder where the same is payable to bearer, may maintain actions thereon in like manner as upon inland bills of exchange. Days of grace are not allowed upon any bill of exchange, note, or draft payable on demand, but are allowed upon all bills of exchange payable at sight or at a future day certain within the state, and on all negotiable promissory notes, and drafts payable at a future day certain within the state, wherein there is no express stipulation to the contrary. The damages upon bills of exchange drawn or indorsed within the limits of the state and payable without the United States, which have been protested for non-acceptance or non-payment, and due notice given of the same, consist of the current rate of exchange at the time of the demand, with five per cent. damages upon the con-

(*a*) R. S. of 1846, 157.

tents of the bill, with interest upon the same from the date of the protest. Upon bills of exchange drawn or indorsed within the state, but payable at any place within the states of Wisconsin, Indiana, Illinois, Pennsylvania, Ohio, or New-York, which have been duly protested for non-acceptance or non-payment, besides interest and costs, three per cent. damages upon the contents of the bill: if payable within either of the states of Missouri, Kentucky, Maine, New Hampshire, Vermont, Massachusetts, Rhode Island, Connecticut, New Jersey, Delaware, Maryland, Virginia, or the District of Columbia, five per cent.: if payable at any other place within the United States, ten per cent.

No person can be charged as the acceptor of a bill of exchange, unless his acceptance be in writing, signed by himself or his lawful agent.

The holder of a bill of exchange or promissory note, instead of bringing several actions against the drawers, makers, indorsers, or acceptors, may include them in one action, and proceed to judgment as though they were joint contractors. (*b*)

Notaries public are authorized to demand payment of foreign and inland bills of exchange and promissory notes, and protest the same for non-acceptance or non-payment, and the certificate of the notary, under his hand and seal, shall be presumptive evidence of such facts, unless the defendant annex an affidavit to his plea, denying having received such notice. (*c*)

Bonds, choses in action, &c.—Some of the most important distinctions at common law, between sealed and unsealed instruments, have been abolished by statute. Thus, a seal affords only presumptive evidence of a consideration, which may be rebutted to the same extent and in the same manner as if the instrument was not under seal. (*d*)

Neither a seal nor scroll is essential to the validity of any bond, deed of conveyance, or other contract in writing signed by a party or his agent.

Wherever an action of covenant or debt may be brought upon an instrument under seal, or a judgment, there an action of assumpsit may be maintained in the same manner in all respects, as upon contracts without seal. (*e*)

(*a*) R. S. 156. (*b*) Ib. 440. (*c*) Ib. 79. (*d*) Ib. 460. (*e*) Ib. 487.

The assignees of bonds or other choses in action, may prosecute the same in their own names, subject to any equity which may have existed between the original parties previous to the notice of the assignment. (*a*)

2. *Interest.*

Parties to a contract may stipulate in writing for the payment of any rate of interest not exceeding ten per cent. Upon contracts which do not fix the amount of interest, and upon judgments at law, or decrees in Chancery, seven per cent. is the legal rate. Where more than the legal rate of interest is reserved, the contract is only void for the excess. Upon all actions brought upon any bills of exchange or promissory notes, payable in money, and to order or bearer, originally given upon an usurious consideration, the indorsee or holder for a valuable consideration before the maturity of the note, and without notice of the usury, may recover to the same extent as if no usury was alleged or proved. (*b*)

3. *Effect of Marriage upon the Rights of Property.*

Any real or personal estate acquired by a feme sole before marriage, or to which after marriage she may become entitled by inheritance, gift, grant, or devise, and the rents, profits, and income of such real estate, shall be and continue her own to the same extent after her marriage as before, liable for her own debts contracted before marriage, but free from liability for the debts or engagements of her husband. The wife is not, however, authorized to dispose of any such personal or real estate during coverture without the consent of her husband, except by the order of the judge of probate, or the proper court of the county; nor is the husband barred of his title by the courtesy, if his wife dies without disposing of her realty. (*c*)

(*a*) R. S. 379, 439. (*b*) Ib. 160. (*c*) Ib. 340.

4. *Frauds.*

The general provisions of the English statutes against fraudulent conveyances, and also to prevent frauds and perjuries, have been adopted in England. It is not necessary, however, that the consideration of any promise, contract, or agreement which is required to be in writing, should be expressed on the face thereof; but it may be proved by any other legal evidence. No action can be brought to charge any person by reason of any representation or assurance as to the ability, credit, character, or trade of another, except the same be in writing.

No mortgage of goods and chattels, nor conveyance of the same by way of mortgage, which is not followed by delivery and continued change of possession, will be valid against the creditors of the mortgagor, unless the same is filed in the proper office. Nor will any sale of goods and chattels be valid against the creditors of either vendor or vendee, unless followed by a change of possession, or unless the persons claiming under the same, can show that it was made in good faith and without any intention of defrauding creditors or purchasers. (*a*)

5. *Limited Partnerships.*

The laws of Michigan allow the formation of limited partnerships upon conditions, and under restrictions, substantially the same as those already enumerated in the chapter on Maine. (*b*)

6. *Limitation of Actions.*

All actions of debt, founded upon any contract or liability not under seal, except such as are brought upon the judgment or decree of any court of record of the United States, or one of the states thereof, all actions of assumpsit or upon the case founded on contract, and all actions of replevin and trover, must be brought within six years from the time the cause of action accrues. This limitation does not apply to actions brought upon

(*a*) R. S. 325 to 329.

the bills, notes, or other evidences of debt issued by a bank. Where the action is brought to recover the balance due upon a mutual or open account current, the cause of action shall be deemed to have accrued at the date of the last item. All personal actions upon other contracts must be brought within ten years, and not thereafter. Infants, feme coverts, persons non compos mentis, insane, imprisoned, or absent from the United States at the time any cause of action accrues on their behalf, may bring the same at any time within the period of limitation after the removal of their disability. Where any person is absent from the state at the time a cause of action accrues against him, or subsequently leaves the state, such period of absence is not to be taken as a part of the limitation. Suit may be commenced within two years from the discovery of any cause of action which has been fraudulently concealed.

In actions upon any contract, express or implied, no new promise or acknowledgment shall withdraw a case from the operation of the statute, unless the same is in writing; nor can one of two or more joint contractors or executors deprive the other of the benefit of the statute by any written acknowledgment. This provision does not vary the common law effect of a partial payment; but no endorsement or memorandum of such payment by, or on behalf of the party to whom it purports to have been made, is to be taken as sufficient proof of such payment. (*a*)

7. *Attachment.*

Any creditor may proceed against the property of his debtor, both real and personal, by attachment in the Circuit or County Court, where the debt, over and above all legal set-offs, exceeds the sum of one hundred dollars, where before executing the writ the creditor, or some one in his behalf, makes and annexes to the writ an affidavit, stating that the defendant is indebted to the plaintiff, and specifying the amount of such indebtedness as near as may be, over and above all legal set-offs, and that the same is due upon contract express or implied, or upon judgment, and containing a further statement, that the deponent knows, or has good reason

(*a*) R. S. 600.

to believe, either, 1st, that the defendant has absconded, or is about to abscond from the state, or that he is concealed therein to the injury of his creditors; or, 2d, that the defendant has assigned, disposed of, or concealed, or is about to assign, dispose of, or conceal any of his property, with intent to defraud his creditors; or, 3d, that the defendant has removed, or is about to remove any of his property out of the state, with intent to defraud his creditors; or, 4th, that he fraudulently contracted the debt, or incurred the obligation, respecting which the suit is brought; or, 5th, that the defendant is not a resident of the state, and has not resided therein for three months immediately preceding the time of making such affidavit; or, 6th, that the defendant is a foreign corporation.

Goods and chattels are bound by an attachment from the time of serving the writ; but to create a lien upon real estate, a certified copy of the writ, with a description of the realty, must be deposited in the office of the register of deeds of the county where the same is situate. If it appears by the return of the writ that either of the defendants has been served personally, the suit proceeds as in ordinary cases; if there has been no personal service, but property of the defendant has been attached, the plaintiff is required to publish in a newspaper of the county, or judicial circuit, for six successive weeks, a notice of the attachment, after which, upon filing an affidavit of the fact, he may file his declaration and proceed as if a copy had been served on the defendant. Where perishable property has been attached, it may be sold pending the proceedings by order of the court. Where there has been no personal service, a judgment is rendered in the ordinary form, but it is not conclusive upon the defendant, and on an execution thereupon, the officer is only authorized to sell the property attached.

In cases of joint indebtedness, the writ of attachment may issue against the separate or joint estate of such debtors, or any of them. (*a*)

There are similar provisions authorizing and regulating attachments in justices' courts. They will be found in the Revised Statutes of 1846, from 389 to 393.

(*a*) R. S. 513 to 517.

Attachment of boats.—The laws of Michigan give a lien upon ships, boats, and vessels used in navigating the waters of the state, for debts contracted by the master, owner, agent or consignee for supplies for its use, or material or labor expended upon it, or for wharfage, or for damages arising from the non-performance of any contract of affreightment or the transportation of persons or property. (*a*)

8. *Insolvent Law.*

There are two classes of provisions for the relief of insolvent debtors; first, those which relieve the debtor from imprisonment on any existing debts; and second, those which discharge him from the obligation of such debts. The petition, in either case, may be presented to a judge of the Supreme Court, or a commissioner of the Circuit Court, or a county judge, provided that he resides in the county in which the petitioning debtor resides or is imprisoned. In the first case, the petition of the insolvent must pray that his estate may be assigned for the benefit of all his creditors, and that his person may thereafter be exempted from arrest or imprisonment, by reason of any debts arising upon contracts previously made, or of any judgments existing against him in civil cases, and if in prison, that he may be discharged from imprisonment. Such petition must be accompanied by a schedule containing an account of his creditors, with the places of their residence, the amount and nature of their debts, and a complete inventory of all the estate, real and personal, legal and equitable, of the petitioner, and also an affidavit of the correctness of the schedule, and that the debtor has not, at any time or in any manner whatsoever, disposed of any part of his estate for his future benefit, or that of his family, or in order to defraud any of his creditors, and that he has not paid or in any way compounded with any of his creditors, with a view to procure them to refrain from opposing his discharge. The officer receiving this order shall make an order requiring the creditors of the petitioner to show cause, at a time and place specified in the order, why the prayer of the same should not be granted; and notice of the contents of this order must be given, by personal service or mail, to

(*a*) R. S. 537

each creditor. Any creditor who opposes the discharge of an insolvent debtor, may file a specification of his objections in writing, and demand a trial of their validity by a jury, who may hear the proofs and allegations of the parties, and determine the matter submitted to them. Upon the hearing of such petition before the jury or otherwise, the insolvent may be examined on oath touching any matters stated in his schedule, and may be required to state any changes which may have occurred in the situation of his property since making the same; and if he has made any transfer of his real or personal estate, or collected any debts since making the schedule, he will be required to pay forthwith to the officer the full value of the property so transferred, or debt so collected, except such as may have been expended in the necessary support of himself and family; and no discharge can be granted unless such payment is made, or secured to be made, within thirty days, to the assignees of the insolvent. If, upon the hearing of the case, it shall appear that the debtor, in contemplation of his insolvency or of his petitioning for a discharge under the provisions of the act, or knowing his insolvency, has made any assignment, absolute or conditional, of any part of his estate, or confessed a judgment, or given any security, with a view to give a preference to any creditor for an antecedent debt, he will not be entitled to a discharge.

Where the jury finds in favor of the petitioner, or the officer is satisfied of the truth of the petition, the latter may direct an assignment to be made to such persons as he shall designate of all the estate of the debtor, excepting articles which are exempted from sale on execution. This assignment will vest in the assignees all the interest, whether legal or equitable, positive or contingent, which the debtor may at that time possess in any real or personal property. The assignment is to be recorded in the office of the register of deeds for the county. The officer shall thereupon grant a discharge, declaring that the person of the debtor shall be forever afterwards exempt from imprisonment upon any debt due at the time of making the assignment, or contracted for before that time, though payable afterwards, or of any judgment in any civil suit existing against him at the time of such assignment, and by reason of any liabilities incurred by him by making or indorsing any promissory note or bill of exchange, or incurred by him in consequence of the payment by any party to such note or bill of the whole or any part of the money secured thereby. This discharge does not affect the liability of the insolvent to arrest for any of the causes enumerated under the title of "*Proceedings in Civil Suits,*" as authorizing the emanation of a capias or a ca. sa. The property of the insolvent, acquired after the execution of the assignment, still remains liable for his precedent as well as subsequent debts. A debtor of the United States cannot be exonerated from imprisonment by such discharge, in any suit or proceeding founded upon such debt. The discharge will be completely vitiated, if there has been on the part of the insolvent any perjury, fraud, composition, or collusion.

An insolvent can only be released from the obligation of his debts, where his petition is also signed by creditors whose claims amount to two-thirds of his entire indebtedness within the United States. Executors or administrators may become petitioning creditors for the discharge of an insolvent. The proceedings in this case, as to the petition schedule, affidavit, notice, trial, and assignment, are precisely similar to those just described. The discharge, when granted, exonerates the debtor from all debts due at the time of the assignment, or contracted for before that time, though payable afterwards, founded upon any contracts made within the state, or to be executed within the state, and from all debts whatever owing to any person uniting in the petition, or who has accepted a dividend from the estate of the insolvent, and from all liabilities incurred by such insolvent by making or indorsing any bill of exchange or promissory note before the execution of his assignment, or incurred by him by reason of the payment by any party to such note or bill of the whole or any part of the money secured thereby, whether such payment be made prior or subsequent to the execution of the assignment. This discharge will be invalid for the same reasons as that which releases the debtor only from imprisonment.

A corporation is deemed a creditor within the meaning of this law, and may present or unite in any petition as other creditors.

Assignees appointed under the provisions of the insolvent law, are deemed to be trustees of the estate of the debtor for the benefit of his creditors, and are subject to be controlled or removed for proper cause by the Circuit Court of the county in which they reside. It is their duty to take possession of the entire estate of the insolvent, to collect its debts, to convert the realty and personalty as speedily as possible into money, to call in all claims against the insolvent, and adjust the same, either personally with the creditor or by reference to arbitration, and within fifteen months from the time of their appointment to call a general meeting of the creditors, at some time not more distant than three nor less distant than two months, for adjusting all demands against the estate, and declaring the amount of the assets. The assignees, after deducting their necessary disbursements and a commission of five per cent. on the amount of assets, shall discharge all debts entitled to a preference by the laws of the United States, and then pay all debts which may be owing by the debtor as guardian, executor, administrator, or trustee. The residue shall be distributed equally among all those who were creditors at the time of making the assignment, and who have presented their claims as such, and whose debts have been ascertained, in proportion to their respective demands. Where the claim of a creditor is not due, he may receive his proportion of the dividend by deducting a rebate of legal interest. Where the whole estate of the debtor is not distributed upon the first dividend, the assignees shall make a similar dividend from year to year so long as any money remains in their hands. A creditor who has neglected to deliver to the assignees an account of his demand before the first dividend, and who delivers the same before the second dividend, shall receive the proportion to which he would have been entitled in the former dividend, before any distribution is made to the creditors. (*a*)

9. *Proceedings in Civil Suits.*

Bail.—Personal actions may be commenced either by a writ of summons, or a capias ad respondendum. In either case, where the plaintiff is a non-resident of the state, the writ must be indorsed by some responsible inhabitant of the state, who thereby

(*a*) R. S. 607 to 625.

becomes liable for costs. In actions upon contracts, express or implied, a capias can only issue where the action is to recover damages for any breach of promise to marry, or for money, collected by any public officer, or for any misconduct or neglect in office, or any professional employment where the plaintiff or some are in his behalf, makes and attaches to the writ an affidavit, stating that he has a claim for damages against the defendant, for the cause of action therein stated, and upon which he believes that he or the plaintiff is entitled to recover a certain sum, being more than one hundred dollars. (*a*) But a warrant to arrest the defendant may issue in other cases, where the plaintiff establishes by his own affidavit or that of some other person, that there is a debt due to him from the defendant, specifying the nature and amount thereof as near as may be, for which the defendant cannot be imprisoned, and one or more of the following particulars:

1. That the defendant is about to remove any of his property out of the jurisdiction of the court where the suit is brought, with intent to defraud his creditor; or

2. That the defendant has property or rights in action which he fraudulently conceals, or that he has rights in action, or some interest in public or corporate stock, money, or evidence of debt, which he unjustly refuses to apply to the payment of any judgment or decree which shall have been rendered against him, belonging to the complainant; or

3. That he has assigned, removed, or disposed of, or is about to dispose of any of his property, with the intent to defraud his creditor or creditors; or

4. That the defendant fraudulently contracted the debt or incurred the obligation respecting which suit is brought.

The defendant may controvert the truth of the plaintiff's allegation, before the court or officer having jurisdiction of the cause, and he will be discharged or committed according to the result of the trial. (*b*)

A defendant arrested upon a capias may release his body by executing a bail bond with sufficient sureties, or he may obtain the liberty of the jail limits, which are coextensive with the county, on giving a bond with sufficient surety that he will not escape.

(*a*) R. S. 432, 434.

(*b*) Ib. 604 to 607.

Organization of courts.—The jurisdiction over civil actions is mainly distributed between the County Courts and the Circuit Courts. The former are courts of record, held in each county on the first Monday of every month, and having original and exclusive jurisdiction in civil actions, where the damages claimed do not exceed five hundred dollars. No cause can be continued in the County Court for a longer term than three months. Where a judgment has been rendered in the County Court, whether upon confession or on trial, the defendant may at any time within ten days, stay the execution thereon, by filing with the clerk satisfactory security in writing for the payment of the judgment, interest, and costs; and if this obligation is broken, execution may at once issue against the surety as well as the principal. (*a*)

The Circuit Courts have jurisdiction in all cases where the damages claimed exceed five hundred dollars. They are held at least once a year in every county, and twice a year in the greater number. There is no provision for the stay of execution upon the judgments of this court.

Judgment and execution. (*b*)—The entire estate of a debtor, both real and personal, including estates in remainder and reversion, and equities of redemption, may be sold upon an execution on a judgment at law or decree in Chancery. The lien, however, of a judgment only attaches from the time of actually levying the writ of execution. Execution may issue as of right, at any time within two years from the rendition of the judgment. Where several executions have issued against the same defendant, that which was first delivered to the officer shall have priority, although a subsequent execution may have been previously levied, provided no sale has taken place under such levy.

The writ of capias ad satisfaciendum, may issue upon a judgment in any of the cases already specified, where the party may be arrested on mesne process, and is subject to the same conditions and restrictions. No female, however, can be imprisoned upon any process in any civil action.

A debtor who has been imprisoned on execution for a certain length of time, as for example nine months where the debt exceeds five hundred dollars, six months where it exceeds one but

(*a*) R. S. 378 to 382. (*b*) Ib. 474 to 480.

not five hundred dollars, may be discharged from confinement on his giving notice of his inability to pay the debt, and his desire to take the benefit of the law for the relief of poor debtors, and making oath, and establishing to the satisfaction of the officer, that he has no estate except such as is exempt from execution, to the value of twenty dollars, and that he has no estate then concealed or conveyed, with design to secure the same to his own use, or that of his family, or to defraud his creditors. The law then provides that the debtor shall not only be exempt from future imprisonment for such debt, but that he shall be discharged from the same. There are many cases in which this clause would impair the obligation of contracts, and as to them it is of course null and void. (*a*) See farther the provisions for insolvent debtors under the title, "*Insolvent Law.*"

Upon the writ of fieri facias, not only the goods and chattels, but in case of their insufficiency, the real estate of the defendant may be sold. Money, bills, or evidences of debt issued by any moneyed corporation and circulated as money, the interest of a stockholder in any joint stock company, the interest of a bailor in goods or chattels pledged by way of mortgage or security for the performance of any contract, and all other goods liable to execution at common law, unless specially exempted, may be taken and sold. The amount of property exempt from execution is very considerable.

Remedy against sheriffs and attorneys.—Any attorney, sheriff, justice of the peace, or other officer, having collected money belonging to another, and refusing to pay it over within a reasonable time after a demand thereof, shall be deemed guilty of a misdemeanor, and on conviction may be punished by imprisonment in the county jail, for not more than one year, or by a fine not exceeding four times the amount thus received, or by both, at the discretion of the officer. (*b*) Where any officer unreasonably neglects to pay over money collected by him on execution, when demanded by the creditor, he is liable for five times the lawful interest in addition to the principal, from the time of the demand until payment. (*c*)

(*a*) R. S. 624. Acts of 1847, 172. (*b*) R. S. 666. (*c*) Ib. 479.

10. *Administration of the Estates of Deceased Persons.*

Letters testamentary or of administration are granted to the proper person by Courts of Probate. It is the duty of executors or administrators to make and return to the Probate Court, within three months from their qualification, a complete inventory of the estate of the deceased, to administer the same according to law and the will of the testator, to pay debts and legacies, and to render an account of his administration to the Probate Court within one year, and at any other time which may be required. The widow of a deceased person, besides her wearing apparel and ornaments, may take any quantity of the household furniture not exceeding in value two hundred and fifty dollars, and any other personal property not exceeding in value two hundred dollars. The widow and children are allowed such provision from the personal estate as the Court of Probate may think sufficient for their maintenance during the settlement of the estate, which, in case of an insolvent estate, is not to continue for a longer period than one year from the time of granting administration, nor for any time after the assignment to the widow of her dower and personalty. Where the deceased person leaves children under seven years of age, having no mother, or where the mother dies before they reach such age, it is the duty of the Probate Court to make an allowance for their maintenance, until they arrive at such age, out of the personal estate and the income of the real estate which would have been assigned to the mother, if living. The personal estate is the primary fund for the payment of debts, but in case of its insufficiency, the real estate (saving the widow's dower) may be sold under a license to be obtained from the Court of Probate, on a petition filed by the executor or administrator, setting forth the necessary facts, and affording an opportunity fo. all persons interested to controvert the same. The proceeds of the sale are deemed assets in the hands of executors or administrators, and their sureties are responsible for the proper application of the same. Where there are any debts existing against a deceased person, it is the duty of the Probate Court, after granting letters testamentary or of administration, to appoint two or more suitable persons as commissioners, to receive, examine, and adjust all claims against the deceased. It is the duty of such commissioners to appoint a convenient time and place for executing their commission, and to give notice of the same within sixty days, to all creditors, and also of the time which the Court of Probate may allow for the presentation of their claims; the notice to be given both by posted advertisement and newspaper publication, for four weeks successively. The Probate Court shall allow such time to creditors for the presentation of their claims as the circumstances of the case may require, not in the first instance to exceed eighteen or fall short of six months, nor to be extended for any case beyond the period of two years from the date of the commission. Creditors not presenting their claim within the time allowed, are forever barred. After the appointment of commissioners, no personal action can be brought against an executor or administrator, nor can any attachment or execution be issued against the estate of a deceased person until after the expiration of the period limited by the court for the payment of debts. The commissioners are empowered and directed to decide upon all claims against the deceased, and to report a list of such as may be allowed, at the expiration of the time limited for presentation. Any executor, administrator, or creditor, may appeal from the decision of the commissioners to the Circuit Court for the same county, upon application filed in the probate office within sixty days from the report of the commission: the appeal to be tried by such court, with the assistance of a jury, if any questions of fact are involved. Contingent claims may be presented to the commissioners, and if allowed, the Court of Probate may direct the executor or administrator to retain sufficient estate to pay the same, or its ratable proportion, when it becomes absolute. Upon the return of the report of the commissioners, the Court of Probate shall make a decree for the distribution of assets among the creditors, within some time, in the first instance not exceeding eighteen months, but which may be extended from time to time, on the application of the executor or administrator, showing good cause, for periods of one year, provided that the entire term thus allowed is not to exceed four years. It is the duty of the executor or administrator to give notice, by publication, for three successive weeks, in some newspaper to be designated by the Court of Probate, of the time limited for the payment of debts; and any creditor neglecting to present his claim for two years from the date of the last publication, is for ever barred.

Where the assets of the deceased are not sufficient for the payment of all his debts, the following order is to be observed, after paying the necessary expenses of administration:

1st. The necessary funeral expenses.

2d. The expenses of the last sickness.

3d. Debts having a preference by the laws of the United States.

4th. Debts due to other creditors.

No creditor of one class is to receive any portion of his debt until all those of the preceding class have been fully paid.

Before the account of any administrator or executor will be allowed, notice must be given to all persons interested, of the time and place of examining the same. Where the executor or administrator neglects to render his account at the proper time after being duly cited by the Court of Probate, he is liable upon his official bond for any damage which may ensue. (*a*)

(*a*) R. S. 282, 307.

WISCONSIN.

1. ASSURANCES OF DEBT.
2. INTEREST.
3. STATUTE OF FRAUDS.
4 LIMITED PARTNERSHIPS.
5. EFFECT OF MARRIAGE UPON RIGHTS OF PROPERTY.
6. LIMITATION OF ACTIONS.
7. ASSIGNMENTS BY INSOLVENT DEBTOR.
8. ATTACHMENT.
9. PROCEEDINGS IN CIVIL SUITS.
10. EFFECT OF DEATH UPON THE RIGHTS OF CREDITORS.
11. COURTS.

1. *Assurances of Debt.*

Book accounts.—Book accounts are made evidence in certain cases, where confirmed by the oath of the plaintiff or his clerk or agent. The books must be produced at the trial of the cause, and the party must swear that they are his account books, that they contain the original entries of charges for goods or other articles delivered, or work and labor or other services performed, or materials found, and that such entries are just to the best of his knowledge and belief: that said entries are in his own handwriting, and that they were made at or about the time said goods or other articles were delivered, said work and labor or other services were performed, or said materials were found. (*a*)

Whenever the original entries are in the handwriting of an agent, the oath of such agent may be admitted to establish the same. But these books shall not be admitted as testimony of any item of money delivered at one time exceeding five dollars, or of money paid to third persons, or of charges of rent.

(*a*) Acts of 1838–39, 249, 250.

When a book has marks which show that the items have been transferred to a ledger, the book shall not be testimony unless the ledger be produced. (*a*)

Effect of scroll.—Any instrument to which the person making the same shall affix any device by way of seal, is to be taken to have the same force and obligation as if it were actually sealed. (*b*)

Bills of exchange and promissory notes.—All notes for a sum of money, payable to any person or order, or to bearer, are negotiable in like manner as inland bills of exchange, according to the custom of merchants, and the payees or indorsees of every such note may maintain an action thereon against the makers and indorsers of the same respectively, as in cases of inland bills of exchange, and not otherwise. (*c*)

Rate of damages upon protested bills.—The drawer or indorser of a bill of exchange drawn upon any person or body politic out of the United States or the territories thereof, which has been duly presented and protested for non-acceptance, and who have been duly notified thereof, shall pay the bill with legal interest, and twenty per cent. damages in addition, together with costs and charges of protest. (*d*)

When such bill is drawn upon a person or body politic, or corporation, in an adjacent state or territory, the damages are reduced to five per cent. (*e*)

When the bill is drawn upon any person or body politic in one of the United States or its territories, but not adjoining this state, the damages are fixed at ten per cent. (*f*)

Notary public.—By act of '41, 26, it is declared that full faith and credit shall be given to the attestations, protestations, and other instruments of publication, under seal, of all notaries public appointed in any state or territory of the United States. (*g*)

It is made the duty of every notary public, when any bill of exchange, promissory note, or other written instrument, is protested by him, for non-acceptance or non-payment, to give written notice thereof to the makers and indorsers; and where the persons protested reside within two miles of the residence of the notary, to

(*a*) Acts of 1838–39, 249, 250. (*b*) R. S. 156. (*c*) Ib. 175. (*d*) Ib. 174. (*e*) Ib. 174. (*f*) Ib. 174 (*g*) Ib. 85.

serve the notice personally. It is also made his duty to keep a record of such notices, and the time and manner of their service, the names of the parties, and which record is declared to be at all times competent evidence to prove such notices. (*a*)

2. *Interest.*

Upon all bills of exchange, promissory notes, contracts, debts, or demands, wherein the rate of interest is not specified, seven per cent. per annum shall be allowed.

No bank or corporation, unless otherwise provided in their charter, shall take, directly or indirectly, more than seven per cent. per annum.

With this exception, the parties to a contract may stipulate for any rate of interest not exceeding twelve per cent. per annum.

When a greater rate of interest than that which is allowed by law has been taken by any person or corporation, the person so paying may recover three times the amount of the excess of interest, in an action of assumpsit before any court of competent jurisdiction: provided that such suit be commenced within one year from the day of payment of such excess. (*b*)

3. *Statute of Frauds.*

In the following cases, every agreement shall be void, unless such agreement, or some note or memorandum thereof, *expressing the consideration*, be in writing and signed by the party charged therewith:

1. Every agreement that by the terms is not to be performed within one year from the making thereof.

2. Every special promise to answer for the debt, default, or miscarriage of another person.

3. Every agreement, promise, or undertaking made upon consideration of marriage, except mutual promises to marry.

4. Every contract for the sale of any goods, chattels, or things in action, for the price of fifty dollars or more, shall be void, un-

(*a*) R. S. 84. (*b*) Ib. 156.

less—1. A note or memorandum of such contract be made in writing, and be subscribed by the parties charged therewith: or, 2. Unless the buyer shall accept and receive part of such goods, or the evidences, or some of them, of such things in action: or, 3. Unless the buyer shall at the time pay some part of the purchase money. (*a*)

4. *Limited Partnerships.*

Limited partnerships for the transaction of agricultural, mercantile, mechanical, mining, smelting, or manufacturing business, and for no other purpose, are authorized by law.

Such partnerships must consist of one or more persons, who shall be called general partners, and be jointly and severally responsible, as general partners are by law, and of one or more persons who shall contribute in actual cash payments, a specified sum as capital, to the common stock, who shall be called special partners, and shall not be liable beyond the fund so contributed.

The general partners only have authority to transact business, and sign for the partnership and bind the same.

The business must be conducted under the name of the general partners only, without the addition of the word company, or any other general term: and any special partner allowing his name to be used in the firm, shall be deemed a general partner.

A special partner may from time to time examine into the state of the partnership concerns, and advise as to their management: but if he transacts any business on its account, or acts as its agent, attorney, or otherwise, he shall be deemed a general partner.

In case of the insolvency or bankruptcy of the partnership, no special partner, under any circumstances, shall be allowed to claim as a creditor, until the claims of all the other creditors of the partnership shall be satisfied.

No part of the sum which any special partner shall have contributed to the capital stock shall be liable for any debts previously contracted by the general partners: nor shall any part of such sum be withdrawn by him, or transferred to him, in the shape of

(*a*) Acts of 1838–39, 163.

dividends, profits, or otherwise, during the continuance of the partnership. And where it shall appear that the original capital has been reduced by the payment of interest or profits to any special partner, such partner shall be bound to make good his share of the capital, with interest. But unless the original capital is thereby reduced, any partner may receive interest and profits on the sum contributed by him.

All sales, assignments, and transfers of the property of the partnership, or of the general or special partners, made in contemplation of insolvency, with intent to prefer some general or separate creditor, to the creditors in general of the partnership, are declared to be void against such creditors: and any special partner concurring in or assenting to such act, renders himself liable as a general partner.

Suits in relation to the partnership may be brought and conducted against the general partners in the same manner as if there were no special partners.

Persons desirous of forming a special partnership must make and severally sign a certificate, containing the name under which the partnership is to be conducted, the general nature of the business, the names of all the general and special partners interested therein, distinguishing which are general and which are special partners, and their respective places of residence, the amount of capital which each special partner shall have contributed to the common stock, and the period at which the partnership is to commence, and at which it is to terminate. This certificate is to be acknowledged and certified in the same manner as if it were a deed, and recorded and filed in the office of the register of deeds of the county in which the principal place of business of the partnership is situated: and where the partnership has places of business in different counties, a transcript of the certificate, duly certified, is to be filed in the office of the register of each. An affidavit of one or more of the general partners must be filed at the same time, stating that the sums specified in the certificate have been contributed by each of the special partners to the common stock, and have been actually and in good faith paid in cash. And until these requisitions have been complied with, the partnership is not to be considered as formed: and for any false statement in the certificate or affidavit, all the persons interested in the partnership shall be liable as general partners.

The partnership is also to be deemed general, unless immediately after the registry, the terms thereof are published in a newspaper of the county where the principal business is carried on; or if there be no newspaper in such county, then in the newspaper published nearest thereto. An affidavit of the publication of such notice, by the printer of the newspaper, may be filed in the registry office of the county where the principal business is carried on, and shall be evidence of the facts therein stated.

The proceedings required on the original formation of a partnership must take place on its renewal or continuance. So, an alteration of any matters specified in the original certificate, is to be deemed a dissolution of the partnership; and if carried on subsequently without any renewal as a special partnership, is to be deemed a general partnership.

No dissolution of a limited partnership can take place by any acts of the parties, previous to the time specified in the certificate of its formation or renewal, until a notice of such dissolution shall have been filed and recorded in the register's office in which the original certificate was recorded, and published once in each week for four weeks in some newspaper published in the county or adjacent thereto. (*a*)

5. *Effect of Marriage upon the Rights of Property.*

Under the constitution of Wisconsin all property, whether real or personal, owned by a woman at the time of marriage, or acquired during coverture, remains her separate property, and is liable for her separate debts, contracted before marriage.

6. *Limitation of Actions.*

In the act concerning executors, administrators, and guardians, it is provided that no suit shall be commenced against any execu-

(*a*) R. S. 153, 156.

tor or administrator, as such, unless within four years from the time of his accepting the trust: provided notice of his appointment be given in the manner prescribed by law. (*a*)

In the act concerning the proceedings of courts of record, there is a provision that the term of eighteen months after the death of any testator or intestate shall not be deemed any part of the time limited by law for the commencement of actions against his executors or administrators. (*b*)

All actions of debt founded upon any contract or liability, not under seal, except such as are brought upon the judgment or decree of some court of record of the United States, or a state or territory thereof; all actions upon judgments rendered in any court not being a court of record; all actions for arrears of rent; all actions of assumpsit or upon the case, founded upon any contract or liability, express or implied, must be commenced within six years after the cause of action shall accrue. (*c*)

The preceding limitation does not apply to any action brought upon a promissory note which is signed in the presence of an attesting witness, by the original payee, his executor or administrator, nor to an action brought upon any bills, notes, or other evidences of debt, issued by any bank. (*d*)

In all actions of debt or assumpsit, brought to recover the balance of a mutual and open account current, the cause of action shall be deemed to have accrued at the time of the last item proved in such account. (*e*)

All other personal actions founded upon contract must be brought within twenty years from the time that the cause of action accrues. (*f*)

Where any cause of action is fraudulently concealed by any party liable thereto, the same may be commenced within six years after the discovery of the liability. (*g*)

Where a party liable to a cause of action is out of the state at the time when it accrues, it may be commenced within the time limited, after his return to the state: so, if after the accruing of a cause of action, the party liable thereto should be absent from the territory, the period of his absence is not to be considered a part of the limitation. (*h*)

(*a*) R. S. 314. (*b*) Ib. 212. (*c*) Ib. 261. (*d*) Ib. 261. (*e*) Ib. 261. (*f*) Ib. 261. (*g*) Ib. 262. (*h*) Ib. 261.

Infants, feme coverts, persons non compos mentis, imprisoned or absent from the United States, may bring any action within the period of the preceding limitations, after the removal of their respective disabilities. (*a*)

7. *Assignments by Insolvent Debtor.*

No conveyance or assignment made by any insolvent debtor to assignees or trustees for the use of any of his creditors, shall be valid or effectual against any attachment or execution in behalf of any creditor who is not a party to it, unless it is so made as to allow all the creditors of the debtor to become parties to it, if they see fit, and unless also it is so made as to give each of the creditors who shall become parties to it, an equal share of the property in proportion to their respective debts, excepting only such creditors as may, by the laws of the United States or of the state, be entitled to a preference. (*b*)

The insolvent law of Wisconsin provides for assignments by insolvent debtors, which shall have the effect of discharging them from all debts due to creditors who may become parties thereto: the discharge however not to operate as a release of any person liable for the same debt with the insolvent, as a partner, joint contractor, endorser, acceptor or surety. (*c*)

A schedule must be annexed to such assignments, containing 1. A full and true account of all the creditors of the debtor to the best of his knowledge and belief. 2. Their places of residence. 3. The amount, nature and security of each debt, as near as may be. 4. The true consideration of each case of indebtedness, and the place where it accrued. 5. A statement of any existing judgment, mortgage, or collateral security for any such debt. 6. A full and true inventory of all the estate, real and personal, legal and equitable, of the insolvent, except such as is exempt from execution; of the incumbrances existing thereon, and the books, vouchers and securities relating thereto. The debtor is to make an affidavit to be annexed to the assignment, of the correctness of the schedule, and that he has not in any manner or at any time disposed of any part of his estate for the future benefit of himself

(*a*) R. S. 261. (*b*) Ib. 172. (*c*) Ib. 171.

or family, or to defraud any of his creditors; and that he has in no instance acknowledged a debt for a greater sum than was honestly due. The assignment must be so made as to give to each of the creditors becoming parties to it, their proportion of the property without any preference, excepting as to such debts as by the laws of the United States or the territory may be entitled to a preference.

All creditors shall have a right to become parties to the assignment, provided they apply before the final dividend is declared: but no creditor who comes in after any dividend, shall be allowed to disturb the same, but he shall receive an equal proportion with the other creditors, so far as the funds then remaining unappropriated in the hands of the assignee, shall be sufficient therefor.

All persons are to be considered as creditors, who are liable as endorsers or sureties upon any bill, note, bond or other contract, made by the debtor before the date of the assignment, and which shall become absolute before the final dividend of the assigned property. The estate is to be distributed by the assignees under the superintendence of the District Court.

The discharge shall not avail the debtor if, upon a suit subsequently brought, the creditor can establish that the debtor has fraudulently concealed or disposed of property which the laws do not exempt from execution, to the amount of one hundred dollars, or that he knowingly made any false statement concerning the amount and disposition of his property, or that at any time after the passage of this law, and in contemplation of such an assignment of his property, he made any transfer thereof or any payment, with a view to give any creditor a preference over others. (*a*)

A debtor, whose body has been taken in execution, may release himself from imprisonment, and future arrest for the same debt, upon taking an oath of insolvency. This discharge, however, is not to impair or in any way affect the right of the plaintiff to take out a new execution against the goods and estate which the debtor may subsequently acquire. (*b*)

But as to imprisonment for debt, see title "Proceedings in Civil Suits."

(*a*) R. S. 170 to 173. (*b*) Ib. 172.

8. *Attachment.*

Foreign attachment.—A creditor may sue out an attachment against his debtor, before a justice of the peace, where the debtor resides out of the county and more than one hundred miles from the residence of the justice before whom suit is brought, (*a*) or where he is a non-resident of the state, or where he has absconded or concealed himself, so that the ordinary process of law can not be served upon him, or where he is about to abscond or remove his property, so as to hinder and delay his creditors, or where there is good reason to believe that he is about fraudulently to dispose of his property, so as to hinder or delay his creditors. The debt must not exceed fifty dollars, or fall below five.

The action must be brought before some justice of the county wherein the property of the defendant may be found. (*b*) The creditor or some credible person must first file an affidavit with the justice, stating that the defendant is justly indebted to him, in a sum above five dollars, after all just offsets and credits; stating the amount, and also his belief of the existence of one or more of the facts which are necessary to entitle the plaintiff to this writ.

Before issuing the writ of attachment, the justice shall take from such applicant a bond to the defendant with at least two sufficient sureties, in the sum of two hundred dollars, conditioned to pay the defendant all damages and costs he may sustain by reason thereof, if no judgment shall be recovered against him. (*c*)

The lands and tenements, goods and chattels, rights and credits, money and effects, of the debtor, except such as by law are exempt from execution, may be attached. (*d*)

The plaintiff may, upon an affidavit filed with the clerk, setting forth that the defendant has lands or chattels in another county, obtain a writ of attachment, directed to the sheriff of such county. (*e*)

Where two or more are jointly bound, either as joint obligors, partners, or otherwise, the writ of attachment may issue against

(*a*) Acts of 1844, 18. (*b*) Acts of 1838–39, 336. (*c*) Ib. (*d*) Acts of 1842, 22. (*e*) Acts of 1838–39, 168.

the separate or joint estates, or both, of such debtors or any of them, in the same manner as in other cases. (*a*)

Where judgment has been rendered in attachment, the officer may sell property in his hands, whether held by legal or equitable title, under the same restrictions and regulations as if the same had been levied upon by execution. The proceeds of sale are to be divided among the first attaching creditors, (if the two first attached at the same time,) and any balance distributed among the creditors who subsequently come in, pro rata, the judgments remaining, if the whole amount is not paid, as security for the residue, and upon which execution may issue as in ordinary cases. (*b*) At or before the second term after issuing the writ of attachment, all other creditors may come in and file their declarations. (*c*)

The writ of attachment is not abated by the death of the defendant. (*d*)

The defendant may at any time release his goods from attachment by executing to the plaintiff a bond in the penal sum of double the amount of the appraised value of the goods so attached, or the claims filed against him, with his sufficient surety, conditioned for the delivery of the property or its appraised value in money, to answer any judgment which may be obtained by the plaintiff. (*e*)

Where the plaintiff will make oath that he has good reason to believe that a garnishee, or other person, indebted to defendant or having his property in possession, will abscond before judgment and execution can be had against him, he may institute an action against such party by capias ad respondendum and hold him to special bail. (*f*)

Attachment of boats.—Boats and vessels which are used in navigating the waters of the state, are made liable for certain debts contracted by owner, master, or agent. (*g*)

Judicial attachment.—A writ of attachment may issue as the first process in personal actions, in the following cases and in no others:—1. In the case of a non-resident. 2. Where the defendant has departed or is about to depart from the state with

(*a*) Acts of 1838–39, 148. (*b*) Ib. 168. (*c*) Ib. 166.
(*d*) Ib. 168. (*e*) Ib. 166, 167. (*f*) Ib. 166. (*g*) R. S. 168.

intent to abscond. 3. Where the defendant is about fraudulently to remove or dispose of his property, so as to hinder or delay the creditor suing out such writ. (*a*)

The cause of action in every case must arise out of, be founded upon, or sound in contract, or upon the judgment or decree of some court of law or chancery. (*b*)

Such attachment can only be issued where the facts necessary to entitle the plaintiff to the writ are proven to the satisfaction of a district judge, or a Supreme Court commissioner of the proper county, by the affidavit of the plaintiff or some credible witness, stating the nature and amount of the plaintiff's demand, and the circumstances upon which the belief of such fact is founded; and the clerk can only issue the writ on the filing of the affidavit, indorsed by such officer with the fact of his satisfaction. It is competent for the defendant to traverse the affidavit, and disprove its allegations.

9. *Proceedings in Civil Suits.*

Bail.—Special bail can only be required in actions upon contracts, where the plaintiff or his agent makes affidavit before some probate or district judge, stating that the defendant is indebted to him, and in what sum, as he verily believes; and also, either that the defendant is a non-resident of the state, and that the debt was contracted therein, or that he is about to remove his residence from the state with intent to defraud his creditors. The officer before whom such affidavit is made, when satisfied of the truth of its statements, shall indorse upon the process an order that the defendant be held to bail in a penal sum double the amount so sworn to be due. (*c*)

Judgment and execution.—Judgments rendered in the district court constitute a lien upon the real estate of the debtor, in the county where such judgment has been rendered, and also in every other county where an attested copy of the judgment has been filed with the clerk of the District Court, from the day of such filing. (*d*)

This lien binds after acquired lands. A judgment remains a

(*a*) Acts of 1842, 21. (*b*) Ib. (*c*) R. S. 264. (*d*) Acts of 1841.

lien upon land for ten years and no longer, unless renewed by scire facias against the judgment debtor, his heirs, devisees, or terree tenants. (*a*)

The time, however, is not to be computed, during which execution is stayed by any order of court, or agreement of the parties, entered of record. There is a special proceeding, by which any debtor, upon notice to his creditors, may have his entire real estate valued, and such portion of his lands released from the lien as, according to the appraisement, exceed the quantity necessary to satisfy the judgment. Trust estate in lands may be taken on execution against the person for whose use they are held. (*b*)

But where judgment has been rendered on a debt secured by mortgage, the sheriff cannot sell the equity of redemption upon an execution under it. The judgment debtor may redeem real estate sold under execution, within two years from the date of the sale, upon payment of the principal sum with interest, at the rate of twelve per cent. per annum, and until the expiration of that period, he is entitled to remain in the possession of the real estate or chattels real. If the debtor does not redeem within two years, any of his creditors may do so, within the three months ensuing, upon payment of the purchase money and seven per cent. interest. (*c*)

Personal property is only bound from the time it is taken in execution. The stock of any incorporated company may be seized and sold as other personalty upon execution.

Under the constitution of Wisconsin, forty acres of land, or any lot or lots in a city, not exceeding one thousand dollars in value, are exempt from sale on execution, as a homestead. There are also the usual minor articles protected for the use of the family.

Execution must be taken out upon a judgment within two years, and may run into any county in the state.

Imprisonment for debt.—Imprisonment for debt was abolished in 1842, upon final process of execution in all civil cases, excepting in actions of trespass or tort. (*d*)

(*a*) R. S. 235. (*b*) Acts of 1838–39, 230. (*c*) R. S. 595.
(*d*) Acts of 1842, 58.

10. *Effect of Death upon the Rights of Creditors.*

The estates of deceased persons are administered under the direction and revision of Probate Courts, established in each county. (*a*)

The real estate of a deceased person may be sold for the discharge of his debts, but it is in no manner bound or affected by any judgment against his executor or administrator. (*b*)

Where the estate of a deceased person is insolvent, it will be distributed equally by the executor or administrator, among all creditors, whose claims have been allowed by two or more commissioners appointed by the judges of the Probate Court—debts to the state or the United States, expenses of funeral and last sickness, debts due for taxes and expenses of settlement, being first paid. (*c*)

11. *Courts.*

Original jurisdiction in civil causes is invested in District Courts, which are held in the spring and fall in each county of the state. The judges of the District Court constitute a Supreme Court, having appellate jurisdiction.

(*a*) R. S. 212. (*b*) Ib. 212. (*c*) Ib. 303.

IOWA.

1. *Choses in Action.*

Assignability of.—All bonds, bills and notes for the payment of money, are rendered negotiable and may be assigned, so as to vest the assignee with the right of action therein. (*a*)

But a suit cannot be brought upon any negotiable instrument against an indorser, without first suing the principal, unless the institution of such suit would have been unavailing, or the maker had absconded, or left the state, when the assigned instrument become due.

Rate of damages upon protested bills of exchange.—Five per cent. as damages, besides interest and charges of protest, are allowed upon all foreign bills duly protested for non-acceptance or non-payment.

2. *Interest.*

Six per cent. is the rate of interest established by law, but the parties may contract for ten per cent.

(*a*) Acts of 1839.

3. *Limited Partnerships.*

Limited partnerships are authorized under similar qualifications to those enumerated under the title, "Wisconsin."

4. *Effect of Marriage upon Rights of Property.*

The real estate of a married woman, possessed before coverture, or acquired after coverture in her own name, and as her own property, from any other source than the gift or purchase of her husband, is not liable for his debts. (*a*)

5. *Statute of Frauds.*

The English statute of frauds is substantially re-enacted. (*b*)

No bill of sale or other conveyance of personal property, where the vendor shall retain the actual possession of the property so conveyed, can pass any right to such property against existing creditors or subsequent purchasers without notice, unless such instrument be acknowledged before some justice of the peace for the county where the same is executed, and recorded in the office of the recorder of deeds for the county where the holder of the property resides. (*c*)

6. *Corporations.*

Under the constitution of Iowa, the real and personal property of the stockholders of any corporation, created after its adoption, are rendered liable for the debts of such corporation.

7. *Limitation of Actions.*

The statute of limitation of personal actions is believed to be the same as that of Michigan.

(*a*) Acts of 1846, 4.

(*b*) Acts of 1840, 76.

(*c*) Ib.

8. *Imprisonment for Debt.*

No person can be arrested, held to bail, or imprisoned upon any original, mesne, or final process or execution, issued in any civil suit. (*a*)

9. *Judgment and Execution.*

Judgments have the operation of a lien upon the real estate of the defendant, situate in the county, where the judgment has been rendered, from the day of the rendition thereof till after the expiration of ten years. A duly attested copy of such judgment, if filed and recorded in the office of the District Court of any other county, will give to it the same operation as a lien, as if it had been originally rendered in such county; but no execution is to issue upon such attested copy. No judgment shall have the effect of a lien upon any equitable interest of the debtor in real estate, unless such interest appears of record in the county where the real estate is situate. (*b*)

The personal and real estate of a debtor, including his equitable and possessory interest in lands, may be taken and sold under execution. But unless personally authorized by the debtor to do otherwise, it is the duty of the officer to seize and sell the personal estate in the first instance. Where real estate has been sold under execution, the debtor may redeem the same within one year from the sale, by paying to the clerk of the court, for the use of the purchaser, the amount of the purchase money with ten per cent. per annum added thereto. If not redeemed within this time by the defendant, it may be redeemed within three months by any judgment creditor of the debtor upon the same terms. (*c*)

Executions issued from any court of record are returnable within seventy days from the date of the same; except that where the execution is issued to any other county than that in which the judgment was rendered, there shall be one additional day for every twenty miles of distance between the seats of the two counties. (*d*)

(*a*) Acts of 1844, 22. (*b*) Acts of 1840, 76; and 1846, 33.
(*c*) Acts of 1849, 197; and 1846, 32. (*d*) Acts of 1839.

When a judgment is obtained in any of the District Courts against a person for a sum exceeding one hundred dollars, he may obtain a stay of execution by procuring one or more sufficient securities to acknowledge him or themselves as bail foi the payment of such judgment with interest and costs.

10. *Attachment.*

In actions founded upon contract, an attachment may be issued upon the affidavit of the creditor or his agent, setting forth, either that the debtor is a non-resident of the state, or that he is about to remove or dispose of his property with intent to defraud his creditors, or that he has absconded, so that the ordinary process of law cannot be served upon him. Before the writ is issued, the plaintiff must enter into bond, with sufficient sureties, to be filed in the clerk's office, conditioned to pay all damages which the defendant may sustain by reason of the attachment. If the defendant desires to contest the allegations of the affidavit, he may have a trial of the same by a jury, and if it is found in his favor the attachment will be dissolved.

11. *Miscellanies.*

The organization of courts, the administration of estates, and other provisions of general interest, are substantially similar to those of Wisconsin.

DELAWARE.

1. CHOSES IN ACTION.
2. INTEREST.
3. FRAUDS.
4. ASSIGNMENT BY INSOLVENT DEBTOR.
5. PRINCIPAL AND SURETY.
6. LIMITATION OF ACTIONS.
7. ATTACHMENT.
8. PROCEEDINGS IN CIVIL SUITS.
9. EFFECT OF DEATH UPON THE RIGHTS OF CREDITORS.
10. COURTS.

1. *Choses in Action*

All bonds and instruments in writing for the payment of money, payable to any person or order or assigns, may be assigned or indorsed, so as to give to the indorsee or assignee any right of action on the same, in his own name; and to deprive the assignor of any power by release or acknowledgment, after the transfer, of prejudicing the interest of the assignee. The assignment, however, of any specialty, must be under the hand and seal of the assignor, and in the presence of two credible witnesses. (*a*)

The assignee of a bond, however, takes it subject to all equities existing between the original parties. (*b*)

A scroll, ink or printed seal, is equivalent to wax in written instruments or contracts. (*c*)

Damages upon protested bills.—Where any bill of exchange drawn upon persons in a foreign country, is returned protested, the drawer and all others concerned shall pay the contents of the bill with twenty per cent. damages, in the same specie in which

(*a*) Revised Code, 43.

(*b*) Oliver for the use of Griffith *v.* Lowery, 2 Harr. 467.

(*c*) Griffith's Register, 1066.

the bill was drawn, or in current money of the government equivalent to that which was first paid to the drawer or indorser. (*a*)

2. *Interest.*

Six per cent. is the legal rate of interest, and all usurious contracts are void, and subject the lender to the forfeiture of his whole debt.

3. *Frauds.*

All promises to answer for the debt of another, in a sum under forty shillings, may be established by the oath of the party in whose favor the promise was made.

No action, however, shall be brought to charge any person upon a promise to pay the debt of another in a sum of the value of forty shillings and not exceeding ten pounds, or to charge an executor or administrator upon any special promise to answer damages out of his own estate, unless such promise be established by the oath of one credible witness, or some memorandum thereof in writing signed by the party to be charged.

No action shall be brought to charge any person upon any agreement made upon consideration of marriage, or upon any contract or sale of lands, tenements, or hereditaments, or any interest in or concerning them, or upon any agreement that is not to be performed within the space of one year, or to charge any person for the debt of another in a sum of the value of ten pounds and upwards, unless the same be reduced to writing, or some memorandum or note thereof be signed by the party or his agent.

Except for goods, wares, and merchandise sold and delivered, and other matters properly chargeable in an account, in which case the oath of the plaintiff, together with a book regularly and fairly kept, shall be allowed as evidence to charge the defendant with the sums therein contained. (*b*)

Items of cash, it has been held, are not properly chargeable in an account.

It is made essential to the validity of a bill of sale of personal

(*a*) R. C. 74. (*b*) Ib. 88.

property, that the possession thereof shall be delivered to the vendee as soon as may be convenient after the execution of the instrument, and if such property afterwards returns to the vendor, it shall be liable to his creditors. (*a*)

4. *Assignment by Insolvent Debtor.*

All assignments in contemplation of insolvency, in which some creditors are preferred to others, are declared fraudulent and wholly void; and such persons are for ever excluded from the benefit of the laws for the relief of insolvent debtors. (*b*)

The courts of Delaware have held that a voluntary assignment preferring creditors, made in Pennsylvania, in contemplation of insolvency, would not be sustained against a subsequent attachment by a citizen of Delaware, of effects of the insolvent found in that state. (*c*)

But where a citizen of Pennsylvania had taken the benefit of the insolvent laws of that state, in respect of a debt contracted there, though with a citizen of Massachusetts, the courts of Delaware, in the exercise of national comity, will so far respect the judgment of the Pennsylvania court as to discharge the insolvent from imprisonment in Delaware, though the assignment in Pennsylvania, as preferring creditors, would have been illegal in Delaware. (*d*)

5. *Principal and Surety.*

Any surety or joint debtor who discharges the obligation to the creditor, is entitled to call for an assignment of the bond, judgment, or other evidence of debt, and is invested with all the rights of proceeding upon the same against the principal debtor, that belonged to the creditor. The assignment must be under the hand and seal of the assignor, and in the presence of two witnesses. The assignee, before resorting to any process by virtue of the rights thus acquired, must exhibit an account of the sum remaining due from the defendant, verified by affidavit. (*e*)

(*a*) R. C. 75. (*b*) R. S. 139. (*c*) Maberry & Pollard *v.* Shisler, 1 Harr. 349. (*d*) Fisher *v.* Stayton, 3 Harr. 271. (*e*) R. C. 43, 44, 45.

It is held in this state that the relation of principal and surety continues after judgment, in the eye of a court of equity, and that the latter may obtain in that forum the benefit of those equitable principles, to which he was entitled under his original character, at law. (*a*)

6. *Limitation of Actions.*

All actions of replevin, detinue, debt not founded upon a record or specialty, account, assumpsit, and upon the case, must be brought within three years from the accruing of the cause of action. This limitation does not run in the case of a mutual and running account between parties, while such account continues open and current; except also, that where the cause of action arises upon a promissory note, bill of exchange, or an acknowledgment under the hand of the party of a subsisting demand, the action may be commenced at any time within six years from the accruing of such cause of action. There is a saving of three years after the removal of their disability, in favor of infants, feme coverts, and persons non compos mentis. Where a cause of action arises within the state, if the person liable thereto is not at the time an inhabitant of the state, or removes from it before the expiration of the limitation, the time during which such person shall have been absent from the state shall be deducted from the limitation, and at least one year shall in every instance after the return of such person be allowed for bringing the action. (*b*)

The promises of an executor or administrator to pay a debt which has been barred by the statutes of limitation, will revive it. (*c*)

It has been held that payment of a part of a debt, or any recognition of an existing debt, or acknowledgment of a subsisting demand, will prevent the operation of the statute of limitations. The acknowledgment is held to revive the old debt, and not to create a new obligation. (*d*)

(*a*) McDowell *v*. The Bank of Wilmington and Brandywine, 1 Harr. 369.
(*b*) R. S 357. (*c*) Bennington *v*. Parkins' Adms. 1 Harr. 128. S. C. 209.
(*d*) Newlin *v*. Duncan, 1 Harr. 204.

7. *Attachment.*

A writ of attachment may be issued either against a resident or a non-resident of the state. In the former case, it is necessary that one writ of capias should be returned non est inventus, and that such proof of the cause of action be exhibited, as the court may think fit; or upon oath being made by the plaintiff, or some other credible person on his behalf, that the defendant is justly indebted to him in the sum of forty shillings and upwards, and has absconded from the place of his usual abode, or has gone out of the government, with intent to deceive and defraud his creditors, as is believed. This oath may be administered by the officer granting the writ, or by any judge of the court out of which it may issue, and must be filed in the court to which the attachment is returnable.

The writ runs against goods and chattels, rights and credits, lands and tenements, and may be served upon any garnishee found by the officer within his jurisdiction, whether an inhabitant of the state or not. Where the plaintiff, or any creditor claiming a benefit under a writ of attachment, makes oath that the garnishee is a non-resident, or that he, as the juror verily believes, is about to depart from the county where the attachment is depending; and the additional oath, that the garnishee has (as he believes) effects of the defendant in his hands, or is indebted to the defendant, the court will require such garnishee to give sureties for his appearance at court and abiding its judgment.

The attachment may be dissolved by putting in special bail before judgment, either by the defendant or some sufficient person for him. Where the garnishee neglects to appear and answer upon oath as to the property of the defendant in his custody, he may be coerced by process of contempt.

Upon the appearance of the garnishee, if he declares upon oath, that he has no property of the defendant under his control, he will be discharged, unless the plaintiff or some other creditor require him to plead, when an issue may be made up between them and tried by a jury; and if upon such trial judgment be rendered against the garnishee, the plaintiff or such other creditor may take out an execution against the garnishee, as for his own proper debt.

Upon the return of the writ of attachment, the justices of the court from which it issued are to appoint three disinterested citizens as auditors, to ascertain and adjust all claims of the plaintiff, and all other creditors who may become parties, after public advertisement of thirty days, and report to the said justices at the ensuing court after their appointment. Their proceedings are subject to the revision and control of the court, who, upon the second court after issuing the writ, may give judgment for the plaintiff, unless the defendant has given special bail, and order the sheriff to sell his goods and chattels, lands and tenements, as in other cases, and deliver the money, arising from the same, to the auditors, who are to make a pro rata distribution among all the creditors. The creditor, before receiving his dividend, must give bond with security, conditioned for the restitution of the money, if the debtor shall come into court within one year, either in person or by attorney, and disprove the claim. (*a*)

In the case of non-residents, a writ of attachment may issue from any court of law within the state, upon oath by the plaintiff or some person on his behalf, that the defendant resides out of the state, and is justly indebted to him in the sum of fifty dollars and upwards.

Proceedings are to be had thereon as in other cases.

Attachment for security.—Where a citizen of the state is apprehensive that a debtor who is a resident, and whose obligation is not yet due, may remove from the state, and take his effects with him, he may, upon oath or affirmation to that effect, and that the defendant is indebted to him in a sum of money exceeding forty shillings, and has refused to give better security for its payment, take out a writ and cause such debtor to be arrested, who upon the return of the writ, if the court think that there was sufficient cause for the proceeding, shall be required to give such security. (*b*)

In Burrows vs. Dumphy, 2 Harr. 308, it was held that the remedy under this section, although given in terms only to the inhabitants of the state, extends to citizens of other states; but

(*a*) R. C. 46 to 53.

(*b*) Ib. 51.

that it is doubtful whether the court could constitutionally require any other security than for the appearance of the party and his answering to a suit.

8. *Proceedings in Civil Suits.*

Imprisonment for debt.—No execution of capias ad satisfaciendum can be issued on a judgment in any civil action against a free white citizen of the state, nor can any such person be imprisoned for the non-performance of a decree for the payment of money, unless the plaintiff, or some credible person for him, shall make oath before the prothonotary of the county where the judgment is of record, or some judge of a Superior Court within the state, or the chancellor, that the defendant in such judgment or decree is justly indebted to the plaintiff in a sum exceeding fifty dollars, and that he or she verily believes that the said defendant has secreted, conveyed away, assigned or disposed of, either money, goods, chattels, stocks, securities for money, or other real or personal estate of the value of more than fifty dollars, with intent to defraud his or their creditors. This affidavit must also specify and set forth the fraudulent transaction. (*a*)

Judgment and execution.—The creditor must first look to the personalty for the satisfaction of his debt, but if that proves insufficient, the real estate of the debtor is liable to be seized and sold under judgment and execution. Lands which are unimproved or yield no yearly profits, may be seized and sold under a writ of fieri facias: and if such lands cannot, upon being offered for sale, find a purchaser, they may be delivered to the plaintiff, at a valuation, to hold as his own, in entire or partial satisfaction of his debt. When the lands are improved and yield yearly profits, they cannot be exposed for sale, if the clear profits shall be found, upon an inquisition of freeholders, sufficient to pay the debt within the space of seven years, but must be delivered to the party obtaining the judgment until the debt and damages are levied by a reasonable extent, as under the writ of elegit in England.

If the land is thus ascertained to be insufficient to pay the debt within seven years, or if during the term of the extent another

(*a*) Acts of 1841, 423.

judgment is recovered against the same debtor, and if that with what remains due cannot all be satisfied out of the yearly profits in seven years, a writ of venditioni exponas may issue for the sale of such lands and tenements.

A judgment constitutes a lien upon the real estate of the debtor, in the county where it was rendered, from the time of its being actually entered or signed. (*a*) With respect to personal property it is bound from the delivery of the writ to the officer. (*b*) No species of personal property is exempt from execution. (*c*)

The writ of capias ad satisfaciendum cannot be taken out against any debtor unless after one or more writs of fieri facias have been issued, and it appears from the sheriff's return, that the defendant has neither real nor personal property within the county sufficient to satisfy the debt, or until the plaintiff has made an oath of a similar purport. (*d*)

Any judgment creditor may take out an attachment as well as any other execution, upon which there shall be an order of summons, and the same proceeding, as in other cases without his oath, appointing auditors, making distribution, or finding security. (*e*)

9. *Effect of Death upon the Rights of Creditors.*

An executor or administrator shall pay the debts of the deceased in the following order:—1. Funeral expenses. 2. The reasonable bills for nursing and necessaries for the last sickness of the deceased. 3. Wages of servants and laborers, employed in household affairs, or in the cultivation of a farm, for a period not exceeding one year. 4. Rent, not exceeding one year's rent. 5. Judgments against the deceased, and decrees of a court of equity against the deceased, for the payment of money. 6. Recognizances and obligations of record for the payment of money. 7. Obligations and contracts under seal. 8. Contracts under hand for the payment of money or delivery of goods, wares, or merchandise. 9. Other demands.

An executor or administrator, after the expiration of six months from the granting letters testamentary or administration, may pay any debt of inferior dignity, notwithstanding the existence of de-

(*a*) R. S. 392. (*b*) Ib. (*c*) R. C. 209 to 217. (*d*) Ib. 215, 216. (*e*) Ib. 51

mands of a superior order, if he has no notice of such demands. It is not necessary, however, that this notice should be by action. The law requires him to take notice of judgments, decrees, recognizances, and mortgages, of record in the county where the letters are granted, unless there has been a failure to insert such judgments in the alphabet of the record. (*a*)

Before an executor or administrator shall pay any debt of the deceased, the claimant shall make an affidavit "that nothing has been paid or delivered towards the satisfaction of said debt, except what is mentioned, and that the sum demanded is justly and truly due." (*b*)

It has been decided under this statute, that the probate must disclose all credits within the plaintiff's knowledge, and that it is not sufficient to make a general reference to the defendant's books, for credits. (*c*)

If this affidavit is not produced in an action against an executor or administrator, for a debt of the deceased, the court will, on motion, give judgment of nonsuit. (*d*)

Where the personal estate is not sufficient for the payment of debts, the real estate may be sold under a decree of the Orphans' Court of the county where it is situate, upon a petition of the executor or administrator, setting forth these facts, and exhibiting a full and true account of the personal estate of the deceased and his debts of every description. The money arising from any sale of lands under the decree of the Orphans' Court, all just charges being first deducted, shall be applied in the following order:—First class; To debts by judgments or mortgages against the deceased, and which constituted liens upon the premises sold; such judgments to be satisfied according to the legal priority of their respective liens. Second class; To judgments against the executors or administrators of the deceased, which before the sale were liens upon the premises. Third class; To other debts outstanding against the deceased, observing the rules of priority prescribed in the administration of personal assets. (*e*)

Executors and administrators are required to render an annual account of their administration until it is completed. (*f*)

(*a*) R. S. 217, 231. (*b*) Rev. Laws, 226.
(*c*) Lolley *v.* Needham's Executors, 1 Harr. 86. (*d*) R. L. 226.
(*e*) R. S. 231 to 235. (*f*) Ib. 227.

When a judgment has been recovered against an administrator or executor before a justice of the peace, and no personal assets can be found to satisfy the debt, the register of the county granting letters testamentary or of administration may, after citation, require the executor or administrator to file a a petition in the Orphans' Court for the sale of the real estate of the deceased. (*a*)

Courts.

The Superior Court has a general and original jurisdiction in all cases at common law throughout the state. The Court of Chancery has jurisdiction of all cases of equitable cognizance. There is also an Orphans' Court, having jurisdiction in all matters of probate.

(*a*) Acts of 1833, 248.

MARYLAND.

1. *Assurances of Debt.*

Book accounts.—The payment and delivery of any money, and the delivery and sale of any goods or chattels whatsoever, by any merchant or person carrying on any trade, and being an inhabitant of any other of the United States, or of any foreign country, may be proven by the oath or affirmation of any disinterested credible person to the delivery of the goods, or payment of the money, &c., made and certified before and by the authorities necessary to authenticate any instrument not required to be recorded in the foreign country. There must also be added to the account, the plaintiff's oath or affirmation, taken at or before the first imparlance court, that the goods, money, &c., were delivered as charged, that he has received no payment or satisfaction therefor, other than is accredited, nor any security for the same, and that the balance charged and claimed is justly due according to the best of his knowledge and belief. Where the plaintiff is a resident this oath may be made before any judge or justice of the state. This oath when made by a non-resident, must be taken and certified by the same authorities as take and certify that of the witness; viz., any court, judge, justice, or other officer of the state or country where made, having authority by law to administer an oath or affirmation, and a certificate under seal from the governor, chief magistrate, or notary public of such state or country, that the court or officer had authority to administer the oath, and that such oath was duly made. (*a*)

Bills of exchange and promissory notes.—Bills of exchange and promissory notes are governed by the statute of 3d and 4th Anne, ch. 9, and by the English Law Merchant generally.

Damages upon protested bills of exchange.—The rate of damages on all bills of exchange drawn in Maryland, upon any person or company in any other of the United States, and protested according to the laws of such state, is eight per cent. upon the value of the principal sum in such bill. The holder may also recover so much money as will purchase a good bill at the current rate of exchange of such bills, and also the costs of protest and legal interest, from the time of protest until the principal, damages, and interest are paid.(*b*)

On all bills of exchange drawn in Maryland upon any person or corporation in a foreign country, which are regularly protested, the person entitled thereto, may recover so much money as will purchase a good bill upon the same place and at the same time of payment, at the current rate of exchange, also fifteen per cent. damages on the value of the principal sum in the bill, costs of protest, and legal interest on the principal from the time of protest until principal and damages are paid. (*c*) The indorser who shall pay the aforesaid value, damages, and interest, may recover the sum paid with legal interest from the drawer or person liable.

Protests which are duly made for the non-payment or non-acceptance of a bill of exchange, foreign or inland, are received as prima facie evidence of the facts therein stated. (*d*)

Assignability of choses in action.—Bonds or other obligations under seal, being assigned under seal, may be put in suit by the

(*a*) 1 Dorsey Laws, 200. (*b*) Ib. 198. (*c*) Ib. 197. (*d*) 2 Ib. 1257.

assignee in his own name against the obligor, or if he is unable to pay, or cannot be found in the place of his usual abode, or from any other casualty, the assignee may be unable to recover his debt from the obligor, the like action may be maintained against the assignor, in case the assignee was not a surety, or unless the debt has been lost by the default of the assignee. (*a*)

Contracts, illegal.—All contracts for the purchase of any public loan, or the stock or bill of any corporation, which contain a clause that the same may be executed at a future period, exceeding five judicial days then next ensuing, are void, and any moneys paid under such contract, may be recovered with a penalty of twenty per cent. (*b*)

Stamp act.—By an act passed in 1844, all bonds, bills, and notes, for the payment of a sum of money above one hundred dollars executed in the state, and all foreign or inland bills of exchange for the same amount are charged with the payment of a duty to the state, and required to be stamped; and no such instrument unless stamped, is allowed to be pleaded or given in evidence or available for any purpose in any court of law or equity in the state. Any holder, however, on making oath that he received any such instrument not stamped, without knowing the requisitions of the law, or in forgetfulness of them, and without any intention of evading its provisions, and paying the duty and the additional sum of ten dollars to the clerk of the county, or of Howard District, or of the City Court of Baltimore, may obtain an endorsement on the instrument of such affidavit and payment, and the same will then be as valid and available as if originally stamped. This act was to remain in force until 1st of May, 1848. (*c*)

2. *Interest.*

Six per cent. interest is the established legal rate of interest. All contracts for the loan of money at a greater rate are utterly void; the usurious lender to forfeit treble the value of the money lent, one-half to go to the state, and the other half for the benefit of any person who will sue for it. (*d*)

(*a*) 1 Dorsey, 108. (*b*) Acts of 1841, 282. (*c*) Acts of 1844, 280. (*d*) 1 Dorsey 5.

The right of any legal or equitable assignee, indorsee, or holder, of any bond, bill, promissory note, or negotiable instrument, to sue thereon is protected, where he has paid a bona fide and legal consideration for such instrument without notice of any usury in its creation. (*a*)

Corporate institutions may be governed in their discounts by the rates of interest which are charged and set forth in Rowlett's Tables. (*b*)

3. *Frauds.*

The property in goods or chattels is not transferred by gift, mortgage, or sale, where vendor, mortgagor, or donor remains in possession, unless the same be in writing and recorded in the county where the vendor, &c., resides. (*c*)

No deed of mortgage or bill of sale is valid or effective, except as against the mortgagor or grantor, unless there be indorsed thereon an affidavit of the mortgagee or grantor, sworn to, before the judge or justice as the case may be, taking the acknowledgment at the time thereof, that the consideration set forth in the bill of sale is true and bona fide. (*d*)

The statutes of 13th and 27th Elizabeth, against fraudulent conveyances, and the 29th Chas. II., against frauds and perjuries, are both in force in Maryland. The latter, however, was never formally published.

4. *Corporations.*

An act was passed in 1838, containing various important provisions in reference to manufacturing companies to be subsequently incorporated: among others, that the stock of the company should be transferable only upon its books, and according to its regulations, that real estate purchased by such corporations should be liable to be sold under execution for its debts, that the directors who are present and do not express dissent when any engagement beyond the actual market value of the assets of the company is contracted, shall become personally answerable

(*a*) 1 Dorsey 200. (*b*) 2 Dorsey 1079. (*c*) Dorsey 1729.
(*d*) Acts of 1847, 271.

therefor in proportion to their stock, and that any mortgage of the company to give one creditor preference over another. shall enure ratably to the benefit of all. (*a*)

5. *Effect of Marriage upon Rights of Property.*

The slaves of which a woman is possessed at the time of her marriage, do not thereby become liable for her husband's debts: (*b*) nor can her real estate be sold for his debts during her life. (*c*)

6. *Limited Partnerships.*

Limited partnerships for the transaction of mercantile, mechanical, or manufacturing business, were authorized by the act of 1836. (*d*)

7. *Factors, Agents, &c.*

In all cases where payments of money, transfers of property, or other dealings are made or had, to or with any person acting under a power of attorney, or other agency duly created by any person within the state, the death of the grantor or the transfer of his interest at the time of the transaction shall not invalidate it, provided that the person having such dealings had no notice of the death of the party or the fact of the assignment. (*e*)

8. *Part Owners of Vessels*

The high Court of Chancery and the several county courts, sitting as courts of equity, are invested with as full jurisdiction in cases of controversy between part owners as in ordinary cases of partnership, provided that the defendants are residents of the county in which the bill is filed. Under this authority they may direct the sale of any ship, vessel or steamboat, held by part owners, and apportion the proceeds among the parties, according to their respective interests. (*f*)

(*a*) Acts of 1828, 267. (*b*) Acts of 1842, 293. (*c*) Acts of 1841, 161.
(*d*) 2 Dorsey 1228. (*e*) Ib. 1244. (*f*) Acts of 1839, 304.

9. *Limitation of Actions.*

Actions of account upon any debt or contract, or upon the case, except such accounts as concern merchant and merchant, their factors and servants, who are non-residents of the state, and actions of debt upon any contract, or lending without specialty, must be brought within three years after the cause of action has accrued. All actions upon bonds, judgments, or writings under seal, must be brought within twelve years after the cause of action first accrues. In the first class of cases, there is a saving of the rights of infants, feme coverts, and persons non compos mentis, for the term of three years after the removal of their respective disabilities; in the latter class for the similar period of five years. (*a*)

10. *Effect of Death upon the Rights of Creditors.*

The personal estate of a decedent constitutes the primary fund for the payment of his debts, and must be exhausted before a creditor can reach the realty. Where the personal estate is insufficient, the Court of Chancery will direct a sale of the real estate upon such application. The Court of Chancery will distribute the proceeds ratably among all the creditors of the deceased. (*b*)

In the distribution of an estate, debts by judgment or decree within the state, are to be first paid; and then all other debts, whether by specialty or simple contract, are put upon an equality.

The executor or administrator, upon giving notice by advertisement six months before the settlement of his account, may close his administration, and bar all creditors whose claims have not been presented within one year.

11. *Attachment.*

A creditor may obtain an attachment against the lands, tenements, goods, chattels, and credits of a debtor, who is either a

(*a*) 1 Dorsey, c. 23, 10. (*b*) Ib. 210. 1 Harr. & Gill. 504; 6 Gils. 29, 424.

non-resident, or being a citizen absconds or secretes himself, with intent to evade the payment of his just debts. (*a*)

Any person residing in any part of the United States, or who may sue out mesne process, may prosecute the writ of attachment. (*b*)

The provisions of the law likewise extend to the case of corporations, whether incorporated by the state or not, and whether plaintiffs or defendants. (*c*)

Where the debtor is not a citizen of the state, the creditor must make an oath or affirmation that he either knows, or is credibly informed and believes that such is the fact, and where the debtor is a citizen, the creditor must make a similar oath that he has either fled from justice, or removed from his place of abode with intent to defraud or injure his creditors. This oath or affirmation may be made before any judge of the General Court, justice of the peace or of the County Court, or before any judge of any other of the United States. In the latter case there must be annexed the certificate of the clerk of the court of which he is judge, or of the governor, chief magistrate or notary public of such state, that he has power to administer such oath. The creditor must also make oath that the debtor is bona fide indebted to him in the sum of $—— over and above all discounts, at the same time producing the bond, bill, or account on which he is indebted. (*d*)

Attachments may be laid upon debts and upon judgments or decrees, or upon stock or other funded property. (*e*)

When the creditor, or any person for him, makes oath that he believes the person against whom the attachment is to be served, has property belonging to the defendant in his possession, or under his care, or is indebted to the defendant in any sum, though not then due, and that he has just cause to fear that said garnishee is about to remove from the county where he resides, the clerk may insert in the attachment a clause of capias against said garnishee, and he shall be held to sufficient bail to appear at court and make answer to the plaintiff's interrogatories, and to render his body to prison, or pay the condemnation money, if judgment shall pass against him. (*f*)

(*a*) 1 Dorsey 320. (*b*) 1 Ib. 832. (*c*) 2 Ib. 1088. (*d*) 1 Ib. 320.
(*e*) 2 Dor. 1067, 1101. (*f*) 1 Ib. 320.

Attachment against a non-resident debtor will not be dissolved unless defendant, or some one for him, enter into bond, with security, to satisfy any judgment that may be obtained against defendant. Where either of the plaintiffs or defendants was a citizen of the state at the time the contract was made, or debt accrued, upon which the attachment issues, the attachment will not be dissolved unless some one of the defendants give bond to be approved by the court, on condition to pay the plaintiff the value of such goods as may have been levied on, in the event of his recovery. (*a*)

Judgments in attachment have preference according to the order of the periods of levying the attachment. (*b*)

12. *Proceedings in Civil Suits.*

Bail.—Bail cannot be required of females, or of executors or administrators sued as such, or of insolvent debtors. It cannot be required in actions of debt upon bonds with collateral condition, or upon judgments where bail was given in the original action. It may be required on producing the evidences of debt, in all actions ex contractu, whatever may be their form, and whether their evidences be the written acknowledgment of the party, or the affidavit of the plaintiff. Where the injury arises from a breach of contract sounding in damages, it is usual to hold to bail upon affidavit stating that the party is injured by the breach of contract set forth in the affidavit, to a particular amount. For the manner in which a debtor imprisoned on mesne process may obtain his discharge, see title "Insolvent Law."

Judgment and execution.—The lands of a judgment debtor are bound from the rendition of the judgment: his goods only from the delivery of the execution to the officer. The equitable interest of a judgment debtc in land, may be taken and sold on an execution at law; (*c*) but not so his equitable interest in personalty. To reach the latter interest, the creditor must levy his execution, and cause it to be returned, by which he acquires a prior right in equity, to be satisfied from its proceeds. (*d*)

(*a*) Acts of 1839, 39. (*b*) Dorsey 946. (*c*) Dor. 1810, 160, 602.
(*d*) Harris *v.* Alcock, 109, 252.

Judgments in a Magistrate's Court do not create a lien upon lands and tenements. (*a*)

The three general executions in use are the writs of attachment, fieri facias, and capias ad satisfaciendum. As to the manner in which the debtor may release himself from the last, see title "Insolvent Law."

Courts.—The county courts have original jurisdiction in all cases where the matter in dispute is of the value of fifty dollars and upwards. They are held twice a year in each county. There are six judicial districts in the state, each comprising two, three or more counties. For each district, there are a chief judge and two associates, who constitute the county courts for the respective districts. There are besides, the Orphans' Court held in each county, and the Court of Chancery, whose jurisdiction is coextensive with the state.

13. *Insolvent Law.* (*b*)

The insolvent system of Maryland, is regulated by the act of 1805, and its numerous supplements. Any debtor wishing to avail himself of its provisions, who has resided sixty days within the state, may make an application in writing to the County Court, or a judge thereof, or to the Orphans' Court, offering to deliver up all his property to his creditors. A schedule of his estate with a list of his creditors, verified by affidavit, must accompany the petition; upon which the court shall direct that notice of such application, and of the time fixed for the appearance of the debtor, shall be given to the creditors; and on the appearance of the debtor at the time fixed, and he must give security for his appearance at that time, the court administers an oath to him, to the effect that he has surrendered all his property, and that he has not directly or indirectly disposed of any part of it, with a view to defraud his creditors or secure the same to himself: whereupon the court shall appoint such persons as a majority of the creditors

(*a*) Acts of 1838, 380.

(*b*) The above outline of the Insolvent Law of Maryland is mainly taken from the Western Law Journal, vol. ii. 389, with the permission of the author, F. W. Brune, Jr., of Baltimore.

in value shall recommend, but in case they recommend no one, such person as the court may think proper, to be trustee for the benefit of the creditors. The trustee shall give bond, and upon the debtor's executing a deed to him of all his property, the debtor shall be discharged from all debts and contracts due or contracted at the time of his application, provided that any property which the debtor may afterwards acquire by gift, descent, or in his own right by bequest, devise, or in the course of distribution, shall be liable for the payment of his debts, and vest in his trustee for that purpose. Any creditor may allege within two years from his application, that the debtor hath disposed of or purchased in trust for himself or his family, or concealed any part of his property to deceive and defraud his creditors, or hath lost more than one hundred dollars by gaming at any one time within three years from the date of the application: and the court may thereupon, at the election of the creditor making these allegations, examine the debtor and the persons to whom he may have transferred his property, on oath, or may direct an issue in a summary way, to try the truth of such allegations: and if the debtor is found guilty of the charges alleged against him, he shall be forever precluded from any benefit of the insolvent law, and be liable to be convicted and punished for perjury. Provision is also made for cases in which the debtor is imprisoned at the time of the application, by which he may in such cases obtain a personal discharge. All conveyances to creditors, or sureties, and all judgments confessed to them, when made by the debtor with a view or under an expectation of applying for the benefit of the insolvent laws, and for the purpose of preferring such creditor or surety, are declared void, and the property attempted to be conveyed or assured, shall vest in the trustee of such debtor.

By the act of 1834, chap. 293, all conveyances and dispositions of property, made by a debtor in Baltimore city or county, with an intent to prefer any creditors or security, when such debtor has no reasonable expectation of being exempted from liability or execution on account of his debts, without applying for the benefit of the insolvent laws, are declared void, except as against persons claiming for a valuable consideration under such creditors or their legal representatives, or where the creditor or security appears to have had no notice of the insolvent condition of the debtor.

Persons imprisoned for fines due to the state, cannot be released under this law.

The insolvent laws of Maryland profess to operate upon all claims, whether the creditors are residents of other states or not, and no matter where the contracts are to be performed ; but they are necessarily qualified by the constitution of the United States, and the decisions of the Supreme Court of the United States, declaring the meaning and effect of the constitution. The bankrupt laws of a state, although constitutional in their action upon the rights of citizens of that state, so far as they affect posterior contracts, are unconstitutional when they affect the rights of the citizens of other states. (*a*)

(*a*) Frey *v.* Kirk, 49 & 9, 509 ; S. P. Cook *v.* Moffat, 5 How. S. C. R. 295.

DISTRICT OF COLUMBIA.

1. *General Observations on the Judicial Organization of the District.*

The laws of Maryland, which were in force in February, 1801, except so far as they have been repealed by acts of Congress, prevail in the District of Columbia, as at present constituted. (*a*)

The laws regulating rights have not been materially changed; but the organization of the courts is of course wholly distinct. The judicial power is vested in a Circuit Court, with subordinate tribunals, consisting of one chief judge and two assistant judges, who have all the powers vested by the law in the Circuit Courts of the United States, and the judges thereof. In some respects even it has been held that the power of the Circuit Court of the District of Columbia is more extensive than that of the Circuit Courts of the United States in the several states, to whom the entire judicial power of the United States under the constitution has not been committed. (*b*)

From the judgment of this court, there lies an appeal in cases where the matter in dispute is of the value of one thousand dollars and upwards, to the Supreme Court of the United States.

(*a*) Statutes at Large, ii. 103.
(*b*) Kendall, Postmaster-General *v.* The United States. 12 Peters 524.

In cases where the debt or demand does not exceed fifty dollars, justices of the peace have jurisdiction.

2. *Interest.*

Upon all judgments rendered on the common law side of the Circuit Court, upon contracts, interest is to be awarded at the rate of six per cent. on the principal sum due, until the judgment is satisfied. (*a*) The law of Maryland as to interest has been in no way altered or modified.

3. *Limitation of Actions.*

The Maryland statute is in force. There is a saving, however, of persons "beyond seas," which was abolished in Maryland in 1819 by an act of the legislature.

4. *Administration of Estates.*

Estates of deceased persons are administered under the superintendence of an Orphans' Court, upon the general rules and principles which have been stated in the chapter on Maryland.

5. *Bail.*

No female can be imprisoned upon any civil process; nor any non-resident for a debt contracted out of the District; nor any person in a civil action, where the debt or claim, exclusive of interest and costs, is less than fifty dollars. (*b*)

No person can be held to bail in any civil suit in the District of Columbia, unless on affidavit filed by the plaintiff or his agent, stating, in cases of debt or contract, the amount which he verily believes to be due, and that the same has been contracted by fraud or false pretences, or through a breach of trust, or that the defendant is concealing or has concealed his property in the District or elsewhere, or is about to remove the same from the District, or place of his residence, in order to evade the payment of the debt,

(*a*) U. S. Statutes at Large, ii. 756.

(*b*) Ib. v. 678.

or that, being a resident of the District and domiciled therein, is about to abscond without paying the debt, and with a view to avoid the payment of the same, setting forth all the facts on which such allegations of fraud or breach of trust are founded, and the grounds, nature, and particulars of the claim. The sufficiency of this affidavit, and the amount of bail, is to be determined, upon application of the defendant, by the court in term time or a judge in vacation. The affidavit may be filed in all cases previously to issuing the writ. (*a*)

6. *Execution.*

No person can be imprisoned upon final process in any civil action, except in cases where he has been held to bail; or where the plaintiff, after judgment has been rendered in his favor, shall make oath according to law, that the defendant has conveyed away, lessened, or disposed of his or her property, rights or credits, or is about to remove, or has removed his or her property from the district, with intent, as the said plaintiff believes, thereby to hinder or delay the recovery or payment of his debt. Where a defendant has been arrested on a ca. sa. issued by reason of this affidavit, he may, on application for a habeas corpus, be brought before one of the judges of the county, and require the plaintiff to establish the truth of his affidavit before a jury impanneled under the direction of such judge, or be discharged. (*b*)

Upon executions of fieri facias, the goods and chattels, lands and tenements of a debtor may be sold. See this subject treated of in chapter upon Maryland.

7. *Insolvent Law.*

Any debtor in close confinement within the District at the suit of his creditor, may petition in writing any one of the judges of the Circuit Court for the District of Columbia for relief. The petition must offer to deliver up all the property, real, personal, or mixed to which the debtor is entitled, for the use of his creditors, annexing thereto a schedule of the same, with a list of his creditors, as far as can be ascertained, verified by affidavit. Notice of

(*a*) U. S. Statutes at Large, v. 498.

(*b*) Ib. 678.

this application, requiring also the presence of the creditors at such time as the judge may direct, is to be published in some newspaper for such period as the judge may think proper. At the time and place designated for the appearance of the creditors, the debtor is to take an oath that he has surrendered all his property, and that he conveyed away or disposed of no portion of the same for his own benefit, or to the injury of his creditors. (*a*)

Any creditor of an insolvent debtor may, either before the oath of insolvency has been administered, or upon reasonable notice to appear at any time within two years after the application, before any court of the United States, where such debtor may be found, file a written allegation that such debtor has been guilty of fraud or deceit toward his creditors by conveying or disposing of a portion of his property to their injury, or that he has assigned a part of his property with intent to give a preference to one creditor or surety, or that at some one time within twelve months before the application, he has lost more than three hundred dollars by gaming. Whereupon the court, or any one judge of the district, may examine such debtor or any other person upon interrogatories on oath touching the substance of said petition, or may direct an issue to be tried in a summary way, without the form of an action, to determine the truth of the same, and if upon the interrogatories or the trial of the issue, either of the allegations shall be established, the debtor shall be precluded from any benefit under the act.

The judge is to appoint such person as the majority of the creditors may recommend, or in default thereof, as he may select, a trustee for their benefit, who is to give bond and security for the faithful performance of his trust. (*b*)

The petitioning debtor, upon conveying all his property to such trustee, and delivering up the same with his books and papers, may be discharged from imprisonment, and cannot be subsequently arrested or imprisoned under process sued out on any judgment or decree rendered against him for a debt contracted or becoming due before the period of such discharge. (*c*)

(*a*) Statutes at Large, ii. 237. (*b*) Ib. ii. 239, 755. (*c*) Ib. 239.

No discharge thus obtained, can operate against any creditor residing out of the District of Columbia, except the creditor at whose instance the debtor may be confined. (*a*)

The acting judge may appoint a time for creditors to exhibit their claims to the trustee, and it is the duty of the latter to report to the judge any claim which he may think proper to contest, and the judge may either submit the same to a jury, having examined the debtor and creditor upon oath, touching the claim, or refer the controversy to arbitrators for their decision, and he may order a portion of the debtor's estate to be set apart for the eventual satisfaction of any contested claim. The trustee is to collect the assets of the insolvent, sell and convey the property of the same at such time and in such manner as the judge may direct, and distribute the proceeds pro rata among all the creditors, after satisfying all liens and incumbrances. No process against the real or personal property of the debtor is to have any effect, except executions and attachments in the nature thereof put into the officer's hands before the application. (*b*)

(*a*) Statutes at Large, iii. 682.

(*b*) Ib. ii. 239.

VIRGINIA.

1. *Assurances of Debt.*

Choses in action.—Bonds, bills, and promissory notes may be assigned, so as to confer upon the assignee thereof the right of suing in his own name, as fully as the original obligee or payee might have done. Suit may be brought at law by the assignee of a note or obligation against any previous assignor. (*a*)

The assignee of a bond or promissory note not negotiable, although for a valuable consideration, and without notice, takes it subject to all the equity of the obligor. (*b*)

Before the assignee of a bond or promissory note can resort to an assignor, he must show the use of due diligence to recover the amount due from the obligor or maker. (*c*)

Bills of exchange and promissory notes.—Inland bills of exchange.—All bills of exchange or drafts for money in the nature of bills of exchange, drawn by any person residing in this state or in the United States, shall be considered as inland bills of

(*a*) Tate's Digest, 30.

(*b*) Norton *v.* Rose, 2 Wash. 233; Pickett *v.* Morris, 2 Wash. 255.

(*c*) Mackie's Ex'rs *v.* Davis, 2 Wash. 219.

exchange; and if such bill or draft be protested for non-acceptance or non-payment, the drawer or indorser shall be subject to one per centum damages thereon, and interest at six per cent. from date of the protest. (*a*) If such bill be lost or miscarry, the drawer shall sign and deliver another of the same tenor, sufficient security being given to indemnify him against the former. (*b*)

Foreign.—Where any foreign bill of exchange, for the payment of any sum of money, in which the value is or shall be expressed to be received, shall be protested for non-acceptance or non-payment, the drawer or indorser shall be subject to ten per centum damages thereon, and interest at six per cent. from the date of the protest. (*c*)

In all foreign bills of exchange for any debt due in current money of this commonwealth, or for current money advanced and paid for such bills, the sum in current money that was paid or allowed for the same shall be mentioned and expressed in such bill: and in default thereof, in case such bill shall be protested, and a suit brought for the recovery of the money due thereby, the sum of money expressed in such bill shall be held and taken as current money, and judgment be entered accordingly. (*d*)

Promissory notes.—All notes and bills made negotiable at the incorporated banks of the state are placed on the same footing as foreign bills of exchange. (*e*)

2. *Interest.*

Six per cent. is the rate of interest established by law. Every contract in which a higher rate is taken or reserved is absolutely void, and the lender receiving such usurious excess is liable to a penalty of twice the debt, to be recovered in a qui tam action. (*f*)

3. *Factors.*

All the property, debts, stocks, and choses in action, acquired by any person trading or transacting business in his own name, with the addition of the words "agent," "factor," and "compa-

(*a*) R. C. c. 125, § 1. (*b*) Ib. (*c*) Ib. 126, § 1; Suppl. c. 199, § 1.
(*d*) Ib. c. 126, § 4. (*e*) Charters of the several Banks. (*f*) Tate's Dig. 318.

ny," or "& Co.," and not disclosing the name of a principal or partner liable for all the debts incurred in the course of the business, shall, as to all creditors of such person, be taken to be his individual property, and liable for his debts, as if it were acquired solely on his own account. (*a*)

4. *Limited Partnerships*

Limited partnerships for mercantile, manufacturing, and mechanical business, may be formed on the following terms, but not for banking, brokerage, or making insurance.

Such partnerships must consist of one or more general partners, responsible as at present by law, and one or more special partners, who shall contribute in cash a specific sum, and not be liable for debts of the partnership beyond the fund so contributed. General partners only are to transact the business, sign for the partnership and bind the firm.

Persons wishing to form such partnership shall sign a certificate, which shall contain,—1. The name or firm under which the partnership is to be conducted: 2. The general nature of the business to be transacted: 3. The names of all the general and special partners, (distinguishing them,) and their respective places of residence: 4. The amount of capital of each special partner: 5. The period of the commencement and termination of the partnership. The certificate is to be acknowledged before a justice by all the parties, and the justice is to certify the same in the usual mode to the clerk of the proper court, to be recorded. The certificate, so acknowledged and certified, is to be filed in the clerk's office of the county or corporation in which is the principal place of business of the partnership, and to be recorded by the clerk at large. If the business is in several counties, a transcript is to be recorded in each. At the time of filing the certificate and acknowledgment, an affidavit of a general partner is to be also filed, that the amount to be contributed by each special partner has been actually paid in cash. No such partnership is deemed to have been formed until the certificate has been made, acknowledged, filed, and recorded, and the affidavit filed

(*a*) Acts of 1839, 45.

as aforesaid; and any false statement will render all liable as general partners.

The parties shall publish the terms of the partnership for at least six weeks after recordation, in two newspapers; if not, they shall all be deemed general partners. Affidavits of the publication by the printers may be filed with the clerk, and are received as evidence.

Every renewal or continuance is to be made on the same terms and in the same manner as the formation.

Every alteration in names of the partners, or nature of the business, or in the capital or shares thereof, or in any other matter specified in the original certificate, shall be deemed a dissolution, and the partnership so carried on afterwards shall be deemed a general partnership, unless renewed on the terms aforesaid. (This section does not refer to losses in the regular course of trade.)

The names of the general partners only are to appear, in conducting the business.

Suits may be brought by and against the general partners, and the special partners are suable by the firm.

No part of the sum contributed by a special partner is to be withdrawn by him, but any partner may annually receive interest, provided the capital stock is not diminished, or profits over interest.

If the capital is reduced by payment of interest or profits to special partner, he may be compelled to refund to creditors.

Special partners may examine into, and advise about the partnership concerns, but must not transact business or be employed as agent, attorney, or otherwise.

General partners are to account to each other, and to the special partners.

Every partner guilty of fraud is liable civilly, and also to indictment and fine, and imprisonment.

Every sale, assignment or transfer of any property or effects of partnership made by such partnership when insolvent, or in contemplation of insolvency, or after or in contemplation of insolvency of any partner, with intent of preferring any creditor of such partnership or insolvent partner over other creditors, and every judgment confessed, lien created, or security given, under like circumstances, are void against creditors.

And so also of such sale, assignment and transfer, or lien created, &c., when made by any partner.

Every special partner who shall violate any of the preceding provisions, is liable as a general partner.

In case of insolvency or bankruptcy of partnership, no special partner shall claim as a creditor until all other creditors are satisfied.

No dissolution of partnership by the acts of parties can take place, previous to the time specified in renewal or original certificate, until notice is filed and recorded in the clerk's office of the original certificate, and published once a week for four weeks in a newspaper printed in each of the counties or corporations where the partnership has its place of business, or if there is no newspaper therein, then in the nearest newspaper, &c. (*a*)

5. *Limitation of Actions.*

The general act of Virginia provides that all actions upon the case, other than for slander, and other than such accounts as concern the trade of merchandise between merchant and merchant, and all actions for account, and all actions for trespass, debt, detinue, and replevin for goods and chattels, shall be commenced and sued within five years next after the cause of such action or suit, and not after. (*b*) This act is copied from the English act, 21 Jac. 1, ch. 16, sec. 3, excepting only the time of the limitation, and English decisions upon their act would probably be held as explanatory of the Virginia law.

To an action of *deceit* in the sale of a chattel, brought more than five years after the sale, plea of the statute of limitations, with general replication, is a good bar, for the cause of action arose when the deceit was practised. (*c*) But to each plea a replication that the deceit or fraud was discovered within five years before the commencement of the action, is a sufficient answer. (*d*)

(*a*) Acts of 1837, 81. (*b*) R. C. c. 128, § 4. (*c*) Rice *v.* White, 4 Leigh. 474.
(*d*) Same case per Tucker J. Shields *v.* Anderson, 3 Leigh. 729.

In reference to merchants' accounts excepted in the above statute, it is said that to bring his case within this exception, the plaintiff must show that both parties were merchants, and besides there must be mutual accounts and reciprocal demands, for if all the items be on one side, it is no account between merchant and merchant. (*a*) An account between merchant and merchant, although closed by cessation of dealing, is not an account stated, and is still within the exemption; nor is it necessary that any of the items in such account be within five years before suit, (*b*) nor is it necessary that in such account the items should altogether consist of merchandise and goods sold. (*c*)

This exemption does not apply to accounts between merchants and their customers, because the customers are not merchants, and because the seventh section of the same act enacts that all actions or suits founded upon any account for goods, wares, or merchandise, sold and delivered, or for any articles charged in any store accounts, shall be commenced and sued within one year (now two years) (*d*) next after the cause of such action or suit, or the delivery of such goods, wares, or merchandise, and not after; except that, in case of the death of the creditors or debtors, before the expiration of the said term, the further time of one year from the death of such creditor or debtor shall be allowed for the commencement of any such action or suit. This act does not apply where the trader has no retail store, but sold his goods at auction; in such case the limitation is not two, but five years. (*e*) This act, too, has been extended, so as to run against a claim asserted for a decedent's estate, not from death of the decedent, but only from the qualification of the executor or administrator, (*f*) and the same would probably be true as to a claim against a decedent's estate (*g*) But the act does not run in favor of executors de son tort. (*h*)

The thirteenth section provides that where one out of this country shall through a factor sell and deliver goods here, and

(*a*) 2 Tuck. Com. 153.

(*b*) Watson *v.* Lyle, 4 Leigh. 249; Coalter *v.* Coalter, 1 Rob. 79.

(*c*) Watson *v.* Lyle, 4 Leigh. 249.

(*d*) Acts 1838, c. 95, § 5.

(*e*) Tomlin *v.* How, I Wash. 190.

(*f*) Hansford *v.* Elliott, 9 Leigh. 79.

(*g*) Clark *v.* Hardiman, 2 Leigh. 347.

(*h*) Hansford *v.* Elliott, 9 Leigh. 79.

such factor shall die within the limitation allowed, this act shall be extended two years from the death of such factor.

Generally, the lex fori alone governs the remedy, but an act passed in 1836 provides, that where suit is brought upon the judgment of a court of any state of the United States, the defendant may plead any act of limitation of force in such state, and that such plea shall have the same force that it would have in a similar action in such state. (*a*)

Under this general act, and up to 1838, the doctrine of new promises remained as in England under her cognate act, capable of being sustained so as to take a debt out of the statute, by re-acknowledgment, part payment, or other evidence of a new promise, expressed or implied. But an act passed in 1838 enacts that in actions of debt or upon the case, grounded upon any simple contract, no acknowledgment or promise made hereafter, by words only, shall be deemed sufficient evidence of a new and continuing contract, whereby to take any case out of the operation of the act before memtioned, unless such acknowledgment or promise shall be made or contained by or in some writing to be signed by the party chargeable thereby; and the third section extends the same to set-offs. (*b*) This statute is, throughout, the same with the English, called Lord Tenterden's act, (*c*) with these two exceptions.

1. The English act provides that nothing in that act shall alter, take away, or lessen the effect of any payment of any principal or interest made by any person whomsoever. This is omitted from the Virginia statute.

2. The Virginia statute provides that every such written promise or acknowledgment shall be held and taken to be a drawing down of the original debt or contract to the date of the said promise or acknowledgment. This is not in the English act.

By all these statutes, specialties are left as they were at the common law, subject, after twenty years, to a presumption of payment which might be rebutted. But a statute passed in 1826 enacts that all actions founded on bonds executed by executors, administrators, guardians, sheriffs, and some other officers men-

(*a*) Acts 1838, c. 62. (*b*) Ib. c. 95.
(*c*) 9 Geo. 4, c. 14. See Act at large in Joynes on Lim. App.

tioned, and other persons acting in a fiduciary character, either public or private, shall be instituted or brought within ten years after the right or cause of action shall have accrued, and not afterwards. (*a*) But the defendant must be fiduciary as to the plaintiff; his being fiduciary as to any other person is not sufficient. (*b*)

6. *Parol Agreements.*

No action shall be brought whereby to charge any executor or administrator, upon any special promise, to answer any debt or damages out of his own estate, or whereby to charge the defendant upon any special promise to answer for the debt, default, or miscarriage of another person, or to charge any person upon any agreement made upon consideration of marriage, or upon any contract for the sale of lands, tenements, or hereditaments, or the making any lease thereof for a longer term than one year, or upon any agreement which is not to be performed within the space of one year from the making thereof, unless the promise or agreement upon which such action shall be brought, or some memorandum or note thereof, shall be in writing and signed by the party to be charged therewith, or some other person by him thereunto lawfully authorized. (*c*) This statute is copied, with but one variation, from 29 Car., 2, c. 3, and hence the decisions of the English courts upon their statute apply to this.

The variation referred to is important. The English statute requires the agreement by which one promises to pay or see paid the debt due by another, to be in writing, whilst the Virginia statute, in the same case, requires the promise or agreement to be in writing. Agreement comprehends the *consideration* of the undertaking, promise does not. Hence, in Virginia the consideration which moved the promisee to undertake, need not be in writing, although in England it is otherwise. (*d*)

As to the promise of one to pay or see paid the debt due by

(*a*) Sup. R. C. c. 200, § 1.

(*b*) Spotswood *v.* Dandridge, 4 H. & M. 139; Redwood *v.* Riddick, 4 Mun. 222.

(*c*) R. C. c. 101.

(*d*) Violet *v.* Patton, 5 Cranch. 151; Colgin *v.* Henley, 6 Leigh. 85; Johnson *v.* Ronald, 4 Mun. 77.

another, this distinction is taken. Where the promiser merely agrees to see the debt paid, and the original debtor is not released from his obligation, so that the creditor has a double remedy, the promise is *collateral* (in the nature of a security), and must be in writing to bind the promiser. But where the promiser undertakes to pay the debt due by another without any reference to that other, the promise is *direct*, for the debt is then his own and no longer another's, and is therefore out of this statute, and need not be in writing. (*a*) This direct promise, when relied on, must be strictly proved. A merchant cannot charge the goods sold to his customer to the promiser, and thereby make him directly responsible, so as to avoid the necessity, under this statute, for a written promise. (*b*)

Though a collateral promise be in writing, a sufficient consideration must have moved to the promiser. (*c*) Part performance of a collateral promise, though not in writing, will take that promise out of this statute. (*d*)

Another statute provides that no action shall be brought whereby to charge any person upon or by reason of any representation or assurance made or given concerning or relating to the character, credit, ability, trade, or dealings of any other person, to the intent or purpose that such other person may obtain credit, money, or goods upon the same, unless such representation or assurance be made in writing signed by the party to be charged therewith. (*e*)

7. *Fraudulent Conveyances.*

By the statute (*f*) every gift, grant, or conveyance of lands, tenements, hereditaments, goods or chattels, or of any rent, common or profit, out of the same, by writing or otherwise, and every bond, suit, judgment or execution had or made and contrived to delay, hinder or defraud creditors of their just and lawful actions, suits, debts, accounts, &c., or to defraud or deceive those who

(*a*) Waggoner *v.* Gray, 2 H. & M. 611. (*b*) Cutler *v.* Hinton, 6 Ran. 518.

(*c*) Waggoner *v.* Gray, 2 H. & M. 611; Colgin *v.* Henley, 6 Leigh. 85.

(*d*) Wilde *v.* Fox, 1 Ran. 165; Anthony *v.* Leftwich, 3 Ran. 238; Rowton *v.* Rowton, 1 H. & M. 99. (*e*) Acts 1840–41, c. 60, § 1.

(*f*) R. C. c. 101, §2.

shall purchase the same lands, tenements or hereditaments, or any rent, profit, or commodity out of them, shall be from henceforth deemed and taken (only as against the person or persons, his, her or their heirs, &c., whose debts, suits, &c., thereby shall or might be in any wise disturbed, hindered, delayed, or defrauded) to be clearly and utterly void, any pretence, &c., to the contrary notwithstanding. And, moreover, if a conveyance of goods and chattels be made, and not on valuable consideration, it shall be taken to be fraudulent within this act, unless the same be by will or deed proved and recorded as therein directed, or unless possession shall really and bona fide remain with the donee. And where any loan of goods and chattels shall be pretended to have been made to any person, with whom or those claiming under, possession shall have remained for five years, without demand made and prosecuted at law, the same shall be taken, as to creditors and purchasers, to be fraudulent within this act, unless the same be by will duly proved and recorded. By the section it is provided that this act shall not extend to any lands, goods, chattels, &c., which shall be upon good (i. e. valuable) consideration, and bona fide lawfully conveyed.

A fraudulent intent seems to be the test of the act, and a valuable consideration will not protect a deed executed with such intent. (*a*)

An absolute sale of chattels, not accompanied and followed by transfer of possession to the vendee is per se fraudulent and void as against creditors of the vendor; yet there are some exceptions, where it may be explained. (*b*)

An important decision has been lately made upon this act to the following effect: A fraudulent intent of the grantor against one of his creditors is fraudulent against all, and that no distinction exists between prior and subsequent creditors; thus, A, expecting to be held responsible as security for a sheriff, fraudulently conveyed away land, with the purpose thereby to avoid such responsibility and afterwards became indebted; and it was held, that the conveyance was fraudulent and void as to this subsequent creditor, inasmuch as it was fraudulent and void at the time it was made, and could never become valid. (*c*)

(*a*) Briscoe *v.* Clark, 1 Ran. 213. (*b*) Mason *v.* Bond, 9 Leigh. 181.

(*c*) Hutchinson *v.* Kelly, 1 Rob. 123.

8. *Effect of Death upon Rights of Creditors.*

Limitations.—In any suit against an executor or administrator for the recovery of a debt due by his testator or intestate upon an account, it is the duty of the court to strike from the account every item thereof, which shall appear to have been due five years before the death of the testator or intestate. (*a*) It will be observed that the terms of this law extend only to open accounts, and not to settlements or assumptions by the testator or intestate within five years. (*b*)

Suits upon the bonds of executors and administrators, as persons in a fiduciary situation, are limited as mentioned under title "*Limitations.*"

The equity of sec. 10 of general act of limitations is extended to executors, &c.; so that if an action of assumpsit be brought in proper time, but the plaintiff or defendant die before judgment and the limitation run out, the executor or administrator may bring a new action, provided he does it within a reasonable time, which, from analogy to the statute, is probably one year. (*c*)

The statute of limitations does not begin to run against a claim asserted for the estate of a deceased person, till the qualification of an executor, &c. (*d*)

If there be several executors or administrators, an acknowledgment to take a debt already barred, out of the statute, must be made by all. (*e*)

Bail.—The words of the act allowing bail as of right do not extend to executors and administrators. But where the suit is upon a personal promise of the executor or administrator, or in debt on a judgment suggesting a devastavit, or upon the executor's or administrator's bond, in all which cases the executor or administrator is directly responsible, bail may be directed, upon proper affidavit made, according to the act. (*f*)

Judgment.—The general judgment against an executor is de

(*a*) R. C. c. 128, §16, (*b*) Brooke *v.* Shelby, 4 H. & M. 266.
(*c*) 2 Lom. Ex. 376; Brown *v.* Putney, 1 Wash. 302.
(*d*) Hansford *v.* Elliott, 9 Leigh. 79; Clark *v.* Hardiman, 2 Leigh. 347.
(*e*) 2 Lom. Ex. 421. (*f*) Ib. 409; 2 Tuck. Com. 234.

bonis testatoris; and this is the judgment given where the executor, &c., has not made himself personally responsible. But a judgment de propriis will be given, where the executor has promised to answer any debt or damage due by his testator out of his own estate. But such promise must be in writing, (*a*) and for good consideration as assets in his hands or forbearance to sue on part of the creditor. (*b*) And where forbearance is the consideration, it seems that without a writing, an executor, &c., is liable, where he promises to pay the debt of his testator. (*c*) A judgment quando assets acciderent is given where the executor pleads plene administravit, and the jury find for him thereon.

Assets.—What shall be assets in the hands of the executor, &c., remains as at common law, being in general the personal estate or whatever the executor, &c., may demand by suit, except so far as altered by these provisions of the statute.

If any person die after the 1st day of March, the servants and slaves of which he was possessed, employed in making a crop, shall be continued on the plantation until the last day of December following, and their crops shall be assets. If decedent die on or after the 1st day of March, all the emblements of his land which shall be severed before the 31st day of December following, shall be assets: but all such emblements growing on the land at that day, or at the time of decedent's death, if that event happen after the 31st day of December and before the 1st day of March, shall pass with the land to the heir. (*d*)

Where any person shall die seized of lands held for the life of another, and shall devise the same, all the interest of the deceased in such lands shall be assets in the hands of such devisee; and if no such devises be made, such lands, for the residue of the term, shall be assets in the hands of the heir, as special occupant; and if there be no special occupant, it shall go to the executors or administrators, and be assets in their hands. (*e*)

Lands.—At the common law, a bond binding the heirs is a lien on the heir, who in default of personal assets is bound to discharge it out of the real assets of the obligor, provided real assets

(*a*) R. C. c. 101, § 1.
(*b*) Taliaferro *v.* Robbs, 2 Call. 258.
(*c*) 3 Mun. 59; 2 Tuck. Com. 139.
(*d*) R. C. c. 104, §§ 53, 54.
(*e*) Ib. § 61.

have descended. This doctrine has been extended by an act passed in 1842, which charges upon lands, &c., all debts due by specialty (whether binding the heirs or not); and also by simple contract, provided they be evidenced by writing, signed by the debtor or some person legally empowered by him. (*a*)

At the common law also, the heir could release himself from all liability upon his ancestor's obligation, by a bona fide alienation of the lands descended before action brought. To prevent this, it has been enacted that where any heir at law shall be liable to pay the debt of his ancestor, in regard of any lands, &c., descending to him, and shall sell the same before any action brought, such heir at law shall be answerable for such debt or debts, in any action or actions of debt to the value of the said land so by him sold. (*b*)

Nor by the common law was land in the hands of a devisee liable for the payment of bonds of the devisor binding the heirs. But the statute declares the devise in such cases, so far as concerns the creditors, to be void. (*c*)

The before recited act of 1842 (*d*) enacts, that where any person shall die seized of or entitled to any estate or interest in lands, tenements or hereditaments, or other real estate, which he shall not by his last will and testament have charged with or devised subject to the payment of his debts, the same shall be assets. The phraseology of this act is very general, embracing all estate or interest which a person may have in any real estate whatever. So that in general terms, whatever real estate a person leaves at his death is liable for all of his debts which are evidenced by writing.

Administration of assets.—The dignity of debts is in the following order:

1. Funeral expenses and expenses of administration, and debts due to the state or United States.

2. Debts due by the testator or intestate, as guardian, curator, or committee to a ward, idiot, or lunatic, or their representatives. (*e*)

3. Debts of record, being by judgment or recognizance.

(*a*) Acts 1841–42, c. 98. (*b*) R. C. c. 105, § 6. (*c*) Ib. §§ 1, 2, and 3.
(*d*) Acts 1841–42, c. 98. (*e*) R. C. c. 108, § 12; ib. c. 104, § 60.

4. Debts evidenced by specialty or writing, signed by the testator or intestate. An act passed in 1831 directs that, in the administration of the personal assets of decedent's estates, debts due by specialty and promissory notes or other writings signed by the decedent or some other person by him or her thereunto lawfully authorized, shall be regarded and taken to be of equal dignity, (*a*) and the act of 1842, before referred to, declares what shall be real assets, and then directs that they shall be administered, in courts of equity, *ratably* for the payment of all the just debts of the decedent, as well debts due on simple contract as on specialty, provided that no debt which is not evidenced by writing signed by the debtor or some person legally empowered by him, shall be charged on the real estate by virtue thereof. Simple contract debts in writing are thus put on an equality with specialty debts, by the one act as to *personal* assets, and by the other act as to *equitable* assets.

5. Debts by simple contract, not evidenced by writing.

6. Judgments or bonds, voluntarily confessed or given by testator or intestate, not for valuable consideration

9. *Remedies to recover Debts.*

Courts and time required to obtain judgment.—The Circuit Superior Courts of Law and Chancery sit twice a year, and the County and Corporation Courts sit four times a year, in every county and corporation. These courts have concurrent jurisdiction in all matters in equity, and also at law, where the amount in controversy is more than fifty dollars, and also in actions of detinue and trover; and in suits at law, where the amount in controversy is less than fifty and more than twenty dollars, the County and Corporation Courts have sole jurisdiction. (*b*) Writs in the Circuit Superior Courts are returnable either to the first day of the next succeeding term, or to some previous rule day; and in the County and Corporation Courts, to the first day of the next succeeding term alone. (*c*) Rules, in both these courts, are held in the clerk's offices on the first Monday of every month, (*d*) except where such court commences its session during the week

(*a*) Sup. R. C. c. 160. (*b*) R. C. c. 71, §7; Sup. R. C. c. 109, §§22, 23.
(*c*) R. C. c. 128, §70; Sup. R. C. c. 212, §2. (*d*) R. C. c. 128, §69.

in which the first Monday comes, in which case, the rules are held on the next preceding Monday. (*a*) Common law suits, in Virginia, are, for the most part, perfected at the rules, by the clerk's entering up, on the second rule day, an office judgment. This office judgment may be set aside by the defendant's appearing at the next term of the court and pleading to issue: (*b*) but none but an issuable plea can be then received. And every office judgment, in which no writ of inquiry is awarded, and which is not set aside as aforesaid, is considered as a final judgment of the last day of the term, and executions may issue thereon. (*c*) So that, where no plea is entered, judgment may be obtained in two or three months from the return day of the writ.

Kinds of actions and parties thereto.—An ordinance of convention in 1776 made the common law of England, and all acts of parliament made in aid thereof, prior to the fourth year of James I. which were of a general nature, the law of Virginia. An act of assembly in 1792 (*d*) referring to this ordinance, directs that no act of parliament shall have any force or authority within this commonwealth, saving however "all and every writ or writs, remedial or judicial" which could have been had previous thereto. Under these, there remain in Virginia all the common law actions of debt, assumpsit, detinue, &c.

A further statute enacts that "an action of debt may be maintained upon any note or writing by which the person signing the same shall promise or oblige himself to pay a sum of money or quantity of tobacco. (*e*) But this writing must acknowledge a sum to be due, which is certain, and subject to no contingency whatever. (*f*) Under this law an action of debt will lie for a payee against the acceptor of an order, although it is not so in England. (*g*)

Attachments against non-residents.—By statute, if any suit shall be commenced in equity against any defendant, who is out of this state, and another within the same having in his hands effects or debts of such absent defendant, upon affidavit such court may make any order and require security if necessary, to restrain the home defendant from paying, conveying away or secreting

(*a*) Acts of 1845–46, c. 74. (*b*) R. C. c. 128, § 77. (*c*) Ib. § 79.
(*d*) Ib. c. 40. (*e*) Ib. c. 125, § 4. (*f*) Beirne *v.* Dunlap, 8 Leigh 514.
(*g*) Hollingsworth *v.* Milton, 8 Leigh 50.

the effects or debts in his hands of such absent defendant, and may order such effects or debts to be delivered or paid to the plaintiff upon his giving security. (*a*) The preliminary steps required, by a literal interpretation of this law, to procure the attachment, were found in practice to be too dilatory—and hence the courts have sanctioned the practice of allowing the clerks to endorse the restraining order on the subpœna, at the time of its issue, which order is binding on the home defendant from the time of the service of the subpœna. (*b*) This attachment may be brought by a creditor residing out of this state (*c*) and against even a corporation of another state. (*d*)

Attachments against absconding debtors.—The same statute, (*e*) section 6, provides that "if any person shall make complaint to any justice of the peace that his debtor is removing out of the county or corporation privately, or absconds or conceals himself so that the ordinary process of law cannot be served on him, such justice shall grant an attachment against the estate of such debtor or so much thereof as shall be sufficient to satisfy the debt and costs of such complainant, which attachment, where the debt or demand shall exceed ten dollars or four hundred pounds of tobacco, shall be returnable to the next County or Corporation Court, and shall be levied upon the slaves, goods and chattels of the party absconding, wherever the same shall be found, or in the hands of any person indebted to, or having any effects of the party absconding. By section 11 the attachment, when for a sum less than ten dollars, is returnable and triable before a single justice instead of the court. By section 13, if any such attachment be returned, executed, and the goods or effects attached be not replevined, or proper defence be not made, the plaintiff shall be entitled to judgment for his whole debt and execution thereof upon the goods and chattels as attached—and where such attachment is returned executed upon a garnishee, upon said garnishee's appearance and examination, as elsewhere pointed out, judgment shall go against said garnishee, for all sums of money due from him to or in his

(*a*) R. C. c. 40.

(*b*) McKim *v.* Fulton, 6 Call. 106; Williamson *v.* Bowie, 6 Mun. 176; Erskine *v.* Staley, 12 Leigh. 406.

(*c*) Williamson *v.* Bowie, 6 Mun. 176.

(*d*) U. S. Bank *v.* M. Bank of Balt. 1 Rob. 573.

(*e*) R. C. c. 123.

custody for the person absconding, and all goods and effects whatsoever in the hands of such garnishee, belonging to such absconding person. This act, being an innovation upon the common law, and a severe remedy liable to abuse, it should be construed strictly, and the plaintiff must bring himself within its words or most obvious intent. (*a*)

Parties to a suit.—Various provisions are found in the acts, regulating the parties to actions, as where one of those in interest dies, &c., but the only material variations from the common law, are these:

1. An assignee of any bond, bill, promissory note or any other writing obligatory whatsoever, may, upon the assignment, maintain any action in his own name which the original obligee or payee might have brought, but shall allow all just discounts, not only against himself, but against the assignee, before notice of the assignment was given to the defendant. (*b*)

2. Such assignee may sue any remote assignor, but such assignor shall have the same defence, as if the suit had been instituted by his immediate assignee, and no action shall be prosecuted against two or more assignors, unless they be joint: and this act shall not abridge any rights to which indorsers of bills of exchange, or assignees of bonds, notes, or obligations, were formerly entitled. (*c*)

Judgment; lien.—There is no statute in Virginia which, in express terms, makes a judgment a lien upon the lands of the debtor, unless a statute passed in 1843 and mentioned below, possesses that effect. As in England, the lien is the consequence of a right to take out an elegit. The whole subject therefore remains as at common law, with the addition thereto of the statute of 1843.

The act in the Revised Code gives the privilege of taking out an elegit, and prescribes the form of the writ. (*d*) From that act, it appears that the elegit binds the goods and chattels, saving oxen and beasts of the plough, and a moiety of all the lands and tenements of which the defendant was seized at the day of the plaintiff's obtaining the judgment or at any time afterwards; and directs the sheriff to deliver the same to the plaintiff as his own proper

(*a*) 3 Call. 415, 416; 2 H. & M. 315; 7 Leigh. 311, 313, 314.

(*b*) R. C. c. 125, § 5. (*c*) Ib. § 6. (*d*) Ib. c. 134, § 1.

goods, chattels and freehold, until he shall have levied thereof, out of the rents, hires and profits, his debt and damages by the judgment. (*a*) As every judgment in a term is of the first day of the term, an elegit binds lands, &c., from the first day of the term in which judgment was obtained (*b*) even in the hands of bona fide purchasers since that time, without notice. (*c*) The plaintiff preserves the lien of his judgment, by issuing his elegit within a year from his judgment or entering upon the roll book in England or record book here, that he elects to charge the goods and half the lands which would be equal to issuing the elegit; and if he does neither, he might, on motion, be allowed to enter the election nunc pro tunc. (*d*) But it is not essential to the existence of the lien, that the elegit shall have issued; some other execution within the year will keep the judgment alive, and preserve the right to an elegit. (*e*) If during the term in which judgment was obtained, the defendant executes a deed of trust, conveying real and personal, estate and the plaintiff, after judgment, without issuing any execution, file a bill in chancery to subject the property as conveyed, the court will dismiss the bill as to the personalty, without injury to the plaintiff's right to the money resulting therefrom, after satisfying the deed, but will also direct the trustees to sell the lands, and out of the proceeds, to satisfy the judgment in the first place, and then the deed. (*f*)

The statute of 1843, before referred to, directs the clerk of every county or corporation court to keep a judgment docket, in which he shall docket all such unsatisfied final judgments and decrees, and such forfeited forthcoming bonds, recognizances, and other bonds having the force of judgments, as any person interested therein shall require him to docket; in such docket plainly setting down the date of such judgment, and the names, descriptions, and residences of the parties, so far as they can be ascer-

(*a*) R. C. c. 134, § 1.

(*b*) Skipwith *v.* Cunningham, 8 Leigh. 271; Coutts *v.* Walker 2 Leigh. 268; Mut. Ass. Soc. *v.* Stanard, 4 Mun. 539.

(*c*) Taylor *v.* Spindle, 2 Grat. 44.

(*d*) Epes *v.* Randolph, 2 Call. 186; Avery *v.* Robinson, 4 Mun. 546.

(*e*) Scriba *v.* Deans, 1 Brock. 166, 170; Taylor *v.* Spindle, 2 Grat. 44.

(*f*) Mut. Ass. Soc. *v.* Stanard, 4 Mun. 539.

tained from the record, the debt, damages, interest, and costs in each case, and the amount and date of credits, if any: and further, that no judgment, decree, bond, or recognizance, thereafter rendered, executed, or acknowledged, shall bind the land of any party to the same, against a bona fide purchaser, for valuable consideration without notice, unless the same shall be docketed in the county or corporation in which the land may lie, within twelve months after the rendition or forfeiture of such judgment, decree, bond, or recognizance, or ninety days before such land shall have been conveyed to such purchaser. (*a*) It is supposed, however, that this statute affects only the manner of acquiring and holding the lien by judgment, leaving the right and law in relation thereto, as it was before, and at common law.

Revivor.—The act allowing executions allows them only within a year from the judgment; (*b*) but where execution hath once issued within the year, new executions may go until satisfaction. (*c*) A judgment, therefore, upon which no execution has issued within a year from its date, cannot support an execution, and is therefore dead; but it may be revived by a scire facias or an action of debt brought thereon, within ten years next after the date of such judgment, and not after. (*d*) And where a suit abates, or a judgment becomes dead, by death of one of the parties, both may be reinstated, where a mere revival is sought, by scire facias, and a bill of revivor is unnecessary. (*e*)

All persons who shall recover any debt, damages, or costs by judgment, may prosecute writs of fieri facias, elegit, and capias ad satisfaciendum within the year, for taking the goods, lands, or body of the person against whom such judgment is obtained. (*f*)

Elegit.—The force and effect of this writ in Virginia, has been sufficiently explained under lien of judgment.

Fieri facias.—This writ or other writ of execution (including the elegit, as far as it is against the goods) shall bind the property of the goods, against which such writ is sued forth, but from the

(*a*) Acts 1842–43, c. 75. (*b*) R. C. c. 134, § 1. (*c*) Ib. § 3; c. 128, § 5.
(*d*) Ib. c. 128, § 5. (*e*) Vaughan *v.* Wilson, 4 H. & M. 480.
(*f*) R. C. c. 134, § 1.

time that such writ shall be delivered to the sheriff or other officer to be executed. (*a*) From the day of delivery of such execution to the officer, the creditor acquires a lien upon the goods of the debtor, of which he cannot be deprived by the act of the debtor—and this lien exists whether the execution is levied or not—and a subsequent sale of his goods by the debtor is void. (*b*) If two or more writs of fieri facias against the same person be delivered to the same officer, they shall take precedence of each other, according to the time of their delivery; but if the two writs be delivered to different officers they take precedence according to the time of their actual execution. (*c*) The writ of fieri facias is privileged in this, that after the discharge of the body of a debtor from custody, either upon his taking the oath of insolvency, or under the law concerning jail fees, the creditor may still, without any notice to the debtor or order of court, sue out his writ of fieri facias; and the same privilege extends to an elegit, but not to the capias ad satisfaciendum. (*d*)

Capias ad satisfaciendum.—All executions of capias ad satisfaciendum shall bind the real estate of the defendant, from the time when they shall be levied, (*e*) and also, the property of the goods, from the same time, (*f*) and shall have priority according to the time when they are levied. (*g*) These provisions, it will be perceived, are entire innovations upon the common law, which, so far from binding the property by the levy of a capias ad satisfaciendum, considered it entirely and for ever discharged. By the actual service of the capias ad satisfaciendum the lien of the judgment is destroyed, and the plaintiff can then only stand on the lien given to the capias ad satisfaciendum executed, as above; (*h*) and therefore, deeds made by the debtor after judgment, and before capias ad satisfaciendum executed, if afterwards capias ad satisfaciendum be served, will be good. But as this doctrine proceeds upon the principle that the levying of the capias

(*a*) R. C. c. 134, § 13.
(*b*) Pegram *v.* May, 9 Leigh. 176; Tate's Dig. 371
(*c*) R. C. c. 134, § 13; Tate's Dig. 371, note 1.
(*d*) Sup. R. C. c. 216, § 3; Acts 1845–46, c. 84.
(*e*) R. C. c. 134, § 10.
(*f*) Sup. R. C. c. 213, § 4.
(*g*) Foreman *v.* Loyd, 2 Leigh. 284.
(*h*) Rogers *v.* Marshall, 4 Leigh. 425.

ad satisfaciendum determines the right of the plaintiff to an elegit, it may possibly be affected by the act of 1846, (*a*) which allows an elegit after capias ad satisfaciendum has been executed and defendant discharged by taking the insolvent oath ; and the lien of the capias ad satisfaciendum executed, which is perfected only by the defendant's release as an insolvent, will not overreach the lien by elegit levied and land extended before such release, although the judgment on which the elegit issued was rendered after the service of the capias ad satisfaciendum. (*b*) Any debtor who shall be taken in execution, may discharge himself from custody, by subscribing and delivering a schedule of his whole estate, delivering over all personal estate contained in said schedule, and conveying all the real estate therein to the sheriff and taking the oath of insolvency, in form prescribed. (*c*) After such discharge no other writ of capias ad satisfaciendum shall issue, except by order of court, upon motion, after ten days' notice of such motion to the defendant. (*d*)

Bail in suits.—The English doctrine of appearance and special bail has been superseded by a statute passed in 1826, which provides that when bail shall be lawfully required on any writ of capias ad respondendum, the officer executing the same shall not discharge the defendant from custody, upon the execution of any bond for the appearance of such defendant, nor shall he take any such bond ; the defendant shall be discharged from custody upon giving good special bail to the action, in the manner therein provided. (*e*)

In all actions of debt founded upon any writing obligatory, bill, or note in writing, for the payment of money or tobacco, all actions of covenant and detinue, and all actions upon statutes especially authorizing bail to be taken, the plaintiff may of right demand bail. (*f*)

In all other personal actions, it shall be lawful for any judge of the General Court, or any justice of the peace for any county or corporation, upon proper affidavit verifying the justice of the plaintiff's action, and showing probable cause to apprehend that

(*a*) Sup. R. C. ch. 216, §3 ; Acts 1845–46, c. 84.

(*b*) Foreman *v.* Loyd, 2 Leigh. 287.

(*c*) R. C. c. 134, §31.

(*d*) Ib. §33.

(*e*) Sup. R. C. c. 208.

(*f*) R. C. c. 128, §43.

the defendant will depart from the jurisdiction of the court so that process of law cannot be served upon him, to direct bail to be taken, by indorsement on the original writ or subsequent process. (*a*)

In any personal action, in which bail shall not have been required, the court may, at any time before final judgment, for good cause shown, rule the defendant to give special bail, and on his failure to do so, may refuse him permission to plead, or may set aside any plea already pleaded by him and award a writ of inquiry, or otherwise proceed to judgment according to law, or may cause him to be arrested and committed to prison. (*b*)

Bonds with collateral conditions, or any collateral engagements whatever, are not within the act. (*c*) Bonds, which although not single bonds, are yet to be defeasanced by payment of an ascertained sum, and where the intervention of a jury is not necessary to judgment, are within the act, and bail is demandable; but if there be in the bond no ascertained sum, for which judgment may be given, and the intervention of a jury be necessary to ascertain what is due, such bond is one with a collateral condition, and bail is not demandable. (*d*) The indorser of a negotiable note is only collaterally liable, and therefore cannot be held to bail as of right. (*e*) The affidavit required by the statute to authorize bail where it is not demandable as of right, may be made by a third person, the plaintiff's agent, (*f*) and it is supposed may be made by a person out of the state.

If bail be not given, when required, the defendant shall be committed to prison. He may then, after reasonable notice to the plaintiff or his attorney, confess a judgment in the clerk's office, for the amount of the plaintiff's demand with interests and costs, or for such part thereof as the plaintiff or his attorney may consent to; and thereupon be forthwith discharged from custody, unless the plaintiff or his attorney shall direct otherwise, in which case he shall be and remain in custody, in the same manner and with the same effect as if under a capias ad satisfaciendum, (*g*)

(*a*) R. C, c. 128, § 44. (*b*) Ib. § 50.
(*c*) Ruffin *v*. Call. 2 Wash. 181; Nadenbonsh *v*. Lane, 4 Rand. 413.
(*d*) Henderson *v*. Hepburn, 2 Call. 238, 239.
(*e*) Metcalf *v*. Battaile, Gilmer 191; Hatcher *v*. Lewis, 4 Ran. 152.
(*f*) Ashby *v*. Kiger, 3 Ran. 50. (*g*) Sup. R. C. c. 217.

and may then discharge himself by taking the insolvent debtor's oath. And if bail be given, and the bail, after judgment, surrender the principal, such principal may discharge himself from custody by taking the insolvent debtor's oath. (*a*)

If bail be given, when required, the bail by bond undertakes that in case the defendant shall be cast in the suit, the said defendant will pay and satisfy the condemnation of the court, or render his body to prison in execution for the same, or that he the bail will do it for him. (*b*) In detinue the bail undertakes that in case the defendant be cast, the said defendant shall restore to the plaintiff the specific property sued for, or pay the alternative value thereof, or render his body to prison in execution for the same, or that the bail will do it for him. (*c*) In consequence, if the plaintiff, recover judgment, and cannot obtain satisfaction thereof and issue execution against the defendant's body, which is returned "not found," the bail becomes liable for the said judgment, upon a scire facias, unless he be discharged or discharge himself by one of these modes.

1. Bail may be discharged by the plaintiff failing to commence proceedings against him within three years after judgment against principal. (*d*)

2. Bail may discharge himself by surrendering his principal at any time before the end of the term next after the scire facias shall have been served upon him. (*e*) In detinue, however, such surrender shall discharge the bail only from the payment of the alternative value of the property recovered and the costs and damages, and not from the obligation to deliver the specific thing. (*f*)

(*a*) Acts 1842–43, c. 74.
(*b*) R. C. c. 128, § 51.
(*c*) Sup. R. C. c. 208, § 5.
(*d*) Acts 1845–46, c. 88.
(*e*) R. C. c. 128, § 54; Sup. R. C. c. 207.
(*f*) Sup. R. C. c. 208, § 6.

NORTH CAROLINA.

1. *Common Law.*

By an act passed in 1778, and which still remains in force, the common law which had been previously in force and use within the colony, is declared to exist in full vigor and effect, except so far as it is inconsistent with the political institutions of the state, or has been repealed or otherwise provided for. (*a*)

2. *Choses in Action.*

Bills, bonds, and promissory notes.—All promissory notes for the payment of money to any person or order, are put upon the same footing, and made negotiable as inland bills of exchange. (*b*)

All bills, bonds, or notes for money, whether with or without a seal, payable to order, or not, are transferable by indorsements, as promissory or negotiable notes are: and the indorsee may

(*a*) R. S. i. 110.

(*b*) Ib. 93.

maintain an action on the case thereon in his own name, or an action of debt, if such action could have been maintained by the original obligee. (*a*)

Upon any order drawn upon any third person, for the payment of money, the drawer and acceptor shall be liable: but before any suit shall lie against the drawer, for non-acceptance, the note must be first protested, and notice thereof given to the drawer. (*b*)

In all cases wherein it may be necessary to prove a demand upon, or notice to, the drawer or indorser of a bill of exchange, or other negotiable security, or a demand upon the acceptor or drawer of a bill of exchange, the protest of a notary public, or in default of one, of a justice of the peace, or clerk of a court of record, setting forth that he has made such demand or given such notice, and the manner in which the same has been done, shall be prima facie evidence of the facts so set forth. (*c*)

Actions may be brought upon protested bills of exchange, against drawers and indorsers, jointly or separately. (*d*)

The acts rendering sealed instruments and other securities not known to the law merchant, negotiable, do not entitle them tc days of grace. (*e*)

Where any negotiable securities, other than bills of exchange, inland or foreign, are indorsed, the indorsement, unless otherwise expressed, shall render the indorser or indorsers liable as surety or sureties to any holder of such instrument, and no demand upon the maker is necessary before proceeding against an indorser. (*f*) This act applies only where the antecedent indorsements, unless expressed to be without recourse, as well as the indorsement in question, have been made within the state. (*g*)

There are, it is believed, no other provisions changing the common law as to the assignability of choses in action.

In Griffith's Law Register, vol. 3, p. 222, a scroll is said to be equivalent to a seal in every case.

Damages upon protested bills.—The rate of damages upon protested bills, where the bill is drawn or indorsed in the state

(*a*) R. S. i. 94. (*b*) Ib. 95. (*c*) Ib. 95. (*d*) Ib. 95.

(*e*) Jarvis *v.* McMain, 3 Hawks 10; Fields *v.* Mallet, ib. 465.

(*f*) R. S. 95. (*g*) Ingersoll *v.* Long, 4 Den. & Batt. 293.

upon any person or body corporate in any other of the United States, or the territories thereof, excepting the state of Louisiana, is fixed at three per cent. on the principal sum: upon bills drawn or indorsed as aforesaid, upon any person or body corporate in any other place in North America, or the islands thereof, excepting the Northwest coast of America, or in any of the West Indies or Bahama islands, ten per cent. upon such principal sum: upon bills drawn or indorsed as aforesaid, upon any person or body corporate in the island of Madeira, the Canaries, the Azores, the Cape de Verd islands, or in any other state or place in Europe or South America, fifteen per cent. on such principal sum: and where such bills shall be drawn or indorsed as aforesaid, upon any person or body corporate in any other part of the world, twenty per cent. on such principal sum. (*a*)

Book accounts.—Book accounts may be received in any action of debt or case, as evidence of goods sold, or services performed, for all charges within two years, on oath of the plaintiff that the matter in dispute is a book account, and that he hath no other means to prove the delivery of such articles, and that such book contains a true account of all the dealings or the last settlement of accounts between them, and that all the articles therein contained, and by him so proved, were bona fide delivered, and that he hath given the defendant all just credits. (*b*)

A copy from the book of accounts proved as in the preceding manner, may be received as evidence, unless the defendant or his attorney has given notice at the joining of the issue that he will require the production of the original book.

No book account verified by the oath of the plaintiff as aforesaid, shall be received to establish any claim, the amount whereof exceeds sixty dollars.

A set-off may be proven where it consists of a book account, in the same manner as if it constituted the foundation of the action.

Similar provisions exist for the reception of book accounts where executors or administrators are either plaintiffs or defendants.

The act authorizing a party to prove his book account by his

(*a*) R. S. 95. Acts of 1841, 3.

(*b*) R. S. 97.

own oath, only removes his incompetency as a witness: it leaves his credibility to be examined by a jury: and the opposite party may in reply prove him to be not worthy of credit on oath. (*a*)

3. *Interest.*

Six per cent. is the established rate of interest, and all agreements for a higher rate are utterly void, and any person receiving more, liable to a forfeiture of double the amount of the loan, one moiety to go to the state, and the other to the informer. (*b*)

Bonds, bills and notes payable on demand, do not bear interest until such demand has been made. (*c*) Securities for the payment or delivery of tobacco and all other specific articles bear interest as moneyed contracts, that is, the articles are valued by a jury at the time they become due, and interest charged accordingly. (*d*)

4. *Frauds.*

All contracts for the sale of lands or slaves, or any interest therein, or a memorandum or note thereof, must be in writing, and signed by the party to be charged. (*e*)

Persons removing or assisting in removing any debtor out of the county in which he has resided for six months, with intent to hinder, delay or defraud his creditors, are made liable for all the engagements of the debtor in such county. Contracts of executors to be answerable out of their own estate, or to charge any person with the debt or default of another, must be in writing, or some memorandum or note thereof, signed by the person to be charged therewith.

The English statutes against fraudulent conveyances are in force.

5. *Corporations.*

Shares of stock in all incorporated joint stock companies in the state, are declared to be personal estate, and as such may be held by aliens, and transferred under such rules and regulations

(*a*) Kitchen *v*. Tyson, 3 Mur. 314. (*b*) R. S. 606. (*c*) Ib. 94. (*d*) Ib. (*e*) Ib. 290.

not inconsistent with the laws of the state, as the corporation may from time to time establish. (*a*)

6. *Principal and Surety.*

The usual summary remedy of judgment upon motion and citation is given to a surety who has paid the debt of his principal. (*b*)

Where any surety has discharged the debt of his principal, his claim against the estate of the latter is put upon an equal footing in the administration of the assets, with that of the creditor who has been paid. (*c*)

7. *Limitation of Actions.*

All actions of account render, actions upon the case, of debt for arrearages of rent, of debt upon simple contract, actions of detinue, replevin and trespass, either for goods and chattels or quare clausum fregit, must be brought within three years after the cause of action has accrued, except such accounts as concern the trade of merchandise between merchant and merchant, and their factors or servants; saving, however, to infants, feme coverts, persons non compos mentis, imprisoned and beyond seas, the period of limitation after the removal of their disability: where any person against whom there is a cause of action is beyond seas at the time of its accruing, the action may be brought within the term of limitation after the return of such person. (*d*)

The limitation thus prescribed applies as well to indorsed bonds and other securities made transferable by law, as to promissory notes.

Upon all judgments, contracts and agreements, a presumption of payment or satisfaction arises after the lapse of ten years. The abandonment of the right of redeeming a mortgage or other equitable interest, and presumption of payment, arises within the same time. Mortgages of personal estate must be redeemed

(*a*) R. S. 121. (*b*) Ib. i. 597. (*c*) Ib. 598. (*d*) Ib. 373, 374.

within two years after forfeiture. (*a*) No scire facias against the bail of any defendant can be sued out after the lapse of four years from the time of rendering the judgment or entering the decree against such defendant. (*b*)

8. *Effect of Death upon the Rights of Creditors.*

Every executor or administrator shall, within two months from the period of his qualification as such, advertise at the court-house of the county where the deceased usually dwelt, and other public places, for all persons having claims upon his estate to exhibit them within the period prescribed by law. The executor or administrator, at the expiration of two years, is to pay over to such persons as may be entitled by law or the will of the deceased, the estate remaining in his hands, taking however from such persons a refunding bond, with two or more sureties, that if any debt truly owing by the deceased, shall be afterwards recovered, or made to appear, then he or they shall respectively refund his or her ratable part of that debt, out of the share so allowed, the bonds so taken to be returned to court for the protection and benefit of any such creditor. (*c*)

All creditors residing within the state shall exhibit their claims within two years from the qualification of the executors or administrators, or if living out of the state within three, or be forever barred, saving however one year to persons non compos, feme coverts, and infants, after the removal of their disabilities. (*d*)

An executor, however, has an honest discretion to plead or not to plead the statute of limitations to a claim against his testator's estate. (*e*)

If the personal estate of the deceased, which is of a perishable nature, and moneys on hand, are not sufficient to discharge his debts, his remaining personal property may be sold by his representative on order of the County Court, obtained for that purpose. No executor or administrator can be required to plead to any original suit brought against him at law, until the expira-

(*a*) R. S. i. 376. (*b*) Ib. 375. (*c*) Ib. 276, 277. (*d*) Ib. 375.
(*e*) Sandridge *v.* Spurgen, 2 Iredell's Equity 267.

tion of nine calendar months from the time of his taking the office. (*a*)

The only alteration of the English rules for the administration of assets, is in the acts of 1786, which places bills, bonds, notes, whether with or without seal, and all liquidated accounts signed by the debtor, upon the same footing. (*b*)

The real estate of a deceased debtor cannot be sold upon a judgment against his personal representatives. But when on a plea of fully administered, in a suit against an executor or administrator, the issue is found for the defendant, the plaintiff may sue out a scire facias against the heirs and devisees of the debtor, to appear and show cause, if any there be, why execution should not issue against the real estate for the amount of such judgment. Upon the return of such scire facias, the heirs and devisees may contest the finding of fully administered, in a collateral issue with the executor or administrator: and if such issue be found against the defendant, or be not made, judgment may pass against the heirs or devisees, and execution issue thereon against the real estate of the debtor in the hands of the heirs or devisees. Where the executor or administrator fails to plead plene administravit, or it is found against him, and he proves insolvent, the creditor, if he has been guilty of no negligence or collusion, may have the same remedy against the heirs or devisees, who may likewise, in such proceeding, contest the insolvency of the executor, or the want of assets.

The creditor may bring a joint or several action against the heirs and devisees.

The lands of a deceased debtor remain liable for the payment of his debts for the space of two years from the probate of the will or granting letters of administration upon his estate. (*c*)

When the goods and chattels of any deceased person are insufficient to pay his debts, the executor or administrator may sell the real estate, of whatever kind, under a license which he obtains on petition, from the County Court, or Superior Court of the county in which the letters have been granted. The proceeds of the real estate thus sold shall be deemed assets, in the same

(*a*) Williams *v.* Maitland, 1 Iredell 92.

(*b*) R. S. i. 276.

(*c*) Ib. 362 to 367.

manner as if the estate had been personal: bonds and obligations binding the heirs being put on the same equal footing with other specialties, bills, promissory notes and liquidated accounts. (*a*)

9. *Insolvent Law.*

Any debtor charged on mesne process, or in execution for debt, and having remained in close prison twenty days, or having taken the benefit of the prison bounds, may, on a petition to two justices or to the County Court, or to a judge of the Superior or Supreme Court, in or out of court, notice having been given to the creditors at whose suit he is imprisoned, be forever discharged from execution against his body on such debts, by taking an oath that he is not worth ten dollars over and above certain trifling articles allowed him by the law, and that he has not, directly or indirectly, disposed of any of his property to defraud his creditors.

Or such debtor may petition to be discharged from imprisonment on surrender of all his property, and upon filing a full and exact schedule of the same, verified by affidavit, and giving notice of his application to the creditors at whose suit he is imprisoned, the court may direct his discharge, and he shall be exempt from future arrest for any debt existing at the time of such discharge. Any creditor may suggest fraud or concealment on the part of the debtor, and if the same is found in an issue against him, he will not be released.

All the property of the debtor contained in the schedule, real and personal, vests in the sheriff of the county where it is filed, whose duty it is to sell and convert the same into money, and pay the proceeds into the Court of Pleas and Quarter Sessions. The court thereupon appoints two commissioners to examine into the claims of all the creditors of the insolvent, and make a pro rata distribution among them of his effects.

Any debtor who has been arrested upon a ca. sa., or is in custody by surrender of bail after judgment, may obtain his release from confinement by giving bond with sufficient security for his appearance at the next court, to which the execution was return-

(*a*) Acts of 1847, 1. (*b*) R. S. i. 320 to 329.

able, to abide such proceedings as the court might take, as to allowing him the benefit of the insolvent act. The debtor having given ten days' previous notice in writing to his creditors of his intention to take the benefit of the act, may, unless some creditor suggests fraud or concealment of his property, and upon an issue made up to try the same, it is found against the debtor, be admitted either to take the oath for the benefit of insolvent debtors, or to swear to a schedule previously filed. And his discharge is to have the effect previously stated.

The suggestion of fraud must be made by the creditor in writing, setting forth the particulars of the fraud or concealment, and accompanied by his affidavit that he verily believes the matter therein stated to be true. (*a*)

10. *Attachment.*

An attachment may issue against the estate of any debtor who absconds, so that the ordinary process of law cannot be served upon him, on an affidavit being made to that fact, before any judge of the Supreme or Superior Courts, or any justice of the County Court, by the creditor, his agent or factor, and a similar affidavit as to the amount of the debt or demand. (*b*)

An attachment may also issue in favor of a citizen of the state against any non-resident debtor, but not in favor of a non-resident creditor against a non-resident debtor. (*c*) Before the writ of attachment can issue, the plaintiff is required to give bond with security, to be returned with the affidavit into court, conditioned to satisfy all costs and damages which the defendant may sustain by reason of the wrongful issuing of the attachment.

The real and personal estate of the defendant are both subject to the attachment.

A surplus of money raised by execution, remaining in the hands of the sheriff, may be attached by the creditors of the original defendant. (*d*)

Any persons having in possession effects of an absconding or

(*a*) Acts of 1845, 45. (*b*) R. S. i. 70.

(*c*) Broghill *v.* Wellburn, 4 Dev. 511 ; Taylor *v.* Buckley, 5 Iredell 383.

(*d*) Orr *v.* McBride, 2 Car. L. R. 257.

absent debtor, or indebted to the same, may be summoned as garnishees, to appear and state under oath the amount of such effects or indebtedness. Where a garnishee appears and confesses, a judgment may be entered and execution awarded for the use of the plaintiff, against such garnishee, for all sums of money due to the defendant, or effects of the defendant in the hands of such garnishee. If any garnishee fails to appear and discover upon oath, as required, the court may enter up against him a conditional judgment, upon which a scire facias may issue, returnable to the next term, to show cause why a final judgment should not be rendered against him, and upon the continued default of such garnishee, the court may confirm the judgment, and award execution for the whole debt of the plaintiff. When the garnishee denies that he owes to, or has in his hands any estate of the defendant, and the party plaintiff shall suggest an opposite statement on oath, the question may be tried by a jury, on an issue made up under the direction of the court, and upon the verdict of the jury the court may give judgment as in other cases.

Where an attachment has been levied upon the goods or estate of a non-resident of the county from which the writ has emanated, the pendency of the same must be made known by the clerk by public advertisement for the space of six weeks, and until the expiration of this period final judgment cannot be rendered upon the attachment. (*a*)

Similar provisions are made for the issuing of writs of attachment, in cases cognizable by a justice of the peace. When real estate is attached, in such case, and condemned by the justice, it is his duty to return the proceeds to the next County Court, who may affirm the same, and issue a venditioni exponas.

The provisions of the attachment law are to be strictly construed, and very trivial objections to the process and to the jurisdiction will be entertained, if brought forward at the proper time. (*b*)

(*a*) R. S. i. 75.

(*b*) Skinner *v.* Moore, 2 Dev. & Batt. 138 ; State Bank *v.* Hinton, et als. 1 Dev. 397.

9. *Proceedings in Civil Suits.*

Bail; judicial attachment.—No clerk or his deputy may grant any writ or leading process, returnable to any court of record, until he has taken sufficient security from the persons applying for the same, conditioned for the prosecution of the suit, and in case of failure of such prosecution, for the payment of such costs and damages as may be awarded by the court to the defendant; and for a violation of this provision the clerk is liable to a penalty of two hundred dollars, to be recovered from him by the defendant in an action of debt, in the court where the offence has been committed. (*a*)

Where the sheriff returns that the defendant is not to be found in his county, the plaintiff may at his election sue out an alias and other process, to compel an appearance, or an attachment against his estate; and if the sheriff returns any goods attached by him, the plaintiff may file his declaration, and proceed as in other cases to judgment; and if the goods attached are not replevied, they may be sold as on an execution of fi. fa., and if the judgment remains unsatisfied, the plaintiff may have execution for the residue. (*b*)

Judicial attachments may issue against the estate of persons who have left the state, after leading process has been executed on them. (*c*)

No female can be taken or imprisoned for debt, upon either mesne or final process. (*d*)

A writ of capias ad respondendum may issue with the ordinary subpœna from courts of equity, where the plaintiff shall specially state upon oath his debt or damages, before one of the judges of the Superior Court of law and equity, or one of the judges of the Supreme Court, or the clerk and master in equity. (*e*)

Upon this writ when thus emanating from a court of equity, or from a court of law, except where executors or administrators are defendants, it is the duty of the sheriff to require sufficient bail, and in case of his failure to take any bail, or that which

(*a*) R. S. i. 152. (*b*) Ib. 155. (*c*) Ib. 75. (*d*) Ib. 155. (*e*) Ib. 177.

upon exception shall be found insufficient, he shall stand as special bail. (*a*)

See under the title, "*Insolvent Law,*" as to the mode by which a debtor may release his body from custody.

Judgment and execution.—Execution of fi. fa. may issue against the real as well as personal estate of the debtor; the former of which may be sold after forty days previous advertisement thereof, in three public places in the county, without any valuation or appraisement. Upon this writ, the goods and chattels of the debtor, if such are to be found, must be first taken, and if these are not sufficient to satisfy the plaintiff's claim, then the writ may be levied upon the lands and tenements. The equity of redemption, and the legal right of redemption in all lands, tenements, rents, and mortgages, may be taken and sold under this execution. The writ may be also levied upon goods and chattels, lands or tenements, held in trust for the person against whom the execution issues. (*b*)

The creditor may, if he prefers, resort to the writ of elegit, and obtain possession of all his chattels, and a moiety of the lands of his debtor, until his debt be levied upon a reasonable extent. In this case, the lands of the debtor are bound from the rendition of the judgment; in the former, from the teste of the writ. (*c*)

Where the elegit is issued, it binds all the lands owned by the defendant at the time of its rendition; where a fi. fa. is sued out, lands are only bound from its teste, and sales made after that time, of land situated where the writ does not run, as in another county, are valid. (*d*)

It has been held that under the peculiar law of North Carolina, an elegit will not divest the title of any purchaser under a fi. fa. issuing upon a junior judgment. The first execution finally acted on, protects both the purchaser under it, and the plaintiff in it.

The sheriff upon executing a writ of fi. fa. may permit the goods and chattels levied on, to remain in the possession of the defendant upon his giving a bond with security, conditioned for

(*a*) R. S. 87. (*b*) Ib. i. 265. 266.

(*c*) Winstead *v.* Winstead, 1 Hay 243; Ingles *v.* Donaldson, 2 Hay 57; Gilkes *v.* Dickerson, 2 Hawks 341. (*d*) Hardy *v.* Jasper, 3 Dev. 158.

(*e*) Ricks *v.* Blount, 4 Dev. 128.

their forthcoming to answer the execution. If such bond is forfeited, the officer may obtain a summary judgment upon ten days notice for the amount of the debt, and the damages which a jury empanneled for the pupose may ascertain. (*a*)

No execution can issue upon a judgment, after a year and a day from its rendition, without a scire facias to revive the same, except that where execution has been taken out during such period, it may continue to issue for the term of a year and a day from the period of the last issuing. (*b*)

A ca. sa. cannot issue on any case unless the plaintiff or his agent make an affidavit in writing before the clerk of the court in which the judgment was rendered, or the justice of the peace to whom the application is made for such process, that he believes the defendant has not property to satisfy such judgment which can be reached by a fieri facias, and has property, moneys, or effects which cannot be reached by a fieri facias, or has fraudulently concealed his property, moneys, or effects, or is about to remove from the state.

No issue of fraud will be made up and tried unless upon the written suggestion of the creditor or his agent, specifying the particulars of the fraud or concealment, and accompanied by an affidavit to their truth. (*c*)

Courts.—The judicial system of North Carolina is very similar to that of Virginia. The Superior Courts of law and equity are held twice each year in every county of the state, once in the spring and once in the fall. County Courts are held quarterly in each county, having concurrent jurisdiction with the Superior Court in cases where the matter in controversy exceeds one hundred dollars.

(*a*) R. S. 278. (*b*) Ib. 170. (*c*) Acts of 1845, 45.

SOUTH CAROLINA.

1. BONDS, BILLS, AND PROMISSORY NOTES.
2. FRAUDS AND FRAUDULENT CONVEYANCES.
3. INTEREST.
4. AGENTS.
5. LIMITED PARTNERSHIPS.
6. LIMITATION OF ACTIONS.
7. ATTACHMENT.
8. INSOLVENT LAW.
9. EFFECT OF DEATH UPON THE RIGHTS OF CREDITORS
10. PROCEEDINGS IN CIVIL SUITS

1. *Bonds, Bills, and Promissory Notes.*

All bonds, bills, and promissory notes, whether payable to order or not, may be assigned or endorsed so that an assignee may maintain an action thereupon in his own name; the defendant however not to be precluded from any discount or defence to which he would have been entitled as against the obligee or payee. (*a*)

The assignees of any judgments or decrees may bring suit thereon in their own names as such, in the same manner and subject to the same equities as the assignees of any bond, bill or note not negotiable. (*b*)

No acceptance of an inland bill of exchange is sufficient unless in writing.

A protest is only necessary upon inland bills of exchange and promissory notes, to recover the interest, damages, and costs allowed by law. Upon all protested bills of exchange suit may be brought against the drawers and endorsers either jointly or separately. Upon such bills, if drawn upon persons out of the state, but within the United States, the rate of damages is fixed at ten per

(*a*) Statutes v. 230

(*b*) Ib. vi. 33.

cent.: if within North America or the West Indies twelve and a half per cent. : on persons in any other part of the world, eighteen per cent. besides interest and charges. (*a*)

A scrawl is equivalent to a seal in all private instruments.

2. *Frauds and Fraudulent Conveyances.*

The English statute of frauds and perjuries, and also of fraudulent conveyances, prevail, without any substantial alteration, in South Carolina. No parol gift of any chattel is valid against subsequent creditors, purchasers, or mortgagors, except where the donee lives separate and apart from the donor, and actual possession at the time of the gift is delivered to and remains and continues in the donee, his representatives or assigns. (*b*)

3. *Interest.*

Interest in South Carolina was changed in 1748 from ten to eight per cent. In 1777, it was changed to seven, at which rate it has remained to the present time. (*c*) Upon any contract where usury is reserved, the person lending or advancing money or other commodity upon such unlawful interest, shall be allowed to recover, in all cases whatsoever, the amount or value actually lent or advanced, without any interest, or costs. (*d*) The acts inflicting a penalty upon usurious loans have been repealed. (*e*) In a case of usury, the borrower is a competent and sufficient witness, un less the lender will deny upon oath in open court what the witness offers to swear. (*f*)

4. *Agents.*

The act of an agent, done after the death of his principal, which would have been lawful, if the principal had been living, will be valid and effectual, if the party treating with the agent, dealt bona fide, and without any knowledge at the time of the death of the principal. Where a note, whether filled up before or after having been signed or indorsed, is passed away after the

(*a*) St. iv. 741. (*b*) Ib. vi. 483. (*c*) Ib. i. 431 ; iv. 364. (*d*) Ib. vi. 409. (*e*) Ib. vi. 409. (*f*) Ib. iv. 364.

death of the drawer or indorser, by an agent duly constituted in his or her lifetime, such transfer will be valid and binding on his or her estate, provided the receiver of such note or bill takes it bona fide, and without knowledge of the death of the principal, and provided the act would have been binding on the principal, if done before his or her death. The act to be done, however, either under the power of attorney, or in relation to the bill or note, must be done within nine months from the death of the principal, or of the drawer or indorser of such note. (*a*)

5. *Limited Partnerships.*

By act passed in 1837, and which was to remain in force for ten years, but which was subsequently, by the act of 1846, extended for twenty years from that date, the formation of limited partnerships was authorized, for the transaction of any mechanical, manufacturing or mercantile business, or for the transportation of passengers, products of the soil, or merchandise within the state. The act is not to be so construed as to authorize any limited partnership for the purposes of banking or making insurance. It contains the general provisions, which have been enumerated under the laws of other states, as to the general and special partners, their respective rights, duties and liabilities, the certificate of the partnership agreement, its recordation with the clerk of the court of those districts where the business of the partnership is transacted, the publication for six weeks after such registry of the terms of the partnership, the requisites for the alteration, renewal, continuance or dissolution of the same, the invalidity of any sale or transfer of the effects of the partnership, or of the individual partners, or of any security executed by all or either of them in contemplation of insolvency, for the purpose of preferring a creditor or creditors of the partnership or of the individual partner, over other creditors of the partnership, &c. (*b*)

(*a*) St. vi. 359. (*b*) Ib. vi. 578; Acts of 1846, 365.

6. *Limitation of Actions.*

All actions of detinue, trover, replevin, account, (except such as concern the trade of merchandise between merchant and merchant,) debt founded upon any contract without specialty, covenant, and case, must be brought within four years. (*a*) There is a saving of five years, after the removal of the disability, in favor of persons beyond seas, feme covert, or imprisoned, and a saving in favor of infants of two years after they come of age, and of three years if they are also beyond seas. (*b*)

All actions against an executor or administrator must be brought within two years after the death of the testator, or the accruing of the cause of action. (*c*)

The statute is not to be so construed as to defeat the rights of minors, when it has not barred the right in the lifetime of the ancestor, before the accrual of the rights of the minor. (*d*)

7. *Attachment.*

In the case of a debtor who is a non-resident, or a citizen who has been absent more than a year and a day, or a debtor who absconds, or is removing out of the county, or conceals himself so that the ordinary process of law cannot be served upon him, his creditor, wherever residing, may obtain a writ of attachment against his estate, both real and personal. The writ is demandable of common right, on the plaintiff's giving bond to the defendant in double the amount for which the attachment issues, conditioned to pay all damages which the defendant may sustain by reason of the illegal issuing of the attachment. The defendant cannot dissolve the attachment, or impair the lien of the writ upon the property originally attached, without putting in bail to the action, but he may appear by attorney duly authorized by a warrant filed in the clerk's office from which the writ emanated, and defend the action. If in such case judgment is rendered against him, it shall be final and conclusive, and the plaintiff may sue out the ordinary writs of execution.

(*a*) St. ii. 586. (*b*) Ib. 586. (*c*) Ib. (*d*) Ib. vi. 238.

It is the duty of any garnishee to surrender the property of the absent defendant in his hands, unless he claims the same under oath as a creditor in possession, or to give bond for the safe keeping and forthcoming of the same, when required. Unless he complies with these requisitions, a personal judgment may be rendered against such defaulting garnishee.

Upon the return of a writ of attachment, it is the duty of the Court of Common Pleas, or any law judge at chambers to appoint one or more assignees, with full power and authority to receive and take from the sheriff or garnishee all the estate, real and personal, of the absent debtor, and to collect the debts and receive the rents and profits of the realty, and whose duty it shall be to dispose of the same according to the order of the Court of Common Pleas. (*a*)

The proceeds of the attachment are for the sole benefit of the attaching creditor. The first writ which is lodged in the sheriff's office is entitled to a priority of lien on the absent debtor's goods, though a second writ of attachment may be first served upon a garnishee. (*b*)

There is some difference between foreign and domestic attachments, but it does not seem necessary to be noted.

8. *Insolvent Law.*

There are two distinct classes of provisions in South Carolina for the benefit of insolvent debtors: the one established and regulated by the act of 1759, and which operates somewhat as a bankrupt law, affording general and permanent relief; and the other depending on the act of 1788, and which only affords a partial and temporary relief from imprisonment. The former and earlier act will be first considered. It provides that persons in custody, or on the prison's bounds, and who desire to surrender their estates to satisfy their debts, may, within one month from their arrest, petition the court from which the process issued, certifying the cause of their imprisonment, and annexing a schedule of their real and personal estate, upon which petition the court shall direct

(*a*) Acts of 1844, 290; Acts of 1843, 256; Statutes at Large, vii. 214, 294; vi. 431; iv. 544; ii. 589, 592.

(*b*) Callahan *v.* Howell, 2 Bay 8.

the petitioner to be brought before it at an appointed time, three months' notice thereof having been previously given to his creditors by publication in some newspaper or otherwise, for the purpose of examining into the matter of the petition in a summary way, and hearing what may be alleged for or against the discharge of the prisoner. The debtor is required at such time to make an oath, in effect, that the schedule he has presented is true and complete, that he has not since his arrest made any disposition of his property for his own benefit or to defraud his creditors, and that he will use his utmost efforts to make the property set forth available to his assignee, &c. If the court, upon examining the prisoner, is satisfied of the truth of his affidavit, it shall set aside certain articles trifling in amount, for the benefit of the prisoner, and order him to make an assignment on the back of his petition, of all his estate, real and personal, to the suing creditor, or such other persons as the court may direct, in trust for such suing creditor, and such other creditors of the petitioner as shall be willing to receive a dividend of his estate, and shall within twelve months from exhibiting the petition, make their demands. By such assignment, the estate of the debtor is completely vested in his assignees, who are authorized to take possession of and collect the same.

The effect of the discharge is to acquit the debtor from all debts, contracts, or demands of the creditors on whose suit he is charged, and all other creditors who have accepted any dividend from his estate, and to debar any creditor whatsoever from bringing any action against the debtor for the period of twelve months from such discharge. The act also provides for the sale, collection, and distribution of the estate among the creditors referred to, by the assignees. The discharge will be invalidated by any fraud or concealment. (*a*)

The act of 1788, provides that any prisoner in custody on mesne process or on execution, may, on petition to one of the judges of the court whence the process has issued, or one of the commissioners appointed for taking special bail in the circuit districts, and ten days' public notice to his creditors, be discharged from confinement and relieved from future arrest by the suing

(*a*) B. D. ii. 148 to 160.

creditor, on assigning his estate, or so much thereof as will satisfy the demand of the suing creditor. This discharge will not affect any other creditor, or exempt after acquired property of the debtor from being taken in execution to satisfy the claim of the creditor from whose execution he has been released, where the estate surrendered by him is insufficient.

Where a prisoner applying for the benefit of this act is charged with fraud, a jury may be summoned to try the facts, according to whose verdict he shall be discharged or remanded. (*a*)

9. *Effect of Death upon the Rights of Creditors.*

There is an ordinary in each district, who has cognizance of the probate of wills, of letters testamentary and of administration, the examination and settlement of the accounts of executors and administrators, the distribution of assets, &c.

Executors or administrators are to pay the debts of the testator or intestate, in the following order:

1. Expenses of funeral and last sickness, and charges of probate of will or letters of administration.
2. Debts due to the public.
3. Judgments, mortgages, and executions, the oldest first.
4. Rents, then bonds or other obligations, and lastly debts due on open account.

No preference whatever is to be given to creditors in equal degree, where there is a deficiency of assets, except in the cases of judgments, mortgages that shall be recorded from the time of recording, and executions lodged in the sheriff's office, the oldest of which shall be first paid; or in those cases where a creditor may have a lien upon any particular part of the estate. Executors and administrators hold as trustees, and cannot pay themselves first, as in England. (*b*)

Executors or administrators are required to give three weeks' notice, by advertisement in the state papers, or at three different places of the most public resort in the county, for creditors to render an account of their demands. They are allowed twelve

(*a*) St. vi. 492. (*b*) Brev. Dig. 335; Griffith's L. R. iv. 860.

months to ascertain the debts of the deceased, and will not be liable to any creditors failing to present their claims within that time. No action can be instituted against an executor or administrator, as such, until nine months from the death of the testator or intestate.

Executors and administrators are required to render an annual account of their receipts and expenditures to the ordinary of the district, and for neglecting the same, they will lose the right to their commissions, and also be responsible in damages for any injury arising to any person interested. (*a*)

Sales of personal property, unless authorized by the will, cannot be made by an executor, without the order of a court of ordinary, or court of equity, which can be obtained, wherever such sale is desirable, either for a division of the property, the payment of debts, or to prevent the loss of perishable articles. (*b*)

Lands are made assets for the satisfaction of debts, in the same manner as real estates are liable in England to the satisfaction of debts due by bond or specialty. (*c*)

Thus, they are liable from the time of a judgment rendered against the debtor himself, if a judgment has been rendered in his lifetime; or they are liable in the hands of the heir, although he is not named in the contract, and although it be simple and by parol; or the heir is answerable for their value if aliened by him before suit brought. (*d*)

10. *Proceedings in Civil Suits.*

Bail.—No person excepting transient persons can be held to bail for a less sum than fifty pounds current money; nor upon any writ of capias ad respondendum for debt, unless an affidavit before some judge or justice of the peace or clerk of the Court of Common Pleas be indorsed or annexed to the writ before service, of the "sum really due;" nor for any other cause, without a judge's order, on probable cause shown, to be indorsed on or annexed to the writ, expressing the sum for which bail shall be given. (*e*)

(*a*) B. D. 335. (*b*) Ib. ix. 5. (*c*) Ib. ii. 2. (*d*) Ib. i. 2, note. (*e*) Ib. i. 53.

No proceedings can be had upon the bail bond, until judgment and execution against the principal. A scire facias may then issue against the bail to show cause why execution for the judgment should not issue against them. On a scire facias returned, or two nihils, judgment may be obtained against the bail. (*a*)

Where a resident of the state, indebted by bond, note or otherwise, is about to remove or abscond from the limits of the state before the maturity of the debt, the creditor upon making affidavit to these facts, and to his ignorance of such contemplated removal when the contract was made, or when he became the holder of the claim, may hold such debtor to bail, to appear at court the day after the day of payment. The proceedings will, however, be dismissed with costs, if the debtor disprove the allegation of ignorance of his intention to remove.

Judgment and execution. (*b*)—Execution may be sued out at any time within three years from the rendition of a judgment against the lands, goods and chattels, or body of the defendant. After that period, the plaintiff must revive his judgment by scire facias or action of debt, before taking out an execution. (*c*)

The only writs of execution that are known in practice, are those of fieri facias and capias ad satisfaciendum. The former runs against the real as well as personal estate of the debtor. (*d*) It takes effect as to personalty, only from the time of its delivery to the officer to be executed, and as between two writs, that has priority which was first delivered; as against purchasers bona fide and for a valuable consideration, it binds the realty only from the day of signing the judgment. (*e*) The writ may be sent to any county to which the debtor may remove, or where his estate may be found.

Trust estates may be taken and sold upon an execution against the party for whose use they are held.

There are no appraisement laws, or any laws authorizing a delay beyond that required to advertise the property.

The body of a defendant cannot be taken in execution

(*a*) Brev. Dig. i. 53. (*b*) St. vii. 226, 227; vi. 5, 218.

(*c*) Broughton *v.* Dawson, 1 Nutt & McChord, 403.

(*d*) Durphey *v.* Nelson, 4 McChord 129. (*e*) B. D. ii. 221.

where the debt or damage is less than twenty pounds current money. (*a*)

A person may be released from imprisonment on a ca. sa. by consent of both parties, without discharging the debt, or in any manner impairing the lien of the judgment, or affecting the right of a plaintiff to sue out subsequent writs of ca. sa. or fi. fa. (*b*)

No female can be arrested on a writ of ca. sa. (*c*)

Remedy against sheriffs.—Any sheriff refusing to pay over money collected by him within ten days, is liable to a penalty of fifty per cent. on the sum so received, to be recovered by action of debt. (*d*)

Courts.—A Court of Common Pleas is held twice a year in each district, having a general common law jurisdiction. There are also four Chancery Courts in the state, among which are distributed all matters of equitable cognizance.

(*a*) B. L. 326. (*b*) St. vi. 1. (*c*) Ib. 237. (*d*) B. D. ii. 448.

GEORGIA.

1. *Choses in Action.*

All bonds, promissory notes, or liquidated demands may be assigned and transferred by indorsement, in like manner as inland bills of exchange, unless the maker of such instrument restrain its negotiability by expressing such intention in the body thereof. The general principles of commercial law as to promissory notes have been materially changed by statute. Demand of the maker and notice of default, are not necessary to bind the indorsers; but they are regarded as sureties on such instruments, and may be sued in the same manner and in the same action with the principal or maker. This provision does not apply to promissory notes, intended to be negotiated at any chartered bank, or which are deposited in such bank for collection. The indorser of any such instrument may require the holder on its maturity, to collect the same, and if the holder does not proceed to do so within three months from the time of such requisition, the indorser will be released from liability. (*a*)

(*a*) Hotchkiss' Statute Laws, 440.

Suits against indorsers.—Where the indorser of a note lives in the same county with the principal, the former cannot be sued without first suing the latter; but they may be sued together in the same action and district. (*a*)

Damages upon protested bills of exchange.—Whenever any bill of exchange, hereafter to be drawn or negotiated (1823), within this state upon any person within the United States, is returned unpaid, and duly protested for non-payment, as in the case of foreign bills of exchange, the holder of such bill may recover from the drawer or indorsers thereof, five per cent. damages over and above the principal sum for which said bill of exchange has been drawn, together with lawful interest, on the aggregate amount of such principal sum from the time at which notice of such protest was given, and payment of said principal and damages demanded. The same damages are recoverable, whatever may be the residence of the drawer or acceptor, where the protested bill was drawn in Georgia, upon or payable at a place within the United States, but without that state. Where any foreign bill of exchange drawn within the state, is returned protested for non-payment, the holder may recover from those liable for the payment of such bill, the amount of the same with costs and charges of protest, and interest upon such sums from the date of the protest, until presentment of the bill for payment in Georgia, at the rate established at the place where the bill was payable; if such bills are at a premium, then the amount of the premium upon the face of the bill, and charges; if such bills are at a discount, then the holder shall deduct the amount thereof from the preceding items. The holder may also recover ten per cent. damages upon the amount of the bill, and the legal interest established in Georgia, upon the entire sum to which he would be thus entitled, from the time of demanding the same, until it is paid. (*b*)

2. *Interest.*

The computation of time is required always to be made by the calendar and not the lunar months. The legal rate of interest is eight per cent. per annum. Where more is reserved, the cred-

(*a*) H. S. L. 663. (*b*) Ib. 439.

itor can only recover the principal of his debt, but he is liable to no forfeiture. (*a*)

3. *Agents.*

All powers of attorney for the sale of lands are to be deemed in full force, until notice to the agent of a countermand, revocation, or death of the principal. (*b*)

4. *Effect of Marriage upon Rights of Property.*

Upon marriage, the real estate of the wife becomes vested in the husband, as fully as if it were personal property. The husband is declared to be the sole heir of an intestate wife; and where the husband dies without issue, the wife may inherit. (*c*)

5. *Frauds.*

The English statute of 29 Chas. II. against frauds and perjuries has been adopted in Georgia without any substantial variation: also the statute of 13th and 27th Eliz. against fraudulent conveyances. (*d*)

6. *Partnerships.*

The following is the act of Georgia as to limited partnerships: (*e*)

By whom formed; for what purposes.—Limited partnerships for the transaction of any mercantile, commercial, mechanical, manufacturing, mining, or agricultural business, within this state, may be formed by two or more persons, upon the terms, with the rights and powers, and subject to the conditions and liabilities herein prescribed; but the provisions of this act shall not be construed to authorize any such partnership for the purpose of banking, or making insurance.

How constituted.—Such partnerships may consist of one or more persons, who shall be called general partners, and who shall be jointly and severally responsible as general partners, and of one

(*a*) H. S. L. 442. (*b*) Ib. 404. (*c*) Ib. 428. (*d*) Ib. 424, 421.
(*e*) Ib. 373 to 378.

or more persons who shall contribute in actual cash, a specific sum as capital to the common stock, who shall be called special partners, and who shall not be liable for debts of the partnership beyond the fund so contributed by him or them to the capital, except as hereinafter provided.

Business, by whom transacted.—The general partners only shall be authorized to transact business, and to sign for the partnership, and to bind the same.

Certificates of partnership; specifications of certificate.—Persons desirous of forming such partnership shall make and severally sign, by themselves or attorney in fact, a certificate which shall contain:

1st. The name of the firm under which such partnership is to be conducted.

2d. The general nature of the business intended to be transacted.

3d. The names of all the general and special partners inserted therein, distinguishing which are general, and which are special partners, and their respective places of residence.

4th. The amount of capital which each special partner shall have contributed to the common stock.

5th. The period at which the partnership is to commence, and the period at which it shall terminate; and when made by an attorney in fact, the power of attorney duly authenticated shall be recorded along with such certificate.

How acknowledged.—The certificates shall be acknowledged by the several persons signing the same, or their attorney in fact, before a judge of the Superior or Inferior Court, or a justice of the peace, or notary public, and such acknowledgment shall be certified by the officer before whom the same is made.

Certificates and powers of attorney, when and where filed.—The certificate and power of attorney in fact, so acknowledged and certified, shall be filed in the office of the clerk of the Superior Court of the county, in which the principal place of business of the partnership shall be situated, and shall also be recorded by him at large, in a book to be kept for that purpose, open to public inspection. If the partnership shall have places of business, situated in different counties, a transcript of the certificate and power of attorney in fact, and of the acknowledgment thereof, duly certified by the clerk in whose office it shall be filed, under his official seal, shall be filed and recorded in like manner in the office of the clerk of the Superior Court in every such county: and the clerk for each and every registry required by this act, shall be entitled to the sum of five dollars.

Affidavit.—At the time of filing the original certificate, with the evidence of the acknowledgment thereof, as before directed, an affidavit or affidavits of the several general partners shall also be filed in the same office, stating that the sums specified in the certificate to have been contributed by each of the special partners to the common stock, have been actually and in good faith paid in cash, and a certified copy of such certificate, power of attorney, and affidavits, shall be evidence in all courts and places whatsoever.

Informal partnerships.—No such partnerships shall be deemed to have been formed, until such a certificate as is herein mentioned, shall have been made, acknowledged, filed and recorded; nor until an affidavit shall have been filed as above directed; and if any false statement be made in such certificate or affidavit, or if such partnership business be commenced before such certificate or affidavit is filed, all the persons interested in such partnership shall be liable for all the engagements thereof as general partners.

How published.—The partners shall publish the terms of the partnership, when registered, for at least six weeks immediately after such registry, in one newspaper in the county in which the place of business is situated, and in one newspaper in the city of Milledgeville. If no newspaper should be published in the county in which the business is to be transacted, the notice shall be published in all the newspapers in the city of Milledgeville as before required, and if such publication be not made within two months from the time of filing such certificate and affidavit, the partnership shall be deemed general.

Evidence of publication.—The affidavits of the publication of such notice by the printers, publishers or editors of the newspapers in which the same shall be published, may be filed in the office of the Superior Court in which the certificate has been filed, and shall be evidence of the facts therein contained.

Renewal or continuance of partnership.—Every renewal or continuance of such partnership beyond the time originally fixed for its duration, shall be certified, acknowledged, and recorded, and an affidavit of a general partner be made and filed, and notice be given in the manner herein required for its original formation; and every such partnership which shall be otherwise renewed or continued, shall be deemed a general partnership.

Alterations of name, &c., deemed a dissolution.—Every alteration which shall be made in the names of the partners, in the nature of the business, or in the capital or shares thereof, or in any other matter specified in the original certificate, shall be deemed a dissolution of the partnership; and every such partnership which shall in any manner be carried on after any such alteration shall have been made, shall be deemed a general partnership, unless renewed as a special partnership, according to the provision of the last section.

Name of firm.—The business of the partnership shall be conducted under a firm, in which the names of the general partners only shall be inserted, without the addition of the word "company," or any other general term; and if the name of any special partner shall be used in such firm, he shall be deemed a general partner.

Suits.—Suits to be brought by any partnership to be formed under this act, shall be in the name or names of the general partners only; and suits against such partnership shall be brought against the general partners only; except in cases where the special shall be rendered liable as general partners, in which cases suits may be brought against all the partners jointly or severally, or any one or more of the special partners may be sued in the same action with the general partners.

Capital stock not to be withdrawn.—No part of the sum which any special partner shall have contributed to the capital stock, shall be withdrawn by him, or paid or transferred to him in the shape of dividends, profits or otherwise, at any time during the continuance of the partnership, but any partner may annually receive lawful interest on the sum so contributed by him, if the payment of such interest shall not reduce the original amount of such capital; and if, after the payment of such interest, any profits shall remain to be divided, he may also receive his portion of such profits, but shall not be liable for any debts previously contracted by the general partners.

Interest and profits, when to be restored.—If it shall appear that by the payment of interest or profits to any special partner, the original capital has been reduced, or the firm shall be unable to pay its debts, the partner receiving the same shall be bound to restore the interest or profits received by him, necessary to make good his original share of the original stock.

Privileges and liabilities of special partners.—A special partner may at any time examine into the state and progress of the partnership concerns, and may advise as to their management, but he shall not transact any business on account of the partnership, nor be employed for that purpose as agent or otherwise. If he shall interfere, contrary to these provisions, he shall be deemed a general partner; but he may act as the attorney or counselor at law or in equity, for the partnership, without being liable to become a general partner.

Liability of general partners.—The general partners shall be liable to account to each other, and to the special partners, for their management of the business of the firm, both in law and equity, as other partners are now by law and equity.

Partners guilty of fraud, how punished.—Every partner who shall be guilty of any fraud in the affairs or business of the partnership, shall be liable civilly to the party injured, to the extent of his damage; and shall also be liable to an indictment for a misdemeanor, punishable by fine or imprisonment, or both, at the discretion of the Superior Court, by which he shall be tried.

Fraudulent assignments invalid.—Every sale, assignment, or transfer of any of the property or effects of such partnership, made by such partnership when insolvent, or in contemplation of insolvency, or after or in contemplation of the insolvency of any partner, with the intent of giving a preference to any creditor of such partnership, or insolvent partner, over other creditors of such partnership; and every judgment confessed, lien created, or security given by such partnership, under the like circumstances and with the like intent, shall be void as against the creditors of such partnership.

By general or special partners.—Every such sale, assignment, or transfer of any of the property or effects of a general or special partner, who may have become liable as a general partner, made by such general or special partner when insolvent, or in contemplation of insolvency, or after or in contemplation of the insolvency of the partnership, with the intent of giving to any creditor of his own, or of the partnership, a preference over creditors of the partnership, every judgment confessed, lien created, or security given, by any such partner, under the like circumstances and with the like intent, shall be void as against the creditors of the partnership.

Liability of special partners for a violation.—Any special partner who shall violate any provision of the two last preceding sections, or who shall concur in or assent to any such violation by the partnership, or by any individual partner, shall be liable as a general partner.

Special partners, when not allowed to claim as creditors.—In case of the insolvency or bankruptcy of the partnership, no special partner shall, under any circumstances, be allowed to claim as a creditor until the claims of all the other creditors of the partnership shall be satisfied.

Dissolutions, how effected.—No dissolution of such partnership by the acts of the parties, shall take place previous to the time specified in the certificate of its renewal, until a notice of such intended dissolution shall have been filed and recorded in the clerk's office in which the original certificate was recorded, and published at least once a week, for four weeks, in a newspaper printed in each of the counties where the partnership has places of business; but if no newspaper be printed in such counties, then the notice shall be published for four weeks in all the newspapers in the city of Milledgeville, which notice shall be signed by all th partners, or their representatives: Provided, that nothing herein contained shall be so construed as to affect the collection of any demand against either of the special partners, which may have been contracted previously to the commencement of such special partnership.

Copartners in general; illegal use of names.—It shall not be lawful for any persons who are partners in trade, or business of any kind, to insert or use in their partnership, firm, style, and name, the name of any person not actually a copartner with them at the time his or her name is so inserted or used, nor shall it be lawful to continue, in any partnership, firm, style, and name, the name of any individual partner, after he or she shall have retired from the partnership: Provided, that this act shall not be so construed as to prevent the collection of debts due to any partnership after its dissolution, or after the retirement of any partner, in the name previously used, in conformity with this act.

Penalty for violation.—Each and every individual violating the provisions of this act, shall forfeit and pay the sum of one hundred dollars for each and every day such name may be used; to be sued for and recovered by any person who may prosecute for the same.

Execution of sealed instruments.—In all suits, either in favor of, or against partners, or persons jointly interested, and in all cases where such partners or persons jointly interested, shall in any wise become connected with any suit or other matter, pending in any of the courts of this state, in any way whatsoever, wherein it shall become necessary for said partners or persons jointly interested to give bond, it shall and may be lawful for any one of said partners or persons jointly interested, to execute the same, by signing the names of all of said partners or persons jointly interested; and the same shall be obligatory, and binding upon every of said partners or persons interested.

7. *Limitation of Actions.*

All actions of trespass, detinue, trover, and replevin, for taking away goods and cattle, all actions upon account and upon the case, other than such accounts as concern the trade of merchandise between merchant and merchant, their factors or servants, all actions of debt grounded upon any lending or contract without specialty, within four years after the cause of action accrues.

All actions founded upon bonds or instruments under seal, must be brought within twenty years from the maturity of the instrument; all actions founded upon notes and other acknowledgments under the hand of the party, shall be commenced within six years from the time such acknowledgment shall be due. There is the usual saving in favor of infants, feme coverts, or persons non compos mentis, of the period of the limitation after the removal of their respective disabilities. (*a*)

10. *Effect of Death upon the Rights of Creditors.*

Within three months from the probate of a will or the grant of letters of administration, the executor or administrator shall make out and return an exact inventory of the personal estate, and shall also return an appraisement of the same, made by three or more respectable freeholders, appointed by the court. (*b*)

Every executor or administrator shall give six weeks' notice by advertisement in one of the papers of the state, or at three different places of the most public resort in the county, for creditors to give an account of their demands.

Executors or administrators are allowed twelve months from their qualification to ascertain the debts due to and from the deceased: and no action may be commenced against them in their representative capacity, until twelve months after the death of the testator or intestate.

They will not be liable to make good the claim of any creditor, who does not present a statement thereof, within the foregoing period.

Debts due by a testator or intestate as guardian, executor or administrator are to be paid before any other debt of such testator or intestate. Executors and administrators are to observe the following order in the payment of debts: first, the funeral and other expenses of the last sickness; second, charges of probate and will, or of the letters of administration; third, debts due to the public; fourth, judgments, mortgages and executions, the eldest first; fifth, rent; sixth bonds, and other obligations; seventh, debts due on open accounts. Where there is a deficiency of assets, no preference is to be given to creditors of an equal degree, except in the case of judgments, mortgages that shall be recorded from the time of recording, and executions lodged in the sheriff's office, the eldest of which shall be first paid, or in those cases where a creditor may have a lien on any part of the estate. (*c*)

(*a*) H. S. L. 541. (*b*) Ib. 476. (*c*) Ib. 485

The real estate of a party who dies charged in execution, may be sold under a new execution, as if such party had never been charged in execution. (*a*)

Heirs and devisees are liable to creditors of the deceased by bond or specialty, to the value of the lands descended or devised. (*b*)

Real estate being liable to execution in the same manner as personal, may be taken and sold on a judgment against an executor or administrator, in his representative capacity.

It is the duty of executors and administrators to render an annual account of their administration upon the first of January, to the register of probate of the county in which they have qualified: and for neglect in this matter an executor or administrator loses his right to commissions, and renders himself liable for any damages that may be sustained by any party in interest. (*c*)

The Inferior Courts of each county have jurisdiction and authority as courts of ordinary in all matters testamentary and relating to the administration of the estates of deceased persons, the appointment and qualification of executors and administrators, the settlement of their accounts, distribution of estates, &c. (*d*)

9. *Insolvent Laws.*

Any person confined for debt, whether charged in execution or otherwise, who may be unable to satisfy the same, or to give bail for his appearance to the action, and is willing to surrender his estate for the benefit of his creditors, may apply for a discharge as an insolvent debtor to any judge of the Superior Court or justice of the Inferior Court.

The creditors at whose suit the debtor is confined, and also all to whom he is indebted, shall be summoned, thirty days beforehand, to appear personally, or by attorney, at a day to be appointed for the examination of the debtor and his condition; the notice to be served personally upon or left at the usual place of abode of creditors residing in the state, or where they reside out of the state, to be served in the same manner upon their attorneys, or if they have no attorney, then the notice is to be published for two months previous in one of the Savannah or Augusta papers. The court at

(*a*) H. S. L. 602. (*b*) Ib. 459. (*c*) Ib. 476. (*d*) Ib. 686.

such time is to examine into the matter of the petition and into any suggestions which may be made of fraud on the part of the debtor, for the trial of which a jury may be impanneled. If the court shall be satisfied of the insolvency of the petitioner, and the fairness of his proceedings, they shall administer to him the usual oath of an insolvent debtor, and direct him to deliver over and assign to some person or persons, who shall be nominated by a majority of the creditors, his whole estate real and personal, in trust for and to the use of his judgment creditors. The debtor is then to be discharged from imprisonment, and his body cannot be taken in execution upon either mesne or final process, on account of any debt contracted previously to such discharge. The property, both real and personal, which such debtor may acquire is however always subject to be taken in execution by his creditors.

A debtor imprisoned upon a ca. sa. may release his body, upon tendering to the officer a bond with sufficient surety, conditioned for his appearance at the next term of the court, from which the process issued, and applying for a discharge as an insolvent. If this bond is forfeited for any other reason than the sickness or death of the debtor, judgment will be entered up against principal and securities, upon which no indulgence will be allowed. If the debtor appears, ten days' previous notice having been given to his creditors of his intention, he may take the oath of insolvency, and upon surrendering his estate be exempted from future imprisonment in every case in which notice has been given to his creditors. Where any creditor suggests fraud or concealment on the part of his debtor, an issue may be made up for the trial of the same by a jury, and if it shall be found against the debtor, he will be committed. (*a*)

10. *Proceedings in Civil Suits.*

Attachment. -Where any debtor is a non-resident, or where he is actually removing without the limits of the state, or of any county, or where he absconds or conceals himself, or defies the sheriff, so that the ordinary process of law cannot be served upon him, any judge of the Superior Court, or justice of the Inferior Court, or justice of the peace, may, on affidavit made of such fact

(*a*) H. S. L. 308 to 315.

by a creditor or his agent, grant an attachment against the estate of the debtor, or so much thereof, as may be necessary to satisfy the plaintiff's demand. It is the duty of the sheriff to levy such writ upon any estate, real or personal, of the debtor wherever to be found, and to summon all persons indebted to, or having in possession effects of the debtor, to appear at the next court to be held for the county, and answer as to the same. If the return of the garnishee is disputed, an issue may be made up to try the same, and judgment will be rendered according to the verdict of a jury.

There are the usual provisions for the sale of property, where it is perishable, the replevy of it by the defendant, judgment against the garnishee, trial of the right of property where it is contested, &c.

The judgment in attachment only binds the property attached, unless the defendant has become a party to the attachment, or has returned to the county after the emanation of the writ, and been served with personal notice of the proceedings ten days before final judgment, in either of which cases a judgment will bind the entire estate of the defendant.

The attachment first served is in every instance to be first satisfied.

Where a debtor whose obligation is not due, is about to remove, or is removing beyond the limits of the state, any creditor or his agent, upon making oath to such fact and also to the amount of the indebtedness, may obtain an attachment against his property.

There are also special provisions for attachments against insurance companies carrying on business in the state of Georgia, and also in favor of securities who have paid the debt of the principal, or against whom process is pending for the collection of the same, or where, before the maturity of the claim, the principal debtor is about removing his property from the state.

Attachments may also issue in all cases where a suit has been instituted, and pending the suit, the defendant places himself in a situation in which the suing out an attachment would have been authorized. (*a*)

(*a*) H. S. L. 550 to 560.

Bail.—The cases in which bail may be demanded depend upon the principles of the common law. The statute has added the requisition of a previous affidavit by the plaintiff of the amount claimed by him, and that he has reason to apprehend the loss of the same, unless the defendant is held to bail. Such affidavit may be made before any judge, justice of the Inferior Court, or justice of the peace within the state, or any judge or justice of a Superior Court of any of the United States. In the latter case, the seal of the state must be annexed thereto, and a certificate of the governor, certifying that the person taking the affidavit is one of the judges of the Superior Court of that state.

Where no bail has been taken on the institution of a suit, or having been required, has been discharged, bail may be required upon a similar affidavit pending the proceedings. (*a*)

Judgment and execution.—Judgments bind the property of the defendant from their date; but judgments rendered at the same term are to be considered as of equal date, and no execution on such judgment can obtain any priority by being delivered to the officer before other executions on similar judgments. Where, however, a purchaser of property bound by a judgment for a valuable consideration, and without actual notice of the judgment, has been in peaceable possession of the same, if real estate, for seven years, if personal, for four, he cannot be disturbed.

A judgment becomes dormant where no execution has been sued out, or if sued out, not returned for seven years after the date thereof. Any party against whom a judgment has been rendered may obtain a stay of execution for sixty days, upon giving security for the payment of the same and costs.

Writs of execution may be taken out, directed to all or any of the sheriffs of the state, to be levied either upon the real and personal estate of the defendant, or upon his body. The discharge of a debtor imprisoned upon a ca. sa., does not operate as satisfaction of a debt, unless it has been actually paid, and the creditor may take out execution of fi. fa. against his estate. Property seized upon execution must be sold on the first Tuesday of each month. Where real estate is sold, thirty days' previous

(*a*) H. S. L. 564, 565.

notice must be given by advertisement in a newspaper, and also in three of the most public places of the county. (*a*)

Besides various minor articles exempt from execution, fifty acres of land may be reserved by the head of each family. (*b*)

Garnishment.—A process of garnishment pending any suit, or after the rendition of judgment, may issue against any person indebted to the defendant, or having effects of the defendant in his hands. Upon this summons, similar proceedings are to be had as in cases of attachment, and judgment entered against the garnishee for the amount confessed or ascertained to be in his hands belonging to the defendant. (*c*)

11. *Courts.*

There is in each county an Inferior Court, which has a general common law jurisdiction, except in cases involving the title to real estate, and which holds two terms in the year. There are also eleven Superior Courts, having a general common law and equitable jurisdiction in their respective circuits, and which also hold a spring and fall term in each of the different counties of the state.

(*a*) H. S. L. 597 to 608. (*b*) Ib. 317. (*c*) Ib. 560 to 564.

FLORIDA.

1. *Bonds, Bills of Exchange, and Promissory Notes.*

The assignment or indorsement of any bond, note, deed, bill of exchange, or other writing for the payment of money, vests the assignee or indorsee with all the rights, powers, and capacities of the assignor or indorser. (*a*)

A scrawl affixed as a seal to any instrument, is as effectual as a seal. (*b*)

Upon foreign protested bills of exchange, five per cent. damages are allowed. (*c*)

All promissory notes and other instruments in writing, not under seal, possess the force and effect of bonds and instruments under seal; and it is not necessary for the plaintiff to prove the execution of any bond, note, or other instrument in writing, purporting to have been signed by the defendant, nor the consideration for which the same was given, unless the same shall be denied by the defendant under oath. An exception is allowed to the last provision, in favor of executors and administrators, who may deny the execution of such instrument, or plead a want or failure of

(*a*) Thompson's Digest, 348. (*b*) Ib. (*c*) Ib. 349.

consideration, by giving reasonable notice in writing of such intention to the plaintiff, his agent or attorney. (*a*)

2. *Interest.*

Judgments, and all contracts in which no higher rate of interest is expressly reserved, bear interest at the rate of six per cent. per annum. Parties may stipulate for interest at the rate of eight per cent. Where more than eight per cent. is reserved upon any contract, the lender shall forfeit the whole amount of interest then due, to be recovered by a qui tam action. Where a suit is brought upon any note given on account of an usurious contract, the maker or obligor of such note is exonerated from the payment of all interest whatever; and in such case he is a competent witness to prove the usurious consideration, unless the party against whom the testimony is to be offered will deny upon oath the truth of the same. (*b*)

3. *Frauds.*

No mortgage of personal property is valid for any purpose, unless recorded in the county where the property is situated at the time of the execution of the mortgage, except where a bona fide and continuing change of possession takes place within twenty days from the execution of the mortgage. (*c*)

All loans of goods and chattels, or limitations of a use or property therein, by way of condition, reversion, remainder, or otherwise, in goods and chattels which have remained for five years in the uninterrupted possession of another, unless declared by will or deed in writing, proved and recorded, shall be taken to be fraudulent and void as to the persons remaining in possession. (*d*)

The statute of frauds is borrowed from the English statute of Chas. II., with no substantial variation, except the addition of the words "promise or" before "agreement." (*e*) The clause as to contracts for the sale of goods enacts that no contract for the sale of any personal property shall be good, unless the buyer shall accept the goods or part of them so sold, and actually receive the

(*a*) Thom. Dig. 331. (*b*) Ib. 234. (*c*) Ib. 183. (*d*) Ib. 217. (*e*) Ib.

same, or give something in earnest to bind the bargain, or in part payment, or some note or memorandum in writing of the bargain or contract made, and signed by the parties to be charged therewith or their lawfully authorized agents. (*a*)

4. *Effect of Marriage upon Rights of Property.*

The husband does not acquire by marriage any right or title to the personal or real property of his wife, which remains her own notwithstanding coverture, and is not liable to be taken on execution for his debts. So, a feme covert may become seized and possessed of such property as fully as a feme sole. Such separate property, to be protected from the husband's debts, must be inventoried and recorded in the county where it is situate, within six months from the marriage or the time of its acquisition The husband is not liable for the debts of his wife, contracted before marriage, but her property continues to be. On the death of a feme covert, her husband has a child's interest in her property, both real and personal, and if there are no children, then her husband is entitled to administration, and to all her property of every description. In all sales, transfers, or conveyances of the property of the wife, the husband must join. (*b*)

5. *Limited Partnerships.*

Limited partnerships, for the transaction of any commercial (other than that of banking or insurance), mechanical, manufacturing, or agricultural business, or for the transportation of persons, produce, or merchandise, were authorized by an act passed in 1838, upon the terms and conditions therein prescribed. Such partnership may consist of one or more persons, who shall be called general partners, and who shall be jointly and severally responsible as in ordinary cases of partnership, and one or more persons who shall contribute a specific sum as capital to the common stock, who shall be called special partners, and who shall not be liable for the debts of the partnership, beyond the sum so contributed by him or them to the capital. The articles of a limited

(*a*) Thomp. Dig. 218. (*b*) Ib. 220.

copartnership must be executed in the presence of two subscribing witnesses, and must be proved before an officer authorized by law to record the same, or some judicial officer of the state, either by the acknowledgment of the parties or the oath of one of the subscribing witnesses. The articles of copartnership so proved, must be filed in the office of the Circuit Court of the county where the principal place of the business of the partnership is situated, and recorded in a book kept for the purpose. If the partnership have several places of business, a transcript of the articles and the probate thereof, duly certified by the clerk of the county where first recorded, shall be filed and recorded in the office of the clerk of the Circuit Court of the other counties. The articles must contain the name of the firm, the names of the general and special partners, distinguishing them, and their respective places of residence, the general nature of the business to be transacted, the amount of capital which has been contributed by each partner to the common stock, and the period at which the partnership is to commence, and at which it is to terminate. At the time of filing the original articles of copartnership one or more of the general partners must file an affidavit, stating that the amount in cash, or its equivalent, specified in the articles, has been contributed by each of the special partners. When property constitutes a part of the stock, it must be appraised by three persons appointed by the judge of the Circuit Court, or where he is a party, by the sheriff of the county, and this appraisement, accompanied by a certificate of the appraisers under seal, must be filed and recorded in the office of the Circuit Court with the articles of copartnership. The terms of the partnership, when registered, shall be published for six weeks immediately succeeding in a newspaper published in the county where the principal place of business is situate, or if there is none such, in one published at the nearest point thereto. Until the articles of copartnership have been made, proved, filed, and recorded, together with the affidavit required to accompany them, the partnership shall not be deemed to have been formed. If any false statement is made in such articles or affidavit, or if the publication required by law is omitted, all the persons interested in the partnership shall.be held liable for all its engagements as general partners.

The business of the partnership must be conducted under a firm, in which the names of the general partners only shall be inserted, without the addition of "company" or any other general term: and any special partner allowing his name to be used in such firm, shall be deemed a general partner. The general partners only are authorized to conduct the business of the firm, and to bind it by signing its name. A special partner may at any time examine into the affairs of the partnership, and advise as to its management, but if he transacts any business on its account, except as an agent under a power of attorney, or in any way interferes with its management, he shall be deemed a general partner.

Any partner, general or special, shall be liable to account to any or all the other partners, either for the management of the business or indebtedness thereto, by suits at law or in equity, as partners ordinarily are by law. Suits may be brought by or against the general partners, as if there were no special partners; and in suits brought against the partnership, it is left optional with the plaintiff to include any special partner who has become liable as a general partner by violating some of the provisions of the act. If by the payment of interest or dividends, the original capital is reduced, the partner receiving the same shall be bound to restore the amount necessary to make good his share of the original stock, or he shall be deemed a general partner from the period when it became so reduced.

All assignments of the property or effects of the partnership, or of a general partner, and all confessions of judgment and other assurances, made by the partnership or any of the general partners, in contemplation of the insolvency of either of the general partners, or of the partnership, and with the intent to prefer any creditor of such general partner or of the partnership, over other creditors, shall be void as against the creditors of the partnership. Any special partner violating this provision, or concurring in or assenting to its violation by the partnership, or any individual partner, shall be liable as a general partner. In case of the insolvency or bankruptcy of the partnership, no special partner will be allowed to claim as a creditor, until the claims of all the other creditors of the partnership shall be satisfied.

Any alteration in the name of the firm, or the partners, or in the nature of the business, or in the articles of copartnership, or in the amount of the original capital by a reduction, if made with the privity of the special partner, shall be deemed a dissolution of the partnership, and any continuance of the business thereafter shall be regarded as a general partnership, unless renewed as a special partnership. Upon any renewal or continuance of a limited partnership, the requisitions of the law as to its original formation must be pursued, or it will be deemed a general partnership. A limited partnership is not dissolved by the death of one or more of the special partners, nor by the death of a general partner where there is more than one, before the expiration of the term specified in the articles for the continuance of the partnership, unless the articles expressly so provide. No limited partnership can be dissolved by the acts of the parties previous to the time specified in the articles, until a notice of such intended dissolution has been filed and recorded in the clerk's office where the original articles of copartnership were recorded, and also published once a week for four weeks in a newspaper printed in each of the counties where the business of the copartnership has been conducted; or if there be no such newspaper, then in the one nearest thereto; the notice to be signed by all the parties or their representatives. (*a*)

6. *Limitation of Actions.*

All actions of detinue, all actions of trover and replevin, for taking away of goods and chattels, all actions of account and upon the case, other than such accounts as concern the trade of merchandise between merchant and merchant, their factors or servants, all actions of assumpsit or debt grounded upon any lending or contract without specialty, must be brought within five years after the cause of action has accrued.

All actions or suits founded upon any account for goods, wares or merchandise sold and delivered, or for any article charged in any book account, must be commenced and sued within two years after the accruing of the cause of action, or the delivery of the

(*a*) Thomp. Dig. 230 to 234.

goods, wares, and merchandise, except that in the case of the death of such creditors or debtors before the expiration of the said term of two years, the further time of two years shall be allowed from such period. The limitation of two years is to be computed from the respective times of delivery of the several articles charged in such account. (*a*)

In suits against an executor or administrator, for the recovery of a debt due by open account, it is made the duty of the court, to strike out every item which shall appear to have been due five years before the death of the testator or intestate, saving to all persons under any of the statutory disabilities, three years after the removal of the same. (*b*)

No action of debt or scire facias can be brought upon a judgment obtained against a testator or intestate, against any person having charge of his estate, after the expiration of five years from the qualification of such person with a similar saving to that just mentioned. (*c*)

Upon the various personal actions, there is a saving of the period of limitation in favor of infants, feme coverts, persons imprisoned, non compos mentis, and beyond seas. The term "beyond seas," in the act, does not extend to persons who at the time of the accruing of the cause of action, or the making of the contract, were residing or domiciled without the limits of the state. (*d*)

The statute does not run in behalf of any debtor, who by absconding or concealing himself, or removing out of the county in which he resided at the time the cause of action accrued, or by any other indirect means, obstructs any persons who have title thereto from bringing any of the aforesaid actions. (*e*)

Where an action upon any contract made out of the state, is barred by the law of the place where such contract was entered into, the defendant may plead such law in effectual bar of a suit thereon, in the courts of Florida. (*f*)

(*a*) Thomp. Dig. 442. (*b*) Ib. 444. (*c*) Ib. (*d*) Ib. 443. (*e*) Ib. 444. (*f*) Ib. 445.

7. *Attachment.*

Attachments of property in the nature of mesne process, for the purpose of compelling attendance, and giving the court jurisdiction to render a judgment, are not authorized; but in the case of a non-resident or absconding debtor, a creditor may resort to a distinct proceeding, the ordinary statutory remedy of attachment, to procure satisfaction of his claim, The party applying for the writ of attachment, or his agent, must first make oath in writing, that the amount of the debt or sum demanded is actually due, and that the party from whom it is due, is actually removing out of the state, or resides beyond the limits thereof, or absconds or conceals himself, so that the ordinary process of law cannot be served upon him, or is removing his property beyond the limits of the state, or secreting, or fraudulently disposing of the same for the purpose of avoiding the payment of his debts; and also enter into bond with two good and sufficient sureties, payable to the defendant, in a sum at least double the debt demanded, conditioned to pay all costs and damages which the defendant may sustain in consequence of improperly suing out the attachment.

Where an executor or administrator resides or has removed beyond the limits of the state, any person having a claim upon the estate of the deceased, may obtain an attachment against any assets within the state, provided the executor or administrator has no legally authorized and publicly known agent in the state, and the creditor or his agent will make oath in writing that the debt demanded is actually due, and that the representative of the estate resides out of or has removed from the state.

On proper affidavit being made, a writ of attachment may issue at any stage of a suit.

The service of a writ of attachment does not operate to dispossess the tenants of any lands or tenements, but they bind the property, except against any pre-existing lien. Personal property unless replevied, or of a perishable nature (when it may be sold) remains in the custody of the officer attaching the same, until it is sold.

An attachment may be dissolved at any time upon motion

founded upon an affidavit and evidence which will satisfy the court, that the allegations of the plaintiff in his affidavit are untrue.

Where several judgments in attachment are rendered at the same term, against the same person in favor of different plaintiffs, they shall be satisfied pro rata out of the judgments obtained against the garnishee in such suit, unless the defendant have sufficient other property to satisfy the same. (*a*)

A writ of attachment may issue where the debt will become due within nine months, if the party applying for the same, his agent or attorney, will make oath in writing and also produce satisfactory evidence that the amount of the demand claimed is actually an existing debt, and that it will become due and payable at a specified time within the term of nine months, and that the party against whom the said writ of attachment is asked, is actually removing his or her property beyond the limits of the state, or is fraudulently disposing of or secreting the same for the purpose of avoiding the payment of his or her just debt or demand. The plaintiff in the attachment must also give bond and security as in ordinary cases.

There is also a statutory remedy by attachment to prevent the fraudulent removal of mortgaged personal property. (*b*)

8. *Proceedings in Civil Suits.*

Bail.—Bail cannot be required upon any original writ or summons emanating from a court of law in any civil action. (*c*)

Service of process, where there are several defendants.—Where there are several defendants in any civil action, and process is served upon one or more of them, and a return made by the sheriff, that the other defendants do not reside in the county, the plaintiff may at his option proceed to judgment against those upon whom the process has been served, or obtain time from the court to perfect service, by directing writs to the sheriffs of the counties in which the other defendants reside, and having them served and returned. (*d*)

Where suit is brought against a mercantile firm, the plaintiff

(*a*) Thomp. Dig. 367 to 311. (*b*) Ib. 380. (*c*) Ib. 326. (*d*) Ib. 327.

may obtain a judgment against the firm, and proceed to execution after a service of process against any one member thereof. (*a*)

Time within which a judgment may be obtained.—A Circuit Court having general jurisdiction in all cases at law or equity, holds a spring and fall term in every county of the state. All writs are to be returned to the next ensuing term of the court, from which they issue; but must be served by the officer ten days before the first day of such term. Where no defence is made, a judgment may be rendered by default, at the term to which a writ is returned; but all controverted cases stand for trial in their order at the term succeeding that to which the first process was returnable. (*b*)

Lien of judgments.—All judgments at law or decrees in equity create a lien upon the real estate of the defendant situate in the county where they are rendered, from the period of their rendition, and upon his or her real estate situate in any other county, from the period when a transcript of the judgment or decree shall have been recorded in such county. (*c*)

Execution may be sued out at any time within three years from the rendition of a judgment, and where execution has once issued during that period, it may be renewed upon the return of the original execution, from time to time for twenty years, unless sooner satisfied. (*d*)

Equities of redemption both in real and personal property may be levied upon and sold under execution upon any judgment at law or decree in equity. (*e*)

Executions.—A capias ad satisfaciendum cannot issue upon any judgment in a civil action; nor the body of a defendant be subject to arrest or confinement for the payment of money, except for fines imposed by lawful authority. (*f*)

Lands and tenements as well as goods and chattels may be sold upon a writ of fieri facias. This writ cannot be issued until ten days after the adjournment of the court by which the judgment was rendered, unless the plaintiff, his agent or attorney, shall make affidavit that there is good reason to believe that the defendant will remove his property from the state before the same

(*a*) Thomp. Dig. 327. (*b*) Ib. 34. (*c*) Ib. 352. (*d*) Ib. 355. (*e*) Ib. 355. (*f*) Ib. 354.

can be levied upon in the usual manner, in which case the writ may be issued immediately. (*a*)

The sheriff is bound, if possible, to collect the amount of any execution coming into his hands, by the next succeeding term of the court. (*b*)

No sale can take place until after the same has been advertised thirty days in the mode prescribed by law: nor at any other period than on the first Monday of the months of December, January, February and March, provided the defendant in the execution will enter into bond with sufficient security to the plaintiff, in a sum double the value of the property replevied to have the same forthcoming at the day of sale. (*c*)

Garnishment.—Upon the judgments or decrees of any Circuit Court, or the judgments of any justice of the peace, a summons may be issued, on the suggestion of the plaintiff or his agent, against any person supposed to be indebted to, or having the custody of property belonging to the defendant: and upon the return of the summons and answer of the garnishee, the court may render judgment in favor of the plaintiff for the amount of indebtedness: or if the garnishee acknowledge the possession of property and refuse to surrender it, a judgment may be rendered against him for the entire amount of the plaintiff's claim remaining unsatisfied. All property belonging to the defendant, in the hands of the garnishee, is bound by service of the process of garnishment.

It is not necessary that execution should be taken out upon a judgment or decree before resorting to the process of garnishment: but no summons can issue until the plaintiff or his agent has made and filed an affidavit, that he does not believe that the defendant has in his possession visible property sufficient to satisfy the judgment upon which a levy can be made. (*d*)

Remedy against sheriffs and attorneys for failing to pay over money collected.—If a sheriff refuses or fails to pay over money which has been collected, within thirty days after the same shall have been received, upon demand being made by the plaintiff or his agent, the amount may be recovered with twenty per cent.

(*a*) Thomp. Dig. 355. (*b*) Ib. (*c*) Ib. 357, 358. (*d*) Ib. 374.

damages, on motion, ten days' previous notice being given. (*a*) For a similar refusal by an attorney he may be stricken from the roll of attorneys, and is liable to a suit for the amount, and a penalty of ten per cent. for each month of detention. (*b*)

9. *Effect of Death upon the Rights of Creditors.*

The personal estate of a deceased person constitutes the primary fund for the payment of debts. But real estate may be considered as assets, and sold either upon an order of the Court of Probate, on a petition filed by the executor or administrator, setting forth the insufficiency of the personal assets for the payment of debts or legacies, or upon a judgment against an executor or administrator, in his representative capacity. The heirs and devisees of a deceased person may contest the application to sell his real estate, and if successfully, the petition will be dismissed with costs. (*c*)

Where any married man dies intestate, or without making any satisfactory provision by his last will for his wife, the widow, in addition to her dower, is entitled to the following share in his personal estate, irrespective of the claims of creditors, and in preference to all other persons, viz.: if there be no children or but one child, to one half, but if there be more than one child, to one third part, in fee simple, except slaves, in which she shall have a life estate. (*d*)

No executor or administrator can be compelled to pay the debts of the testator or intestate, until after the expiration of six months from the taking out letters testamentary or of administration: and no costs can be recovered upon any suit brought against him within that period, nor execution taken out on a judgment obtained thereon until its expiration. (*e*)

It is the duty of an executor or administrator, on taking out letters testamentary or of administration, to cause an advertisement to be published once a week for the space of eight weeks, in some newspaper printed in the county in or nearest to that wherein the letters have been granted, calling upon all persons

(*a*) Thomp. Dig. 358. (*b*) Ib. 323. (*c*) Ib. 202 to 205. (*d*) Ib. 185. (*e*) Ib. 205.

who have debts or demands against the estate to present them. All debts or demands, not exhibited within the space of two years from the granting of the letters, are barred, provided notice of that fact has been given for four weeks previous, by advertisement once a week in some newspaper printed in the state. The rights of infants, feme coverts, persons non compos mentis, imprisoned, and beyond seas, are protected for the additional term of two years after the removal of their respective disabilities. (*a*)

Debts are to be discharged in the following order:

1. The necessary funeral expenses.

2. Debts due for board and lodging during the last sickness of the deceased.

3. Bills for medical attention, nursing, or medicines furnished during the last sickness.

4. Judgments of record rendered and docketed in the state during the lifetime of the deceased, and all debts due to the state. And finally all other debts, whether by specialty or otherwise, without distinction of rank. (*b*)

Executors and administrators are required to render an annual account of their administration to the Courts of Probate, and any neglect of this requisition will subject them to the loss of their commissions. The court, however, will not allow any account to be settled, unless the executor or administrator has given previous notice for two months, by written advertisement, of their intention to present their accounts for such purpose. An executor who fails to settle his accounts at the proper period, may be compelled to do so by coercive process issued by the respective probate judges. (*c*)

(*a*) Thon.p. Dig. 205. (*b*) Ib. 206. (*c*) Ib. 211.

ALABAMA.

1. CONTRACTS AND CHOSES IN ACTION.
2. INTEREST.
3. CORPORATIONS.
4. LIMITED PARTNERSHIPS.
5. STATUTE OF FRAUDS.
6. ASSIGNMENTS BY INSOLVENT DEBTOR.
7. EFFECT OF MARRIAGE UPON THE RIGHTS OF PROPERTY.
8. LIMITATION OF ACTIONS.
9. ATTACHMENT.
10. EFFECT OF DEATH UPON THE RIGHTS OF CREDITORS.
11. PROCEEDINGS IN CIVIL SUITS.

1. *Contracts and Choses in Action.*

All joint bonds, covenants, bills, promissory notes, or judgments of any court of record within the United States, are to be respectively deemed and construed in law, as joint and several instruments. (*a*)

All bonds, obligations, promissory notes, and all other writings for the payment of money, or any other thing, may be assigned by indorsement, whether the same be made payable to the order or assigns of the obligee or payee or not, or whether made payable to a fictitious person or bearer; and the assignee may sue in his own name, and maintain any action which the obligee or payee might have maintained thereon previous to assignment, the defendant, however, to be allowed the benefit of all set-offs, discounts, and payments made or acquired before notice of the assignment; and the assignee may also maintain an action against the person assigning or indorsing the same, as in cases of inland bills of exchange. (*b*)

(*a*) Clay's Digest, 323. (*b*) Ib. 382.

The assignee of any instrument for the payment of money, except a bill of exchange foreign or inland, or a promissory note payable in bank, in order to hold the assignor responsible, must bring suit, to the first court of the county where the maker resides, to which the writ can be properly returnable, unless suit be delayed with the consent of the assignor. A return of "nulla bona" upon a writ of fieri facias, on a judgment against the maker, shall be sufficient evidence of insolvency to authorize a recovery against the assignor or indorser upon his assignment or indorsement. (*a*)

Bills of exchange, foreign and inland, and promissory notes payable in bank, are governed by the rules of the law merchant as to days of grace, protest, and notice. Bills drawn and payable within the state, are deemed inland bills, and those drawn here and payable out of the state, are deemed foreign bills. (*b*)

Bonds and other instruments payable in bank, are governed by the rules of the law merchant as to days of grace, demand, and notice, in the same manner that bills of exchange and notes payable in bank are, and also as to set-offs and defence. (*c*)

Any instrument in writing, signed by the owner of a cotton-gin, or his agent, acknowledging the receipt of a certain quantity of cotton, may be assigned as inland bills of exchange are by the custom of merchants in England, so as to vest in the indorsee a right of action thereon. (*d*)

Rates of damages upon protested bills.—On all bills of exchange drawn by any persons in the state, and payable at any place within the state, and on all bills of exchange, or drafts drawn by any person in the state, upon any person either in or out of the state, and payable at any bank or other place in the city of New Orleans, that may be purchased or discounted by the bank of the state of Alabama, or any branch thereof, and which may be protested for non-acceptance or non-payment, the damages are five per cent. On bills of exchange drawn upon persons within the United States, but without the limits of the state, the damages on protest for non-payment are ten per cent. besides legal interest, from and after the date of such protest. On all bills drawn upon persons resident out of the jurisdiction of the United

(*a*) Clay's Digest 383. (*b*) Ib. (*c*) Ib. 384. (*d*) Ib. 380.

States, which are protested, the damages are twenty per cent. on the principal sum mentioned in such bills respectively, and all charges incidental thereto, with lawful interest until paid. (*a*)

The protest of a notary public setting forth a demand, refusal, non-acceptance, or non-payment of any inland bill of exchange or other protestable security; and that legal notice, expressing in said protest the time when given of such facts, was personally or through the post-office given to any of the parties entitled by law to notice, is made evidence of the facts it purports to contain. (*b*)

Promissory notes always import a consideration till the contrary is shown.

2. *Interest.*

Eight per cent. is the rate of interest allowed by law; but contracts and assurances in which a higher rate of interest is reserved, are only void as to the interest. The principal sum loaned may be recovered. Where more than eight per cent. interest is taken, the lender is liable to a qui tam action for the whole value or amount together with the entire interest. Where a suit is brought upon any instrument alleged to be usurious, the borrower is a good and sufficient witness to prove the usury, unless the lender will deny upon oath in open court the facts which such witness proposes to establish. (*c*)

3. *Corporations.*

No corporation invested with the privileges of banking and the authority to discount bills of exchange and promissory notes by any other state, can exercise such privileges by agent or otherwise in the state of Alabama. (*d*)

4. *Limited Partnerships.*

By an act passed in 1837, limited partnerships are authorized in Alabama. The provisions of this law are identical with

(*a*) Clay's Digest 381. (*b*) Ib. 380. (*c*) Ib. 589. (*d*) Ib. 133.

those already detailed under the same title as existing in New Jersey. (*a*)

5. *Statute of Frauds.*

The statute of Alabama as to parol contracts is a transcript of the English statute of frauds, except in the last clause of the statute, the word "promise" as well as "agreement" is used. (*b*)

When the possession of goods and chattels has remained in one person for the space of three years, as loanee, without any demand made and pursued by due course of law, on the part of the pretended lender, they shall be taken as to the creditors and purchasers of the person in possession to be fraudulent, unless such loan be declared by will or deed in writing, proved and recorded. (*c*)

6. *Assignments by Insolvent Debtor.*

A debtor in failing circumstances may make an assignment of his property, preferring creditors, provided he does not reserve any benefit to himself. The instrument of conveyance, if it contains personal property, must be recorded within thirty days, in the office of the county where it lies or if lands, within sixty days.

It seems to be essential to the passing of title to a trustee in a deed of trust, that the creditors intended to be secured, should assent to it, unless the deed is absolute, conveying the whole estate of the debtor, and providing for the equal payment of all his creditors. (*d*)

7. *Effect of Marriage upon Rights of Property.*

The property of a woman at the time of her marriage, or which she subsequently receives by descent, gift, or bequest, is not subject to the debts or liabilities of the husband contracted

(*a*) Clay's Digest 389. (*b*) Ib. 254. (*c*) Ib. 255.

(*d*) Article on the Law of Debtor and Creditor in Alabama, in Hunt's Merchants' Magazine, vol. xvi. p. 58, from the pen of the Hon. B. F. Porter.

before marriage, nor is the husband liable for the debts of the wife contracted before mariage, beyond the amount of the estate which he receives by her; but such property of the wife remains liable for her debts, notwithstanding the termination of the coverture. (*a*)

8. *Limitation of Actions.*

All actions of trespass, detinue, trover and replevin for taking away of goods and chattels, all actions of debt founded upon any contract or lending without specialty, or for arrearages of rent due on a parol demise, all actions of account, and upon the case, except such actions as concern the trade of merchandise between merchant and merchant, their factors or agents, must be brought wiihin six years after the cause of action has accrued. There is a saving of the period of limitation in favor of infants, feme coverts, and persons non compos mentis, after the removal of their disability. Actions of debt or covenant upon any lease under seal, or upon any sealed instrument for the payment of money, or upon any award under seal, must be brought within sixteen years after the cause of action has accrued; unless a payment has been made upon such instrument, when the limitation is to commence running from the time of payment. The time during which any person entitled to one of these actions is an infant, feme coverts, or non compos mentis, is not to be taken as a part of the period of limitation. Judgments in any court of record within the state may be revived by action of debt or scire facias within twenty years next after the date of the judgment. There is a similar saving to this limitation, as to that immediately preceding. (*b*) The period during which a person liable to any of the actions which have been enumerated, may be absent from the state, is not to be accounted as a part of the limitation.

All actions brought to recover any money due by open account, must be commenced within three years from the time of their accruing, unless they concern the trade of merchandise between merchant and merchant. (*c*)

An important decision has been made in Alabama, upon the effect of an acknowledgment upon the bar of the statute. It has

(*a*) Acts of 1845, 25. (*b*) Clay's Digest 326. (*c*) Ib. 328.

been held that a verbal acknowledgment by the obligor of a bond will not prevent the operation of the statute, nor revive the remedy upon it, after the bar of the statute has become complete.(*a*)

9. *Attachment.*

Original attachments, foreign and domestic, may be issued by any judge of the Circuit or County Courts, or any justice of the peace. Before any attachment can issue, the applicant or his agent must make an affidavit in writing, that the person against whom it is prayed absconds, or secretes himself, or resides out of the state, or is about to remove out of the state, so that the ordinary process of law cannot be served upon him, or is about to remove his property out of the state, whereby the plaintiff may lose his debt, or be compelled to sue for it in another state; and also, of the amount due to the plaintiff, and that the attachment is not sued out for the purpose of vexing or harassing the defendant, The plaintiff must also give the usual bond to indemnify the defendant. It is not necessary to the issuing of an attachment, that the debt should be due.

Attachments may be granted when both plaintiff and defendant are non-residents, and the defendant has any property in the state. (*b*)

Attachments may be levied on real as well as the personal estate of the defendant; and the levy of the attachment creates a lien upon the property. An attachment may be sued out against one of several partners, without joining the others. (*c*)

The provisions for the replevy of the goods by the defendant, the sale of perishable property, the trial of an adverse claim to the property attached, and for proceedings and judgment against garnishees, are similar to those which have been detailed under this title in the chapters on other states.

The attachment law, it is declared, shall not be strictly construed, and defects of form may at any time before or during the trial, be amended, where the judge is satisfied that the defects were not made for the purpose of defrauding the defendant.

Judicial attachment.—On a return of non est inventus to a

(*a*) Crawford *v.* Childress' Ex'rs. 1 Ala. 483. (*b*) A. D. 37 to 43.
(*c*) Green *v.* Pyne, 1 Al. Rep. 235.

writ of capias ad respondendum, the plaintiff at his option may sue out a new process, or an attachment against the personal estate of the defendant; and if he fails to appear upon the return of this process, the plaintiff may have a judgment or his debt, upon which the property attached will be sold, and if it is not sufficient to satisfy the debt, execution may issue for the balance.

Judicial attachments do not issue as a matter of right, when the sheriff returns upon an execution that his defendant is not to be found in the county: but the plaintiff or his agent must first make an affidavit before the clerk of the court to which the writ is returnable, that he has reason to believe the defendant avoided the execution of such writ. (*a*)

10. *Effect of Death upon the Rights of Creditors.*

The personal estate constitutes the primary fund for the payment of debts: but if it is not sufficient, the real estate, saving to the widow her right of dower, is chargeable with the deficiency. (*b*) The real estate may be sold, either under the order of the Orphans' Court of the county in which letters of administration or testamentary were granted, upon the petition of the executor or administrator setting forth the insufficiency of the real estate; (*c*) or upon a scire facias sued out by any judgment creditor, suggesting that real estate has descended to the heirs, and that a sale of the same or a part thereof is necessary for the satisfaction of said judgment, and that the executor or administrator has failed or refused to make application for a sale thereof, and requiring the heirs and personal representatives of the deceased to show cause, if they can, why said plaintiff should not have execution against such real estate. (*d*) That an executor or administrator may have an opportunity of ascertaining the situation of the estate of his testator or intestate, no suit shall be commenced against him in his representative capacity until the expiration of six months from the time of proving the will of the testator, or taking out letters of administration on the estate of the deceased. (*e*)

Where the estate is insolvent, the debts due for the last sick-

(*a*) Acts of 1845, 137. (*b*) Clay's Digest 191. (*c*) Ib. 224. (*d*) Ib. 197. (*e*) Ib. 192.

ness and necessary funeral expenses are to be first paid, and then the balance of the assets accruing from the sale of the real as well as personal estate is to be distributed among all the creditors in proportion to the sums respectively owing to them. The executor or administrator of such estate is required to file in the office of the Orphans' Court by which he was appointed, a written allegation, setting forth that the estate is insolvent, and praying that it may be declared such, and accompanying such allegation by three several schedules, all to be verified by affidavit; one schedule containing a full statement of the personal estate and its estimated value; a second, a similar account of the real estate; and the third, an inventory of all claims against the estate, the amount and nature of each, and the names and residences of the several creditors. (*a*) To obtain this information, the executor or administrator, within two months after his qualification, is required to give notice by a weekly publication in some newspaper of the state for the space of six weeks, to all creditors to exhibit their claims within the period allowed by law or be forever barred. (*b*)

Upon the filing of such allegation, the judge, or in his absence the clerk of the court, shall appoint some day not less than thirty nor more than sixty days distant, for hearing and determining the same; and the clerk, by advertisement in a newspaper and otherwise, and by notice personally served, or sent by mail to creditors out of the county, shall inform them of the time designated for this purpose. If no opposition is made by any creditor, the estate may be declared insolvent. If the allegations of the executor are contested by any creditor, an issue will be made up to try the same under the direction of the court, and if it is decided against the executor, the allegation shall be dismissed with costs. If the estate is declared insolvent, the court shall order the executor or administrator to appoint a day for the settlement of his accounts, not less than thirty nor more than sixty days off, and direct the clerk to give notice to the creditors to attend at such time. On this day, the creditors, voting in person or by attorney, in proportion somewhat to the amount of their respective claims, may elect any resident citizen as an administrator de bonis non upon such estate: or in the event of their making no election, the judge may

(*a*) Clay's Digest 192. (*b*) Ib. 223.

appoint such a person. All persons having claims against such insolvent estate, shall file the same in the clerk's office of the said Orphans' Court, within six months from the time that the estate is declared insolvent, verified by their affidavit, and if no opposition is made to such claim within nine months after the estate is declared insolvent, it shall be allowed without further proof. But within this period the administrator, or any creditor proceeding in his name, may file written objections to the allowance of any claim, and the question thus arising may be tried under the form of an issue made up by the court; the party cast to pay the costs. The court may fix a period for the executor or administrator of an insolvent estate to settle his accounts; which shall be not less than nine nor more than twelve months from the time of declaring such estate insolvent: and at such time the court may decree to each creditor whose claim has been allowed, his ratable portion of all moneys then found due from the executor or administrator, reserving nevertheless a ratable portion of such moneys for any claims which may then be contested and undivided; and a similar settlement is to be made at least every six months thereafter, until the estate shall be finally distributed. (*a*)

All claims against the estates of deceased persons, which shall not be presented within eighteen months after the same shall have accrued, or within eighteen months after letters testamentary or of administration have been granted, shall be forever barred: except those of infants, feme coverts, persons non compos mentis, and those arising upon debts contracted out of the state. (*b*)

11. *Proceedings in Civil Suits.*

Imprisonment for debt.—Imprisonment for debt is not allowed either upon mesne or final process, except in cases of fraud. A party cannot be held to bail to answer for a civil demand, or his body taken in satisfaction of a debt, unless the creditor or his agent establish by affidavit a prima facie case of fraud, or that either the debtor is about to abscond, or has fraudulently conveyed, or is about fraudulently to convey his estate or effects, or has money liable to satisfy his debts, which he fraudulently with-

(*a*) Clay's Digest 194. (*b*) Ib. 195.

holds. The debtor may release his body if arrested, by swearing that the particular ground of the creditor's affidavit is untrue, or by rendering a schedule of his estate, exceeding twenty dollars, and not exempt from execution, unless the truth of such schedule is controverted by the creditor, when an issue shall be made up immediately to try the question.

Judgment and execution.—Lands and tenements, as well as goods and chattels, may be taken in execution and sold on judgments at law or decrees in chancery. (*a*) The writs of execution in use are the fi. fa., ca. sa., and elegit. The former runs against the real as well as personal estate. Goods and chattels are bound from the time the writ of execution is delivered to the officer. Lands are bound from the time of the rendition of the judgment, and not from the first day of the term. (*b*) The lien created by a judgment on lands is coextensive with the state; but a bona fide purchaser under a fieri facias issued on a junior judgment, will be protected. (*c*) An execution loses its priority if not sued out from term to term, and an execution upon a junior judgment delivered to the sheriff at any intermediate term, will acquire a priority. (*d*) A mere equity of redemption in personal property, unaccompanied by possession on the part of the mortgagor, (*e*) or any mere equitable title to real estate, cannot be sold upon execution issuing out of a court of common law. Such interest can only be subjected to the payment of debts by a suit in Chancery. (*f*) Besides various articles of personal property, forty acres of land, where the same is not embraced within the corporate limits of any town or city, and where it does not exceed the value of four hundred dollars, are exempt from execution. It is the duty of the sheriff to expose property taken on execution, for sale, upon the first Monday in each month, ten days' previous notice of the time and place of sale being given. The defendant may retain goods and chattels in his possession on giving a bond with security, conditioned for the forthcoming of the property at the time and place of sale. If this bond is forfeited, it is the duty of the sheriff to

(*a*) Clay's Digest 199 to 220. (*b*) Quinn et als. *v*. Wiswall, 7 Ala. Rep. 645.

(*c*) Campbell *v*. Sponce et als. 4 Ala. R. 543.

(*d*) McBrown *v*. Turner, 1 S. 72.

(*e*) Perkins & Elliot *v*. Mayfield, 5 S. 182. (*f*) Clay's Digest 350.

return the same with the execution in ten days, to the clerk of the court from which it issued: and the clerk shall within five days issue a new execution against all the obligors, upon which no indulgence is to be allowed.

Creditor's bill.—Whenever an execution issued on a judgment at law shall have been returned unsatisfied, the plaintiff in the execution may file a bill in Chancery against the defendant, or any other person, to compel the discovery of any property, money or thing in action belonging to the defendant, or held in trust for him, and to prevent the transfer of any such property, money or thing in action, or the payment or delivery thereof to the defendant, except where the trust has been created by some other person than the defendant himself.

The Chancery Court shall have power to compel such discovery, to prevent such transfer, and decree satisfaction of the sum due on the judgment, out of the money, property or thing in action belonging to or held in trust for the defendant (with the above exception), which shall be discovered by the proceedings in Chancery, whether the same were originally liable on execution at law or not.

A bill of discovery may likewise be filed when defendant has fraudulently confessed judgment. (*a*)

The following points were decided in reference to this act in the case of Brown, Dimmock et. als., vs. Bates, 10 Alab. 432:

1. The act extends the remedy in favor of judgment creditors, and it is permissible to allege in the bill the supposed interests of the defendant in property, &c., in the general terms of the statute, either positively or in the alternative.

2. A creditor's bill need not allege a fraud on the part of the defendant, or the concealment by him of property or effects, with the intention to delay or hinder the complainant or other creditors in the collection of their debts.

3. Several plaintiffs having distinct judgments may join in filing a creditor's bill, or one creditor may file a bill in behalf of himself and all other judgment creditors (whose executions have been returned unsatisfied) who may choose to come in and contribute to the expense of the suit. So, one creditor by judgment

(*c*) Acts of 1843–4, 107.

and another by decree, who may have acquired liens upon their debtor's property, may join in such a bill.

4. It is no objection to a bill filed in a Chancery Court of this state, that the judgments the complainants are seeking to enforce, were rendered in the District or other Court of the United States.

Attachments in chancery.—The real or personal property of either a legal or equitable nature, or choses in action within this state, or debts (whether due or not due) of a non-resident or absconding debtor, or of a debtor who is disposing of his property with a fraudulent intent, may be attached, and applied to the satisfaction of the complainant's claim, through the medium of a bill in chancery verified by affidavit, and to which the person who owes the non-resident, or absconding, or fraudulent debtor, or the person in whose possession the choses in action proceeded against may be, must be made defendants. Accommodation indorsers, and other securities, may in the same way attach the property, choses in action, or debts of their principal, who is about to remove, or is removing, or absconding or disposing of his property fraudulently, whether the debt for which he is security is due or not, affidavit to be made as in the case of non-resident debtors. All transfers, sales, &c., of property, effects, &c., thus attached, are inoperative and void, as against the complainant, in the attachment bill. (*a*)

Remedy against sheriffs and attorneys.—Whenever any clerk, sheriff or coroner fails or refuses to pay over money collected or received upon any execution, on the application of the plaintiff or his agent, the court to which the execution is returnable may, upon one day's notice, render judgment against such officer and his securities, for the amount of the money thus received, and five per cent. damages on the same for every month in which it has been detained after demand made, and costs of suit. (*b*) The same remedy is given against attorneys. (*c*)

Courts.—The judicial system of Alabama is very similar to that of Virginia. The Circuit Courts, which are held in the spring and fall in each county of the state, have general civil jurisdiction both at law and in equity.

(*a*) Acts of 1845–6, 17. (*b*) Clay's Digest 218. (*c*) Ib. 65.

MISSISSIPPI.

1. CHOSES IN ACTION.
2. INTEREST.
3. FRAUDS.
4. EFFECT OF MARRIAGE UPON RIGHTS OF PROPERTY.
5. LIMITED PARTNERSHIPS.
6. LIMITATION OF ACTIONS.
7. EFFECT OF DEATH UPON THE RIGHTS OF CREDITORS.
8. ATTACHMENT
9. PROCEEDINGS IN CIVIL SUITS.

1. *Choses in Action.*

Bonds, bills, and promissory notes.—All bonds, bills, and notes for the payment of money may be assigned by indorsement, so as to vest the assignee with a right of action thereon in his own name, against the maker or indorser, whether the same be payable to order or assigns or not: but the defendant is allowed the benefit of all set-offs, or defences, which he may have possessed before notice of the assignment. (*a*)

All joint bonds, covenants, &c., are to be construed as joint and several, so also all contracts, promises and liabilities of copartners. Suits may be brought against any one or more of such promissors or obligors, either severally or jointly. (*b*)

Damages upon bills of exchange.—By an act passed in 1837, no damages are allowed for default made on any bill of exchange drawn by any person within the state on any other person within another state of the United States. Damages at the rate of five per cent. are chargeable on all domestic or inland bills of exchange which may be protested for non-payment, and are chargeable as well against the acceptor as other parties to the bill. Upon all

(*a*) Howard & Hutchinson's Statute Law, 373, 374.

(*b*) Ib. 595.

bills drawn upon persons resident without the jurisdiction of the United States, which are protested, ten per cent. damages on the principal sum, with charges and interest are allowed. (*a*)

Cotton receipts.—Cotton receipts are assignable, like promissory notes, in Mississippi as well as in Alabama. Where no time is expressed on their face for the payment or delivery of the cotton therein mentioned, the same shall be construed as payable, and deliverable four months after the date or delivery of the receipt. If a cotton receipt, after it becomes due, is not paid within fifteen days' time from a lawful demand by the holder, the latter may recover fifteen per cent. damages upon the value of the cotton specified in the receipt, unless indeed the owner or holder of the receipt has failed to supply the necessary bagging and cordage. (*b*)

2. *Interest.*

Eight per cent. per annum for the bona fide use of money, and six upon all other contracts, is the established rate of interest. The reservation of a greater rate will expose the lender to the loss of the entire interest, but not the principal. (*c*)

3. *Frauds.*

The English statute of frauds has been substantially re-enacted in Mississippi. The only material variation is in the addition of the words "promise or" before the clause "agreement upon which the action shall be brought." (*d*)

4. *Effect of Marriage upon Rights of Property.*

No husband is liable for the debts of his wife, contracted before marriage, until her separate property has been exhausted: nor for any debts contracted after marriage, if the wife has a separate estate. (*e*)

Any married woman may acquire both real and personal

(*a*) Howard & Hutchinson's Statute Law 376. (*b*) Ib. 372.
(*c*) Acts of 1842, 212. (*d*) H. & H. 376.
(*e*) H. & H. 332. Acts of 1846, 152.

estate, at law and in equity, independent of her husband, by bequest, demise, gift, purchase, or distribution.

Any woman possessed of slaves, or of real estate, at the time of her marriage, shall hold and possess the same to her own separate use, notwithstanding the coverture, and may also hold or acquire all such stock, or implements of husbandry as may be necessary to conduct the business of a plantation.

5. *Limited Partnerships.*

In 1838 a law was passed authorizing the formation of limited partnerships. (*a*) Its provisions are nearly identical with those already detailed under the title of "*Florida.*"

6. *Limitation of Actions.*

All actions of trespass quare clausum fregit, of trespass, detinue, trover and replevin for taking away goods and chattels, all actions of debt founded upon any lending or contract without specialty, all actions of account and upon the case, except such as concern the trade of merchandise between merchant and merchant, their factors, agents, &c., must be commenced and sued within six years next after the cause of action has accrued. Minors, feme coverts, and persons non compos mentis at the time any cause of action may accrue, shall have the period of the limitation to institute suit, after the removal of their disability. The time during which any person liable to a cause of action may be out of the state, is not to be reckoned a part of the limitation. All actions founded upon any account for goods, wares or merchandise sold and delivered, or for any article charged in any store account, must be commenced and prosecuted within three years after the accruing of such cause of action. Every action of debt or covenant for rent or arrearages of rent, founded upon any lease under seal, and every action of debt on a bill, obligation and award for the payment of money, must be commenced and sued within sixteen years next after the cause of action has accrued. (*b*) Judgments of any court of record may be revived

(*a*) H. & H. 378. (*b*) Ib. 568.

by scire facias or action of debt thereon, at any period within twenty years from the date of the judgment.

7. *Effect of Death upon the Rights of Creditors.*

The estates of deceased persons are administered under the supervision of Courts of Probate. The validity of a will may be contested, either when it is offered for probate, or at any time within five years afterwards, by bill in Chancery. After that period, the probate becomes conclusive, except that infants, feme coverts, persons non compos mentis, and absent from the state, may have a like period after the removal of their respective disabilities. (*a*)

The personal estate is the primary fund for the payment of debts; but in the event of its deficiency the real estate, saving to the widow her right of dower, is also chargeable. Where an estate is insolvent, the widow is only to be endowed of the lands and tenements. Where the personal estate is insufficient, it is the duty of the executor or administrator to exhibit to the Orphans' Court of the proper county, a full account under oath of the amount of the estate, and the debts so far as they can be discovered; whereupon a citation issues against all persons interested in the real estate, to show cause why so much of the same should not be sold as may be sufficient to discharge the balance of the decedent's debts remaining unsatisfied. And unless upon the return of such citation the allegations in the petition of the personal representative are denied and refuted, the court will direct a sale, upon sufficient notice being given by the executor or administrator, of so much of the realty as may be necessary.

All claims against the estate of a deceased person must be presented within two years after the executor or administrator has advertised the grant of letters testamentary or of administration.

The executor or administrator is not authorized to pay any claim against the estate of his testator or intestate, until the same shall have been first probated by the court in which the estate is

(*a*) H. & H. 389.

administered, been recorded therein, and certified by the judge thereof under his hand, "as examined and allowed." (*a*)

Before any open account can be allowed, the complainant must make an affidavit that it is just and due, and also prove the contract or transaction upon which it is founded by other competent testimony. (*b*) Where any claim which has been exhibited before the Probate Court is contested by the executor or administrator, the same may be referred to the decision of auditors.

That the executors or administrators may ascertain the situation of the estate of the testator or intestate, no suit can be brought against them as such until after the expiration of six months from the probate or grant of letters of administration; and if he represents such estate as insolvent, no action whatever is to be brought against him. The Orphans' Court in such case, after ordering the real estate of the deceased to be sold, shall appoint two or more fit persons as commissioners to examine and adjust all claims against the same, who shall give notice to the creditors of the estate, of a place and time for the presentation and proof of such claims, and report to the court such as they think proper to allow, who shall thereupon order accordingly. Debts not due may be exhibited as if they were, a rebate of legal interest being deducted. The estate shall be equally distributed among the creditors in proportion to the amount of their claims, as thus ascertained, the necessary funeral expenses being first paid. (*c*)

8. *Attachment.*

An attachment is known in Mississippi both as a form of process to compel an appearance in a civil suit, and lay the foundation of a general judgment, and as an original and summary action. (*d*)

Any creditor, or if out of the state, his agent, upon making affidavit before any judge of the Supreme Court, or any justice of the peace, or the County Court, that his or her debtor has removed

(*a*) Acts of 1846, 147. (*b*) Ib. 151. (*c*) H. & H. 408–410.
(*d*) Ib. 583, 548.

or is removing out of the state, or so absconds or privately conceals him or herself, that the ordinary process of law cannot be served on such debtor, and also as to the amount of his or her debt, to the best of his or her knowledge or belief, may obtain a writ of attachment, returnable to the next term of the court where such suit is properly cognizable, against the estate, both real and personal, of such debtor; and also a summons of garnishment against any person supposed to be indebted to such debtor. Before granting any writ of attachment, the judge or justice must take a bond with security from the applicant or his agent, conditioned to satisfy all costs and damages which the defendant may recover by reason of the wrongful issuing of the attachment, which bond is to be returned to the court where the writ is returnable.

An attachment may issue in the case of a non-resident debtor against any estate, real or personal, belonging to him within the limits of Mississippi; and in the event of his death, against such estate in the hands of his executor or administrator. In the case of non-resident debtors, who are jointly indebted, either as joint obligors or partners, a writ of attachment may issue against the separate and joint estate of such debtors or any of them.

A writ of attachment may issue where any creditor has sufficient grounds to suspect that his debtor will remove with his effects out of the state, before his debt becomes payable, or where such debtor has removed, leaving effects, upon his making affidavit as to the amount of his debt, and the time when it will be payable, and that he has just cause to suspect and verily believes that such debtor will remove himself with his effects out of the state before the said debt will become payable, or hath actually so removed, and that he had no knowledge when the said debt was contracted, of the intention of such debtor so to remove.

The provisions of the law as to the levy of attachments, the mode of replevying them, the proceedings against garnishees, and the trial of the right of property to any portion of the attached estate, are so similar to the details of other states already enumerated, as to require no repetition.

9. *Proceedings in Civil Suits.*

Imprisonment for debt.—Imprisonment for debt upon either mesne or final process, has been abolished in every instance except where, upon an issue submitted to them, a jury shall declare that the debtor has fraudulently concealed his property. (*a*)

The effect of this statute has been to render unnecessary the various provisions for the relief of insolvent debtors from imprisonment.

Judgment and execution.—All judgments operate as liens from the date of their rendition upon the property of the defendant in the county in which they are rendered. In order to give to a judgment any operation as a lien upon the property of the defendant situate in other counties, an abstract of the same duly certified must be recorded in the office of the Circuit Court of such county. (*b*)

It is the duty of the clerk of the Circuit and Chancery Courts, within thirty days from the adjournment of any term, to enroll all judgments and decrees of such court in the order of time in which they may have been rendered; and the liens of such judgments as between themselves shall take effect according to the priority of time in such rendition. (*c*)

The writ of fi. fa. runs against the lands and tenements, as well as the goods and chattels of the defendant. It cannot, however, be levied upon mere equitable interests, The aid of Chancery must be invoked to reach this species of interests. A summons of garnishment, may however, issue upon any judgment or decree, and be served upon any person suggested on the oath of the plaintiff to be indebted to the defendant, if such defendant or judgment debtor has no property or effects upon which levy can be made; and a garnishee thus summoned may be compelled to pay the amount due from him to such defendant or judgment debtor, whether the same be due on judgment or otherwise. (*d*)

Execution may be taken out at any time within one year from

(*a*) Acts of 1840, 40. (*b*) Acts of 1841, 93. (*c*) Acts of 1846, 190.
(*d*) Gray *v.* Hanly, 1 Smed. & M. 598.

the period of rendering a judgment, or the expiration of a stay of execution indorsed thereon. (*a*)

When the officer returns "no property found" on an execution, and the plaintiff suggests that the defendant has fraudulently conveyed his property, the question may be tried upon an issue made up before a jury, after serving a notice in the nature of a scire facias upon the person on whose hands is the property, and if such issue be found for the plaintiff, the property thus conveyed shall be subject to his execution. (*b*)

Where land is sold upon execution, the debtor or any other bona fide creditor, may redeem the same at any period within two years, on tendering to the purchaser the amount of the purchase money, with ten per cent. interest thereon, and all lawful charges.

Where an execution is levied upon personal property, and the debtor tenders the sheriff a bond with sufficient surety in a penalty double the amount of the debt, conditioned for the forthcoming of the same upon the day of sale, it is the duty of the officer to restore the property to the possession of the defendant. If the condition is broken, by a failure to deliver the property or discharge the debt, the bond, upon being returned to the court from which it issued, has at once the force and effect of a judgment, upon which execution at once issues against all the obligors, without the privilege being extended to any of them of executing a new forthcoming bond.

Besides the property usually exempted from execution, the debtor in Mississippi is entitled to retain his homestead; if in the country, one hundred and sixty acres of land, if in town, a house and lot to the value of one thousand five hundred dollars.

Courts.—The organization of courts in Mississippi, is very similar to that in Virginia. There are County and also Circuit Courts held in each county, the former four times, the latter twice a year. The Circuit Courts have a general common law jurisdiction. All matters of equitable cognizance are confided to a Court of Chancery.

(*a*) McIntyre *v.* The Agricultural Bank, Freeman's Ch. 105; Money *v.* Dorsey, 7 Sm. & Mars. 15; ib. 630; ib. 657.

(*b*) H. & H. 635.

TENNESSEE.

1. *Choses in Action.*

Promissory notes are negotiable in the same manner, as are inland bills of exchange according to the custom of merchants.(*a*) The Tennessee statute is substantially a copy of 3rd and 4th Ann, chapter 9.

All bills, bonds, or notes for money, whether under seal or not, or whether expressed to be payable to order or for value received or not, are negotiable, and may be transferred by indorsement in the same manner and under the same restrictions as promissory notes, and the indorser may maintain any action thereon, which could have been brought by the obligee or payee. (*b*)

The assignee of any bond with collateral condition, or of any bill or note for specific articles or the performance of any duty, may sue thereon, in his own name, at law or in equity. (*c*)

The holder of any bill of exchange, foreign or inland, promissory note, or writing obligatory, may institute a joint or several action against the makers and indorsers. (*d*)

Book accounts.—A creditor may in some cases prove a book

(*a*) Tennessee Digest 550. (*b*) Ib. 500. (*c*) Ib. 130. (*d*) Ib. 416.

account, when it does not exceed seventy-five dollars, by his own oath. (*a*)

Rate of damages upon protested bills—Whenever any bill of exchange drawn or indorsed within the state, upon any persons or body corporate in any other state, or place, is returned unpaid with a legal protest, the holder may recover from the drawer or indorser of such bill, the damages hereinafter specified, over and above the principal sum for which the bill has been drawn, and the charges of protest together with lawful interest upon the amount of such principal sum, damages and charges of protest, from the time at which notice of such protest was given, and payment of the amount due demanded, viz.: where the bill is drawn upon any person within the United States, three per cent.: where it is drawn upon any person in any other place in North America, bordering upon the Gulf of Mexico, or in the West India islands, fifteen per cent.: where it is drawn upon any person in any other part of the world, twenty per cent. These damages are to be in lieu of interest and all other charges, except charges of protest, to the time when notice of the protest was given, and demand of payment made.

The entry of a notary on the protest, is prima facie evidence of notice of dishonor; and where such entry was not made, and the notary is dead, then a similar entry in his record book of protests, is to be taken as prima facie evidence of the fact. (*b*)

2. *Interest.*

Interest is allowed upon bonds, bills, notes, or bills of exchange, liquidated and settled accounts, signed by the parties, in the absence of any agreement to the contrary. Where an instrument is payable on demand, such demand must be made by the creditor or his agent before interest can be allowed. Securities for the payment and delivery of property and all specific articles bear interest as moneyed contracts; that is to say, the articles shall be valued by a jury at the time they become due, and interest shall be paid accordingly. The legal rate of interest is six per cent. per annum. If more than six per cent. is reserved,

(*a*) T. D. 131. (*b*) Ib. 126.

the defendant can only avoid the usurious excess, and the plaintiff may recover a judgment for the principal of his debt, with legal interest. (*a*)

3. *Frauds.*

The English statutes of 13th and 27th Elizabeth, against fraudulent conveyances, and also the statute of 29th Charles II. against frauds and perjuries, have been substantially re-enacted in Tennessee. The word "promise" is added to the last clause of the latter statute, in reference to the necessity of a writing. (*b*)

4. *Limited Partnerships.*

Limited partnerships for manufacturing purposes were authorized by act passed in 1842. The provisions of this law are similar to those already detailed. A special partner may however transfer his interest in the partnership by a deed in writing, acknowledged, or proved and registered, without producing the effect of a dissolution. (*c*)

5. *Limitation of Actions.*

Actions of account and upon the case, except such accounts as concern the trade of merchandise between merchant and merchant, their factors or servants, actions of debt for arrearages of rent, actions of detinue, replevin, and trespass, quare clausum fregit, within three years next after the cause of action accrues. (*d*)

The statute of limitations of 21 James I, chap. 16, sec. 3, is is in force in Tennessee, and bars any contract or lending without specialty in six years from the time the cause of action accrues. (*e*)

The same limitation applies to bonds, bills, and other securities made transferable by law, after their assignment or indorsement, as is applicable to promissory notes. (*f*)

There is the usual saving in favor of infants, feme coverts,

(*a*) T. D. 406, 407. (*b*) Ib. 350 to 353. (*c*) Acts of 1842, 149.
(*d*) T. D. 440. (*e*) Tisdale *v.* Munro, 3 Yer. 320. (*f*) T. D. 441.

persons non compos mentis, imprisoned beyond seas, of the term of the limitation, after the removal of their respective disabilities. (*a*) The phrase "beyond seas" is declared to mean beyond the limits of the United States. (*b*)

6. *Attachment.*

Wherever a debtor so absconds or conceals himself, or removes privately, as that the ordinary process of law cannot be served upon him, or wherever a debtor or defendant in any suit, or judgment is removing, or about to remove himself or his property beyond the limits of the state, or shall be absconding or concealing himself, or his property or effects, or wherever a debtor is a non-resident, and his creditor or his agent makes an affidavit of such fact, and also of the amount of his claim, any judge of the Circuit Court, or justice of the County Court may issue a writ of attachment against the estate of such debtor, both real and personal, including choses in action. Debts and choses in action, whether due or not, may be attached. (*c*)

Property exempt from execution is also exempt from attachment. Persons who are bound as accommodation indorsers or securities, although the debt for which they are responsible may not be due, can sue out writs of attachment where their principal is about to remove, or is removing, absconding or carrying off his property beyond the limits of the state; no decree, however, to be made until such debt becomes due.

Attachments against non-residents must be stayed for a period not less than six nor more than twelve months from the time of the return of the process.

The act of Tennessee contains the usual provisions for the replevy of property by the defendant, the sale of it by the officer when perishable, for proceedings of garnishment against any person indebted to or having in his possession effects of defendants.

An attachment is a lien upon the property attached from the time that the writ is returned and becomes a record. (*d*)

Attachments in Chancery.—It has been held that the courts

(*a*) T. D. 441. (*b*) Ib. 444. (*c*) Acts of 1843, 30; R. S. 101, 107.
(*d*) Cook 254.

of Tennessee have no jurisdiction of an original attachment, where neither the plaintiff nor defendant are citizens of the state, and can render no judgment against a garnishee summoned upon such an attachment. (*a*) But since this decision, by the act of 1836, where non-residents have any property, real or personal, legal or equitable in Tennessee, or where any resident of Tennessee is indebted to such person, a creditor of the non-resident, whether a citizen of Tennessee, or any other state, may file a bill in Chancery, without having first recovered a judgment at law, to attach such real or personal property, or choses in action, (*b*) upon an affidavit that the defendants are indebted as charged, and are non-residents. This proceeding may also be had against absconding debtors. No final decree will be rendered in a case of this character, until the second term after the bill is filed, nor unless notice has been given by publication in some newspaper designated by the court. Where these requisites have been complied with, the decree will be as binding upon the property attached, as if personal service of process had been made. Where the proceeds arising from the sale of the property attached are not sufficient to satisfy the claim of the complainant, an execution may issue for the balance, to be levied upon any property of the defendant in the state, or summons of garnishment may be issued against any person indebted to him, and proceedings had as upon attachments at law.

Judicial attachment.—Upon the return of "not found" on any civil process, the plaintiff may sue out an attachment against the estate of the defendant; and upon the return of any goods attached, may proceed to final judgment, if the defendant does not appear and make defence; and if the judgment is not satisfied by a sale of the goods attached, the plaintiff may have execution for the residue. This process cannot issue against the estate of a non-resident, unless grounded on original attachment, or unless the leading process has been executed on the person of the defendant while within the state. (*c*)

(*a*) Webb & Co. *v.* Lea, 6 Yer. 473. (*b*) R. S. 106. (*c*) Ib. 108.

7. *Effect of Death upon the Rights of Creditors.*

Every executor or administrator shall within two months from his qualification, give notice to all persons having claims against the deceased, to present them. (*a*)

No executor or administrator shall pay any debts of a testator or intestate, or confess a judgment for the same, until the expiration of six months from the grant of letters testamentary or of administration, and if he pays any debts within that period, and the estate proves insolvent, he will be liable to every creditor for his pro rata share of the estate. (*b*)

Creditors of the deceased, if residents of the state, must demand and sue for their claims within two years, if non-residents, within three years from the qualification of the executors or administrators, saving the rights of infants, feme coverts, and persons non compos mentis, for one year after the removal of their respective disabilities.

No execution may issue against an executor or administrator, until twelve months after his qualification. (*c*)

Although the personal estate is the primary fund for the payment of debts, upon its proving inadequate, the real estate may be sold under the direction of the Court of Chancery, for the district where the lands are situate, upon the application of the executor or administrator, setting forth the insufficiency of the personal assets. The heirs are necessary parties to such proceeding.

In the payment of debts, those due by bills, bonds and promissory notes, whether with or without seal, and all settled and liquidated accounts signed by the debtor, are to be regarded as of equal dignity.

There is no other restriction as to the right of preferring one creditor to another by the executors or administrators, than that of time which has been previously mentioned. (*d*)

(*a*) R. S. 75. (*b*) Acts of 1841, 22. (*c*) R. S. 80. (*d*) R. S. 73.

8. *Proceedings in Civil Suits.*

Imprisonment for debt.—No female can be imprisoned upon either mesne or final process in any civil action.

The original process in all civil actions is a summons. A capias can only issue upon an affidavit at the commencement, or during the progress of a suit, that the cause of action is just, and that the defendant has removed or is about to remove his property beyond the jurisdiction of the court. (*a*)

By an act passed in 1842, the right to issue a capias ad satisfaciendum in any civil action, has been abolished.

The operation of this act has been to render useless the various provisions for the release of insolvent debtors from imprisonment.

Judgment and execution.—All judgments of a court of record are a lien upon the lands of the debtor, from the time of their rendition, provided the judgment is obtained in the county where the debtor is then residing, and that execution, unless stayed by some legal order, is issued within twelve months.

Judgments are a lien upon the lands of the debtor in other counties from the period of their registry in such counties, provided execution, unless stayed as before, issue thereon and the lands be sold within one year from the rendition of the judgment. (*b*)

Process is levied first upon the personalty of the debtor, and if that be insufficient, then upon his realty. (*c*)

Any person whose land has been sold on execution may redeem the same, upon paying or tendering to the purchaser, or any one claiming under him, the amount bid with ten per cent. interest, and other costs and charges. Any bona fide creditor of the judgment debtor may also redeem within the same time, upon tendering to the purchaser the amount bid, with ten per cent. interest, and offering to credit the debtor with ten per cent. on the amount bid at the execution sale. (*d*)

Lands sold under a judgment of the federal court, cannot be redeemed upon this provision. (*e*)

(*a*) R. S. 383. (*b*) Ib. 419. (*c*) Ib. 292. (*d*) Ib. 565. (*e*) 6 Yerg. 209.

Where the officer levies upon personal property, the debtor may retain the possession, upon giving bond with security for its delivery at the day and place appointed for the sale. If this bond is forfeited, the officer may immediately levy upon any property of the defendant in the execution, and if sufficient cannot be found to satisfy the debt, then upon any property of the securities in the forfeited bond, and expose the same for sale. (*a*)

Courts.—Original jurisdiction in all civil cases belongs to Circuit Courts, which hold a spring and fall term in every county in the state.

(*a*) R. S. 129.

KENTUCKY.

1. BILLS OF EXCHANGE AND PROMISSORY NOTES.
2. INTEREST.
3. FRAUDS.
4. CORPORATIONS.
5. EFFECT OF MARRIAGE UPON RIGHTS OF PROPERTY.
6. LIMITATION OF ACTIONS.
7. ATTACHMENT.
8. EFFECT OF DEATH UPON THE RIGHTS OF CREDITORS.
9. PROCEEDINGS IN CIVIL SUITS.

1. *Bills of Exchange and Promissory Notes.*

All bonds, bills, and promissory notes, whether for money or property, are assignable; and the assignee may sue for the same in the same manner the original payee or obligee might sue; but the defendant shall be allowed all discounts, under the rules and regulations prescribed by law, either against the plaintiff, or the original obligee or payee, before notice of the assignment. But the above provision shall not affect the nature of the defence, either in law or equity, that any defendant may have against an assignee or assignees, or the original assignor. (*a*)

All bills, drafts, and checks, drawn in this state or payable in this state, and all bills, drafts, and checks, drawn by banks or individuals in one state on banks or individuals in another state, in favor of, or held, or indorsed, by citizens of this state, for bank notes, or currency, or current funds, shall be deemed negotiable, and treated in all respects as if drawn for money. (*b*)

A scrawl affixed to an instrument as a seal, confers upon it all the force and obligation of one. (*c*)

(*a*) Morehead & Brown's Digest, 150.

(*b*) Loughborough's Digest, 108. (*c*) M. & B. D. 326.

Ten per cent. interest is allowed on all foreign bills which are protested from date until paid, in lieu of damages, but they must be demanded of the drawer within eighteen months from the date of the bill.

2. *Interest.*

By the act of 1819, the rate of interest is fixed at six per cent.; but the contract is not absolutely void. The lender may recover the amount actually loaned, with lawful interest. If the lender refuse to receive the principal with lawful interest, on a tender thereof previous to a suit, he shall pay the costs of the suit.

The act of 1798 rendered the contract itself utterly void. (*a*)

Six per cent. is held in the courts of the commonwealth to be the prima facie rate of interest authorized to be received in the several states and territories of the Union; but either party may prove the rate to be different. (*b*)

3. *Frauds.*

The English statute of frauds and perjuries is in force in Kentucky. (*c*)

4. *Corporations.*

By an act passed in 1841, certain provisions were made for all corporations, carrying on any kind of manufacture.

It is enacted, inter alia, that every transfer of stock shall be made by deed, and acknowledged before some justice of the peace, and recorded by the clerk of the corporation in a book to be kept for that purpose.

All the members of the corporation are jointly and severally liable for all debts of the company, until the whole amount of the capital stock shall have been paid in and a certificate thereof recorded in the clerk's office of the County Court of the county

(*a*) Morehead & Brown's Digest, 856, 852.

(*b*) Loughborough's Digest, 280.

(*c*) M. & B. D. 734

where the manufactory is established. This certificate must be made within thirty days after the last instalment is paid in, and is signed and sworn to by the president, clerk, treasurer, and a majority of the directors.

The corporation shall make an annual publication of its condition, and on failure to do so, the president and directors are made individually liable for all debts of the company then existing, or that may be contracted before the notice is given.

The corporation is prohibited, on pain of forfeiting its charter, from issuing any notes to pass as currency. (*a*)

5. *Effect of Marriage on the Rights of Property.*

The estate of the husband is not liable for the debts or engagements of the wife, contracted before marriage. On the other hand, neither the land nor slaves of a married woman, possessed at the time of marriage or acquired during coverture, are liable for his debts, nor can his estate in them during her life be taken on execution. But such property, both land and slaves, excepting the husband's right of courtesy, may be sold in payment of her debts created before the marriage, or in payment of debts contracted by her in writing jointly with her husband, for necessaries furnished to any member of the family. The slaves of the wife may be sold by the husband and wife jointly in the same manner as real estate. Upon the death of the wife, her slaves descend to her heirs at law, as realty, subject to a life estate of the husband in them. (*b*)

6. *Limitation of Actions.*

Actions on the case, other than for slander, actions for account, actions of debt grounded on any lending or contract without specialty, all actions for arrearages of rent, all actions of detinue and replevin, all actions of trespass, quare clausum fregit, or to goods and chattels, must be brought within five years; actions of assault and battery, wounding and imprisonment, within three years; and actions of slander within one year after the words spoken.

(*a*) Lough. Dig. 149. (*b*) Acts of 1846, 43.

All actions or suits founded upon account for goods, wares, and merchandise, sold and delivered, or for any article charged in any store account, shall be commenced within twelve months next after the cause of such action, or the delivery of such goods, except that in case of the death of the creditor or debtor before the expiration of the twelve months, the further time of twelve months from such death shall be allowed before the commencement of the action. Any merchant who shall post-date his account is liable to a penalty of ten times the value of the article sold. If the merchant should obtain judgment, and the judgment be reversed or arrested, he may commence a new action in one year thereafter. From the first of July, 1838, all sureties are discharged from liability on judgments, on bonds in appeals, supersedeas, sale, and replevin, on bonds in attachment, ne exeat, for the forthcoming of property, or to abide by the decree of a court, or for costs, when seven years shall have elapsed without execution on the judgment, unless delayed by dilatory proceedings on the part of the defendant; or when seven years after the cause of action accrued, shall have elapsed, without suit on the bond which is the foundation of the action.

On administration and guardian-bonds, sureties are discharged from liability to distributees, devisees, or wards, when five years have elapsed without suit after the youngest have arrived at majority. On all other written obligations, sureties are discharged from liability when seven years have elapsed without suit.

But if the surety should abscond or conceal himself, or use any indirect ways to defeat or obstruct his creditor, he cannot claim the benefit of the above provisions.

The statute of limitations does not begin to run until the usual disabilities are removed, viz., infancy, coverture, imprisonment, insanity, and absence beyond seas. (*a*)

7. *Attachment—Foreign and Judicial.*

A justice of the peace may issue a writ of attachment whenever a creditor makes complaint before him that his debtor is

(*a*) Morehead & Brown's Dig. 1132–37, Lough. Dig. 558.

privately removing out of the county, or absconds so that the ordinary process of law cannot be served upon him. The attachment is levied upon the slaves and goods and chattels of the defendant, and may be served by any constable or sheriff. If the debt is not more than fifty dollars, the writ is returned to the magistrate, but if the debt exceeds that sum, it is returned to the Circuit Court. Where the levy has been made by the constable, and the debt is over fifty dollars, he is to deliver the property attached to the sheriff. The justice must take bond and good security for the payment by the complainant of all damages and costs to the defendant in case the plaintiff is cast in his suit. The property may be replevied, but if it is not, judgment is given for the plaintiff, and the goods sold in the same manner as goods taken on a writ of fieri facias. Property in the hands of a garnishee may also be attached. It is also provided that where there is a return of "not found" on a capias or warrant, the plaintiff may sue out an attachment against the estate of the defendant to force an appearance, and proceed substantially as above. (*a*)

Where any debtor is about to remove his property from the commonwealth, or to dispose of the same with the intention of delaying or defrauding his creditors, the Courts of Chancery are authorized, upon a bill filed by any creditor, whether the debt be due or not, to attach the property and arrest such fraudulent sale or removal, and upon the establishment of an intention on the part of the debtor either to remove or fraudulently to dispose of his property, to cause the same to be applied to the payment of the debt. The bill of the creditor must be sworn to, and bond given with sufficient security for the payment of any damage that may be sustained by the wrongful emanation of the order, before such injunction can be granted. (*b*)

8. *Effect of Death upon the Rights of Creditors.*

By an act passed in 1839, all debts are declared of equal dignity in the administration of estates, and are to be paid ratably, except that burial expenses, and costs and charges of administra-

(*a*) Lough. Dig. 46. (*b*) Acts of 1838, 213.

tion, and the costs of such suits as the personal representative is directed by law to institute, shall be paid in full before any distribution: also, where a creditor has a lien which is not sufficient to discharge his debt, he shall not be entitled to any portion of the residue of the estate, until all the creditors not having liens shall have received a sum equal, pro rata, with such lien creditor.

Where the personal estate is not sufficient to pay the debts, the personal representative may file a bill in Chancery to subject the realty to the payment thereof, making the heirs, devisees, legatees, and distributees, and creditors, parties. The court may decree a sale, after proper notice, and upon reasonable credits; and distribute the proceeds among the creditors, as above directed. A master commissioner shall be appointed to ascertain the condition of the estate, and before whom the creditors shall prove their claims. The holders of fraudulent conveyances may be made parties to the bill, and the property subjected to the payment of the debts of the estate. (*a*)

Where any person dies intestate, leaving a widow, that portion of his estate which would be by law exempt from execution, is not considered assets, but the same, together with a sufficiency of provisions to sustain the widow and infant children, if there be any, for the term of twelve months, shall be appropriated by the administrator to their use: and if there be not a sufficiency of provisions on hand, so much of the live stock and growing crop shall be set aside by the commissioner appointed to appraise the estate, as may be necessary to supply the deficiency. (*b*)

9. *Proceedings in Civil Suits.*

Imprisonment for debt.—Imprisonment for debt is abolished in Kentucky, (*c*) except that a capias ad satisfaciendum may be issued on a judgment in trespass, vi et armis, or for words spoken or written, or for seduction, in which cases the defendant may release his person by availing himself of the law for insolvent debtors, on giving the plaintiff ten days' notice. (*d*)

No person can be arrested on any original or mesne process

(*a*) Lough. Dig. 240.

(*b*) Acts of 1845, 35.

(*c*) M. & B. Dig. 195.

(*d*) Ib. 630.

or held to bail, unless the plaintiff make an affidavit that he verily believes the defendant will leave the commonwealth, or move his property out of the same before judgment; or otherwise abscond, so that the process of the court after judgment cannot be served upon him. Upon such affidavit being filed, the clerk shall indorse that bail is required, and in what sum. (*a*)

Any person arrested under an order requiring bail, or on a writ of ne exeat, may avail himself of the act for the relief of insolvent debtors, on giving reasonable notice to the plaintiff or his agent, if in the state; if not, by filing such notice in the office which issued the process against him. (*b*)

Insolvent debtor.—Any person taken or charged in execution, may apply to two justices of the peace, deliver in a schedule of his estate and effects, and take the oath of an insolvent debtor. His person is released, but any estate he may subsequently acquire is liable for his debts.

The schedule is filed in the clerk's office, and the property therein enumerated is vested in the sheriff, who sells the same and distributes the proceeds among the creditors. (*c*)

Judgment and Executions.—The writs of fieri facias and elegit are in use in Kentucky, but the former runs against the real as well as personal estate of the debtor. The personalty must however be first taken and sold.

The estate of the defendant is bound from the time of the delivery of the writ of execution to the officer, who indorses thereon the exact date of its reception. A landlord who reserves rent in money, has a preference over any executions; creditor for one year's rent. (*d*) Various articles, too numerous to mention, principally furniture and tools, and provisions for six months are exempt from execution. (*e*)

The equitable interest of a mortgagor in any real or personal estate may be sued, subject to the incumbrance, and saving to the mortgagor the right of redeeming the same within the year. The

(*a*) M. & B. Dig. 195. (*b*) Ib. 196.

(*c*) Lough. Dig. 273. As a capias ad satisfaciendum may be issued on judgments in certain actions of tort, the above law is still in force. See Imprisonment for Debt.

(*d*) M. & B. Dig. 625, 631. (*e*) Lough. Dig. 235, 236.

purchaser of such equitable interest in personalty is required to give bond, with approved security, that he will not remove the same from the commonwealth, but hold it subject to the order of any court of competent jurisdiction.

Where goods and chattels are levied upon an execution, the same shall be restored to the owner upon his executing an obligation with security for their forthcoming at the time and place appointed for the sale: which obligation, if forfeited, has the force of a judgment, and execution may be issued thereon against the principal and security, upon which no indulgence will be allowed. A defendant may also at any time before sale replevy his property for the space of three months, by giving bond with sufficient security for the payment of the debt, interest, and all costs, at the expiration of that period; which bond, if forfeited, is to have the effect of a judgment, on which execution may be issued as in the case of a forfeited forthcoming bond.

Where real estate is taken in execution and offered for sale, it will, unless it brings two thirds of its appraised value, be subject to redemption by the debtor at any time within one year from the sale, on payment of the purchase money, and ten per cent. interest. (*a*)

Remedy against sheriffs and attorneys for misconduct.—Any sheriff failing to pay over money collected on an execution, or failing to pay over the amount of the debt and costs where he has suffered a defendant in custody under a ca. sa. to escape, may, upon a motion by the creditor in the execution, of which ten days' notice has been given, be amerced, for the benefit of such creditor, in a sum equal to the amount specified in the writ, with interest at the rate of fifteen per cent. from the return of the execution until discharge of the judgment. (*b*) In order to entitle a plaintiff residing out of the county to recover from the sheriff the amount of money collected by him, the former must have appointed an agent in the county, or made a personal or written demand therein. (*c*)

An attorney who fails to pay over money which he has collected may be suspended from practice; and a judgment upon motion

(*a*) M. & B. Dig. 650. (*b*) Ib. i. 624.

(*c*) Davis *v.* Armstrong, 1 Mars. 366; Allen *v.* Grant, 1 Mars. 409.

after ten days' notice may be also rendered against him in favor of the creditor, for the amount due, and cost of the motion. (*a*)

Courts.—The judicial system of Kentucky is so similar in its general features to that of Virginia, that the discrepancies need not be pointed out.

(*a*) M. & B. D. 173, 178.

MISSOURI.

1. *Choses in Action.*

Contracts.—All contracts which are only joint according to the common law, are directed by statute, to be construed as joint and several, and the effects and incidents of a several contract attaches to them. (*a*)

All instruments of writing professing on the face thereof to be sealed, and to which the person executing the same, shall affix a scrawl by way of seal, are to be adjudged as sealed. (*b*)

All notes in writing for the payment of a sum of money or property therein mentioned, to any person or order, or to bearer, shall import a consideration. (*c*)

All bonds or promissory notes for money or property may be assignable by an indorsement thereon, and the assignee may bring an action thereon in his own name; the obligor being allowed every just discount against the assignor before assignment, and every defence to the instrument which he might have made, had it remained in the hands of the assignor. (*d*)

Bills of exchange and promissory notes.—All promissory notes, which express on their face, to be for " value received, negotiable and payable without defalcation," are rendered negotia-

(*a*) Revised Statutes 216. (*b*) Ib. (*c*) Ib. 189. (*d*) Ib. 190.

ble, in like manner as inland bills of exchange; and the payees and indorsers of every such negotiable note, payable to them or order, and the holder of every such note payable to bearer, may maintain actions thereon against the makers and indorsers respectively as in cases of inland bills of exchange. (*a*)

Under this statute it has been held that a note for money payable "to M. or bearer," was not negotiable, but subject to any defence in the hands of the holder, to which it would have been liable in the hands of the maker. It is not even sufficient that the note contain the words "for value received, without defalcation." It must be drawn in the form prescribed by statute. (*b*)

No person can be charged as acceptor of a bill of exchange, unless his acceptance is in writing, signed by himself or his lawful agent. (*c*)

An acceptance upon a separate paper will only bind the acceptor in favor of persons to whom the acceptance has been shown, and who on the faith thereof have received the bill for a valuable consideration. (*d*)

An unconditional promise to accept a bill before it is drawn, shall be deemed an actual acceptance in favor of the same class of persons. (*e*)

A refusal to write an acceptance upon a bill, is declared equivalent to a refusal to accept, and the bill thereupon may be protested for non-acceptance. (*f*)

These provisions, however, are not to abridge or impair the right of any person to whom a promise to accept a bill may have been made, and who on the faith of such promise shall have drawn or negotiated the bill to recover damages from the person making such promise, on his refusal to accept the bill.

The destruction of a bill, or a refusal to accept it within twenty-four hours after its delivery for that purpose are rendered equivalent to acceptance. (*g*)

A notarial protest is declared to be evidence of a demand and refusal to pay a bill of exchange, or negotiable promissory note, at the time and in the manner therein stated. (*h*)

(*a*) R. S. 175.

(*b*) Beatty *v.* Anderson, 5 Missouri 447; Austin & Haines *v.* Blue, 6 Miss. 265; Muldron *v.* Caldwell, 7 Miss. 563.

(*c*) R. S. 175. (*d*) Ib. (*e*) Ib. (*f*) Ib. (*g*) Ib. (*h*) Ib.

Rate of damages upon protested bills.—The provisions as to damages upon protested bills are somewhat novel and minute. To entitle a party to damages upon a protested bill of exchange, drawn or negotiated within the state, the bill must express to be "for value received." (*a*) When such a bill, drawn upon any person, at any place within the state, shall have been presented for acceptance or payment, and protested for non-acceptance or non-payment, the holder may recover from the drawer and indorsers, having due notice of the dishonor of the bill, four per cent. damages; if the bill shall have been drawn upon any person at any place out of the state, but within the United States or its territories, ten per cent. damages; if upon any person at any place without the United States or its territories, twenty per cent. damages. The same rate of damages is fixed in cases where a bill has been accepted, but is not paid at its maturity. No damages are allowed upon bills drawn within the state, upon any person at a place within the same, if payment of the principal sum, with interest and charges of protest, is tendered within twenty days after demand or notice of the dishonor of the bill.

The damages are to be in lieu of interest, protest, and all other expenses incurred previous to the time of giving notice, or to the time when the principal sum shall become payable, when no notice of the dishonor is required to be given; but from such period the holder of the bill may recover lawful interest upon the aggregate amount of the principal sum and the damages.

Where the bill is expressed to be payable in the money of the United States, the amount due thereon, and damages shall be ascertained without any reference to the rate of exchange; but if payable in foreign currency they are to be determined by reference to the rate of exchange, or the value of such foreign currency at the time and place of payment. (*b*)

2. *Interest.*

By an act passed in 1847, the former laws of Michigan as to usury, were repealed, and new provisions declared. Six per

(*a*) Riggs *v.* The City of St. Louis, 7 Miss. 438.
(*b*) R. S. 174.

cent. was established as the legal rate of interest. In cases where a higher rate of interest is reserved than six per cent., the borrower may be relieved from the usurious excess, and the interest at six per cent. will be set apart for the benefit of common schools. The lender is liable to a forfeiture of the whole interest agreed to be taken, to be recovered in an ordinary action, and go to the benefit of common schools. (*a*)

3. *Corporations.*

Where the debts of any corporation, excepting banking companies or literary or benevolent institutions, shall exceed the amount of its capital stock actually paid in, the directors under whose administration it shall happen, unless absent at the time, or if present objecting thereto, and giving notice of the fact to the stockholders, are rendered jointly and severally liable to the extent of such excess, for all debts of the company then existing, or which shall be contracted subsequently, so long as they shall continue in office, and until the debts shall be reduced to the amount of the capital stock. (*b*)

4. *Fraudulent Conveyances.*

All sales made by a vendor of goods and chattels, in his possession or under his control, unless accompanied by delivery within a reasonable (regard being had to the situation of the property) time, and followed by actual and continued change of the possession, shall be presumed to be fraudulent and void as against the creditors of the vendor, or subsequent purchasers in good faith. (*c*)

5. *Statute of Frauds.*

The English statute is substantially re-enacted. In the class of cases which it embraces, the agreement, or some note or memorandum thereof, must be in writing.

Contracts for the sale of goods for the price of thirty dollars

(*a*) Acts of 1847, 63. (*b*) R. S. 234. (*c*) Ib. 528.

or upwards, are not valid, unless part are delivered, or earnest given, or a note or memorandum made of the bargain in writing.

No action can be brought to charge any person, by reason of any representations as to the character, credit or dealings of a third party, unless such representations are in writing. (*a*)

6. *Assignment.*

Wherever a debtor assigns his real and personal estate, in whole or in part, for the benefit of his creditors, or any of them, it is made the duty of the assignee to distribute the same among the creditors generally, under the superintendence of the Circuit Court. It is the duty of the assignee to give notice to the creditors by advertisement, of the time and place of adjusting and allowing demands against the estate, and all the creditors who, being duly notified, shall fail to attend, are precluded from having any of the benefits of the assignment. The decision of the assignee as to any claim exhibited before him, shall be final, unless the creditor request a reference to a jury, when the case shall be certified to the Circuit Court, and tried on an issue formed for that purpose. (*b*)

7. *Statutes of Limitation.*

All actions founded upon any writing, sealed or unsealed, for the payment of money or property, must be commenced within ten years after the cause of action accrued: all actions upon open accounts for goods, wares or merchandise sold and delivered, or for any article in a store account, within two years: all actions of account, detinue, assumpsit, trover, trespass on the case, or debt founded upon any contract or liability, and not otherwise specially limited, within five years. There is the usual saving in favor of infants, married women, persons non compos mentis, or imprisoned on a criminal charge.

There is no limitation on suits brought to enforce payment of bills, notes or other evidences of debt issued by moneyed corporations. A promise in writing is necessary to revive action

(*a*) R. L. 530. (*b*) Ib. 121–132.

barred by the act. No acknowledgment or promise, in writing or otherwise, by one joint contractor, shall deprive his co-contractor of the benefit of this act. Bonds, judgments and decrees are presumed to have been paid after the lapse of twenty years: such presumption being liable to be repelled by proof of payment of part, or written acknowledgment of the indebtedness. (*a*)

8. *Attachment.*

A creditor may resort to the process of attachment to secure his debt in the following cases:

1. Where the debtor is a non-resident of the state.

2. Where the debtor conceals himself so that the ordinary process of law cannot be served upon him.

3. Where the debtor has absconded or absented himself from his usual place of abode, so that the ordinary process of law cannot be served upon him.

4. Where the debtor is about to remove his property or effects from the state, with intent to hinder, delay, or defraud his creditors.

5. Where the debtor has fraudulently conveyed or assigned his property so as to hinder or delay his creditors.

6. Where the debtor has fraudulently concealed or disposed of his property or effects so as to hinder or delay his creditors.

7. Where the debtor is about fraudulently to convey or assign his property or effects so as to hinder or delay his creditors.

8. Where the debtor is about fraudulently to conceal or dispose of his property or effects so as to hinder or delay his creditors.

9. Where the debt was contracted out of this state, and the debtor has absconded or secretly removed his property or effects into this state, with the intent to defraud, hinder or delay his creditors.

Where the demand sworn to is not less than fifty, nor more than one hundred and fifty dollars, and is evidenced by a bond or note for the direct payment of money, or where the demand sworn to is not less than fifty, nor more than ninety dollars, and

(*a*) R. S. 715 to 724.

is founded upon a contract other than a bond or note, the Circuit Court and justices of the peace have concurrent jurisdiction. Where, in either case, the amount falls below fifty dollars, the justices have exclusive jurisdiction.

The remedy by attachment is not confined to citizens of the state. It has been repeatedly held that a non-resident may have an attachment in the state against a non-resident. (*a*)

On affidavit by a creditor whose claim exceeds five dollars, but falls below fifty dollars, that the debtor has no goods or chattels within the state, liable to attachment issued by a justice of the peace, he may sue in the Circuit Court.

A creditor, before he can obtain an attachment, must file, either with the clerk of the Circuit Court, or with the justice, as the case may be, an affidavit, made either by himself or by some person on his behalf, stating that the defendant is justly indebted to the plaintiff, after allowing all just credits and offsets, in a sum to be specified, and on what account, and shall also state that the affiant has good reason to believe and does believe the existence of one or more of the causes which entitle him to the writ of attachment.

The creditor, or some responsible person as principal, and one or more sureties, must also file a bond, whose sufficiency is to be judged of by the clerk or justice, as the case may be, in a penal sum at least double the demand sworn to, payable to the state of Missouri, and conditioned that the plaintiff shall prosecute his action without delay, and pay all damages which may be sustained by the defendant or any garnishee, by reason of the attachment, or any proceeding in the suit, or any judgment or process thereon.

Where the creditor sues in the Circuit Court, and there are several defendants who reside or have property in different counties, or where a single defendant in any such action has property or effects in different counties, separate writs may issue to every such county.

No property or effects exempt by law from execution, shall be attached or seized, in any suit against a defendant who is a resident of the state. In a proceeding before the Circuit Court, the

(*a*) Posey *v.* Buckner, 3 Miss. 605; Graham *v.* Bradbury, 7 Miss. 281.

lands, tenements, goods and chattels, moneys, or credits of a defendant, are liable to be taken upon attachment. The interest of a joint obligee may be attached for his individual debt, in the hands of the obligor. (*a*)

Debts not yet due may be attached, but no execution shall be awarded against garnishee until they become due.

Where judgment in this proceeding is entered against a defendant by default, it will bind only the property and effects attached, and no execution thereon can issue against any other property of the defendant, nor against his body, nor shall such judgment be any evidence of debt against the defendant in any subsequent suit.

Attachment against vessels.—Boats or vessels used in navigating the waters of the state are subject to a lien, which may be enforced by a proceeding against them (among other cases) for all debts contracted by the master, owner, agent or consignee of such vessel, on account of stores or supplies furnished for the use thereof: and for all demands accruing by reason of the non-performance of any contract of affreightment, or of any contract touching the transportation of persons, entered into by the master, owner, agent, or consignee of the boat. (*b*)

9. *Proceedings in Civil Suits.*

Imprisonment for debt.—A party cannot be held to bail or imprisoned upon any contract or debt whatsoever. (*c*)

Judgments and executions.—Judgments constitute a lien upon real estate in any county in which they may be rendered or recorded, from the time of their rendition, for the period of three years. During this term, execution may at any time be issued. The lien of a judgment extends to lands acquired after its rendition. A judgment and lien may at any time within ten years be revived by scire facias. (*d*)

No execution shall create a lien upon any personal property, or upon any real estate to which the lien of the judgment does not extend, but from the time of its delivery to the officer. (*e*)

(*a*) Miller & Irvine *v.* Richardson, 1 Miss. 310. (*b*) R. S. (*c*) Ib. 574. (*d*) Ib. 621. (*e*) Ib. 479.

An execution of fieri facias may issue upon the judgment or decree of a court of record, against the goods, chattels, and real estate of the defendant. It may be directed to and executed in any county of the state. Shares of stock in any incorporated company, evidences of debt issued by any moneyed corporation, or by the government of the United States, or of any state, and equitable as well as legal interests in real estate may be taken and sold upon execution. Leases upon land for any unexpired term of three years or more, are subject to execution and sale as real estate, and cannot be sold on an execution issued by a justice of the peace.

The defendant in execution may elect what property or what part thereof shall be sold by the officer. By giving a bond with good security, conditioned for the forthcoming of the property at the day and place of sale, the defendant may retain possession during the intermediate period. If the condition of the bond is broken, the defendant may obtain a summary judgment at the return term of the execution, and upon an execution on this judgment, no such privilege shall be accorded to the debtor or his sureties.

If the officer cannot find sufficient property to satisfy an execution, the plaintiff or his agent may direct him to summon as garnishees any debtors of the defendant, against whom proceedings may be had similar to those which take place in suits originating by attachment. (*a*)

Courts.—General and original jurisdiction in all civil causes is confided to the Circuit Courts, which hold a term every spring and fall in each county of the state.

10. *Effect of Death upon the Rights of Creditors.*

The personal estate is the primary fund for the payment of debts under the laws of Missouri. But where it is insufficient, upon a petition by the executor or administrator, or in event of his default, by any creditor, to the proper County Court, the real estate will be ordered to be sold. (*b*)

(*a*) R. S. 473 to 489. (*b*) Ib. 84.

The debts of a decedent are distributed into the following classes, and are to be paid in the order of their enumeration :—

1st. Funeral expenses.

2d. Expenses of the last sickness.

3d. Debts due the state.

4th. Judgments rendered against the deceased in his lifetime; but if these judgments constituted liens upon the real estate of the deceased, and the estate shall be insolvent, such judgments are to be paid without reference to classification, except as to the first and second classes of demands.

5th. All demands, without regard to quality, which shall be legally exhibited against the estate, within one year after the granting the first letters thereon.

6th. All demands thus exhibited after the end of one year, and within two years after letters granted.

7th. All demands thus exhibited after the expiration of two years, and within three years after granting of such letters. (*a*)

Where any person residing in another country at the time of his decease, leaves property in Missouri, it is to be distributed in such a manner, if practicable, as that all his creditors, without regard to the nature of their debts, should receive an equal proportional share of his estate. For this purpose, no non-resident is to receive any share of the assets, until the citizens of Missouri have received a just proportion of their claims, calculated upon an estimate of the entire value of the estate of the deceased, wherever found. If there be any residue after such payment to the citizens of Missouri, it may be appropriated to satisfy the claims of any foreign creditors which have been duly proven. (*b*)

If any person commence a suit of any kind in the Circuit Court against an estate, within one year from the date of administration, he may recover judgment, but shall pay all costs.

All demands against the estate of a deceased person, not exhibited within three years after the granting of letters to the executor or administrator, are barred, saving to infants, persons of unsound mind, imprisoned, or absent from the United States, and married women, three years after the removal of their disabilities. (*c*)

(*a*) R. S. 90. (*b*) Ib. 103. (*c*) Ib. 91.

All actions pending against any person at the time of his death, which by law survive against the executor or administrator, and all actions commenced against such executor or administrator after the death of the deceased, shall be considered demands legally exhibited against such estate, from the time of reviving the action or serving the original process on the executor or administrator, as the case may be. A notice in writing, served upon an administrator or executor, stating the nature and amount of a claim, with a copy of the instrument of writing or account upon which it is founded, is to be deemed a demand legally exhibited from the time of serving such notice. (*a*)

Every executor or administrator is required to make an annual exhibit of his account for settlement, with proper vouchers at the end of each year from the date of his letters, until his administration is completed.

(*a*) R. S. 91.

ARKANSAS.

1. *Common Law.*

The general principles of the common law, and the statutes in aid thereof, made prior to the fourth year of James I, so far as the same are applicable to our country, and not inconsistent with the laws or constitution of the United States, or the state of Arkansas, constitute the rule of decision in all civil controversies. (*a*)

2. *Choses in Action, Bills of Exchange, and Promissory Notes.*

All bonds, bills, notes, and agreements in writing for the payment of money, may be assigned, so that the assignee may sue thereon, in the same manner as the original payee; the obligor, however, not to be precluded from any defence or set-off which he might have made to the action before the assignment. The indorsers or assignors of any instrument in writing assignable by law for the payment of money alone, on receiving due

(*a*) R. S. 182.

notice of the non-payment or protest of such instrument, are equally liable with the original maker, and may be sued jointly or separately with him. (*a*)

The provisions relative to discount and set-off, do not apply to promissory notes, or bills of exchange payable to order at any bank of the state, or which may be discounted or negotiated therein. (*b*)

No person can be charged as the acceptor of a bill of exchange, unless the acceptance be in writing; nor if the acceptance be written upon any other paper than the bill, except in favor of a person to whom the acceptance shall have been shown, and who on the faith thereof has given a valuable consideration for the bill. The remedy upon bills of exchange both foreign and inland, and upon promissory notes payable in bank, is governed by the rules of the law merchant, as to days of grace, protest, and notice.

All joint obligations are to receive the same construction, and have the same effect as if they were joint and several. (*e*)

A scrawl affixed as a seal to an instrument which professes on its face to be sealed, shall have the force and effect of one. (*d*)

Damages upon protested bills of exchange.—Upon bills of exchange expressed to be for value received in the state, drawn upon any person at any place within the same, if protested for non-acceptance, or non-payment, damages will be allowed at the rate of two per cent. on the principal sum specified in the bill; if drawn within the state, but payable in any of the states of Alabama, Louisiana, Mississippi, Tennessee, Kentucky, Ohio, Indiana, Illinois, Missouri, or any point on the Ohio river, four per cent. damages; if drawn within the state, but payable at any place within the United States, not already mentioned, damages at the rate of five per cent. on the principal sum; if drawn within the state and payable beyond the limits of the United States, damages at the rate of ten per cent. Damages may also be recovered by the holder from the acceptor, at the rate of two per cent. on inland bills; at the rate of six per cent. on bills drawn upon any person at a place within the state, by a person

(*a*) R. S. 107, 149. (*b*) Acts of 1838, 10. (*c*) R. S. 475. (*d*) Ib. 187.

without the state, but within the United States; at the rate of ten per cent. on bills drawn on a person within the state, by a person at a place without the limits of the United States. In addition to the damages thus allowed, the holder may recover besides costs of protest, interest at the rate of ten per cent. from the date of the protest until payment. (*a*)

3. *Interest.*

Parties may stipulate for any rate of interest not exceeding ten per cent. on a contract, whether under seal or not, for the payment of money. When no rate of interest is fixed by the parties in their agreements, six per cent. is the rate established by law. All contracts in which more than ten per cent. interest is reserved, are void, except in the case of bills of exchange and promissory notes which have passed into the hands of an innocent holder, for a valuable consideration without notice of the usury. The usurious lender is liable to no penalty, but the borrower who has paid the usury may recover the same, by action at any time within one year following the payment. (*b*)

4. *Frauds.*

The English statute of frauds and perjuries has been adopted, except in the addition of the words "agreement, promise, or contract" in the clause requiring a writing. (*c*)

The statutes against fraudulent conveyances, have been adopted without any material alteration. (*d*)

5. *Limited Partnerships.*

Limited partnerships were authorized by an act passed in 1838. The details of the act are almost identical with those of Wisconsin. (*e*)

(*a*) R. S. 149. (*b*) Ib. 469. (*c*) Ib. 186. (*d*) Ib. 413. (*d*) Ib. 599.

6. *Effect of Marriage upon Rights of Property.*

A married woman may acquire the legal title to any real or personal estate, which may come to her during coverture by bequest, demise, gift, or distribution, unless the same comes from her husband. A woman possessed of slaves at the time of her marriage, or who may become entitled to the same during coverture, shall hold them as her separate property, exempt from any liability for the debts or contracts of her husband. The title to such slaves is to be transferred in the manner required by law for the disposition of the real estate of feme coverts. The husband, however, may manage such slaves, and receive and enjoy the proceeds of their labor during coverture. To entitle a married woman to the benefit of these provisions, the law requires that she and her husband should make out a schedule of the property derived through her, under oath, to be verified by the oath of some other reputable person, and filed in the recorder's office of the county within which the property is, as well as within which they live. (*a*)

7. *Limitation of Actions.*

Actions upon promissory notes or other writings not under seal, must be commenced within five years after the cause of action accrues; upon all sealed instruments, judgments, and decrees, within ten years; all actions of account, assumpsit, or case, founded on any other contract or liability, three years. There is the usual saving in favor of infants, feme coverts, and persons non compos mentis, after the removal of their respective disabilities, for the period of limitation. Non-residents are subject to the limitation equally with residents, except where a debtor has absconded from another state into Arkansas, without the knowledge of his creditor. (*b*)

Any acknowledgment to take a case out of the operation of the statute, or to bind a person for a debt contracted during infancy, must be in writing. One joint contractor or executor is not bound by the promise of another. (*c*)

(*a*) Acts of 1846, 38. (*b*) Ib. 39. (*c*) R. S. 528, 531.

8. *Attachment.*

Any creditor who will make an affidavit or procure that of some credible person, stating that a person is justly indebted to the plaintiff in a sum, to be named, exceeding one hundred dollars, and that such person is a non-resident of the state, or is about to remove from the state, or to remove his goods and effects out of the state, or so secretes himself that the ordinary process of law cannot be served upon him, and at the same time files a bond with sufficient security, conditioned to prove his debt or demand on a trial at law, or to pay such damages as may be adjudged against him, may obtain a writ of attachment against any estate, real or personal, of his debtor, in whose soever hands to be found, within the county. Process of garnishment may be served at the same time upon any person supposed to be indebted to the defendant. The usual proceedings are had, when the plaintiff disputes the return of the garnishee, to try the truth of the same, and a judgment is rendered accordingly; as also where any third person contests the title of the defendant to a portion of the property claimed. After the ordinary notice by publication, a judgment may be rendered against the defendant, and so much of the property attached may be sold as is necessary to satisfy the claim of the plaintiff.

There are similar provisions for attachments before justices of the peace, when the debt does not exceed one hundred dollars. (*b*)

Attachment of vessels.—Boats and vessels of all descriptions, navigating any of the waters of the state, are made liable for debts contracted by the owners, masters, supercargoes, or assignees thereof, on account of work done or supplies furnished to such boat. (*c*)

9. *Proceedings in Civil Suits.*

Process.—Suits may be commenced in civil actions in one of three modes, viz.: by a writ of summons, a capias ad respondendum, or an attachment of property. The latter of these modes

(*a*) R. S. 115. (*b*) Ib. 109. (*c*) Ib. 125.

has been considered under a separate title. The second can only be resorted to in the cases pointed out under the title "*Imprisonment for Debt.*" The first is the ordinary mode.

Organization of courts.—General civil jurisdiction is confided to the Circuit Courts, which are to be held twice a year in each county of the state.

All writs taken out at a longer interval than fifteen days before the first day of an ensuing term of the Circuit Court shall be returnable to such term; otherwise, to the first day of the next ensuing term. Where a writ is executed thirty days before the return day, the suit, unless good cause is shown for a continuance, will be tried at such return term. Where a party is served with process fifteen days before the return day, he must appear at the term to which the process is returnable and plead to the action. The suit may be continued for good cause at the first and second term, but the party so continuing is bound to be ready for trial at the third term.

Imprisonment for debt.—Imprisonment for debt upon either mesne or final process is allowed in no case, except that of fraud, alleged by the plaintiff and supported by his own affidavit and that of some other creditable and disinterested person as to the facts upon which the allegation is founded. (*a*)

This act would seem to have virtually superseded the Insolvent Law of Arkansas, whose provisions seem intended for the benefit of persons imprisoned or liable thereto.

Judgments and execution.—Judgments in the Circuit Court, constitute a lien upon the lands of the defendant, situate in the county for which the court is held, for the term of three years, subject to be revised afterwards by scire facias. The term "real estate" includes all interest in land, legal or equitable, which can be sold on execution. (*b*) Execution against the body of the defendant is only allowed in cases of fraud. The ordinary writ of execution is a writ of fieri facias, which runs against the goods and chattels, lands and tenements of the debtor: it may issue from a court of record into any county in the state, and is returnable on the second day of the next term of the court.

The right of pre-emption upon public lands within the state,

(*a*) Acts of 1843, 118. (*b*) R. S. 477.

cannot be sold under execution. (*a*) But all other interests in land, whether legal or equitable, goods and chattels, slaves, rights and shares in the stock of any incorporated company, bills or evidences of debt issued by any moneyed corporation, may be taken and sold.

Personal estate, or real estate to which the lien of the judgment does not extend, is bound only from the time of the delivery of the writ of execution to the officer of the proper county.

Executions are returnable on the second day of the next term of the court thereafter. Before any sale of personal property, the officer must give at least ten days' notice of the time and place of sale, by public advertisement. The defendant may retain possession of the property in the interim, by giving a bond with sufficient surety conditioned for its forthcoming on the day of sale. (*b*) If such bond is forfeited, judgment may be entered up thereon without notice at the first term after the bond was given, (*c*) and upon this judgment no delivery bond will be allowed. (*d*)

Whenever an execution is returned, "no property found," the plaintiff may file a bill in Chancery and subject to the satisfaction of his judgment any equitable interest or chose in action of his debtor. (*e*) When the plaintiff in a judgment believes that any third person is indebted to the defendant, or has effects of his in possession, he may sue out a writ of garnishment against such person, whereupon proceedings are had similar to those which take place in attachments. (*f*) A judgment debtor of the defendant is not however subject to this process. (*g*)

Remedy against sheriffs and attorneys for failure to pay over moneys collected.—Where an officer who has collected money upon an execution, fails to have the same in court ready to pay over to the proper person, the party aggrieved may, upon motion, after two days' previous notice, obtain a judgment against the officer for the amount in his hands with lawful interest, and ten per cent. damages per month thereon, to be computed from the time when the execution was returnable until paid: or the same may be recovered in an action against the officer and his securities. (*h*)

(*a*) Acts of 1840, 9. (*b*) R. S. 372 to 386. (*c*) Acts of 1843, 49.
(*d*) Acts of 1840, 59. (*e*) R. S. 173. (*f*) Ib. 424.
(*g*) Trowbridge *v.* Means, 5 Ark. 135. (*h*) R. S. 384.

The court may also render a summary judgment, upon motion, against any attorney for the amount of money received by him for the use of his clients and costs. (*a*)

10. *Effect of Death upon the Rights of Creditors.*

The administration of the estate of decedents is conducted under the eye and control of Courts of Probate. It is the duty of the executor or administrator, within thirty days after letters testamentary or of administration have been granted upon any estate, to give notice of the fact by publication for six weeks in some newspaper printed in the state, and by advertisement at the door of the court house, requiring all creditors to exhibit their claims properly authenticated, within one year from the date of the letters. The lands and tenements, improvements upon the public lands, as well as the personal estate of a deceased person, constitute assets in the hands of his executors for the payment of debts. Real estate will only be sold for the payment of debts where it appears to the satisfaction of the Court of Probate, upon a petition filed by the executor or administrator that the personal estate is not sufficient for that purpose. Demands may be exhibited against the estate of a deceased person either by instituting a suit against the personal representative, or by serving upon him a written notice stating the amount and nature of the claim, and accompanied by a copy of the instrument of writing or account upon which it was founded: in either case, the demand to be verified by the affidavit of the complainant. Where an executor allows a claim, it is to be filed, with his indorsement thereon to that effect, in the clerk's office of the Court of Probate; if rejected by the executor or administrator, it may be presented to and allowed by the Court of Probate. The following order is to be observed in the payment of debts: first, funeral expenses; second, expenses of last sickness; third, judgments rendered against the deceased in his lifetime, and which are liens on the lands of which he died possessed; fourth, all demands, without regard to quality, which have been exhibited to the executor or administrator properly authenticated, within one year after the first granting of letters on the estate; fifth, all

(*a*) R. S. 129.

such demands as may have been so exhibited, after the expiration of one year, and within two years from the grant of letters on the estate. All demands not exhibited before the expiration of two years, to be absolutely barred.

It is the duty of the representative to present to the Court of Probate at the expiration of one year from the grant of letters of administration, and at a corresponding term each subsequent year until his administration account is closed, a complete statement of his accounts with the estate, its creditors and debtors: and in default thereof he may be compelled by the Court of Probate. Such account is to be continued until the next term of the court, that any person interested may file exceptions to any item therein, to be rejected or confirmed by the Court of Probate, or auditors to whom it may refer the examination of the same. (*a*)

Upon the death of a married man his widow is not only entitled to dower in his real estate, but to a life estate in one third of his slaves, and an absolute estate in one third of the personalty owned by him at the time of death, or where there are no children, one half of the personalty, by a right paramount to that of creditors, and without regard to the amount of the husband's indebtedness. (*b*) Her title to this interest stands upon the same footing as to her dower in realty. The choses in action of the husband are not however embraced under the term of personal estate.

(*a*) R. S. 65 to 97. (*b*) Hill's Administrators *v.* Mitchell, 5 Ark.

LOUISIANA.

1. *Bills and Notes.*

The general principles of the English common law prevail in Louisiana, except where they have been altered by statute. There is no distinction, however, between sealed and unsealed instruments.

No bill of exchange, promissory note, or other obligation for the payment of money, can be received as evidence of debt, where the whole sum expressed in such instrument is only expressed in figures, unless the same is accompanied by proof that the bill, note, or obligation, was given for the sum therein declared to be due and payable. The cents or fractional parts of the dollar may be expressed in figures only.

The first of January, the eighth of January, the twenty-second of February, the fourth of July, the twenty-fifth of December, Sundays, and Good Friday are days of public rest. When the third or both third and second day of grace upon a bill of exchange or promissory note falls upon a day of rest, such note or bill shall become due, in the one case, on the second, and in the other, on the first day of grace. In computing the delay allowed for giving notice of non-payment or non-acceptance of a bill of exchange or promissory note, the days of public rest are not counted.

Damages upon bills of exchange drawn or negotiated within the state, which have been protested for non-acceptance or non-payment, are thus regulated; upon bills drawn on and payable in foreign countries, ten per cent. upon the principal sum therein specified; upon bills drawn on and payable in any other state of the United States, five per cent. upon the principal sum. These damages are in lieu of interest and all charges incurred up to the time of protest and notice, but from such time the holder may recover lawful interest upon the aggregate amount of the principal sum and damages. Where the contents of the bill are expressed in the money of account of the United States, the amount of the principal sum and damages are to be determined without any reference to the rate of exchange existing between the place at which the bill was drawn and that upon which it was drawn. When the contents of the bill are expressed in the money of account, or currency of any foreign country, then the principal sum and also the rate of damages, are to be determined by the rate of exchange; but if the value of such foreign coin is fixed by the laws of the United States, that value must prevail. (*a*)

2. *Contract of Sale.*

Not only all corporeal objects, such as movables and immovables, slaves, live stock and produce, but also incorporeal things, such as a debt, an inheritance, a servitude, or any other right, may be sold. (*b*) The assignee may sue in his own name, for a cession of actions takes place between assignor and assignee.

Possible or contingent interests may also be sold. (*c*)

The succession of a living person cannot be sold. The sale of a thing claimed as the property of another, cannot be made, pending an action therefor, so as to prejudice the right of the claimant. (*d*)

(*a*) Ballard & Curry's Digest, 40. (*b*) Civil Code, 2424. (*c*) Ib. 2426. (*d*) Ib. 2428.

Whenever the contract between the parties is to give one thing, whatever it may be, except money, for another, it is called an exchange, and not a sale.

He against whom a litigious right has been transferred, may release himself by paying to the transferee the real price of the transfer, with interest from its date. (*a*)

This provision does not apply where the transfer has been made to a co-heir or co-proprietor of the right, or to a creditor on payment of a debt, or to the possessor of the inheritance subject to the litigious right. (*b*)

The sale of a thing includes that of its accessories, and of whatever has been destined for its constant use, unless there is a reservation to the contrary. (*c*)

The sale or transfer of a debt includes every thing which is an accessory to the same, as suretiship, privileges and mortgages. (*d*)

The vendor of a debt or incorporeal right warrants its existence at the time of the transfer, but does not, without some express stipulation, warrant the solvency of the debtor. (*e*)

The transfer of debts and incorporeal rights is complete by the consent of the parties and transferring the evidence of claim. But as to third persons, the assignment is incomplete until notice has been given to the debtor. This notice is equivalent to the delivery of movables, and until it has been given, the debt assigned is liable to be attached in the hands of the debtor by the creditor of the original creditor or assignor.

According to the Code, 2421, a contract between husband and wife is only valid in the following cases:

1. When one of the spouses makes a transfer of property to the other, who is judicially separated from him or her in payment of his or her rights.

2. When the transfer made by the husband to the wife, although not separated, has a legitimate cause, as the replacing of her dotal or other effects alienated.

3. When the wife makes a transfer of property to her husband, in payment of a sum promised to him as a dowry.

(*a*) C. C. 2622. (*b*) Ib. 2624. (*c*) Ib. 2436. (*d*) Ib. 2615.
(*e*) Ib. 2616, 2617.

3. *Frauds.*

The law does not recognize as against third persons acting in good faith, a sale of movables unaccompanied by delivery. The creditors of the vendor may treat the sale as a nullity and seize the property under a fi. fa. without resorting to an action to annul the sale. (*a*)

No provisions similar to those of the statute of frauds, chapter 2, prevail in Louisiana in reference to personal property. A verbal sale of all movable effects, whatever may be their value, is valid. Any agreement, however, relative to personal property, where the value exceeds five hundred dollars, must be proved by at least one credible witness, and other corroborating circumstances. (*b*)

The debt of another is a sufficient consideration to support a contract or promise to pay it. (*c*)

All sales of immovable property or shares must be made by authentic act, or under private signature. (*d*)

A verbal disposition of such property will be good as against the vendor, as well as against the vendee, who confesses it upon oath, provided actual delivery has been made of such property.(*e*)

There are various contracts which the code declares fraudulent as to the creditors of the debtor, and allows to be set aside upon an action brought for that purpose. To set aside a deed as fraudulent, the creditor bringing the action must have been one at the time of its execution, unless it can be proved that the deed was made with an actual intention to defraud future creditors.(*f*)

Every contract is deemed fraudulent towards creditors, when the obligee knew that the obligor was in insolvent circumstances, and when such contract gives to the obligee, if he be a creditor, any advantage over other creditors of the obligor. (*g*)

The proceeding to set aside such a contract where it was made for the purpose of securing a just debt, must be brought within one year after its execution. The knowledge of a person's insolvency

(*a*) C. C. 1916, 1917. Jorda *v*. Lewis, 1 Louisiana Annual R. 59.

(*b*) C. C. 2257.

(*c*) Lastique *v*. Baldwin, 5 Mart. Rep. 194; Flood *v*. Thomas, 5 N. S. 41.

(*d*) C. C. 2415. (*e*) Ib. 2255. (*f*) 17 Mart. La. 96. (*g*) C. C. 1979.

will not invalidate any sale of property, or other contract made in the usual course of business, or any payment of a just debt in money.(*a*) Any gratuitous contract will be presumed to have been made in fraud of creditors, if at the time of making it the debtor had not, over and above the amount of his debts, twice the amount of the property passed by such contract. (*b*)

4. *Interest.*

There are two rates of interest; the legal and conventional. The former is five per cent., the latter eight. The reservation of usurious interest does not subject the lender to the loss of his debt, but of the usurious excess only.

Interest is not a necessary incident to a claim for money due. It must be expressly provided for, or it cannot be recovered save from the time when a demand was made for payment of a debt, or a suit instituted to recover it. (*c*)

.5 *Effect of Marriage upon Rights of Property.*

The law of Louisiana upon this subject differs essentially from the civil, the French or the common law. Every marriage contracted in the state, superinduces of right, if there be no stipulation to the contrary, a partnership or community of gains, in relation to their future acquisitions. A marriage contracted out of the state, between persons who afterwards come to live in it, is subjected to this community of gains with respect to all property acquired after their arrival. The property which is owned by the wife at the time of marriage, of whatever nature it may be, composes no part of the stock in trade; but remains her separate property, as also that which she may acquire during marriage, by inheritance, or donation to her particularly. The common property consists only of the profits of the property of which the husband has the administration, of the produce of their reciprocal industry, and of all the property acquired during the marriage by both or either, except donations made to one of the parties or an inheritance falling to either. The debts of both husband and

(*a*) C. C. 1981. (*b*) Ib. 1975, (*c*) Ib. 1929 to 1939.

wife anterior to marriage must be acquitted out of their personal and individual effects; but debts contracted during the marriage enter into the partnership or community of gains, and must be acquitted out of the common fund. The wife or her heirs may exonerate themselves from the payment of any debts by renouncing the community. On renouncing, the wife loses all right to the effects of the partnership, but she is entitled to take back what she brought into marriage. The husband in relation to the common acquisitions is the absolute head and master of the partnership; he may dispose of the whole without the wife's consent. But he cannot convey the common estate, or the gains, to the injury of the wife during coverture, and she may by an action brought after the husband's death, set aside such alienation. During the existence of the community the wife has a right to the administration of her separate estate, though she cannot alienate it without her husband's consent, and upon her death the same descends to her heirs, as well as all moneys received by her husband on account of it. Upon the dissolution of the marriage, all the effects the husband and wife reciprocally possess, are presumed common effects, unless they satisfactorily prove which of such effects they brought in marriage, or have been given them separately, or they have respectively inherited. These common effects are divided equally at the dissolution of the marriage, between husband and wife, or their heirs, however unequal the portions which they brought in marriage.

The most usual convention by marriage contract is the settlement of dowry, or the marriage portion. By dowry is meant that property which the wife brings to the husband, to aid in supporting the charges of matrimony. Whatever is settled on her by the contract, either by herself or parents, or even strangers, whether in money or otherwise, constitutes her dowry. It can neither be settled nor augmented during marriage. The husband cannot be deprived of the administration of it, except on a separation of property when it is in danger from his dissipation or extravagance. If it consists of movable effects, estimated by the contract, they become the property of the husband, and the estimated value, which he owes her constitutes the dower, and its restitution is secured by a tacit mortgage on all the immovables of the husband, and of the community, and a privilege on his immovables. But immovables settled as dowry, even at an estimation, remain the property of the wife unless expressly declared otherwise. The dowry is inalienable even with the consent of both husband and wife, unless express authority be given for the purpose by the marriage contract, except for the establishment of the wife's children by a former marriage with the husband's consent, or for the establishment of their common children. There are some other cases in which the dowry may be sold by authorization of the judge, such as for the purpose of liberating husband or wife from jail, paying debts of the wife or the person who settled the dowry of a date certain, anterior to the marriage, or for the purpose of making heavy repairs indispensably necessary for preserving the immovables.

Whenever adequate provision has not been made for the surviving husband or wife, by testament or otherwise, he or she is entitled to a marital portion; that is, one-fourth of the estate in full property, if there be no children, the same for life, if there be but three or a smaller number of children, and if there be more than three, only a child's portion for life, independent of any legacy in his or her favor.

The parties may, by a contract previous to marriage, regulate their pecuniary interest as they please, provided their agreement does not tend to alter the legal order of descents, not to derogate from the legitimate authority of the husband as the head of the family, and contains nothing contrary to good morals. They may stipulate that their future acquisitions shall be regulated by the laws of any state of the Union, and renounce the laws of Louisiana in that particular, that there shall exist no community, or a modified one. (*a*) Such a stipulation must be made by an act before a notary, and two witnesses.

6. *Partnerships.* (*b*)

The law of partnership differs so widely in the jurisprudence of Louisiana from the principles of the common law, that a brief sketch of its most important features is submitted. It is defined

(*a*) C. C. 360 to 376. (*b*) C. C. 425 to 438.

as a contract for the mutual participation in the profits which may accrue from property, credit, skill or industry, furnished in determined proportions by the parties. The proportion of profits which any partner is to receive, or of the losses and expenses which he is to bear, may be regulated by stipulations between themselves; but a stipulation that one of the contracting parties may share in the profits, but be exempt from any liability for the losses of the partnership, will be void, both as respects the partners and third persons. The partnership property is liable to creditors of the partnership in preference to those of the individual partner; but the share of any partner may, in due course of law, be seized and sold to satisfy his individual creditors, subject to the debts of the partnership; such seizure however, if legal, working a dissolution.

Partnerships are divided as to their objects, into commercial and ordinary partnerships. There is also a provision for anonymous or limited partnership, which will be detailed. There is also a contract or relation, called partnership in commendam, which may be attached as an incident to, or incorporated with either of the several kinds of partnership.

Commercial partnerships are either general or special, and may be formed:

1. For the purchase of any personal property and the sale thereof, either in the same state, or changed by manufacture.

2. For buying or selling any personal property whatever, as factors or brokers.

3. For carrying personal property for hire, in ships or other vessels.

Under the last article, which in this respect has altered the general commercial law, the joint owners of a ship or other vessels are, in all transactions relative to the use of such vessel, or for the objects of the association, as to third persons, commercial partners, and responsible as such in solido. (*a*)

Ordinary partnerships are such as are not commercial. They are divided into universal and particular partnerships. Ordinary partners are not bound in solido for the debt of the partnership, and no one of them can bind his partners, unless they have given

(*a*) Banchor *v.* Bell, 2 Robin. 182.

him power to do so, either specially or by the articles of partnership. In an ordinary partnership, each partner is bound for his share of the partnership debt, calculating such share in proportion to the number of the partners, without any attention to the proportion of stock or profits each is entitled to. If a debt be contracted by one of the partners of an ordinary partnership, who was not authorized, either in his own name or that of the part nership, the other partners will be bound each for his share, provided it be proved that the partnership was benefited by the transaction.

Universal partnership cannot be created except by a writing signed by the parties and registered in the manner prescribed by law. It is a contract by which the parties agree to make a common stock of all the property they possess ; it may embrace both real and personal estate, or be restricted to personal only ; it may provide that the property itself shall be common stock, or the fruits only ; any stipulation that property which may subsequently accrue to one of the parties, by donation, succession or legacy, shall be common stock, will be void. Where nothing more is agreed between the parties than there shall be a universal partnership, it will extend only to the profits of the property which each shall possess, and their credit and industry. If commercial business is carried on under an universal partnership, it must as to that business be governed by the rules applicable to commercial partnerships.

Particular partnerships are such as are formed for any business not of a commercial nature. There is nothing worthy of special comment in reference to them.

Partnership in commendam is formed by a contract in which one person or partnership agrees to furnish another person or partnership a certain amount, either in property or money, to be employed by the person or partnership to whom it is furnished in his or their own name or firm, on condition of receiving a share in the profits, in the proportion determined by the contract, and of being liable to losses and expenses to the amount furnished, and no more. A partner in commendam is rather viewed as a simple furnisher of funds, than as a partner. The parties may regulate by their covenant the proportion of profits which the partner in commendam is to receive, and also as respects each other, the proportion of losses and expenses to be borne by each partner; but as respects third persons, the whole sum furnished or agreed to be furnished by such partner is liable for the debt of the partnership. If he has paid that sum, and it has been lost in the business of the partnership, he is exonerated from any other payment. A partnership in commendam must be made in writing, and recorded in the manner prescribed by law, or such partner will be subject to the same responsibilities towards third persons as attach to the other partners. The contract must state the amount to be furnished by the partner in commendam, its nature, and whether it has been advanced in the proportion of profits he is to receive, and of the expenses and losses he is to bear. It must be signed by the parties in the presence of one or more witnesses, and recorded in full by the officer authorized to record mortgages in the place where the principal business of the partnership is carried on, and if it be a commercial partnership, consisting of several establishments in different parts of the state, it must be recorded in each of such places.

The partner in commendam has no authority to bind the other partners by any act of his. The business of the concern to which he has made the advance must not be carried on in his name, either singly or jointly with others, or by him, or by his agency as agent for the other parties, but by the person or persons to whom he has made the advance. If the partner in commendam takes any part in the business of the partnership, or permits his name to be used in the firm, or by the single person to whom he has made the advance, except as a partner in commendam, he will be liable to all the responsibilities of a general partner in the business.

An act was passed in 1837, authorizing the formation and prescribing the rules of limited or anonymous partnerships. The first section of the act authorizes the formation of such a company, by any number of persons who may be willing to unite, for the purpose of carrying on manufacturing, farming, or any other branch of industry, or of making roads or canals, or of making insurances; such association not to embrace more than one branch of industry.

The second section limits the capital stock of such company to five hundred thousand dollars.

The third section provides for the execution and deposit, with a notary public at the time of the formation of such partnership, of an act, containing,

1. The name and style under which the partnership is to be conducted, and the place where the company is to be located.

2. A full description of the business to be carried on.

3. The amount of capital and mode of payment.

4. The names of the partners and amount of their respective contributions.

5. The period at which the partnership is to commence and at which it is to dissolve.

6. The number of directors or agents to be appointed to transact the business of the company.

7. The power of such officers.

8. The duration of their services.

9. The provision for liquidating the affairs of the company on its dissolution.

10. The powers of the persons intrusted with such duty.

11. The time when the dividends of the clear profits are to be declared and paid.

When such act has been executed and signed by the parties, the notary, and two competent witnesses, it shall be published at full length in the paper published in the parish where the company is formed, and in two newspapers of the city of New Orleans, both in French and English, at least twice a week for thirty days. Such company is only to be sued at the domicil which is the place of its location.

There are minute provisions as to the mode in which the stock of such company is to be paid in, and in which it may be transferred; no transfer, however, to relieve the transferor from any liability previously incurred by the company. A full record is to be kept of the administration of the company. The contracts of such company must be made in their joint name; and they are prohibited from doing any banking or mercantile or commission business of any kind. The individual partners of such company are only liable upon its obligations for the amount of stock at its par value which they respectively hold. For any fraud or false statement in the publications required by the law, such partners are to be liable as general partners. No part of the capital stock can be withdrawn before the dissolution and final liquidation of the concerns of the partnership. No partner who is a creditor of the company can claim as such in the event of its insolvency, until all other creditors have been satisfied.

There are various minute provisions in the act which it seems unnecessary to enumerate. (*a*)

7. *Privileges.*

According to the code, the property of the debtor is the common pledge of his creditors, and the proceeds of its sale must be distributed among them ratably, unless there exist among the creditors some lawful cause of preference—such as a privilege or a mortgage.

A privilege is a right growing out of the nature of the debt which entitles the creditor to a preference over other creditors, even those who have mortgages. Creditors who are in the same rank of privileges, are to be paid on an equal footing. Privileges may attach to either movables or immovables, or to both at once.

These privileges may be asserted by original suit or by intervention in another proceeding, where the property is capable of identification.

Privileges which embrace both movables and immovables.—They are:

1. Funeral charges.
2. Judicial charges, or taxed cost of legal proceedings.
3. Expenses of last sickness.
4. Wages of servants for the year past.
5. The salaries of clerks, secretaries, and other agents of that kind.

The wife has not a privilege upon the immovable property of her husband for her dotal rights, but a mere right of mortgage.

General privileges on movables.—Besides the debts enumer-

(*a*) Ballard & Curry's Digest, 612.

ated in the preceding section, the following claims are privileged on all the movables in general:

1. Claims for supplies of provisions made to the debtor or his family during the last six months by retail dealers, and during the last year by keepers of boarding-houses and taverns.

2. Dotal rights due to wives by their husbands. This privilege can only be enforced upon such effects as were in the husband's possession at the time of the dissolution of the marriage or copartnership.

Privileges on particular movables.—Of these we shall only enumerate the more important:

1. The debt of a workman or artisan for the price of his labor on the movable, which he has repaired or made, if the thing continues still in his possession.

2. The debt on the pledge which is in the depositor's possession.

3. That of the depositor on the price of the sale of the thing by him deposited.

4. The debt due for money laid out in preserving the thing.

5. The price due on movable effects, if they are yet in the possession of the purchaser.

6. The claims of innkeepers, carriers, &c.

7. Merchants, consignees, &c., have a privilege for a general balance over any attaching creditor, on the goods consigned to them, provided, that such goods or an invoice of them has been received previous to the attachment. (*a*)

The privilege of the vendor of movable effects, is not affected by the circumstance that the sale was made upon a credit, or that he has taken a note, bond, or other acknowledgment from the buyer.

Privilege on ships and merchandise.—The following debts are privileged on the price of ships or other vessels in the order in which they are placed:

1. Charges incurred in obtaining the sale of a ship or vessel, and the distribution of the price.

2. Debts for pilotage, wharfage, and anchorage.

(*a*) B. & C. D. 165.

3. Expenses of keeping the vessel from the time of her entrance into port, until sale.

4. The rent of stores in which the rigging and apparel are deposited.

5. The maintenance of the ship, and her table and apparatus, since her return into port from her last voyage.

6. The wages of the captain and crew employed in such last voyage.

7. Sums lent to the captain for the necessities of the ship during the last voyage, and reimbursement of the price of merchandise sold by him for the same purpose.

8. Sums due to sellers, those who have furnished materials, and workmen employed in the construction, if the vessel has never made a voyage; and those due to creditors for supplies, labor, repairing, victuals, armament, and equipment, previous to the departure of the ship, if she has already made a voyage.

9. Money lent on bottomry, for refitting, victualing, arming, and equipping the vessel before her departure.

10. The premiums due for insurance.

11. The amount of damage due to freighters for the failure in delivering goods which they have shipped, or for the reimbursement of damage sustained by the goods through the fault of the captain or crew.

These privileged claims are not only to be preferred to those of ordinary or attaching creditors, but even to those of creditors who, by a contract of pledge or mortgage with the debtor, have acquired a special property in the vessel. Creditors having these privileges may, where the vessel has been sold under compulsory process, claim the price from the purchaser. Where the sale was voluntary and the vessel in port, they may enforce their rights over the ship itself, up to the period when the vessel has made a voyage, in the name and at the risk of the purchaser, without any interposition of their claim. Where the ship was on a voyage at the time of a voluntary sale, the privilege of the creditor only becomes extinct after the vessel has returned to her port of departure, and started upon another voyage for the account of the purchaser, without any claim by the creditor.

Privileges on immovables and slaves.—The vendors of an

estate or a slave, whether sold on or without credit, for the price unpaid, mechanics for their labor in building or repairing a house, and any person for materials supplied by them for this purpose.

Some privileges must be recorded to be preserved, as that of the vendor of immovables or slaves. There are various provisions, somewhat varying the order in which privileged creditors are to be paid. If the movables of the debtor, by reason of the special privileges affecting them, or for any other cause, are not sufficient to discharge the debts having a privilege on the whole movable property, the balance is to be raised from the immovables and slaves of the debtor.

A privilege is destroyed by the extinction of the subject or its acquisition by the creditor, or by the extinction of the debt, or by prescription. (*a*)

8. *Prescription.*

The operation of the lapse of time to discharge debts or to confirm titles, is called prescription. (*b*) A person may relinquish rights which he has acquired by prescription, unless a creditor or other party in interest, interpose to claim its benefit. A tacit renunciation of prescription results from a fact which authorizes a presumption of the relinquishment of the right thus acquired. Prescription ceases to run, whenever the debtor or possessor makes acknowledgment of the right of the person whose title is prescribed. The acknowledgment of a debt by the joint debtor interrupts the prescription with regard to all the other partners. The acknowledgment of a debt by the maker of a note does not interrupt prescription as to the indorser. They are not debtors in solido, within the meaning of Articles 2092, 3517 of the Civil Code, which declare that a suit brought against one of the debtors in solido, or his acknowledgment of the debt, interrupts prescription as to the rest. Solidarity, in the meaning of the code, exists where several persons bind themselves to another for the same sum, at the same time, and in the same contract; and so obligate themselves that each may be compelled to pay the whole debt, and that payment made by one of them exonerates the others towards the creditor.

(*a*) C. C. 477 to 493. (*b*) Ib. 519 to 533.

The maker and indorser do not bind themselves at the same time or by the same contract, but by different and successive contracts without any privity or reciprocity.

Nor is an accommodation indorser a surety in the meaning of Art. 3518 of the Civil Code, which declares that a citation served on the principal debtor or his acknowledgment interrupts prescription as to the surety. The suretiship between an accommodation indorser and the maker of a note exists only as between themselves: as to the holder their liability depends on the rules applicable to negotiable instruments in general. (*a*)

Prescription does not run against minors, and is generally suspended during marriage. The common law doctrine that the statute of limitation having once begun to run against a debt, is not arrested by the intervention of any disability to assert the claim, does not exist in reference to the civil law prescription. (*b*) The following are the most important commercial prescriptions.

The prescription of one year operates upon the claim of the retailers of provisions and liquors, upon actions for the delivery of merchandise or other effects shipped on board any kind of vessel, or for damage sustained by merchandise on board of ships. The prescription of three years runs upon actions for arrearages of rent charge, annuities, and alimony, or for the hire of movables or immovables, for the payment of money lent, unless there be an account acknowledged, note or bond given, or action commenced before that time.

The prescription of five years runs upon actions, on bills of exchange, notes payable to order or bearer, except bank notes, on all effects negotiable or transferable by indorsement or delivery. The action of nullity or rescission of contracts, testaments or other acts, are prescribed by five years, when the person entitled to exercise them is in the state, and ten years if he be out of it.

All other personal actions are prescribed by ten years if the creditor be present, and by twenty years if he be absent.

9. *Effect of Death upon the Rights of Creditors.*

The estates of deceased persons are administered under the general superintendence of Courts of Probate. They have the exclu-

(*a*) Jacobs *v.* Williams, 12 Rob. 183. (*b*) Merchants' Magazine, xv. 474.

sive power of opening and receiving proof of last wills and testaments, and ordering their execution, of appointing and removing curators and administrators, of making inventories and sales of the property of successions, of compelling administrators to render accounts at the periods fixed by law.

The representative of the deceased cannot be required to pay any claims until the lapse of three months. If the estate is sufficient, interest is allowed on debts from the death of the deceased, if they were due at that time, or from their maturity, if they became due subsequently. Claims which are acknowledged by the representative must be so indorsed, and submitted to the probate judge, that they may be ranked among the acknowledged debts of the succession. If a claim is disputed, the holder may bring an action in the ordinary way before the Court of Probate where the succession, was opened, and obtain judgment, as in other cases.

It is the duty of all representatives to render to the Probate Court, at least once in every twelve months, a full account of their administration; and on failure so to do, they shall be dismissed from office, and pay ten per cent. per annum interest on all sums for which they may be responsible, from the expiration of such twelve months.

The order in which debts are to be paid is discussed under the title of "Privileges."

10. *Insolvency.*

The provisions of the insolvent law for the relief of debtors in actual custody, possess little practical importance since the passage of the act to abolish imprisonment for debt. Any debtor, although not imprisoned, who shall be unable to meet his engagements, may avoid all proceedings against his person, by a bona fide surrender of all his estate for the benefit of his creditors. The after acquired property of the debtor is, however, liable for so much of the debts as remains unsatisfied.

But the respite or delay of payment which the debtor may obtain, is of more interest to distant creditors than the cessio bonorum.

Respite.—A respite is an act by which a debtor, who is unable to satisfy his debts at the moment, transacts with his creditors, and obtains from them time or delay for the payment of the sums which he owes to them. It may be voluntary, where all the creditors consent; or forced, when a part of the creditors refuse to accept the debtors proposition, and when the latter is obliged to compel them by judicial authority to consent to what the others have determined in the cases directed by law. The opinion of three-fourths of the creditors in number and amount (now a majority) is essential to the taking place of a forced respite. In order, however, to make it binding upon the other creditors, it is necessary,

1. That the debtor should deposit in the office of the clerk of the court of his domicil, to whom he presents his petition for calling his creditors, a true and exact schedule, sworn to by him, of all his movable and immovable, property, as well as of his debts.

2. That a meeting of the creditors of such debtor domiciliated in the state, shall be called on a certain day at the office of a notary public, by order of the judge, at which meeting the creditors shall be summoned to attend, by process issued from the court, if the creditors live within the parish where the meeting shall take place, or by letters addressed to them by the notary, if they are not residing in the parish.

3. That the creditors be ordered to attend in ten days, if they are all living in the parish of the judge who gives the order, and in thirty days if there are some of them residing out of the parish.

4. That this meeting as well as its object be advertised in English and in French, by papers posted up in the usual places, and also by three publications in English and French in the newspapers, if any be printed within the extent of the jurisdiction of the judge who grants the order.

5. That the creditors explain exactly the amount of the sums which they claim, and make oath before the notary holding the meeting, that they are justly and lawfully due.

Absent creditors are not summoned to the meeting, but they are represented by an attorney appointed by the judge, whose duty it is to establish their debts, and see to the legality of the proceedings.

The creditors who have opposed the granting of the respite, may require that the debtor shall furnish security, that the property of which he is left in possession, shall not be alienated, or in case it is, that the money arising from the sale, shall be employed in paying the debts existing at the time of the respite. The time allowed to a debtor in a forced respite cannot exceed three years. Any one who has claimed the benefit of the cessïon of goods, cannot afterwards pray for a mere respite. Privileged creditors, or those having a special mortgage by public act, wives for their dotal rights or that of reclaiming their property, minors for the balance of account of their tutorship, cannot be compelled to enter into any contract of respite. Privileged or mortgage creditors, however, can only seize the property affected by their lien, until the term granted by the respite has expired. But creditors having a general mortgage, are bound by a respite as much as ordinary creditors. (*a*)

11. *Remedies to recover Debts.*

Imprisonment for debt.—By the act of 28th March, 1840, the writ of capias ad satisfaciendum was in all cases abolished. Since the passage of this act it has been held that no order of arrest can legally issue after a judgment rendered, as a means of coercing payment. (*b*) But where a debtor has been arrested before judgment, under the conditions pointed out by the statute, and which will be presently detailed, the rendition of a judgment does not convert the writ of arrest into a writ of ca. sa. or authorize the discharge of the debtor, except upon the terms prescribed by the statute. (*c*)

Before any creditor can arrest his debtor, he or his agent must swear that he believes such debtor is about to leave the state permanently, and that such oath is not taken with the intention of vexing the defendant. No debtor is to be detained under a writ of arrest for a longer period than three months, provided that if he is a resident of the state he may be detained until, if required

(*a*) C. C. 3051 to 3065. (*b*) Thornhill *v.* Christmas, 10 Rob. 543.
(*c*) Anderson *v.* Brinkley, 1 La. Ann. Rep. 127.

by the creditor, he makes a surrender of his property, upon which proceedings shall take place as in the case of insolvent debtors.

No citizen of another state can be arrested in Louisiana at the suit of a non-resident creditor, unless it is made to appear that such debtor has absconded from his residence. This proviso has been held to mean the debtor's last place of residence, and cannot apply to a case where the debtor has absconded only from the place where the debt was contracted, but has resided for several years in another place. (*a*) The fact that one member of a commercial partnership, doing business in Louisiana, resides and does business in another state, does not bring the resident partners within this prohibition. They may avail themselves in the collection of partnership demands of the same remedies in the assertion of their individual rights. (*b*)

The debtor may be released from arrest upon executing a bond with security to the plaintiff, conditioned that he will not leave the state within ninety days: and if this bond is forfeited the surety becomes absolutely liable for the debts.

Judgment and executions.—Judgments bind the real estate of the debtor, from the time of their registry with the recorder of mortgages. Any species of property which can be seized may be taken on execution of fieri facias, except various minor articles which are protected for the use of the debtor and his family. Property taken on execution must bring two-thirds of its appraised value, or it shall be sold on twelve months' credit: and if the bond for the price is not paid at maturity, execution will issue thereon against the property of principal and security, and sale thereof be made for cash. (*c*)

Where the judgment creditor has reason to believe that any third person is indebted to the defendant or has effects belonging to him, under his control, such party may be cited to appear and answer interrogatories touching the same, and be charged with the debt of the plaintiff, or discharged, according to the judgment which may be rendered by the court upon his answers and the evidence.

(*a*) Hand *v.* Taliaferro, 1 La. Ann. Rep. 26.
(*b*) Broadnax *v.* Thomason, 1 La. Ann. Rep. 382.
(*c*) C. of P. B. & C. D. 135.

Remedy against sheriffs.—A sheriff who fails to return a writ or pay over money collected at the time required by law, may, upon motion, after ten days' notice, be compelled to pay the amount claimed in the writ. (*a*)

Attachment.—The provisions of the attachment law of Louisiana, do not differ very materially from those of the states, whose jurisprudence is founded upon common law. An attachment or mandate commanding the seizure of any property, real or personal, credit or right belonging to a debtor in whatever hands found, to satisfy the demands of a creditor, may be obtained where either 1, the debtor resides out of the state; or 2, where the debtor has left the state never to return; or 3, where the debtor is about leaving permanently the state, without there being a possibility, in the ordinary course of judicial proceedings, of obtaining or executing judgment against him previous to his departure. It is not essential that the debt should be due. The creditor must personally, or by agent, make an affidavit to one of the preceding facts, and also, of the amount of the indebtedness of the defendant; and execute a bond with sufficient surety to the defendant, conditioned to satisfy all damages which he may sustain by reason of the wrongful emanation of the attachment. Any person indebted to or having possession of property of the defendant, may be cited as garnishee. If the garnishee fails to answer, or admits that he is indebted to, or has in his possession effects o the defendant, judgment may be rendered against him for that amount. The attachment may be set aside upon a rule to show cause, by disproving the oath upon which it has been granted, or the debtor may release his property by executing a bond to the officer, conditioned for its forthcoming on the day when it may be required to satisfy an execution on the judgment in attachment. (*b*)

There is also a species of attachment, known as a sequestration or provisional seizure, by which the officer may be ordered, in certain cases, to take and keep a thing of which another has possession, until a controversy respecting it is decided. This writ may be obtained in every case where a party has a lien or privilege upon the property. The plaintiff must not only make

(*a*) B. & C. D. 435. (*b*) C. of P. 239 to 268; B. & C. D. 18.

an affidavit of the grounds upon which he asks a sequestration, but also execute his bond to the defendant, conditioned to pay all damages which may result from the order. (*a*)

Courts.—Under the constitution of Louisiana, the judicial power is vested in a Supreme Court, District Courts and Justices of the Peace. The first court has only appellate jurisdiction. There is no such distinction as that between legal and equitable jurisdiction.

Proceedings are according to the forms of the civil law; the essential features of the trial by jury being preserved. Any person who is interested on the subject matter of any pending controversy, may by intervention become a party to the proceeding.

(*a*) C. of P. 269 to 283; B. & C. D. 774.

TEXAS.

1. CHOSES IN ACTION
2 INTEREST.
3. FRAUDS.
4. EFFECT OF MARRIAGE UPON RIGHTS OF PROPERTY.
5. LIMITATION OF ACTIONS.
6. EFFECT OF DEATH UPON THE RIGHTS OF CREDITORS.
7. REMEDIES TO COLLECT DEBTS.

1. *Choses in Action.*

The assignee of any negotiable instrument may maintain an action in his own name, allowing all reasonable discounts against himself, or the original owner, according to the date of the assignment. The assignee of a bond or other written instrument being the assignee of another assignee, may also maintain an action in his own name: but to hold the assignor as security, he must use due diligence to collect the same. The assignor or indorser may be sued, without previously or concurrently suing the maker or obligor, when he either resides out of the state, or in such part of it that the ordinary process of law cannot be served upon him, or where he is notoriously insolvent. (*a*)

In other cases, indorsers, guarantors, or securities, must be sued simultaneously with the principal. (*b*)

It is not necessary to protest bills of exchange, &c., for non-acceptance or non-payment; or to give notice of dishonor to the drawer, indorser, or assignor; provided in all cases due diligence is used to collect the same. (*c*)

Due diligence consists in instituting suit against the drawer or maker of the instrument, before the first term of the District

(*a*) Dallam's Digest of the Laws of Texas, 28. (*b*) Acts of 1846, 361.
(*c*) D. D. 35.

Court, after the right of action accrued, or show good cause for not so doing; and institute suit before the second term of such court.

2. *Interest.*

The distinction between legal and conventional interest is recognized. The former is eight per cent., at which rate all judgments bear interest, rendered upon contracts in which no more was reserved. The latter is twelve per cent. No interest can be recovered upon contracts, in which more than twelve per cent. was reserved, but only the principal. (*a*)

3. *Frauds.*

The most important provisions of the English statutes against fraudulent conveyances, and to prevent frauds and perjuries, have been adopted in Texas. The clause of the Texan statute requires the "*promise or* agreement, or some memorandum thereof," to be in writing, &c. (*b*)

4. *Effect of Marriage upon Rights of Property.*

The constitution of Texas provides that the real and personal estate owned by a woman at the time of her marriage, or acquired afterwards by gift, devise, or descent, shall be and remain her separate property.

Before this provision, the statutes of Texas had followed the civil and not the common law, in relation to marital rights.

5. *Limitation of Actions.*

All actions of trespass for injury to property, all actions of trover and conversion, all actions for taking away the goods and chattels of another, all actions upon open accounts, other than such as concern the trade of merchandise between merchant and merchant, their factors and servants, must be commenced within

(*a*) D. D. 105. (*b*) Ib. 60.

two years; all actions of debt, grounded upon any contract in writing, shall be commenced and sued in four years next after the cause of action accrues.

All actions or suits founded upon any account for goods, wares, or merchandise, not sold and delivered, or for articles charged in any store account, shall be commenced and sued within two years after the cause of such action, except where the debtor or creditor dies, or the debtor removes before the expiration of two years; in which case the further term of one year is allowed, for the commencement of the action, from such death or removal. In suits for recovery of debts upon open account, against executors and administrators, the court shall cause to be expunged from such account every item which shall appear to be due two years before the death of the testator or intestate. Judgments in any court of record, when execution has not issued within twelve months from its rendition, may be revived by scire facias, or an action of debt, brought thereon within ten years after date of the judgment, and not after: or where execution hath issued and no return is made thereon, the party in whose favor it was issued may move against the sheriff or other officer, or their securities, for not returning the same within five years from the day when it was returnable.

The limitations do not begin to run against infants, married women, persons imprisoned or non compos mentis, until the removal of their respective disabilities. No acknowledgment will take any claim out of the operation of the statute of limitations, unless made in writing by the party to be charged therewith. No action upon a contract, barred by the limitation of the country where it was made, can be sustained in Texas. (*a*)

6. *Effect of Death upon the Rights of Creditors.*

There is in every county in the state, a Court of Probate, under whose supervision the estates of deceased persons are administered. It is the duty of executors and administrators, after qualification, to give notice to all creditors of the estate, by six weeks' successive publication in some newspaper of the county,

(*a*) D. D. 159, 160, 161.

to present their claims for acknowledgment within twelve months. Before any claim for money, or personal property, or land can be acknowledged, it must be verified by the affidavit of the owner before a notary public, or the judge of probate; and if accepted by the executor it must then be presented to the probate judge, for his approval or rejection. No action can be brought upon any claim before its presentation for acknowledgment; but if a claim be rejected by the executor or administrator, or if accepted by him and disapproved by the judge, the owner of the claim may institute suit thereon before a justice of the peace or the District Court of the county; but a judgment thereon will give no claim to priority. No sale, except of perishable property, will be ordered, for the payment of debts, before the fourth regular term of the court after letters have been granted; the court is held once in every two months. Land and negroes may be directed to be sold for the payment of debts, where other personal property is not sufficient, upon petition by the executor or administrator and due notice to all persons interested. In the administration of assets, the following order is to be observed in the payment of claims which have been acknowledged and approved, or have been established by judgment: first, funeral expenses; second, debts due to the late republic of Texas; third, debts due to the government of the United States; fourth, taxes assessed for the state; fifth, recorded mortgages and liens upon specific property, then judgments of the courts of the state of Texas, the oldest first; sixth, all other debts, debts not due being considered after a discount of the legal interest, as due. Claims in suit are to be taken into the pro rata estimate; but claims not presented within twelve months from the publication of notice, shall be postponed, in their payment, until those presented have been paid: to be barred, however, only by the general law of limitations. The preceding classes of creditors are entitled to be paid in their full or pro rata proportions at the sixth regular term (that is, within twelve months) after granting letters. (*a*)

The widow, besides her dower, is entitled to have set aside for her use and that of her family, property of the same amount and the same kind as is exempt from sale under a fieri facias.

(*a*) Acts of 1846, 308 to 318.

It is the duty of the representatives of a deceased person to close the administration of his estate as soon as practicable; and for this purpose they are required to render an account at the expiration of each year of their transactions, and the condition of the estate, and may be compelled to do so upon the petition of creditors, heirs and legatees.

7. *Remedies to Collect Debts.*

Imprisonment for debt.—Imprisonment for debt does not exist in Texas.

Judgment and execution.—Judgments of courts of record bind the real estate of the defendant in the county where they have been rendered from their date; but such lien will expire unless execution is taken out upon a judgment within twelve months. If the defendant has not sufficient property in the county where the judgment was rendered to satisfy the debt, writs of execution may be sent to any county in the state. Executions are made returnable on or before the first day of the next term of the court from which they issue. They run alike against real and personal property. Where the defendant does not designate the property to be levied on, it is the duty of the sheriff to take first the personal property, then the uncultivated lands, then the slaves, and if then the debt cannot be made from these, then the improved lands of the defendant. Any person supposed to be indebted to the defendant, may be summoned to appear as a garnishee, and proceedings had as upon attachment. (*a*)

It is provided by the constitution of Texas, that the homestead of a family not exceeding two hundred acres, if in the country, or the value of two thousand dollars, if in town or city, shall be exempt from sale on execution for any debts subsequently contracted.

All property offered for sale on execution must bring two-thirds of its appraised value, the defendant selecting one of the appraisers, the plaintiff another, and they calling in an umpire in case of disagreement. When the levy is made upon slaves, or

(*a*) D. D. 90.

personal property, the defendant may retain possession by giving bond with security conditioned for their forthcoming on the day of sale; and if this bond is forfeited, execution issues at once against principal and security, upon which no indulgence can be allowed. (*a*)

Remedy against sheriffs, &c.—Where the sheriff or other officer fails to pay over money collected under an execution, when demanded by the person entitled to receive the same, he shall be liable to pay ten per cent. per month on the amount collected, besides interest and costs, to be recovered of him and his sureties by motion before the court from which execution issued, three days previous notice being given. (*b*)

Courts.—The District Courts sit twice a year in each county of the state, and have original jurisdiction in all civil cases involving more than one hundred dollars.

Attachment.—Attachments, both original and judicial, belong to the jurisprudence of Texas. An original attachment may be issued by any judge of the Circuit or County Courts, or any justice of the peace, upon affidavit by the plaintiff or his agent, that the person against whom the attachment is prayed, either absconds or secretes himself, or resides or is about to remove beyond the jurisdiction of the court, so that the ordinary process of law cannot be served upon him, or is about to remove his property beyond the jurisdiction of the court, so that the plaintiff may probably lose his debt, and an affidavit also of the amount of the indebtedness, and that the attachment is not sued out for the purpose of vexing or harassing the defendant. It is not necessary that the debt upon which the attachment is issued should be due. Attachment may be granted in behalf of non-resident creditors, against any estate of a non-resident debtor in Texas, when the latter hath not sufficient property in the place of his residence to satisfy the debt. In the case of a non-resident, the attachment runs against his real estate, in case of a deficiency of his personal property. The law contains the usual provisions for the bond of the plaintiff, the replevy of the property by the defendant, the sale of any perishable property, proceedings of garnishment, &c. (*c*)

(*a*) D D. 90. (*b*) Ib. (*c*) Laws of Texas, ii. 89.

Judicial attachments may be resorted to upon the return of any original writ, "non est inventus." Before judgment can be entered on attachment by any District Court, public notice must be inserted in some newspaper nearest the court, for four weeks successively, pending the cause, stating the amount, property attached, names of parties, and the court wherein proceedings are pending.

CANADAS.(a)

1. GENERAL OBSERVATIONS UPON THE LAWS OF UPPER AND LOWER CANADA.
2. LAW AS TO RIGHTS IN ACTION, IN LOWER CANADA.
3. INTEREST IN LOWER CANADA.
4. FRAUDS IN LOWER CANADA.
5. LIMITATION OF ACTIONS IN LOWER CANADA.
6. EFFECT OF MARRIAGE UPON THE RIGHTS OF PROPERTY, IN LOWER CANADA.

1. *General Observations upon the Laws of Upper and Lower Canadas.*

The laws in force in Lower Canada are,

1. The acts of the British Parliament which extend to the colonies.

2. Capitulations and treaties.

3. The laws and customs of Canada, principally founded on the jurisprudence of Paris as it stood in 1663, the edicts of the French kings and their colonial authorities, and the Roman civil law.

4. The criminal law of England as it stood in 1774, and as explained by subsequent statutes.

5. The ordinances of the governor and council established by the act of that year. And,

6. The acts of the provincial legislature since 1792.

Of the laws, it may be said in general, that the criminal is English, with some provincial statutes not repugnant thereto; the admiralty is wholly English; the commercial laws of evidence

(a) The chapter on Canadas has been compiled from Howard's, Clark's, and Martin's Colonial Law, and from Burge's Commentaries on Foreign and Colonial Law.

are English. Trial by jury is universal in criminal cases, but in civil matters the appeal to trial by jury is confined to certain cases, viz., the demand must exceed ten pounds sterling, the parties, merchants or traders, and the subject matter grounded in debts, promissory contracts, and agreements of a mercantile nature only; or else, the cause of action must arise from personal wrongs to be compensated in damages; in all other cases, the bench are judges, both upon the law and upon the facts. The court of general original civil jurisdiction, is the Court of King's Bench, which has a jurisdiction similar to the King's Bench and Common Pleas at Westminster.

Intimately connected with the laws of the country are the tenures by which land is held; all lands granted since the conquest, are in free and common socage; in the French districts, lands are held according to the old Norman law.

The civil and criminal law of Upper Canada is substantially the same as that of England; administered in the same manner and by similar functionaries. It is therefore unnecessary to recapitulate the English statutes, as to frauds, limitations, usury, promissory notes, &c. The bankrupt laws of England have not been introduced into either province.

Upon all bills of exchange drawn in Upper Canada, on any person in Europe or the West Indies, which may be protested for non-payment, ten per cent. damages with six per cent. interest upon the principal sum furnished here, from the day of date of protest to the time of payment, and charges of protest, may be recovered by the holders of such bill; the principal sum to be reimbursed to the holder at the par of exchange, that is, at the rate of one hundred and eleven pounds and one-ninth currency, for every hundred pounds sterling. Where the bill is drawn upon any person in North America, the West Indies excepted, four per cent. damages and six per cent. interest upon the principal sum, may be recovered.

Real estate may be taken in execution in either province upon judgment, and sold for the payment of debts. It must first appear, however, that the goods and chattels are not sufficient for this purpose. Lands, however, cannot be sold until the expiration of twelve months from the period of delivering the writ to the officer.

In Lower Canada, where the coutume of Paris prevails, the movable and real estate of the deceased are equally liable for the satisfaction of his debts; that is, the heirs are personally liable according to the value of their interest in the whole succession, composed of movable and real estate, and the heirs of property, which is *propre* must contribute to debts which may have been contracted in purchasing *acquets,* although the heir to the *propre* may be heir to the *acquets,* and on the other hand, the heir to *biens acquets* must contribute to debt, even contracted for the annual cultivation of an estate which was *propre.*

In Upper Canada, where the English law prevails, the real estate of all persons whether traders or not, is assets for the payment of the simple contract debts of the deceased. But in the administration of such assets by courts of equity, creditors by specialty in which the heirs are bound, shall be paid the full amount of the debts due to them before any of the creditors by simple contract, or by specialty in which the heirs are not bound, are paid any part of their demands. The personal estate of the deceased, both at law and in equity, vests in the executor or administrator, and he is bound to apply the same to the payment of the debts of the deceased, first discharging the funeral and testamentary expenses; then, debts due to the government; then, those by judgment, decree, recognizance, specialty; and lastly, simple contract, in the order enumerated, subject to the right which a simple contract creditor may exercise of marshaling the assets.

2. *Laws as to Rights in Action in Lower Canada.*

By the civil law, debts and all such rights and causes of action as would devolve on the heir as part of his succession, and also judgments, are the subjects of sale or mortgage. The sale or cession imports a warranty by the vendor that the debt is in existence at the time of the transfer; but without an express warranty, the vendor is not responsible for the solvency of the debtor. The cession transfers to the cessionary the whole debt which was due to the cedent, and not merely the sum which the cessionary has paid as the consideration for the cession. Where the sale is of a debt in litigation, the debtor may redeem it on paying the cessionary the price of purchase. The right of acquiring the debt at the price paid by the cessionary, does not exist:

1. Where the cession has been made to a co-heir or joint owner of the right ceded; or

2. Where it has been made to a creditor in payment of that which is due to him; or,

3. Where it has been made to the possessor of the heritage subject to the right in litigation.

The sale comprises the accessories to the debt, such as the surety, privilege, and mortgage.

The cedent is not divested of his property in the debt, until intimation of the sale has been given to the debtor. By failing to give this intimation, the cessionary is exposed to the risk of a payment by the debtor to the cedent, which would discharge the debt, and to a loss of the same from its being taken in execution by a creditor of the cedent.

3. *Interest.*

The rate of interest upon all contracts for the loan of money, and upon all debts from the time of their maturity, is fixed at six per cent. All agreements and assurances for a higher rate are void, and the lender receiving usurious interest is liable to a penalty of three times the amount of the debt. Legal interest is levied upon all executions from the date of the judgment. No interest is demandable upon any note made within the province in which the penalty or sum to be secured is expressed in New-York currency.

4. *Frauds.*

Under the civil law, creditors were as effectually protected from a fraudulent alienation by their debtors, as under the common law. The alienation is liable to be set aside when the debtor makes it with the intention of defrauding his creditors, knowing that he is insolvent, and that he will thereby diminish his substance. The creditor cannot, however, recover the property which has been fraudulently alienated, unless the alienee was privy to such fraud; or unless the conveyance was voluntary. A payment by a debtor to one of his creditors is not fraudulent unless the payment was made before the debt became due, and was followed by the failure of the debtor.

5. *Limitation of Actions or Prescriptions.*

All actions relative to bills of exchange, and bills to order, subcribed by tradesmen, merchants and bankers, or for matters of commerce, prescribe themselves by five years reckoning from the day of protest or the last suing out any judicial process, if there has been no judgment, or if the debt has not been acknowledged by any separate act.

Bargains concerning movables or sums of money, as sales, hirings, loans, deposits and pledges provable by witnesses, are only provable by writ or oath of party, if the same be not pursued for within five years after the making of the bargain.

Infants, persons absent or imprisoned, are barred by these prescriptions.

6. *Effect of Marriage upon Property in Lower Canada.*

Under the coutume of Paris, which stills prevails in Lower Canada, there exists a community of property between husband and wife. This community commences, unless there be some stipulation to the contrary, from the moment that the nuptial blessing is bestowed. The property of which the community is composed, consists of all the movable or personal property of every description, corporeal or incorporeal, which belonged either to the husband or the wife, before or at the time of the marriage, or to which either may become entitled at any time afterwards during the continuance of the community, whether it belonged to or was acquired by them by succession or otherwise. It also includes all such immovable or real property as either of them may have acquired during the marriage, if in the language of the French law, it consists of biens conquets, or property acquired by industry or other means. There is not admitted into it any immovable or real property, which belong to either at the time of the marriage, or which either may have acquired during the marriage by such a title as to be deemed in the law of succession, *biens propres*, or property held by descent. Property which by the marriage contract is given to either of the conjoints, is the propre of that conjoint, and excluded from the community.

The property of which the community consists is charged with all the movable or personal debts which the conjoints had respectively contracted before or during their marriage, or which were due by the successions which had devolved upon them. This liability results from a principle of the French law, which makes the personal debt of an individual a charge on his entire movable estate; and as by the marriage the whole of that movable estate passes into the community, the debts also pass with it. The debt with which the community is chargeable must be movable, that is, it must be money or some other movable, due by or demandable from the conjoint. Damages for the non-delivery of a specific thing would be deemed a movable debt. The community is charged with a debt, for which the conjoint is liable in solidum with others, or which is secured by mortgage. The community is charged with debts contracted by the wife, with the husband's sanction, for the affairs of the community, or in a trade which he permits her to carry on: but if she has contracted them without his sanction, but with the authority of the law, they are chargeable only so far as they are advantageous to the community. The community is not chargeable with the immovable debts of either conjoint; e. g. the amount due by a conjoint for the price of an estate purchased by him before, and of which he was possessed at the time of the marriage, &c. During the continuance of the community, not only the property of the husband, together with that of the wife comprised in the community, but the husband himself is liable personally for the debts contracted by the wife before the marriage. The wife's creditors, who have obtained a judgment against her before the marriage, cannot however execute it against the husband, until they have obtained a sentence rendering it executable against him. After the termination of the community, the husband continues liable for the whole of the debts contracted by himself before the marriage, and for those which, during the community, were contracted by himself, or by his wife acting under his authority. In respect of the debts contracted by the wife before her marriage, the creditors can proceed against him or his heirs for a moiety only of those debts. After the termination of the community, the wife is liable to creditors for the whole of the debts due by her at the time of marriage, but as the community is charged with them, she is liable to recover one moiety from the estate of her husband. As the wife may have accepted the community under a misapprehension of the amount of debts with which it was charged, her liability and that of her heirs, to creditors, is limited to the amount of the profit which they have derived from it. To secure this privilege, there must be no fraud or default on the part of the wife or her heirs; and they or she must, upon the dissolution of the community, make out a just and true inventory, showing the state of her accounts with it.

The husband has the exclusive administration of the property in community, and an absolute power of alienating it. He is also vested with the sole administration and management of the wife's separate property; but he can make no disposition of it, without her consent. The wife cannot, of her own authority, exercise any power of administration or alienation over the property in community. She becomes, by operation of law, a party to the debts contracted by her husband, and liable to the extent of her interest in the property of the community, without any actual concurrence on her part, and by the effect alone of the marital power. If she becomes, in fact, a party to the debt, having been authorized by her husband to concur in it, she incurs a liability in respect not only of that interest, but also personally, and in respect of all her separate property.

INDEX.

ALABAMA.

ARKANSAS.

CANADAS.

CONNECTICUT.

DELAWARE.

DISTRICT OF COLUMBIA.

FLORIDA.

GEORGIA.

ILLINOIS.

INDIANA.

IOWA.

KENTUCKY.

LOUISIANA.

MAINE.

MARYLAND.

MASSACHUSETTS.

MICHIGAN.

MISSISSIPPI.

MISSOURI.

NEW HAMPSHIRE.

NEW JERSEY.

NEW YORK.

NORTH CAROLINA.

OHIO.

PENNSYLVANIA.

RHODE ISLAND.

SOUTH CAROLINA.

TENNESSEE.

TEXAS.

VERMONT.

VIRGINIA.

WISCONSIN.